Pre-Industrial England

PRE-INDUSTRIAL ENGLAND
GEOGRAPHICAL ESSAYS

EDITED WITH AN INTRODUCTION BY
JOHN PATTEN
Fellow of Hertford College, University of Oxford

DAWSON

Published in 1979

Wm Dawson & Sons Ltd, Cannon House
Folkestone, Kent, England

British Library Cataloguing in Publication Data

Pre-industrial England.
   1. England – Social conditions
   2. Anthropogeography – England
   I. Patten, John
   309.1'42   HN385

   ISBN 0–7129–0824–2

Printed and bound in Great Britain
by W & J Mackay Limited, Chatham

Contents

Publisher's Note

Acknowledgements

My thanks are due to Mark Overton of Emmanuel College, Cambridge, for a number of references on agriculture. Equally, I am indebted to Mary Dobson of Nuffield College, Oxford, for her help not only with references on population but for considerable assistance with that section in my Introduction to this volume of articles.

Most of all I am indebted to Paul Coones of Christ Church, Oxford, not only for his help on industry and manufacturing, but for his advice and assistance on the Introduction and the volume as a whole.

John Patten
Hertford College, Oxford

October 1978

Introduction

JOHN PATTEN

The period immediately before the economy and society of England began to experience the great eighteenth-century transformation has its own fascination. It was very different from today, yet not so totally different as to be absolutely alien. Some of the characteristics of modern post-industrial society can be seen, however imperfectly developed, in an England which has not yet experienced industrialisation, but which was to some extent modernising.

Although most of the features of a modern society, such as mass production, multifarious sources of power, rapid technological change and a proportionally tiny agricultural workforce, are totally absent in the England of the sixteenth and seventeenth centuries, some may be found there. For example, wider education had begun, producing a slow spread of literacy and numeracy, a process speeded from the mid-sixteenth century by the liberating influence of the printing press, which equally importantly improved communications in general. The book, the bookseller and the bookbinder all flourished, and books circulated more widely alongside pamphlets and broadsheets. Relaying news of a devastating fire, the state of play in the current theological debate, or the last speech of some transient folk hero from the gallows, they gave currency to affairs which had previously been the preserve of word of mouth alone. In the capital, by the end of the seventeenth century, recognisably modern newspapers containing advertisements and gossip were on sale. A regularity was beginning to enter life, and some dependable timetables existed for the stage coaches and waggons that linked the country. Provincial shopkeepers could thus obtain goods from London by mail-order and know more or less when they would arrive. Some towns were acquiring residential suburbs from which people were even beginning to commute daily on horseback, if only over a very short distance. Equally, work habits and work psychology were becoming more recognisably modern. According to Blanchard ('Labour productivity and work psychology in the English mining industry, 1400–1800', *Economic History Review* 31, 1978), the seventeenth century witnessed the birth of a new work psychology, free from the constraints of the hierarchical attitudes of the village. For the first time people were becoming more ordered and professional in their attitudes to the use of their labour.

None of these portents of modernisation should be overstated; there was much that was still more medieval than modern. In the England of the sixteenth and seventeenth centuries we seem to have an example of how far a traditional society could go in its development, in what we might hesitatingly call its modernisation, without concomitant industrialisation. One valid view of the period would be not as a staging post on, or launching pad for, the run-up to industrialisation, but as the climax of the development of post-Conquest England before the onset of industrialisation.

Pre-industrial England has been studied by many scholars—political and social historians, anthropologists, historical geographers and economic historians. Much of the writing of economic historians in particular has been dominated by the twentieth-century preoccupation with growth. Hoskins observed that 'Henrician England was a country of very slow economic growth, if any' (W. G. Hoskins, *The Age of Plunder* (1976), 85). Clarkson, in his turn, felt that in England 'the pre-industrial economy was also character-ised by stagnation' (L. A. Clarkson, *The pre-industrial economy in England 1500–1750* (1971), 10). Ashton wrote: 'the seventeenth century had ended in gloom' (T. S. Ashton, *Economic Fluctuations in England, 1700–1800* (1959), 140), and, on a more regional level, Chambers suggests: 'In the local iron industry the seventeenth century lasted until 1750' (J. D. Chambers, 'The Vale of Trent, 1670–1800. A regional study of economic change,' *Economic History Review Supplement* (1957), 9). The training and outlook of most English economic historians has predetermined their views of pre-industrial Eng-land. Too often they have judged it on how little it grew compared with later times, and on just how much or how little it contributed to that later growth. That is a tendency to which the viewpoint of the historical geographer can give a valuable corrective. This is not only because the methods of the geographer, often based on maps and descriptive cross-sections through time, introduce a more stable (and paradoxically timeless) element into the study of the past, less inclined of itself to look for growth at all costs, but also because the study of geographical change forces the period to be examined in its own terms. These themes are examined in this introduction, and exemplified by the reprinted articles which follow it. The collection will be of particular interest to those beginning to study the geography of the period.

Pre-industrial England, notwithstanding the caveats about modernity entered above, had a small population, largely agrarian and rural-dwelling and organised into a very different social structure from our own, with a different technology, using different resources and profoundly influenced by the forces of nature and physical factors. Further-more, contemporaries then viewed the country in a way markedly distinct from the way we look at England today. Emery has produced an invaluable study of contemporary percep-tions of region and environment (see F. V. Emery, 'English regional studies from Aubrey to Defoe', *Geographical Journal*, 1958), in which he tried to show the viewpoints and conventions of English writers on 'place' in Elizabethan and Restoration times. Differ-ences in style and method between these *chorographers* and *natural historians*, in Emery's terms, would then reflect in part the differences in English society, national economy, and scientific scholarship that had occurred between the late sixteenth and the late seventeenth centuries. Some of the Restoration naturalists and polymaths are peculiarly modern in their approach to what might be termed 'environmental problems' and they saw the utilitarian value of new knowledge in improvements of many kinds. Most were by com-parison profoundly unmodern. All were, however, dominated by the English environ-ment; equally, most from the evidence of other writings were not looking for growth, nor were they surprised or upset not to find it. Contemporaries, with their instinct for restrictive practices whether in manufacturing at home or in trading abroad, clearly felt that their world was one in which the economic cake was of finite size and needed to be carefully and equitably shared out, rather than one in which that cake could easily be made to expand and grow. They saw things as much in terms of change as of expansion. Nothing can more aptly characterise the economy of the period than the example of cloth manufac-ture. Increased profit opportunities were not usually found through technological break-through, the spread of new innovations, the growth in scale of production, nor even in the application of new sources of power. Rather they came from simple product change. A new colour, some new weave, a bright new name, these were often enough to boost sales substantially. In agriculture, too, genuinely new developments, such as the floated water meadow, often led at first as much to simple change in farming practice as to actual growth in production, and even the pace of that change was often slow.

The geographer's contribution to the study of England in the pre-industrial period has not been enormous in volume, although the quality has been very high, as the articles of very wide interest reprinted in this volume clearly demonstrate. Many of the studies undertaken so far, both published works and unpublished theses, have been mainly descriptive and often concerned with one particular cross-section, as Sheail's article on the distribution of wealth and tax-payers in the 1520s demonstrates. Such studies are vitally important in mapping out the past for the first time, and until such information is available, discussion of change is difficult to undertake; theory without empirical underpinning is of limited scholarly value.

All the articles reprinted here are by those who called themselves 'historical geographers' when they were written, and almost all still teach the subject. They thus represent the geographer's view of England in the sixteenth and seventeenth centuries. It is a view which is, for the moment, largely static and descriptive in nature, but one which sets the stage for the next important task: the explanation of geographical change in the period *in its own terms* as much as for the impact of those changes on later periods. This introduction will, therefore, consider directions for new research into the patterns of, and processes behind, geographical change in the pre-industrial period, in addition to sketching out a necessary background to the reprinted articles which cannot of themselves cover more than part of the whole. Even discounting its inherently prefatory and descriptive nature, the collection does starkly illustrate one thing. It brings out the fact that *growth* as a phenomenon is not to the forefront as a factor in any of the geographies of the day, except in the runaway growth of London itself which is clearly the exception. Reflecting the chosen order of the articles themselves, this introduction will now consider in more detail pattern, process and change in population, agriculture, manufacture and mining, towns and transport.

Population

There has been a lively and developing interest in recent years in the population of Britain in the pre-industrial period. The main thrust has come from history and for this reason the population of England has usually been discussed either on a national basis, or at the local level where one or two parishes are studied according to availability of sources rather than their intrinsic demographic or geographical significance. The two main papers on population in this book show, however, that historical geographers have begun to make a determined move to examine spatial patterns and spatial processes of population in this period. One of the most important facts to remember in considering the pre-industrial world is that economy and society were local or regional, rather than national, and that population geography and history should follow suit. A national, stationary population may in practice conceal a wide range of rates of growth and decline, and overall growth may be composed of quite different local phenomena. To speak on the one hand in terms of national aggregates or on the other to generalise from individual local examples, is, therefore, to risk seriously distorting the geographical pattern of population change in the pre-industrial period.

The papers reprinted here together with the bibliography on population, point, first, to the methodological approaches used by historical geographers in the field of population; secondly, to some empirical information concerning the population distribution and dynamics of change during the pre-industrial period; and, thirdly, to the main deficiencies in our knowledge of this subject and to fields of future research.

Two main approaches have been used to examine the geography of population in this period: the cross-sectional approach and the process approach. The papers reprinted here by Patten (1975) and Sheail (1972) are both examples of the cross-sectional method in which a static picture is drawn of the population distribution at a single time period or, as in Patten's paper, at a series of separate time periods. A chronology of change can be built up by linking these separate pictures. On the other hand Wrigley's (1968, 1969) classic papers on Colyton describe the population processes of fertility and mortality which explain changes in population parameters. Taken together, they comprise a good example of what has been achieved. Wrigley thus suggests that the fairly static nature of population growth experienced in many late seventeenth-century parishes may have been the result of late age at marriage, low fertility within marriage and high infant and child death rates. Similarly, Patten's paper on rural–urban migration in East Anglia (1976) goes a little way towards explaining some of the regional differences in population distribution of this area discussed in his earlier paper. But a clearer picture of the patterns and processes will only be gained by linking studies at the local (Wrigley, 1968, 1969) and regional scale (Patten, 1975) with the more general geographical studies at the national scale (Sheail, 1972).

The third methodological feature of these papers is the different demographic techniques and sources which they incorporate. The main source used by Wrigley in his classic local studies are parish registers, and his use of both aggregative analysis and family reconstitution show that we have come a long way from the early works of Short, Graunt and King. For technical reasons family reconstitution studies are only feasible in a limited number of areas, but by selecting parishes from different economic, social and geographical zones the more subtle demographic variables will be analysed in contrasting parishes. The papers by Patten and Sheail show that fiscal and ecclesiastical sources, collected for purposes other than demography, may be used to map relative population distribution over large areas. Both consider in detail the representiveness of their sources, for in no instance do they relate to the total population, but rather are measures of parts of it.

Two broad spatial patterns of population distribution are highlighted by these articles and by other case studies listed in the bibliography: first, there was a concentration of population in the south-eastern half of the country below a line drawn between the Severn and the Humber estuaries; and, secondly, a clear difference between population in rural and urban environments. Sheail's paper gives a broad indication of the distribution of the taxable population in the sixteenth century. Pockets of high density can be seen in the part of England south of the Trent–Severn line, with especially high concentrations of over twenty taxpayers per square mile in the East Midlands and East Anglia. During the following two and a half centuries the growth of population in England was accompanied by some redistribution. The exact increase of population in this period is hard to estimate. It is likely, however, to have been over 2 million in 1500, increasing to about 5·2 million by the time Gregory King was writing in 1695 and to 6·3 million by 1750. Lancashire, the West Riding, and Durham, amongst the poorest and least populated counties in 1500 had become, 250 years later, as densely populated as counties in the once dominant south-east region. The main belt of population was beginning to shift from its east/west axis to a north/south axis, marking the prelude to the distribution of population for the following period of industrialisation.

Moreover, during this period a more definite distinction could be drawn between the crowded cities and the more sparsely peopled countryside. At the top of the urban hierarchy was London. At least half the urban increase in the pre-industrial period was due to the growth of London, whose population expanded from about 60,000 in 1500 to 400,000 in 1600, and then to 575,000 in 1695, so that by the mid-eighteenth century at least one in ten of England's population lived in the metropolis. Gregory King (1695) suggested that England could be divided into three settlement categories: London with half a million contained ten per cent of the population of the country; the 'other Cities and Market Towns' contained 870,000 or nearly 16 per cent and the 'Villages and Hamlets' with a population of 4,100,000 or over 74 per cent. The majority of Britain's population was still scattered in the country villages and hamlets.

Patten's paper mirrors some of these national phenomena on a regional scale. In East Anglia the lowest densities were found in the fenland areas which were badly drained and in the relatively infertile sand of Suffolk and Norfolk. Areas of richer farming land in north-east and central Norfolk were by contrast densely populated, as were the major textile regions. The rural picture remained relatively constant over the two centuries and the greatest change was in the urban landscape. The population living in towns increased from 20 per cent in the 1520s, to 25 per cent in 1603 and 33 per cent by the 1670s. Between 1603 and 1670 the towns increased in population size by 50 per cent compared with 11 per cent in the countryside. Simultaneously, the share of Norwich's population in Norfolk increased from 4 per cent in 1520 to 7 per cent in 1603 and 11 per cent in the 1670s. Chambers's study (1957) of the Vale of Trent shows that during the eighteenth century the agricultural parishes in this region increased their population by 38 per cent, the industrial parishes by 36 per cent and the town of Nottingham itself by 170 per cent.

These national and regional studies thus reveal three important facets of demographic change in the pre-industrial period: the beginnings of clearly defined pockets of population growth, a shifting of population from the south-eastern axis to the north and west, and a movement towards the towns at the expense of the countryside. What were the *dynamic variables* responsible for this pattern? The role of mortality, fertility and migration have been discussed at length by historical demographers. The emphasis, however, has been on the temporal rather than the spatial changes in these variables. Wrigley (1968, 1969) suggests that population in the sixteenth century was characterised by negative feedback, when each period of population growth carried with it the seeds of its own destruction. This period of high growth rates, low age at marriage and low mortality was cut short in the late seventeenth century. After 1720, however, the process no longer continually reached the point of reversal. Instead positive feedback set in and previous negative influences became less important. Thus, both burials and baptisms began their long upward trend, culminating in the major population growth of the eighteenth century. Historical demographers have debated the cause of this revolutionary population growth. Yet arguments concerning an increase in fertility (e.g. the position held by Krause, Hollingsworth and Wrigley) in response to changing economic and social conditions, or a decline in mortality (e.g. the position held by Chambers, Russell and McKeown) either through a fortuitous reduction in epidemics or changes in resistance to disease, often have failed to recognise that these temporal fluctuations had significant regional variations. Any decline in rural mortality over this period, for example, was undoubtedly counterbalanced on the national level by the growth of relatively unhealthy cities such as London, Manchester, Liverpool and Nottingham. As Deane and Cole (1962) have pointed out, 'we know that the increase in population was accompanied by fundamental changes in distribution and before we can hope to give a convincing explanation of the national upsurge we need to know more about these regional variations in the pattern of growth'. This comment remains as true now as when it was first suggested.

The difference in the death rate and expectation of life between town and country is quite significant in this period. In an era when public hygiene and private sanitation were sadly lacking, the spread of disease is likely to have been more severe in towns and cities where populations are closely concentrated. Moreover, the constant movement of people into and out of towns increased the risk of speedy transmission of infection. These dangers of urban life were compounded by the fact that the majority of an urban population would be wage-earners who during a harvest failure would be affected to a greater degree than country-dwellers. Mortality in the pre-industrial period depended to some extent on the fortuitous spread of disease but in many instances environmental factors, drainage, hygiene, poverty and nutrition, played an important role in man's susceptibility to disease, and the spatial differences in mortality thus become as significant as the temporal.

It is equally likely that there were marked regional differences in fertility and in the rates of change of this variable. Contemporaries believed that country places were both more healthy and more prolific. Short (1720, p. 121) held that 'in general country Breeders are more fruitful in proportion to their Numbers than in large Towns'. This statement poses an interesting question for it has often been assumed that fertility was higher in the manufacturing towns of the north and west. Did the towns furnish their own labour supply by increasing fertility rates, or did they rely on migration from surrounding rural areas of high fertility? Studies of migration in the pre-industrial period suggest that the population was extremely mobile. On a local scale, movement was often concentrated within a few miles of individual villages. On a regional level, Patten's paper on migration in East Anglia (1976) shows that the towns of Norwich, Ipswich and Great Yarmouth were significant catchment areas for the surrounding rural hinterland and for other more distant parts with similar economic backgrounds. Likewise, towns like Bristol, Newcastle, Hull, Manchester and Liverpool produced hinterlands to draw on for their human resources. On a national level Deane and Cole (1962, ch. III), using Rickman's parish register abstracts, have suggested that the birth rate increased in those districts which felt the direct influence of industrial growth and that much of the migration which took place in the early part of the eighteenth century was from north to south and had little to do with the expansion of the newer industrial areas. The relative contribution of fertility and migration to the growth of the manufacturing towns and provincial centres cannot, as yet, be accurately analysed.

It is probably more feasible to present fairly accurate plots of rural–urban migration fields, and this is considered later in the discussion of towns in pre-industrial England. It is important to recognise that such immigration undoubtedly contributed a great deal to both the economic and the demographic health of towns in the period. Actual rates will always remain hard to quantify, but what is clear is that most towns of any standing could not really have grown in size, or prospered, without continuous influxes of population. It seems that the relative contributions of fertility and migration to urban growth changed in their importance over the sixteenth and seventeenth centuries until, at some time during the earlier part of the eighteenth century, more and more towns became capable of reproducing themselves and growing on their own account, London probably last of all of them.

If the impact of the flow of immigrants into towns cannot be quantified, it can be clearly demonstrated. How else could London have achieved its great rate of growth, have replaced its dead? John Graunt, writing in 1662 of earlier plagues, rejoiced: 'In two years the city hath been repeopled, let the mortality do what it will.' The spectre of death, depersonified almost from its medieval role, was progressively vanquished by streams of people pouring in from near and afar. Smaller towns, by comparison, attracted most of their migrants from their surrounding countryside. Such short-distance movements may well have been temporary, and even if permanent, may not have seemed remarkable to the migrant; for the immediate everyday urban sphere of influence of perhaps five, or ten miles radius may have represented a comparative whole within which movements in or out of town would have been looked on as nothing unusual, simply reflecting deep and long-established rural–urban relationships. Such short-range movement might be better characterised as local and relatively undynamic *mobility* rather than dynamic *migration*.

Such local mobility did not lift the mover out of his or her immediate context. It must be realised that many smaller towns, of a thousand people or even less, had intimate connections with the countryside. They may have been much more like country areas in their mortality/fertility patterns; like the countryside too, they often grew more slowly than larger towns. Such lesser places needed, and attracted, the migrant less. In the movement of people from country to town there was a distinct trend down a 'gradient of movement' from genuine migration to that which should be thought of as local mobility.

Regional variations in population distribution and changes over time were, thus, affected by the spatial differences in the processes of dynamic growth. Our knowledge of these differences is, however, no more than cursory and much work remains before we can map the population geography of the pre-industrial period. The following suggest some areas of future research. First, more regional variations in population density at selected time periods and at different scales of analysis must be determined. It would be interesting to map population totals from the Hearth Tax Returns for the late seventeenth century in order to compare them with Sheail's sixteenth-century maps, for example. Some attempt should certainly be made to calculate when the shift of population to the north and west first commenced and the different rates of growth of town and country parishes in different parts of the country. Secondly, there is a need to examine variations in rates and changes in mortality and fertility not simply on a national scale, but rather across different parts of the country. Thirdly, there is much scope for mapping the diffusion of epidemics in pre-industrial England: typhus, smallpox, plague, influenza and other major epidemics are likely to have spread hierarchically and geographically. Fourthly, we still have little idea of the exact contribution of population movement to the growth of towns or the reasons for the very rapid turnover in population of certain areas. Fifthly, explanations of population change must be assessed on a regional and local scale. It is important that demographic variables are linked with economic, social and environmental trends within the study area.

Much historical demography and historical population geography including Wrigley's Colyton study, have, so far, proceeded in a virtual 'economic' vacuum. Sixthly, the case studies listed in the bibliography demonstrate the uneven distribution of existing detailed work in population. Finally, the problem of accuracy of the source material ought to continue to be thoroughly investigated. In most regional and comparative studies, the historical geographer need often, however, not be concerned with levels of accuracy of data *per se* but rather the degree to which the recorded statistics are internally consistent across space.

Agriculture

The great majority of the population of pre-industrial England worked on the land. At least three-quarters were directly involved in full-time agricultural activity. Of the remainder of the gainfully employed workforce (which, we must remember, involved far more of the total population than today, including very young children and very old people, male and female alike) many had some part-time attachment to the land. Spinners and weavers, nailers and wire drawers, were all likely to suspend these activities to get the harvest in, whether it was corn or cider apples. Urban craftsmen and tradesmen often kept pigs, owned orchard ground inside towns and fields outside them. They were as anxious about the weather as any yeoman or husbandman. The wills and inventories left by these people were as likely to list sacks of corn and milch cows as tools and stock-in-trade. In some parts of the country, particularly the pastoral areas whether wooded or open, bi-employment was the norm, not the exception; spinning and knitting were as much part of the annual rhythm of life as lambing and market time. Those who study the historical geography of pre-industrial England have agriculture on their hands, whatever aspects of its patterns and processes are under scrutiny. Not only did agriculture provide virtually all the food and drink consumed by Englishmen, it was also the source of the bulk of the raw materials used in their manufactures and of the majority of the goods carried on England's rivers and roads, around the coasts and overseas.

A basic division of English farming systems into 'lowland' and 'highland' remains a valid framework for the examination of agriculture in the sixteenth and seventeenth centuries, particularly if the quite strong contrasts between 'scarp' and 'vale' within lowland areas is also recognised. Until quite late in the sixteenth century much of the kingdom's tillage was concentrated on the deeper and more moisture-retentive soils of the vales, as well as on river valleys of the uplands, where open fields could easily be laid out. Much of the considerable volume of work by historical geographers on the agriculture of sixteenth- and seventeenth-century England has been concentrated on the study of its fields systems. Such work is deliberately not, however, represented in the collection of articles in this book. For a major recent volume, *Studies of field systems in the British Isles* edited by Baker and Butlin (1973) encompasses much, though not all, of the regional diversity of field systems in England, and epitomises the sort of work done on them, particularly concerning their progressive reorganisation and the processes of private and parliamentary enclosure which brought it about. The sixteenth and seventeenth centuries saw the beginning of the long-drawn-out end for the open field. This period also witnessed the extension of brand new fields into the fens, marshes and uplands, where no plough had been before. Quite rapid changes in the nature of English society and in landownership then gave rise to new types of legal and quasi-legal survey, and a wealth of new documentation relating to the holding and reorganisation of land becomes available. This documentation has been assiduously mined to elucidate changes in pattern, and the processes that lead to these changes. They were both numerous.

For example, the contemporary scientist and topographer, Robert Plot, writing in his *Natural History of Staffordshire* (1686), distinguished three major regions in that county. These were the moorlands and fringes of the Pennines; the rich arable lowland to the west and south of the river Trent; and the woodlands in the middle part of the county. Most English rural environments thus were represented in Staffordshire, save those of marsh and fen, though there were some wet levels near the Trent. Much of the field systems characterising pre-industrial England were also to be found here. On many of the dairy-lands of Staffordshire, and so also those of the country as a whole, some private and piecemeal enclosure had taken place; much remained unenclosed, and the land here was managed under a three-course rotation, as on the basis of two, three or more open fields per village. Elsewhere on the poorer soils of the uplands in particular, common land was probably being farmed in a way that approximated to an infield-outfield system. In this, there was the bringing into cultivation of the waste or only grazed land on a rotating basis for a number of years to supplement the permanent infield arable. Sometimes this taking-in of the outlands became permanent.

The picture, whether gained from a contemporary's account of Staffordshire or present-day analysis of the considerable body of documentary evidence (see, e.g., Baker and Butlin 1973) points clearly to a period of agricultural transition. Change was expressed in the landscape most often in the shift from the common management of open fields and commons to their enclosure into usually much smaller permanent fields. This restructuring was often, though not always, accompanied by the introduction of improved farming practice.

We now have a number of good studies of field systems of much of the country and of the basic patterns of agricultural activity carried on in some of them. For example, the articles by Yelling reprinted in this volume examine crop and livestock practices in Worcestershire. It is to the process of agrarian change and its diffusion that much attention will have to be paid. The paper by Emery reprinted here, which looks at the diffusion of the new fodder crop of clover from England into Wales, does what is essential in such investigations. It closely examines the processes of spatial change brought about by an innovation in the full context of information circulating at the time of its first impact. E. L. Jones (*Agriculture and the Industrial Revolution* (1974), 83, n. 18) has criticised the work of historians for being carried out too much within conventional administrative units which often blur agricultural distinctions. Historical geographers, by contrast, he says, have hardly generalised their findings or pursued their economic implications. It would also be true to say that, until they have plotted out the directions and chronologies of the processes of agrarian change, in the way that Emery has done, it will be difficult to pursue much further than hitherto these economic implications in their spatial context.

What can be said with certainty of English agriculture after 1500 is that the outstanding need was to raise the low level of productivity, above and beyond that which could be achieved by the considerable but still unmapped extension of cultivable land which was to occur in the next two or three hundred years. Over the huge acreage of wheat and barley under cultivation in fields old or new, output was probably often not far above the natural minimum. There were also limits on the amount of usable land that might be taken from the waste into relatively intensive use, because the balance between arable and pasture could not, as yet, be radically and permanently altered. Pasture was essential for livestock; unless sufficient numbers of sheep and cattle were kept on the farms there could be only insufficient farmyard manure for maintaining, let alone raising, corn yields. A good deal was achieved before 1700 to make this vicious circle more virtuous. It could not however be fully broken before the inorganic fertilisers, imported foodstuffs and mechanisation all came in during the course of the nineteenth century. These were the challenges which faced the pre-industrial English farmer.

What was done by the farmer as population, and thus demand for both food and raw materials, increased? The problem of productivity was most acute in the still largely open-field and corn-producing regions of central England. A basis for change at the outset lay in the predominant two- and three-course rotations. On claylands, pulses such as peas and beans, together with vetches were increasingly grown in the spring shift at the expense of oats and barley. They were even grown in the hitherto fallow furlongs within open fields. A more fundamental and widespread answer to the fodder crisis was found by putting down arable furlongs and fields to grass, either permanently or as temporary leys. This helped farmers to keep additional livestock, especially by the provision of more hay for winter feeding, even when population pressed particularly hard on food resources between 1550 and 1650. So-called 'convertible husbandry' emerged as an identifiable entity in its own right along this path; it was equally feasible in both common and enclosed fields. It offered a less rigid alternation of tillage and grazing than in the past, but as fallowing was still necessary most farmers went for the temporary grass leys after three or four years under the plough. Convertible husbandry was the foundation stone of the modernisation of agriculture to come, and the focus of most innovation.

Ley farming, once established, was itself in its turn to be revolutionised by the appearance of new crops. Foremost amongst them were various sown grasses, notably clover, sainfoin, refoil and rye grass. These were initially adopted in many regions in the early and mid-seventeenth century; the patterns of their diffusion, both geographically and socially, are only now being worked out (Emery, 1976). At first, grass seed was imported from Flanders, France and the Netherlands, but farmers quite quickly discovered how to become self-sufficient in the seed. On the other hand, they seemed to decide to adopt the new grasses fairly slowly. Clover was the most widespread of them. It was best adapted to short leys of up to three years, and for acting as a fallow break crop in a rotation of crops (particularly wheat) while providing invaluable fodder. It had early successes in the West Midlands. The use of another popular grass, sainfoin, in semi-permanent leys was more typical of the light, dry soils on limestone and chalk in all parts of England.

Such grasses raised the farmer's potential for keeping more livestock and also for feeding them better. In the Fenland and East Anglia, the introduction of oil seed, rape and the important new root crop of turnips produced a similar effect but one which was more localised. The turnip has perhaps too often been hailed as a key innovation of national importance, while clover was in fact probably more far-reaching in raising productivity. Thus its spatial advance is a major indicator of the slow and uneven spread of the new agriculture. The detailed chronology of the diffusion of such grass substitutes from the seventeenth century remains to be worked out. As late as the mid-eighteenth century all of these innovations, especially the turnip, still had much ground to conquer. In the course of the seventeenth century they had been grafted on to an agriculture which had already been changed from that of the early sixteenth century by the creeping consolidation of holdings. Other innovations, too, such as the forcing of early grass by the technique of deliberately flooding or 'floating' water meadows, had a similar impact in that they allowed more stock to be kept, they provided more dung per acre.

In the whole of the earlier part of the pre-industrial period, between the beginning of the sixteenth and the middle of the seventeenth centuries, the major innovation was the slow insertion of grass leys into rotation. Notable structural change though this was, it was unlikely to produce an effect on productivity as great as the later introduction of new grasses and fodder crops. Ley husbandry by itself improves soil texture much more than it improves soil fertility, and simple environmental and biological constraints make any substantial rise in productivity impossible. The extension of cultivatable land in this period was much more likely than ley husbandry by itself to lead to increased productivity. Thus it seems that the ideas expressed by Kerridge (1967) suggesting a sixteenth-century 'agricultural revolution' based on the introduction of leys, plus some cropping innovations and the floating of water meadows, are less than likely in practice. More acceptable is to view the (well-studied) years of the sixteenth century as providing the foundation for a further grass-seed and turnip-based advance beginning in the (less well-studied) years of the seventeenth century. These later advances can only be satisfactorily analysed through painstaking examination of the records of probate inventories of individuals (see, e.g., an important article by Overton, 1977) as the pace of change quickened.

The scope for successful innovation of this kind was certainly not restricted to lowland as opposed to upland England, nor to enclosed rather than open fields. Just as it is wrong to think of new crops invariably being introduced in southern and eastern England, and thereafter diffusing north and west across the island and down a regular gradient of time and space, so it would be wrong to regard England as an area in which the scope for innovation was everywhere equal. It would certainly be mistaken to regard the long-established arable regions as those most suited to innovations. It must be remembered that these were traditionally the heavy clays. Light soils had usually been too infertile for permanent tillage. They were often dry enough to maintain stock, especially sheep, during the winter to feed off the fodder crops, thus retaining manure for any following cereal crop. Now, suddenly, light land could be kept more fertile by the sowing of new fodder crops. Cereals could also be more easily grown on them than on the traditional clays which were wetter, heavier to work and with higher traction costs. New grasses were more likely to be taken up on light soils, the turnip even more so, as it grows very well in the finely textured light soils and is much more difficult to lift by hand from heavier, wetter clays. Consequently, such innovations were often more slowly adopted in the traditional clay tillage areas. Moreover, by the later seventeenth century some areas, particularly in the Midlands, went down to permanent grass (helping to preserve, *inter alia*, the splendid agrarian landscape feature, ridge and furrows). These areas increasingly specialised in cattle, both for fattening and dairying, while traditional sheep-rearing light lands such as the South Downs or the sand lands of the Sherwood Forest area could begin to grow corn regularly for the first time. The most important spatial change in pre-industrial agriculture was undoubtedly this shift of activity from heavier to lighter lands, itself consequent on the innovations of new grasses and roots.

Such a generalisation, naturally enough, breaks down on the local and regional scales. It is only a broad environmental and ecological division. Not every light-soil farmer accepted the innovation, nor did every heavy-soil farmer refuse it, or move to other forms of activity. Even where some new crop does appear, it does not automatically mean that agricultural practice was transformed. In Herefordshire, for example, the turnip was found quite early, by the 1650s. Yet it was then not part of any new rotation, nor did it transform the agriculture of this border country—it simply appeared as a supplement to other animal foods here and there. It is interesting to note how innovations such as the turnip were to be found almost as early in the western counties as the eastern, just as clover was in Wales. Chances of modernisation of agriculture were clearly not heightened just by a south-eastern location. If the process of innovation cannot be expressed by the progressive transmission of new crops over the country, what can be put in its place? New crops, it seems, were much more likely to be adopted through a hierarchy based on social status, and to a lesser extent education and interest. This was to be the case regardless of location, other than in the first few years of an innovation being introduced to the country when it could be highly localised: around the point of entry it also seemed unrelated to the balance of farm enterprises. It is probable that fashion, in the shape of fashionable innovation, was as important a factor in the adoption process for new crops as it was later to be, for example, in the decision to set up turnpike trusts.

Later in the eighteenth century, fashion was to play an important role in the breeding of new strains of livestock. It was inevitable, however, that, parallel with the introduction of new crops, a more specialised mixed farming would emerge from the sixteenth century, aimed at animal products of all kinds. Mutton and beef, cheese and butter, came to compete with wool and hides, skins and tallows. This was the outcome of competition for grazing which had helped to evolve enclosure and ley-farming. Natural marshland from Holderness to Romney became more and more used by butcher-graziers for fattening livestock driven from far afield. Cross-breeding and the selective improvement of local strains of cattle, sheep, pigs and horses, was undoubtedly going ahead in the seventeenth century. Some time before the emergence of great stock-improving figures such as Bakewell, longhorn cattle, for example, were progressively being replaced by shorthorns. The rate and nature of this change, characterised by slowly improved breeding, was less apparent and remarkable than the sudden introduction of exotic new crops from the continent. The subsequent diffusion of new crops can quite easily be plotted where documents such as probate inventories can be found, particularly when these have been taken at the 'right' time of the year for the recording of crops, i.e. especially after the harvest. Their very names when recorded—clover, sanfoin, etc.—are clear indications of crop innovation. Livestock innovations by comparison as yet had far fewer new names to be recorded. Thus the 'two cows' or 'kine', or 'three hogs' that are recorded in inventories could either be improved or unimproved strains. Yet there is as pressing a need for the study of the process of livestock improvement as there is of crop innovation in pre-industrial England.

The focus for agricultural change was clearly the seventeenth rather than the sixteenth century, and this is reflected in both the content and the division of the select bibliography on agriculture. There was a period of depressed prices for agricultural goods (notably corn) after 1650 when rents and wages remained high. These circumstances themselves acted as a spur to innovation, improvement and change. Some of the more enterprising farmers increased their profit margins by intensive methods and specialisation, though sometimes innovation seemed almost independent of price changes: fashion or the failure of other fodder sources could be as important. Much specialisation was undoubtedly due to increased demand from a growing urban population, and above all that of London. Market specialisation and the more efficient handling of corn went together. In particular, wheat acreages expanded at the expense of barley, wheat becoming the rent-payer of most midland and southern clay farmers. On the other hand while barley acreages were reduced in total, specialised production for malting increased. Throughout the seventeenth century, London maltsters and exporters drew vast supplies from East Anglia, Kent and Sussex. By comparison with both wheat and barley, rye faded in demand, except in the harshest upland or most sterile lowland environments. Yield rates need to be calculated, especially in the immediate hinterlands of towns and near navigable waterways leading to them, to assess market impact on agrarian productivity. More evidence on yields would also help to set in context the amount of increased productivity attributable to innovation rather than growth in cultivatable acreage.

Simply because agriculture is the most highly studied aspect of pre-industrial England it cannot be implied that less remains to be done on that subject compared with, say, population or manufacture. The amount of work to date has posed as many questions as it has answered. A better chronology of the abandonment of collective rotations within still unenclosed communities ought to be elaborated, parallel with a better chronology of the introduction of new crops, cropping practices and livestock improvements. The variety of pre-parliamentary enclosure which could be brought about or the reclamation of farms and marshes or the enclosure of common fields, must be separated, as must the processes behind them. The agricultural experience of the two centuries, with their slow but constant improvement and innovation coming into sharper focus in the later seventeenth century is making it more and more apparent that to search for the beginnings of an agricultural 'revolution' as such in a particular decade of the sixteenth or seventeen century, is a fruitless and pointless exercise. The modernisation of agriculture was there and it was both slow but constant, of that we can be certain. By contrast, such topics as the effects of weather and climatic periodicity, or of other environmental constraints on agricultural activity, remain largely unknown. They present important possibilities for future research.

Manufacture and Mining

Manufacture in pre-industrial England was overwhelmingly concerned with the provision of the basic necessities of life: food and drink, clothing and shelter. Most of the raw materials were organic and supplied by agriculture, in which the vast majority of the population were employed according to an annual round of iron regularity which was at the mercy of the elements. The 'heart-beat' of the whole economy was the harvest, the pivot of pre-industrial existence; manufacturing labour was by comparison irregular, seasonal, and inextricably linked with the agricultural rhythm: a truly separate 'industrial' sector did not yet exist. Power was provided by human or animal muscle, or the seasonal and erratic forces of wind and water. Most economic activity was thus dependent upon the availability of 'pairs of hands', production of manufactured goods being small-scale and labour-intensive. Although there were important regional specialisations, reflecting varying conditions and resources in England, the nature of essential manufacturing activities was reflected in their generally widespread distribution, coincident with that of the population more than anything else.

The nature of manufacturing activity then, and the apparent paradox of industry in an economy labelled 'pre-industrial' have been insufficiently discussed. Pre-industrial England cannot be viewed simply as a prelude to industrial revolution, as a search for the first germs of heavy industry and their inexorable growth and domination of the life of a later society, as a stage for early industrial revolutions, or the source of technical change: such pictures would be unrecognisable to the pre-industrial labourer, to whom mines and metals, if they affected him at all, gave no promise of their future roles. His life was characterised rather by monotony, simplicity, limited movement, poverty for part or all of the time, and the adverse effects of the interference of natural phenomena and environmental constraints. In an age when technology was governed more by practice than theory and was used more in attempts to control and exploit the forces and opportunities of nature rather than to save labour, the impediments to expansion, rather than positive stimuli assessed in retrospect, may form a more fruitful field of study. Technology was limited, localised, little understood and even may have seemed in a sense magical to some; superstition permeated cloth manufacture, mining, and the beliefs of building masons; industry and rationalism were not yet equated. Despite this, attitudes to work, the work place and regularity of labour were becoming more rational and modern (Blanchard, 1978). The iron furnaces of the late fifteenth century inspired Bosch's hell; but the first true industrial paintings with their initially buoyant optimism were yet to come, with the landscapes which they depicted.

Labour, not raw materials or demand, was thus the central element of production; fixed capital equipment able to operate in a situation free from the vagaries of nature was largely absent, and output was increased by taking labour from the great pool of underemployed, governed by seasonal fluctuations and limited markets. 'Demand' in the truly modern sense did not exist. It was not until the late seventeenth century that the substitution of capital for labour began; the amount of fixed capital had been limited, certainly in relation to circulating capital, although by this time there seemed to be little real shortage. It is dangerous to assume that the industrial elements in the economy were striving towards capitalisation, technological development and large-scale organisation: in pre-industrial England they tended as much in the opposite direction.

The main manufactures of pre-industrial England were cloth, iron, leather and wooden goods. No satisfactory geography of the manufactures of the sixteenth and seventeenth centuries has been written, so a brief outline is one of the necessary tasks of this introduction. The manufacture of *cloth* in pre-industrial England is the subject of an extensive literature which should not lead to an overestimation of the importance of cloth on account of its value in exports, an exaggerated view of its degree of spatial concentration, the writings of contemporaries, or its architectural legacy, largely the creation of a few wealthy and famous individuals or families. In many districts other basic crafts (such as leather, food and drink, and building) employed a similar proportion of the workforce. Nevertheless, owing to its links with agriculture, the ubiquity of demand and the nature of its organisation, textiles may be concluded to be the greatest single national manufacture in 1700 as in 1500.

The domestic origins of cloth-making were never obliterated, despite the changes of the pre-factory era. There were few technological advances made while labour was used to increase output or lower costs. The stages of manufacture fitted splendidly into a family and domestic economy, and while the putting-out system prevailed, mechanical developments were restricted. The great changes in the types of cloth produced during this period did not result from any revolution in technique. The traditional English products were true woollens, spun from short-staple wool, carded and fulled, by which the mass of fibres was felted. The result was a high quality but heavy 'broadcloth'. Worsteds were made from combed, long-staple wool, and were not fulled; they were of increasing importance and were associated with the rise of many new fabrics known as the 'new draperies', whose techniques of manufacture had been brought from abroad. These tended to be lighter, cheaper, of lower quality, and reflect the vagaries of fashion. The replacement of the traditional broadcloths by the new draperies has been the focus of a large proportion of the literature. Bowden (1956) proposed that the decline of broadcloths was related to the changing character of English wool. The increase in long wool (as a result of enclosures), produced a decline in quality and quantity of short wool, with an adverse effect on broadcloth, where quality was vital and costs relatively inelastic. The distribution of sheep breeds and the nature of their wool precludes simple generalisation, but it is clear that a diversification of wools (and hence of their products) was related to a lengthening and coarsening of the fleece, as well as to foreign competition, changing markets and fluctuating tides of taste, which caused major changes in woollen manufacture. The origins of the new draperies are to be found in peasant techniques, their subsequent commercialisation and the modification of Italian models initially by merchants in Flanders; there was no major act of invention. The techniques involved were simple and even retrogressive, employing the spindle and distaff, and far greater emphasis was placed on finishing and modification rather than the more difficult process of cheapening in the face of competition.

The role of immigrants in the introduction of the new draperies into England was considerable. Many of them, and their skills, came from Flanders and the Low Countries, also at the same time the source of numerous agricultural innovations like grass and root crops. Their diffusion was intimately related to the migrations caused by warfare and persecution, and the economic and social effects of the influx of these foreigners was greater than their numbers might suggest. Although hostility towards the newcomers was to be expected, especially in times of depression, the advantages of their activities were appreciated, and they were encouraged by the Crown. Their beneficial effects on the ailing sectors of the East Anglian textile manufacture are undeniable. Norwich worsteds were revived by the aliens in the late sixteenth century; the wool was combed not carded, rock-spun on the distaff, not spun on the wheel, and was pressed not fulled. The new draperies were similar to worsteds, and the early seventeenth century saw the peak of 'Norwich stuffs': the impact of the immigrants with their 'bays' and 'says' on north Essex was considerable too.

The changing distribution of textile manufactures in England reflects the fundamental impact of the new draperies. Bowden's (1971) maps of centres and products in 1500 and 1700 illustrate the diversity of textiles made. The wool-producing regions and the manufacturing districts were not coincident in their distributions. The Midlands supplied the long-fibre wool for the new draperies of East Anglia, while counties like Leicestershire, Lincolnshire, Northamptonshire and Cambridgeshire, which had 'most of wool' had 'least

of clothing therein'. Wool production was very widespread, and wool was easily transported: local wool had not in medieval times, and did not in pre-industrial times, make a
cloth industry by itself. In 1500, fine woollens were produced in the Cotswolds and
Somerset, and medium woollens were restricted to west Yorkshire and Lancashire, and
worsteds to the Norwich region. Broadcloths and kerseys (similar to worsteds in carrying a
visible pattern of weave, but in fact a coarser, thinner woollen) were made in the Midlands,
Suffolk, the Gloucester-Wiltshire-Somerset region, the South-East, west Yorkshire and
the South-West; the last two regions also produced cloths known as 'dozens' and
'straights'. East Yorkshire made coverlets and broadcloths; Lancashire and the Lake
District specialised in 'cottons', 'friezes' and rugs, and west Yorkshire produced penis-
tones. By 1700 a host of new names reflect the spread of the new draperies: shalloons,
serges and tammies in Yorkshire and the Midlands; bays, says and perpetuanas in Suffolk;
Norwich stuffs; and shalloons and druggets in the South. Yorkshire still concentrated on
lighter, old draperies, and the South-West produced Spanish medleys and serges, an easy
step from lighter, worsted-type cloths. The transformation was often related to the nature
of the old cloths traditionally made in the district, and to successful specialisations. The
widespread nature of textile manufacture is further shown by its presence in most regions
of England, if on a less all-embracing scale than in the centres described above. Broadcloths were important at Worcester, plush and horse-clothing at Banbury, blankets at
Witney, and the production of various textiles at Shrewsbury, Kidderminster, Reading and
other towns, whilst 'homespun' was made everywhere.

Early attempts to provide explanations of the distribution of textile manufacture rested
to a considerable degree on raw material availability and physical factors. Later ones have
concentrated on other social and economic forces. The local presence of wool supplies
ranges from a secondary consideration to a totally irrelevant one. But environmental
considerations cannot be ignored in pre-industrial society. To consider them is not automatically to be a determinist or to be in favour of mono-casual explanations. Until the end
of the sixteenth century, wool from different regions or different breeds of sheep may have
displayed little variety, and was widely available. Great stress has sometimes been laid
upon water supply as the chief stimulus to concentration of textile manufacture. The swift
streams of the Cotswold escarpment were the basis of the hill-phase of the Cotswold
manufacture, using over-shot wheels; woollens required fulling, and water-power was
essential. A good fall of water, of sufficient and reliable volume was required, and the steep
gradients of the Cotsworld streams allowed the close siting of large numbers of mills.
Precise location was related to reservoir construction and the nature of the valleys. In East
Anglia where the worsteds were made, water-power was not required as the cloth was not
fulled. Streams were utilised in the Mendips, Devon and West Riding; even the placid little
river Windrush obliged by flowing faster over the eastern edge of the Cotswolds. Soft
water was required; the role of soft water is difficult to assess, but it seems that it was
difficult to produce an even colour using hard water while dyeing in the woven piece.

Explanations finding any validity in physical geography have long been less fashionable
than they were. Exceptions may be found to all the background influences outlined above,
yet the fault may lie chiefly in their over-simplicity. Thirsk (1961) has also convincingly
demonstrated the importance of the socio-economic structure of rural communities, and
the pattern of agricultural economies. The existence of occupations additional to agriculture was characteristic of those farming systems which left enough spare time to engage in

them. Such economies often embodied a community of small farmers involved in dairying in early enclosed lands where manorial organisation was weak. Alternatively the poorer countryside (supporting only sheep-farming or -rearing), or the forest areas, actually created considerable spare labour and an incentive to augment income. Essentially, arable, manorial lands were not conducive to bi-employment, with a fully-occupied, co-operative labour force. James I's failure to establish the new draperies in Hertfordshire reflects this basic contrast. The manufacture of cloth was particularly suited to pastoral regions, usually with plentiful water supplies: Thirsk gives examples from Wiltshire, Suffolk, the Weald, Westmorland and Lincolnshire. A mass of evidence bears out this thesis. However, it is no less geographical for its initial concentration on economic factors; it is based on the essential elements of the agricultural geography of England. The comparison of Thirsk's map of farming regions of England (1967) with maps of geology and the related maps of relief, soils and climate often reveals close correlations: that the physical environment permeated the pre-industrial economy throughout is only to be expected.

The organisation of textile manufacturing is intimately associated with the spatial contrasts discussed above. Out of the basic manufactures of food and drink, shelter and clothing, only textiles became the basis of a 'putting-out industry', a term not synonymous with 'domestic industry'. It involved the use of a rural worker's household and was centred on hand-work of himself and his family, but was commercially organised for markets, involved division of labour and constituted low-cost production on a massive scale. The technology was that of the Middle Ages, and advanced very little, restricted by the putting-out system; in the words of Coleman (1973), 'textile manufacture provides the supreme example of the pre-industrial revolution multi-product industry; and, moreover, of a consumer-oriented industry, effecting little or no change for centuries in the basic techniques of its main production processes . . .' The clothiers' power was based on their control over the workers, and it was the cheap labour of Norwich that maintained the worsted manufacture in the arable region of Norfolk. The widening markets, diversity of products (due to fickle fashion), and division of labour, contributed to the rise of the middle-man, illustrated by the growth of the Shrewsbury drapers. Oswestry was the chief avenue of export of north Wales cloth, owing its status of border entrepôt to its geographical position, attracting the products of the scattered Welsh weavers unable to travel to London, but able to travel to Oswestry and back in a day. The powerful Shrewsbury drapers, controlling labour and based on rural capital, captured the market in 1621 and completed their monopoly of the border cloth trade.

The *leather* crafts were, in many districts, no less important than textiles as a source of employment. The availablity of hides, the widespread market for uses of leather and, in the light crafts, the small amount of skill and capital required and the inexpensiveness of the tools, rendered leather a typical pre-industrial manufacture based on an agricultural product: hide, bark and water were the essential requirements. The so-called 'heavy' leather crafts (tanning, currying) and shoemaking, were independent concerns requiring specialised skills, but the 'light' leather crafts (leather dressing and glove-making) were well suited to the putting-out system; such goods were made in the pastoral districts of the west. Northamptonshire made boots and shoes, and leather clothing, harness, belts and buckets were made in many districts of the Midlands and South-East. London was an important centre, as hides were a by-product of the city's meat consumption, in addition to the supply of tanned leather for shoes from the dairying region of High Suffolk. The Welsh Borderland leather crafts were associated with the metal trades and made horse furniture; Chester was a key centre, using local and imported raw materials, the labour of an extensive poor sector and containing some large concerns connected with farming and serving a national market. In Leicestershire between the mid-sixteenth and mid-seventeenth centuries the leather craftsmen were the largest manufacturing group in the town.

The processing of food and drink too has attracted very little attention considering its importance. Given the pattern of demand and the perishable nature of the goods, much of it took place in the home, but it was a major occupation in towns as well. Brewers met a steady demand, as beer was the standard drink in an age when tea and coffee were unknown, but the most numerous craftsmen in the food trade were the butchers. *Salt* was essential, as the only culinary preservative, and until the later sixteenth century, was largely imported from the warmer continent, where evaporation could occur naturally. In England it was crystallised from sea water on the north-east coast of England and from brine pits cut in the salt-bearing Triassic rocks, as at Droitwich and in Cheshire. The demand, as so often for manufactured goods in pre-industrial England, was limited, the manufacture was small-scale, and the brinemen only worked a limited number of days a year in Cheshire. The substitution of coal for wood as the fuel led to a rise in output in the seventeenth century, concentrating the industry and broadening its scale: in the North-East it focussed on the mouths of coal-exporting rivers.

The hitherto little-studied *building* trade was much more widespread, involving many part-time tradesmen and labourers, and a wealth of specialisations, especially at the time of the Perpendicular churches and later the rebuilding of rural England in the late sixteenth and early seventeenth centuries. Hoskins (1953) suggests that it must have been as important as cloth in Devon and elsewhere; building was also a significant element in urban occupations. Associated with building was quarrying, naturally intimately connected with the diversity of stone provided by the richly varied geology of England.

Iron manufacture by comparison boasts a vast literature, but probably assumes greater significance in retrospect than it did to contemporaries. The annual charcoal blast furnace pig-iron output rose from a minute amount in 1500 to over 20,000 tons by the late seventeenth century, accompanied by a growth of secondary metal trades and important industrial linkage. In the medieval period, iron was made by the direct or bloomery process; bloomeries were mobile and produced a mass of malleable iron (the bloom) which was reheated and hammered. The quality of the iron could be high, but the quantities were small. At the very end of the fifteenth century the charcoal blast-furnace was introduced in the Weald. The indirect process produced a highly carbonised, brittle iron, which, on going to the forge had to be decarburised by oxidation in a finery before being reheated and hammered in the chafery, thus introducing a new stage. Although bloomeries continued to be built, the sixteenth and seventeenth centuries constituted the age of the charcoal blast furnace. This had a significantly greater productive capacity and organisational requirements, and these characteristics sharply defined a locational pattern that was unique amongst the manufactures of pre-industrial England.

In the sixteenth century the iron industry was overwhelmingly concentrated in the Weald, reaching a peak in 1574, with 47 furnaces out of a total of 73 for England and Wales in 1600. The others were confined mainly to the West Midlands. By 1717, however, the Forest of Dean had taken first place in the production of pig-iron, followed by Cheshire and north Staffordshire, south Yorkshire and Derbyshire, with the Weald in fourth place. Next in importance came south Wales, north Lancashire, central Shropshire, the Clee hills, Flintshire and Denbighshire, and Birmingham. The iron industry was distinctly concentrated owing to the operation of a set of very powerful locational factors, of which availability of iron ore was but one.

The supply of charcoal to the ironworks has been the subject of a great debate. It has been argued that the fuel supply was the vital factor in the life of a furnace, that the furnaces consumed the woods, and that the industry struggled to transfer to coal as its fuel. Contemporary accounts of woodland destruction certainly provide apparently frightening pictures to modern eyes—calculations of the amount of wood used would seem at first sight to support the view of Ashton that 'salvation could be found only in solitude, and the industry of smelting and refining was literally fleeing to the wilderness to escape destruction', leaving it 'scattered, migratory, intermittent in operation and probably declining' by the early eighteenth century (P. Deane, *The first industrial revolution*, 1965). In reality coppicing was a widespread practice, landowners were eager to sell or lease their otherwise unsaleable woods, timber near the coast was used far more in ship-building than charcoal-making, the cost of charcoal reflected the labour involved (often seasonal) as much as the value of the wood, supply increased enormously with only a limited rise in prices, sites were generally constant, involving no search for fuel, and contemporaries such as Defoe, Yarranton and Evelyn noted no wholesale destruction, rather an increase due to the ironmasters. The fuel supply problem was in fact a local question, usually settled by coppicing within a radius sufficient to transport fragile charcoal. The transfer to coal was certainly slow and even casual. The geographical expansion was not centrifugal but rather an attempt to expand without increasing costs, and to locate nearer raw materials, in a nineteenth-century fashion but was slow due to difficulties of transport which the nineteenth-century spatial expansion did not experience.

The seventeenth century saw the growth of the West Midland iron industry. The famous Foley partnership grew to become an integrated and united concern spread over the Welsh border, using the key resource of the navigable Severn. Pig-iron was transported to the central forges for manufacture into bar iron, concentrating on the Stour; large amounts were sent from the Forest of Dean. There was progressive refining nearer the market to exploit the weight loss, but the movement was not all centripetal; Stour products were sent far afield, as well as to local nailshops and smithies where coal fuel could be used. The momentum of the proto-Black Country was in its initial stages, overriding local considerations cited to explain precise locations. The beginnings of large-scale, highly organised, full-time concentrated industry were apparent in some parts of the pre-industrial English iron manufacture, unique amongst its manufacturing fellows. Even in 1700, before the great changes of the eighteenth century, the iron industry represented an atypical, nascent true industry in the twentieth-century sense, although all activity could still come to a halt for the harvest.

Early *coalmines* like so many iron furnaces, were run by landowners. The pits were simple, small, shallow, unmechanised, often worked seasonally, restricted to the outcrop, and abandoned when drainage problems became acute, which was invariably very quickly. They are examined by Langton in one of his articles (1972) reprinted in this volume. Demand was limited, and problems of transport restricted the supply. The subsequent history of the coal industry facilitates an overestimation of its role in pre-industrial England, and the small production totals make the rates of increase seem greater. Nef's (1932) massive study, demonstrating the fundamental and revolutionary nature of early coal production and its uses has been supported to a certain extent by those examining its substitution for wood and its use in metal trades, but appears less acceptable in the light of the tiny numbers employed, the small output for other than local markets and the significant failure of larger enterprises. Regional contrasts are vital considerations, as in most aspects of English manufacturing at this time; the 'virtual stagnation' in seventeenth century south-west Lancashire is fully discussed by Langton (1972); a work which is amplified in his *The South-West Lancashire coal industry, 1590–1799: the geography of change in the Industrial Revolution* (C.U.P., forthcoming, 1979). The coasting trade transported coal from the Tyne to London, and coal was used as fuel in most industries except iron and chemicals, but these were themselves still small-scale.

Coal was increasingly utilised in the secondary metal trades, but not in furnaces until the eighteenth century. The Birmingham region produced edge-tools, locks, cutlery, nails, 'toys' (a general term for small metal objects), horse furniture and a host of small wares easily transported; the use of suitable mill-sites and complete absence of manorial or guild control were additional stimuli to the advantageous position. The Forest of Dean also supported an exceptional range of industries: coal, iron, copper, quarrying, glass, wire, woodcrafts, steel, lime-burning, pin-making and nail-making, but the whole economy was relatively distinctive, and contrasts with the rest of the country. These regional differences demonstrate the dangers of generalisation, but undoubtedly local concentration resulting from extensive use of inorganic raw materials was gaining momentum.

Among the non-ferrous metals, *tin-mining* was an important element in the local economies of parts of Cornwall and Devon, large proportions of the population being dependent on it to some degree. Stream-tinning produced an unreliable income, requiring little capital; many tinners ran smallholdings in the diversified economy of Cornwall, and shaft-mining encountered the omnipresent drainage difficulties. Similar pictures emerge of *lead-mining* in the Mendips, the Shelve district of Shropshire, Derbyshire and the Pennines. Lead had a variety of uses, particularly for buildings, pewter, and printing type. The failure of the metallurgical industry to advance beyond small-scale enterprises was fundamentally due to the limited demand, and is exemplified in the story of the *copper* industry in pre-industrial England. Copper was made irregularly in Cumberland, Cornwall, Staffordshire and the Forest of Dean, the last using Cornish ore, but filled no major gap in the economy. Hammersley notes that 'economic historians have sometimes been inclined to discuss the metallurgical industries as if all metal was always useful and as if nobody could ever get enough of it' (1973). Demand in a twentieth-century sense for manufactured goods, however, did not really exist. England was still pre-industrial, mines and smoke still a novelty, its manufacturing space-economy disparate and scattered.

A number of other manufactures need only be mentioned briefly. *Glass-making* had been a forest-fringe activity, using wood fuel, potash, sand and clay. It was common as a dual employment, concentrating and expanding after the substitution of coal and the growing sophistication of buildings. The fragility of the product encouraged market orientation, and the industry spread from its Wealden location. *Papermaking* required skill, a supply of rags, clear water and fast streams. It developed late, owing to French competition, and did not advance in technology, encountering quality problems and the interruptions of drought, flood and frost. The mills were concentrated in the Home Counties, near the rags, patronage and printers of London, and in Worcestershire, with a thin dispersal elsewhere by the mid-seventeenth century, thereafter extending into West-morland and Durham. Mills were often converted, or shared, a typical state of affairs in pre-industrial manufacture. Other local sources of employment lay in pottery, woodcrafts and a host of minor manufactures such as candles, sugar, lime-burning, bricks, ships, clocks and watches, bells, gunpowder, and the ill-fated alum mines. The few large-scale concentrated enterprises, such as the *naval dockyards* on the Thames estuary and the south coast at Portsmouth, were locally important but atypical.

Permanent employment in occupations other than agriculture or those manufactures based on its products was thus limited to a small minority fraction of the population. Dual economies, although not peculiar to pre-industrial England, were characteristic of it; they made maximum use of varied resources, changing seasons and the labour of different members of the family. Dual economies were essential not accidental in pre-industrial England; their very success was a stimulus to manufacturing. Agriculture and manufacture were not opposites: the stimulus to concentration provided by technology, large-scale production and a high purchasing power and the locations they created were of the future; labour not capital, and raw materials not entrepreneurs were central to the space economy of pre-industrial England. Real entrepreneurs in any numbers came later, symptoms of a different process based on new resources, technology, society and capital/labour relations. Comparatively few works have been written by historical geographers on manufacturing in pre-industrial England, and not an enormous number by historians, other than on iron and textiles. Much of the best published material is concerned rather with the 'industrial revolution' and the period immediately before. Too often the manufacturing activity of sixteenth and seventeenth century England is examined as a prelude to industrialisation, just as the period is studied for the beginnings of agricultural revolution or of demographic explosion. The centuries should rather be seen in their own light, and England viewed as a country where trade was more important than manufacture, for which a new spatial and conceptual framework is demanded.

Towns

A small fraction of the population of England lived in places that twentieth-century eyes would immediately recognise as towns. More lived in places that were perceived as 'towns' by contemporaries, small and informal as urban centres though these mostly were. There was only one place in England that was a true city in the continental sense, and that was London. It had grown to a population of more than half a million by 1700. The biggest English provincial city by comparison had barely reached a population of 10,000 in the early sixteenth or 20,000 by the end of the seventeenth century. The majority were much smaller. At most, depending on what is accepted as a town in pre-industrial England, no more than 20 per cent of its population was urban. Many of this number, as we have seen, had deep agricultural interests in the countryside which surrounded towns; many of the smaller towns in which they lived must themselves have seemed little other than over-grown villages, comprising nothing more than a couple of streets running out into the surrounding fields. Despite this small scale of urban life, much more has been written on towns in recent years than, for example, has been devoted to England's manufacturing in this period or to her transport and trade. (Useful introductions are given in Clark and Slack, 1976; Patten, 1978; and Corfield, 1976).

Problems nonetheless still remain. The search for a satisfactory definition of what a town was in these two centuries must be continued. Whatever urbanism meant in pre-industrial society it was certainly something very different from today's definition. 'Towns' were so much smaller; some which seemed to have urban life barely reached a population of a thousand or so. They were deeply influenced by the countryside, out of which most of them had organically grown and which most of them served as their way of life. Many had markets, some fairs, though not all had both. A number of places which had the right to hold markets, and held them, seemed in practice to be no more than mere market villages. Their routine, and their population of a few hundred, was only disturbed by the weekly appearance of some countryfolk who spread out country produce for sale, to be joined by tinkers, chapmen, and other travelling salesmen with their goods. This disturbance to a basically rural round was as slight as was the contribution to the economy of the settlement coming from such small-scale exchange and sale. These centres which had been the lynchpins of much of the limited local space economy of medieval England very often declined completely by the eighteenth century. The competition of larger, better organised towns, linked by increasingly rapid (and regular) transport systems was too much for them.

Whatever actually differentiated a town from other lesser settlements, a clear urban hierarchy existed. At the top of the urban tree was London, both a 'world' city and a 'great capital' of the day. As we have seen, at the beginning of the sixteenth century its population was probably about 50,000 or 60,000; by the end of the seventeenth century two hundred years of exponential growth had brought it to more than half a million. Such figures are approximate, of course, dependant both on imperfect sources and an imperfect perception of where London's burgeoning—and poorly mapped—suburbs ended. What is much clearer is that London was the only settlement in pre-industrial England to experience real urban growth in the sense that we understand it of contemporary society. The next set or group of towns, the provincial capitals like Exeter, Bristol, Norwich, York and Newcastle-upon-Tyne, barely more than doubled in size over the same period: a yawning gap had opened out between the largest of them (with a population of 20,000 or 30,000 in 1700) and London, so many times larger and growing fast past the half-million mark at the same time. It was a truly primate city relationship. The same sort of stability characterised the very slow growth and rather static interrelationships of the third level of the urban hierarchy, the 'middling towns' of the day, many of them ancient county capitals such as Leicester or Northampton. Few of these had reached a population of 10,000 by 1700. And for the great majority of the remainder of the towns that both made up the fourth level of the urban hierarchy and filled in the urban network of pre-industrial England, the story was the same. These small market towns experienced but slight growth in a population that was often no more than a couple of thousand. Regional urban change for most of the characteristic pre-industrial hierarchy has been examined for one area of the country, East Anglia; the picture obtaining there is described in the article by Patten (1975) reprinted in this volume. It shows that the two counties of Norfolk and Suffolk experienced only very slight growth in population in the sixteenth and seventeenth centuries, and that any density of population could usually be attributed to particularly good agricultural conditions or the concentration of textile manufacturing. By the seventeenth century, towns were growing much faster than the countryside; in addition, the larger towns were growing relatively faster than the smaller ones. Whether this pattern was being repeated in other regions remains to be seen. What seems certain is that East Anglia's urban structure was, like that of the country's as a whole, very stable.

This apparent structural stability is further emphasised, both in East Anglia and the country as a whole, by the examples of the few deviations from the overall hierarchy which existed. These were towns which experienced much more rapid population and economic growth than average, sometimes relatively as much as London. In almost all cases such growth was a seventeenth-century phenomenon, and was characterised by three sorts of places. First, there were the spa towns like Tunbridge Wells and Epsom which owed their rapid growth to the increasingly fashionable activity of taking the waters. Starting as a transient summer pastime, water-taking and its attendant social round became more permanent and attracted shops, parades and arcades, lodgings, hotels and eventually residential houses. Some of these inland resorts took off in the same way as Brighton was to do in the early nineteenth century. Secondly, there were the shipyard and port centres such as Portsmouth and the Medway towns or Liverpool which grew equally fast on building, repairing and provisioning the naval fleet or the colonial trade. And thirdly, there were some burgeoning manufacturing towns, such as Birmingham with its metal trades, which were beginning to take on something of the style of the towns of the industrial revolution. Such places were starting to grow quite fast by the end of the seventeenth century, but were still relatively few in number.

Indeed, specialised towns as such were very few in number in European pre-industrial society. There were few single-economy 'coke' or 'rail' or textile towns as were to typify nineteenth-century England. In pre-industrial England even noted centres of cloth manufacture such as Norwich or Exeter had a broadly based urban economic structure; only a limited though important proportion of their workforce engaged in textiles. When one looks at a wide range of towns in different regions such as Preston or Newcastle-upon-Tyne or York or Norwich or Exeter, the picture is always the same. A considerable proportion of each town's economic activity, as shown in their occupational structures by lists of freemen and apprentices, or wills and inventories, was involved simply with 'taking in its own washing' and that of the surrounding countryside. Thus, there were many in the provisioning, clothing and building trades, and all the rest, though these became progressively more sophisticated and diversified in their activities. The shop rather than the market increasingly stood as the focus for much buying and selling of non-perishable goods and dry groceries. Equally, many of the wholesale-type functions such as buying and selling corn and malt in bulk were being taken out of the open market, and into the back rooms of inns and taverns, themselves in a way the forerunners of the nineteenth-century corn exchange.

If the nature or urban economies is a quite well-studied aspect of town life, one other which demands much more future attention is their socio-economic structure. We may know a little about the geographical distribution of poverty within sixteenth-century Norwich (Pound, 1962) or a little about residential segregation in later seventeenth-century London within the walls (Glass, 1966, 1968), but much remains to be done in satisfactorily mapping-out and explaining the internal structure of pre-industrial towns. Langton has pointed the way, both in his article on later seventeenth-century Newcastle-upon-Tyne, reprinted in this volume, and in another article on Gloucester in the late fifteenth century (Langton, 1977). Small and not particularly important though it was, late medieval Gloucester is revealed as geographically very complex. Open ground stood cheek by jowl with subdivided and extended buildings. Extremes of poverty were obviously located close-by (relative) extremes of affluence. A single, dominant, rich core was not, however, clearly present. Different occupational activities were loosely patterned, almost zoned, along the main streets. There are also hints of spatial differences in social status. The sources which could spread further light through the details they give of residence or occupation, such as rentals and court records, are rather intractable and present a considerable challenge.

The picture is clearer by the relatively better documented late seventeenth century, and the important alternative models of Sjoberg and Vance purporting to explain the pre-industrial city are explained and tested in the article on Newcastle-upon-Tyne by Langton reprinted in this collection. The picture he found is of a hybrid between those suggested by the two models. There was a merchant clique pre-eminent in wealth, and therefore power, given the urban socio-economic conditions of the day. Its dominance was expressed spatially by its concentration in one part of the city where mercantile purposes were best served and where the institutions through which it documented the city were located. But it was also true that people of dissimilar occupations and widely divergent levels of affluence lived mixed up together in other parts of the city—as appeared to be the case in Gloucester two centuries earlier. The relationship between workplace and home in the pre-industrial English town, the size and composition of its households, the nature of the housing and land markets, the relative degree of residential occupational zoning, are all important areas for future exploration. Increasing understanding of the social geography of the pre-industrial English town and the behaviour of its residents as expressed in their socio-economic differentiation is likely to tell us much about the nature of their slow 'modernisation', which was taking place before much later industrialisation. For by 1700 some of the larger ones were developing a number of modern characteristics: some streets had paving and some street lighting, and even newspapers were to be found in the glass-fronted shops that lined them in London.

So, too, there is a further need for the examination of the role of mobility and migration. Virtually nothing is known of patterns of mobility within the English pre-industrial town, save that they were 'walking cities'. A little more is understood of patterns of migration into English towns. It is clear that as the population growth of any of them in an era of high mortality depended on considerable immigration, so their economic well-being was equally dependent on continuous influxes of labour to fill urban manufacturing, trading and service occupations. The study of geographical patterns of rural–urban migration reveals much of the social and economic strands linking towns and other parts of the country. In the case of three fair-sized provincial towns, Norwich, Great Yarmouth and Ipswich, examined in an article by Patten (1976) reprinted in this volume, quite clear patterns of migration to them emerged. The most apparent and important migratory movement in pre-industrial England was a tremendous flow of people into London, lifting them right out of their home environment and from the stage of local mobility into that of the capital. This process has been charted in the seminal article by Wrigley (1967) reprinted in this volume. He demonstrates the way in which this process integrated the country with London quite as much as did its insatiable demand for food. What seemed to be present in pre-industrial England was a quite clear hierarchical migratory system, characterised by the declining size of local migration fields around smaller towns. On this was superimposed important longer-range networks of migratory movement, both over-land and coastal, particularly from the north and west of the country (in some parts upland 'regions of difficulty') to the south and east, and especially to the overpowering lure of the capital. Such a generalisation will undoubtedly be subject to considerable modification at the regional level.

If it is important to work out the spatial patterns of rural–urban migration, it is equally important to try to understand something of the behaviour of the migrants themselves. More needs to be discovered of the available information that encouraged or discouraged movement, and this then related to such things as income, employment, opportunity and demographic pressure at home, as well as to the costs and difficulties of movement, and intervening opportunities. The task will be most difficult: the key relationship between information and distance in the migratory process is likely to remain little understood except by implication in pre-industrial society. Overall, a closer examination of national rural–urban migratory patterns will, first, aid in plotting the course of incipient urbanisa-tion; secondly, give a fuller understanding of the role of London in the social and economic geography of the period; and, thirdly, illustrate connections between country and town at local, regional and national scales. Such connections were also expressed in the transport and trading systems of the day, perhaps the least studied aspect of the historical geography of pre-industrial England. These were not all dominated by urban centres, though increas-ingly tended to be so.

Transport and Trade

Much is known from Customs records of English foreign trade, and there is equally quite a substantial literature on it, represented in the select bibliography. Of the internal trade of the country, much less is available, though Everitt in particular (1967, 1973) has brilliantly charted its main outlines. Very little is known in detail of how that trade was carried within the country, whether by land or water; much of the existing literature is rather dated, and the whole topic seems to present numerous possibilities for future research. This impres-sion is only reinforced by a reading of the most comprehensive recent work on internal trade by Chartres (1977). Very few historical geographers have recently worked on transport, and no articles on the subject are reprinted here in this volume.

One thing is clear. Much of the transport system of pre-industrial England was informal and small scale; in the case of land as opposed to river carriage it was not likely even always to be along fixed lines, for roads in the modern sense hardly existed. Despite attempts to ensure their repair and upkeep they did not have surfaces, and were rather routeways, or lines along which people conventionally travelled. The boats that plied around the coast were usually very small; those that travelled along England's difficult, unimproved but reasonably navigable rivers, even smaller. The carts that carried some of the nation's trade were heavy and cumbersome—sprung carriages for personal use were exceptionally rare outside a few main towns, even by 1700. Horses bore some goods, and some people; most of the rest of the goods, and most of the people, walked. The archetype of the countryman or countrywoman trudging to market with goods for sale carried on their backs is undoub-tedly correct. Whilst regularity did exist for some men working the footpost, or increas-ingly for some waggoners travelling to larger centres and especially to London, the idea of the accurate timetable for transport services is an inappropriate one for earlier pre-industrial England. So, too, is any idea of an integrated transport system; where river and land carriage did interrelate it was often only on a seasonal basis.

Yet the sixteenth and seventeenth centuries did see a relatively immense growth in population, increasing regional specialisation of agriculture, diversification in manufacture, and especially of urban demand. These developments caused an increase in trade and the movement of goods which must have been very substantial. Spatial relationships and time budgets were altering. In addition, trade was being concentrated into fewer centres and urban market areas were widening, with most successful market towns standing in the middle of an ever enlarging circle of commerce. London was the epitome of this process, but its expansion was probably symptomatic of other places. Changes in transport and communications, it may reasonably be argued, must have been made to underwrite these developments. The trend towards more integrated markets, for example, could not have been sustained without it. Yet no new mode of transport was introduced and there were none of the great technical or organisational advances which were so to alter the face of English transport in the eighteenth century with the advent of the canal and the turnpike. Methods of transport and of trading were becoming less medieval. The big question is, how quickly were they modernising? Evidence is emerging as we saw, for example, in the discussion of agriculture for the steady modernisation of that sector; the same was demonstrated for towns. Because of the great increase in trading consequent on population growth and other developments we can reasonably imply that there must have been parallel changes in transport. The question is, what were they? Were these demands simply met by an increase in wholly traditional ways and means of carriage, more goods and men travelling in traditional ways along traditional routes, or were they met by real changes in transport methods and systems? These questions are the major challenges presented by the topics of transport and trade, and can conveniently be examined in turn with reference to water and land carriage.

The heart of the pre-industrial transport problem was the relationship between the value of goods on one hand and their weight and bulk on the other. Thus weighty and bulky goods of low value could not stand the cost of land carriage over any distance. The effective land-carried range of corn was no more than five or ten miles; by water this was increased enormously. Midland grain near to the Ouse system could be transported long distances along those rivers, down to Kings Lynn. From here it could go around the coast, or overseas on the thriving bread grain export trade. Much of this grain was sent around the coastal shipping network to the north. Small boats (by modern standards) navigated from headland to headland in the sailing months up the east coast to Newcastle-upon-Tyne. These same boats carried coal in return to southern markets. Coal was another commodity which provides almost the classic example of comparative advantage of water-borne carriage for heavy goods in pre-industrial society. The cost of land carriage effectively doubled the pithead price of coal within every ten miles, so that many bulky goods, such as coal, were carried around the coast since the sea shared the manifest advantages for the carriage of such goods that rivers enjoyed. It was no faster than they were, however, and shared their two main comparative disadvantages: travel on it was slow, and its use was seasonal. In a pre-steam age, any boat's motive force was restricted to the wind, and to rowing; inland, the horse-towing of barges and boats that was to typify the canal age seems hardly to have been in existence. Just ascoasting boats had to be laid up in the winter season because of the hazards to navigation presented by gales and fogs, so their riverine cousins were often halted by ice. Not only that, summer weather with low water running down unimproved rivers over shoals and sandbanks could just as easily impede navigation; so could the obstacles presented by mills and fishtraps all the year round. The best brief description of river and coasting transport and trade is to be found in chapter one of T. S. Willan's important book, *The inland trade: studies in English internal trade in the sixteenth and seventeenth centuries* (1976): the main elements of the systems are set out there. Nonetheless, it is still not possible to say with certainty how many pre-industrial rivers were navigable, and what was the limitation of navigation on them.

Some rivers were slowly being improved here and there. They were generally looked after by the Commissioners of Sewers who had some powers to levy rates and clean them up. But their remit was only to prevent flooding and increase drainage and they had no brief for river improvements as such; these powers were executed by acts of parliament or letters patent. Acts were introduced to improve the river Lea for bringing corn to London in 1571, and the river Thames in 1606, 1624 and 1695. The seventeenth century definitely saw increased activity, with a number of acts in the 1660s for the improvement of the Stour, Wye, Medway and other rivers; some improvements were also being carried out by letters patent on the Warwickshire Avon, the Soar, and other rivers. The level of improvement actually effected is not always clear; the passing of an act enabling or allowing improvement is, of course, in itself an administrative statement which does not necessarily mean that any improvement was ever carried out. Only one actual scheme of canalisation was carried out, in the 1560s on the Exeter Ship Canal. The level of innovations connected with river transport was very low, as pound locks were not generally used on rivers, only flashes of water released from the weirs to lift boats over shallow and difficult stretches. The sixteenth century, in particular, remains a dark age as much in terms of water transport as of road transport. Notably, there is a lack of any full and systematic comparison of the modal properties of both, let alone regional studies of either.

Road transport may only have been able to carry smaller loads than water transport, but it was by comparison less open to seasonable variations, more flexible and a good deal faster. The differential in journey time between them was quite marked. Winter stoppages on land were not as total as they were on water, though travel was undoubtedly much hampered by snow which blocked traffic, or wet weather which slowed down wheeled traffic in particular as it fought its way through ruts and puddles, especially on clay lands. Our existing conceptions of the nature and difficulties of road transport are still largely impressionistic, however, based particularly on evidence derived from accounts of the discomforts and difficulties of travel by a few contemporaries. They need closer examination. It is clear that the quality and maintenance of road surfaces was poor and was to remain so until the widespread diffusion of turnpiking in the eighteenth century. Pressure of trade on roads increased into the seventeenth century, and eventually helped to lead to the turnpiking boom from the 1690s onwards. The level of innovation on road surfaces and in the vehicles travelling on them was very low. There was no major innovation in road transport any more than in river transport in the sixteenth and seventeenth century. This does not mean however that there could not be a great increase in the volume of traffic, even if its speed did not increase. Much land transport was by packhorse; what was needed to accommodate this traffic was more horses, not better roads. Indeed for the Elizabethan period Willan suggests (1976, p. 4) that its population and economy 'needed a network of roads which would be usable, but which in practice, even with a considerable movement of people and goods, would be lightly used in comparison with modern roads. To have brought, or to have tried to bring, such roads up to a high standard might not have reduced the cost of transport appreciably'. There was no real economy of scale in movement yet to be had on land. This did not prevent quite large amounts of such high value goods as cloth being regularly transported in the sixteenth century between Kendal and Southampton, summer and winter, a month-long round trip. By the seventeenth century, in addition, there was an extensive and increasing carrying service between the provinces and London. How widespread such services were is another matter, but some regular schedules—a sure sign of modernisation—were being advertised between provincial and metropolitan inns, the usual points of departure and destination. The friction of distance, and the constraints of regionalism, were broken down, it seems, as much by these means as by the introduction and diffusion of any transport innovation as such.

Putting aside foreign trade overseas, which is a subject of its own and one almost totally ignored by historical geographers (as is England in a European context at the time), it is clear that the increasing movement of goods as a whole, by land, river and sea suggests that a national market was emerging, and that the frontiers or regional economies were breaking down. Distance seems to have begun to shrink, people's perception of it to alter. Thus an enormous amount remains to be carried out on the historical geography of pre-industrial England, its changing regionalism and changing spatial relationships. Nothing illustrates this more than our paucity of knowledge on its transport, which is reflected by the few works on the subject that can be cited in the select bibliography which follows this introduction.

This bibliography follows in its major divisions the order in which the different topics such as population and agriculture have been discussed in the introduction, and is subdivided into topics in order to guide further reading as appropriate.

Select Bibliography

Population

General

J. D. Chambers, *Population, economy and society in pre-industrial England* (1972)

P. Deane and W. A. Cole, *British economic growth 1688–1959* (1962)

M. Drake, 'An elementary exercise in parish register demography', *Econ. Hist. Rev.,* XIV (1962)

M. W. Flinn, *British population growth 1700–1850* (1972)

D. Glass and D. E. C. Eversley, *Population in history: essays in historical demography* (1965)

D. Glass and R. Revelle (eds.), *Population and social change* (1972)

J. Hatcher, *Plague, population and the English economy* (1977)

K. Helleiner, 'The vital revolution reconsidered', *Can. Jour. Economics and Pol. Sci.,* 23 (1957)

T. Hollingsworth, 'Demography of the British Peerage'. Suppl. to *Pop. Studies* XVIII (1964)

T. Hollingsworth, 'Methods of using old documents to study population trends in the past' (UN World Pop. Conferences, Belgrade 1965)

T. Hollingsworth, *Historical demography* (1969)

P. Laslett, *The world we have lost* (1965)

R. Lee, 'Population in pre-industrial England: an econometric analysis', *Quart. Journ. Econ.,* LXXXVII (1973)

D. J. Loschky, 'Urbanization and England's eighteenth century crude birth and death rate', *Jour. Eur. Econ. Hist.,* 1 (1972)

T. McKeown, *The modern rise of population* (1976)

A. Saritini, 'Techniques and methods in historical demography in the seventeenth and eighteenth century', *Jour. Eur. Econ. Hist.,* (1972)

R. Schofield, 'Historical demography: some possibilities and limitations', *Trans. Roy. Hist. Soc.,* 21 (1971)

G. S. L. Tucker, 'English pre-industrial population trends', *Econ. Hist. Rev.,* XVI (1963)

L. J. White, 'Enclosures and population movements in England 1700–1800', *Explor. in Entrep. Hist.,* 6 (1969)

E. A. Wrigley, *An introduction to English historical demography* (1966)

E. A. Wrigley, *Population in history* (1969)

Studies using cross sectional sources such as censuses, taxes, etc.

K. J. Allison, 'An Elizabethan village census', *Bull. of the Inst. of Hist. Research,* 36 (1963)

J. D. Gould, 'The inquisition of depopulation of 1607 in Lincs', *Eng. Hist. Rev.*, LXVII (1952)

E. L. Guildford, 'Nottinghamshire in 1676', *Trans. Thoroton Soc.*, XXVIII (1924)

W. Harrison, 'A list of the householders in the town of Douglas, Isle of Man, with their names 1730', *Manx Soc.*, XXX (1880)

F. G. James, 'The population of the Diocese of Carlisle in 1676', *Trans. Cumb. West Antiq. Soc.*, II (1952)

P. Laslett and J. Harrison, 'Clayworth and Cogenhoe', in H. Bell and R. Ollard, (eds.), *Historical Essays 1600–1750* (1963)

L. A. Parker, 'The depopulation returns for Leics. in 1607', *Trans. Leics. Arch. Soc.*, XXII (1947)

J. Patten, 'The hearth taxes, 1662–1689', *Local Population Studies*, 7 (1971)

J. Patten, 'Population distribution in Norfolk and Suffolk during the sixteenth and seventeenth centuries', *Trans. Inst. Brit. Geogr.*, 65 (1975)

J. F. Pound, 'An Elizabethan census of the poor', *Univ. Birm. Hist. Jour.*, VIII (1962)

V. Smith, 'The analysis of census-type documents', *Local Population Studies*, 2 (1969)

P. Styles, 'A census of a Warwickshire village in 1698', *Univ. Birm. Hist. Jour.*, 3 (1951)

Local and regional population studies

J. D. Chambers, 'The Vale of Trent 1670–1800', *Econ. Hist. Rev.*, Suppl. No. 3 (1957)

I. Doolittle, 'Population growth and movement in Colchester and the Hundred from 1500–1800', *Essex Jour.*, 7 (1972)

D. H. Dury, 'The population of Guernsey: an essay in historical geography', *Geog.*, XXXIII (1948)

D. Eversley, 'A survey of population in an area of Worecestershire from 1660–1850 on the basis of parish registers', *Pop. Studies*, X (1957)

F. R. Grace, 'The population of East Bergholt 1653–1836: an analysis of parish registers', *Suffolk Rev.*, 3 (1970)

W. G. Hoskins, 'The population of an English village 1086–1801', *Trans. Leics. Arch. Soc.*, XXXIII (1957)

P. E. Jones and A. V. Judges, 'London population in the late seventeenth century', *Econ. Hist. Rev.*, 1st Ser. VI (1935)

D. A. Kirby, 'Population density and land values in County Durham during the mid-seventeenth century', *Trans. Inst. Brit. Geog.*, 57 (1972)

D. Mills, 'The Poor Laws and the distribution of population c.1600–1800, with special reference to Lincs.', *Trans. Inst. Brit. Geog.*, XXVI (1959)

N. Pounds, 'Population movement in Cornwall and the rise of mining in the eighteenth century', *Geog.*, XXVIII (1943)

R. Ripley, 'Parish register evidence for the population of Gloucester 1562–1641', *Trans. of the Brist. and Gloucs. Arch. Soc.*, 91 (1972)

S. Sogner, 'Aspects of the demographic situation in 17 parishes in Shropshire 1711–60. An exercise based on parish registers', *Pop. Studies*, 17 (1963/4)

R. Speake, 'The historical demography of the ancient parish of Audley, 1538–1801', *North Staffs Jour. of Field Studies*, II (1971)

Marriage and fertility

J. T. Krause, 'Some implications of recent work in historical demography', *Comp. Studies of Soc. and Hist.*, 1 (1959)

L. Lloyd, 'Multiple births in Shropshire 1601–1800', *Local Population Studies*, 3 (1969)

G. C. Morell, 'Tudor marriages and infantile mortality', *Jour. of State Medicine*, XLIII (1935)

R. B. Morrow, 'Family limitation in pre-industrial England: a reappraisal', *Econ. Hist. Rev.*, XXXI (1978)

R. B. Outhwaite, 'Age at marriage in England from the late seventeenth century to the late nineteenth century', *Trans. Roy. Hist. Soc.*, 23 (1973)

D. Roberts and C. Rowling, 'Secular trends in genetic structure: an isonymix analysis of Northumberland parish records', *Annals of Human Biol.* (1974)

E. A. Wrigley, 'Family limitation in pre-industrial England', *Econ. Hist. Rev.*, XIX (1966)

E. A. Wrigley, 'Baptism/marriage ratios in late-seventeenth century England', *Local Population Studies*, 3 (1969)

E. A. Wrigley, 'Clandestine marriages in Tetbury in the seventeenth century', *Local Population Studies*, 10 (1973)

E. A. Wrigley, 'Births and baptisms: the use of Anglican baptism registers as a source of information about the numbers of births in England before the beginning of civil registration', *Pop. Studies*, 31 (1977)

E. A. Wrigley, 'Marital fertility in seventeenth-century Colyton; a note.' *Econ. Hist. Rev.*, XXXI (1978)

Disease and mortality

A. Appleby, 'Disease or famine? Mortality in Cumberland and Westmorland 1580–1640', *Econ. Hist. Rev.*, XXV (1973)

A. Appleby, 'Nutrition and disease: the case of London 1550–1750', *Jour. of Interdisc. Hist.*, V (1975)

J. Bean, 'Plague, population and economic decline in the later Middle Ages', *Econ. Hist. Rev.*, XV (1963)

C. Cipolla, 'The plague and pre-Malthus Malthusians', *Jour. Eur. Econ. Hist.*, 3 (1974)

I. Doolittle, 'The plague in Colchester 1579–1666', *Trans. of Essex Arch. Soc.*, 4 (1972)

F. J. Fisher, 'Influenza and inflation in Tudor England', *Econ. Hist. Rev.*, XVIII (1965)

M. W. Flinn, 'The stabilization of mortality in pre-industrial Europe', *Jour. Eur. Econ. Hist.*, 3 (1974)

W. E. Godfrey, 'The plague of Chesterfield 1566–7', *Jour. Derby Arch. Nat. Hist. Soc.*, IXXIV (1954)

A. Gooder, 'The population crisis of 1727–30 in Warwickshire', *Midland History*, 1 (1971–2)

M. F. and T. H. Hollingsworth, 'Plague mortality rates by age and sex in the parish of St. Botolph's without Bishopsgate, London, 1603', *Population Studies,* 25 (1971)

W. G. Howson, 'Plague, poverty and population in parts of N.W. England 1580–1720', *Trans. Lancs. and Chesh. Hist. Soc.*, LXII (1960)

J. A. Johnson, 'The impact of epidemics of 1727–30 in South-West Worcestershire', *Med. Hist.*, 15 (1971)

T. McKeown and R. Brown, 'Medical evidence related to English population change in the eighteenth century', *Pop. Studies*, 9 (1955)

T. McKeown *et al*., 'An interpretation of the decline of mortality—England and Wales during the twentieth century', *Pop. Studies*, 29 (1975)

D. W. Palliser, 'Epidemics in Tudor York', *Northern Hist.*, VIII (1973)

R. Pickard, *The population and epidemics of Exeter in pre-census times* (privately printed, Exeter, 1947)

P. Razzell, 'Population change in eighteenth-century England: a reinterpretation', *Econ. Hist. Rev.*, XVII (1965)

P. Razzell, 'An interpretation of the modern rise of population in Europe', *Pop. Studies*, 28 (1974)

E. A. Wrigley, 'Mortality in pre-industrial England. The example of Colyton, Devon, over the centuries', *Daedalus*, 97 (1968)

Migration: general and local studies

J. Cornwall, 'Evidence of population mobility in the seventeenth century', *Bull. Inst. Hist. Research*, XL (1967), 143–52

F. R. Grace, 'The population of East Bergholt, Suffolk 1653–1836', *Suffolk Review*, 3 (1970)

B. Maltby, 'Easingwold marriage horizons', *Local Population Studies*, 2 (1969), 36–9

R. F. Peel, 'Local intermarriage and the stability of rural population in the English Midlands', *Geography*, XXVII (1942), 22–30

S. A. Peyton, 'The village population in the Tudor Lay Subsidy Rolls', *Eng. Hist. Rev.*, XXX (1915)

P. Slack, 'Vagrants and vagrancy in England, 1598–1664', *Econ. Hist. Rev.*, 2nd series. XXVII (1974), 360–79

P. Spufford, 'Population movement in seventeenth-century England', *Local Population Studies*, 4 (1970), 41–50

Agriculture

1500–1650—early patterns and changes

K. J. Allison, 'The sheep-corn husbandry of Norfolk in the sixteenth and seventeenth centuries', *Agricultural History Review*, 6 (1957)

A. R. H. Baker and R. A. Butlin, *Studies of field systems in the British Isles* (1973)

I. Blanchard, 'Population change, enclosure, and the early Tudor economy', *Econ. Hist. Rev.*, 23 (1970)

A. R. Bridbury, 'Sixteenth-century farming', *Econ. Hist. Rev.*, 27 (1974)

M. Campbell, *The English yeoman under Elizabeth and the early Stuarts* (1942)

J. P. Cooper, 'The social distribution of land and men in England, 1436–1700', *Econ. Hist. Rev.*, 20 (1967)

F. J. Fisher, 'The development of the London food market, 1540–1640', *Econ. Hist. Rev.*, 1st Ser. 5 (1935)

F. J. Fisher, 'Tawney's century', in Fisher, F. J. (ed.), *Essays in the economic and social history of Tudor and Stuart England* (1961)

N. S. B. Gras, *The evolution of the English corn market* (1926)

C. J. Harrison, 'Grain price analysis of harvest qualities, 1465–1634', *Agric. Hist. Rev.*, 27 (1971)

W. G. Hoskins, 'The Leicestershire farmer in the sixteenth century', *Trans. Leicestershire Archaeol. Soc.*, 22 (1945)

W. G. Hoskins, 'Harvest fluctuations in English economic history, 1480–1619', *Agric. Hist. Rev.*, 2 (1953)

E. L. Jones, 'The condition of English agriculture, 1500–1640', *Econ. Hist. Rev.*, 21 (1968)

E. Kerridge, 'The movement of rent, 1540–1640', *Econ. Hist. Rev.*, 6 (1953)

E. Kerridge, *The agricultural revolution* (1967)

E. Kerridge, *Agrarian problems in the sixteenth century and after* (1969)

E. Kerridge, *The farmers of old England* (1973)

E. Kneisel, 'The evolution of the English corn market', *Jour. Econ. Hist.*, 14 (1954)

E. Lipson, *The economic history of England* vol. 2, chapter 3 (1931)

M. Overton, 'Computer analysis of an inconsistent data source: the case of probate inventories', *Journal of Historical Geography*, 4 (1977)

V. Ponko, jnr., 'N.S.B. Gras and Elizabethan corn policy: a re-examination of the problem', *Econ. Hist. Rev.*, 17 (1965)

R. S. Schofield, 'The geographical distribution of wealth in England, 1334–1649', *Econ. Hist. Rev.*, 18 (1965)

J. Sheail, 'The distribution of taxable population and wealth in England during the early sixteenth century', *Trans. Inst. Brit. Geog.*, 55 (1972)

V. T. H. Skipp, 'Economic and social change in the Forest of Arden, 1530–1640', *Agric. Hist. Rev.*, Supplement 18 (1970)

L. Stone, *Social change and revolution in England, 1540–1640* (1965)

J. Thirsk, *Fenland farming in the sixteenth century*, Leicester University Department of English Local History, Occasional Paper No. 3 (1965)

J. Thirsk (ed.), *The agrarian history of England and Wales,* vol. IV, chapters 1, 3–9 (1967)

I. M. Wallerstein, *The modern world system: capitalist agriculture and the origins of the European world economy in the sixteenth century* (1974)

J. A. Yelling, 'The combination and rotation of crops in East Worcestershire, 1540–1660', *Agric. Hist. Rev.*, 17 (1969)

J. A. Yelling, 'Probate inventories and the geography of livestock farming: a study of east Worcestershire, 1540–1750', *Trans. Inst. Brit. Geog.*, 51 (1970)

J. A. Yelling, *Common field and enclosure in England, 1450–1850* (1977)

Agrarian development after 1650—the quickening pace of change

T. S. Ashton, *An economic history of England: the eighteenth century*, ch. 2 (1955)

D. G. Barnes, *A history of the English Corn Laws, 1660–1846* (1930)

J. Carswell, *From revolution to revolution: England 1688–1776* (1973)

C. Clay, 'Marriage, inheritance and the rise of large estates in England, 1660–1815', *Econ. Hist. Rev.*, 21 (1968)

D. C. Coleman, 'Labour in the English economy of the seventeenth century', *Econ. Hist. Rev.*, 8 (1956)

H. C. Darby, 'The age of the improver: 1600–1800', ch. 7 of *A New Historical Geography of England* (1973)

M. W. Flinn, 'Agricultural productivity and economic growth: a comment', *Jour. Econ. Hist.*, 26 (1966)

J. D. Gould, 'Agricultural fluctuations and the English economy in the eighteenth century', *Jour. Econ. Hist.*, 22 (1962)

C. Hill, *The century of revolution* (1961)

W. G. Hoskins, 'Harvest fluctuations and English economic history, 1620–1759', *Agric. Hist. Rev.*, 12 (1968)

A. H. John, 'The course of agricultural change, 1660–1760', in L. S. Pressnell (ed.), *Studies in the industrial revolution* (1960)

A. H. John, 'Agricultural productivity and economic growth in England, 1700–1760', *Jour. Econ. Hist.*, 25 (1965)

E. L. Jones, 'Agriculture and economic growth in England, 1660–1750; agricultural change', *Jour. Econ. Hist.*, 25 (1965)

E. L. Jones, *Agriculture and economic growth in England, 1650–1815* (1967), editor's introduction

E. Kerridge, *The farmers of Old England* (1973)

G. E. Mingay, 'The size of farms in the eighteenth century', *Econ. Hist. Rev.*, 14 (1962)

G. E. Mingay, *English landed society in the eighteenth century* (1963)

E. H. Phelps Brown and S. V. Hopkins, 'Seven centuries of the prices of consumables, compared with builders' wage rates', *Economica*, 23 (1956)

J. Thirsk, 'Seventeenth-century agriculture and social change', *Agric. Hist. Rev.*, supplement 18 (1970)

F. M. L. Thompson, 'Landownership and economic growth in England in the eighteenth century', in E. L. Jones and S. J. Woolf, *Agrarian change and economic development* (1969)

C. P. Timmer, 'The turnip, the new husbandry and the English agricultural revolution', *Quarterly Journal of Economics*, 83 (1969)

B. H. Slicher Van Bath, *The agrarian history of Western Europe, 500–1850* (1963)

J. A. Yelling, 'Changes in crop production in East Worcestershire, 1540–1867', *Agric. Hist. Rev.*, 21 (1973)

Innovations

G. E. Fussell, 'Adventures with clover', *Agriculture*, 62 (1955)

R. M. Garnier, 'The introduction of forage crops into Great Britain', *Journal of the Royal Agricultural Society of England*, third Series, 7 (1896)

E. Kerridge, 'The sheepfold in Wiltshire and the floating of watermeadows', *Econ. Hist. Rev.*, 6 (1954)

E. Kerridge, *The agricultural revolution* (1967), chs. 3–9
H. C. Prince, 'The origins of pits and depressions in Norfolk', *Geography*, 49 (1964)

Innovators

C. J. Bates, 'The brothers Collings', *Journal of the Royal Agricultural Society of England*, third Series, 10 (1899)
G. E. Fussell, 'The Norfolk improvers: their farms and methods', *Norfolk Archaeology*, 33 (1964)
W. Housman, 'Robert Bakewell', *J.R.A.S.E.*, Third Series, 5 (1894)
R. A. C. Parker, 'Coke of Norfolk and the agrarian revolution', *Econ. Hist. Rev.*, 8. (Reprinted in Carus-Wilson, vol. 2) (1955)
J. H. Plumb, 'Sir Robert Walpole and Norfolk husbandry', *Econ. Hist. Rev.*, 5 (1952)
J. Thirsk, 'New crops and their diffusion: tobacco-growing in seventeenth-century England', in C. W. Chalklin and M. A. Havinden, *Rural change and urban growth* (1974)

Communication of ideas

W. H. Curtler, *A short history of English agriculture* (1909)
F. V. Emery, 'The mechanics of innovation: clover cultivation in Wales before 1750', *Jour. Hist. Geogr.*, 2 (1976)
Lord Ernle, 'Obstacles to progress', ch. 3 of *The land and its people* (1925), reprinted in Jones (1967)
Lord Ernle, *English farming past and present* 6th edn. (1961)
G. E. Fussell, 'Early farming journals', *Econ. Hist. Rev.*, first series, 3 (1932)
G. E. Fussell, 'Agriculture in rural England in the seventeenth century', *Econ. Geog.*, 9 (1933)
D. McDonald, *Agricultural writers, 1200–1800* (1908)
W. F. Perkins, *British and Irish writers on agriculture* 3rd edn. (1939)

The origins and spread of innovations

G. E. Fussell, 'The Low Countries' influence on English farming', *Eng. Hist. Rev.*, 74 (1959)
D. B. Grigg, *The agricultural revolution in south Lincolnshire* (1966)
A. Harris, *The rural landscape of the East Riding of Yorkshire, 1700–1850* (1961)
M. A. Havinden, 'Agricultural progress in open-field Oxfordshire', *Agric. Hist. Rev.*, 9 (1961)
J. A. Hellen, 'Agricultural innovation and detectable landscape margins: the case of Wheelhouses in Northumberland', *Agric. Hist. Rev.*, 20 (1972)
E. L. Jones, 'Eighteenth-century changes in Hampshire chalkland farming', *Agric. Hist. Rev.*, 8 (1960)
G. E. Jones, 'The diffusion of agricultural innovations', *Jour. of Agricultural Economics*, 15 (1963)

E. Kerridge, 'Turnip husbandry in High Suffolk', *Econ. Hist. Rev.*, 8 (1956)
J. J. Murray, 'The cultural impact of the Flemish Low Countries on sixteenth- and seventeenth-century England', *American Hist. Rev.*, 23 (1957)
W. C. Socville, 'Minority migrations and the diffusion of technology', *Jour. Econ. Hist.*, 10 (1950)
W. C. Socville, 'The Huguenots and the diffusion of technology', *Jour. Pol. Econ.*, 60 (1952)

Manufacture

General

I. Blanchard, 'Labour productivity and work psychology in the English mining industry, 1400–1600', *Econ. Hist. Rev.*, 31 (1978)
L. A. Clarkson, *The pre-industrial economy in England 1500–1750* (1971)
D. C. Coleman, 'Industrial growth and industrial revolutions', *Economica*, 23 (1956)
D. C. Coleman, 'Labour in the English economy of the seventeenth century', *Econ. Hist. Rev.*, 8 (1956)
D. C. Coleman, 'Technology and economic history, 1500–1750', *Econ. Hist. Rev.*, 11 (1959)
D. C. Coleman, *Industry in Tudor and Stuart England* (1975)
D. C. Coleman, *The economy of England 1450–1750* (1977)
D. C. Coleman and A. H. John (eds.), *Trade, government and economy in pre-industrial England, essays presented to F. J. Fisher* (1976)
F. J. Fisher, 'The sixteenth and seventeenth centuries: the Dark Ages in English economic history?' *Economica* (new series), 24 (1957)
R. M. Hartwell, 'Economic growth in England before the Industrial Revolution: some methodological issues', *Jour. Econ. Hist.*, 29 (1969)
B. A. Holderness, *Pre-industrial England: economy and society 1500–1750* (1976)
W. G. Hoskins, *The age of plunder, King Henry's England 1500–1547* (1976)
S. M. Jack, *Trade and industry in Tudor and Stuart England* (1977)
J. U. Nef, 'The progress of technology and the growth of large-scale industry in Great Britain, 1540–1640', *Econ. Hist. Rev.* 1st Ser. 5 (1934)
E. A. Wrigley, 'The supply of raw materials in the Industrial Revolution', *Econ. Hist. Rev.*, 15 (1962)

Dual economies

J. Hatcher, 'A diversified economy: later medieval Cornwall', *Econ. Hist. Rev.*, 22 (1969)
J. Hatcher, 'Myths, miners, and agricultural communities', *Agric. Hist. Rev.*, 22 (1974)
D. G. Hey, 'A dual economy in South Yorkshire', *Agric. Hist. Rev.*, 17 (1969)
R. I. Hodgson, 'First threat to the environment', *Geographical Magazine*, 43 (January, 1971)

W. G. Hoskins, 'Harvest fluctuations and English economic history, 1480–1619', *Agric. Hist. Rev.*, 12 (1964)

W. G. Hoskins, 'Harvest fluctuations and English economic history, 1620–1759', *Agric. Hist. Rev.*, 16 (1968)

E. L. Jones, 'Agricultural origins of industry', *Past and Present*, 40 (1968)

V. H. T. Skipp, 'Economic and social change in the Forest of Arden, 1530–1649', being pp. 84–111 of J. Thirsk (ed.), 'Land, Church and People. Essays presented to Professor H. P. R. Finberg', *Agric. Hist. Rev.*, 18 (1970), *supplement*

J. Thirsk, 'Industries in the countryside', being pp. 70–88 of F. J. Fisher (ed.), *Essays in the economic and social history of Tudor and Stuart England in honour of R. H. Tawney* (1961)

J. Thirsk, 'Seventeenth-century agriculture and social change', being pp. 148–177 of J. Thirsk (ed.) (1970) *op. cit.*

Particular manufactures

(a) Cloth

K. J. Allison, 'The Norfolk worsted industry in the sixteenth and seventeenth centuries: 1. The traditional industry', *Yorkshire Bulletin of Economic and Social Research*, 12 (1960). '2. The new draperies', *ibid.*, 13 (1961)

R. P. Beckinsale, 'Factors in the development of the Cotswold woollen industry', *Geographical Journal*, 90 (1937)

P. J. Bowden, 'Wool supply and the woollen industry', *Econ. Hist. Rev.*, 9 (1956)

P. J. Bowden, *The wool trade in Tudor and Stuart England*, new impression (1971)

D. C. Coleman, 'An innovation and its diffusion: the "new draperies"', *Econ. Hist. Rev.*, 22 (1969)

D. C. Coleman, 'Textile growth', being pp. 1–21 of N. B. Harte, and K. G. Ponting (eds.), *Textile history and economic history, essays in honour of Miss Julia de Lacy Mann* (1973)

R. H. Kinvig, 'The historical geography of the West Country woollen industry', *Geographical Teacher*, 8 (1916)

N. Lowe, *The Lancashire textile industry in the sixteenth century* (1972)

J. de L. Mann, *The cloth industry in the West of England from 1640 to 1880* (1971)

B. McClenaghan, *The Springs of Lavenham and the Suffolk cloth trade in the fifteenth and sixteenth centuries* (1924)

T. C. Mendenhall, *The Shrewsbury drapers and the Welsh wool trade in the sixteenth and seventeenth centuries* (1953)

R. Perry, 'The Gloucester woollen industry, 1100–1690', *Trans. Bristol and Glos. Archaeol. Soc.*, 66 (1945)

J. E. Pilgrim, 'The rise of the "new draperies" in Essex', *University of Birmingham Historical Journal*, 7 (1959)

K. G. Ponting, *The woollen industry of south-west England* (1971)

G. D. Ramsay, *The Wiltshire woollen industry in the sixteenth and seventeenth centuries*, 2nd edn. (1965)

J. Thirsk, 'The fantastical folly of fashion: the English stocking knitting industry, 1500–1700', being pp. 50–73 of N. B. Harte, and K. G. Ponting (eds.), (1973), *op. cit.*

C. Wilson, 'Cloth production and international competition in the seventeenth century', *Econ. Hist. Rev.*, 13 (1960)

(*b*) Leather

L. A. Clarkson, 'The organization of the English leather industry in the late sixteenth and seventeenth centuries', *Econ. Hist. Rev.*, 13 (1960)

L. A. Clarkson, 'The leather crafts in Tudor and Stuart England', *Agric. Hist. Rev.*, 14 (1966)

D. M. Woodward, 'The Chester leather industry, 1558–1625', *Transactions of the Historic Society of Lancashire and Cheshire*, 119 (1967)

(*c*) Salt

T. C. Barker, 'Lancashire coal, Cheshire salt, and the rise of Liverpool', *Transactions of the Historic Society of Lancashire and Cheshire*, 103 (1951)

E. K. Berry, 'The borough of Droitwich and its salt industry, 1215–1700', *University of Birmingham Historical Journal*, 6 (1957–8)

P. Pilbin, 'A geographical analysis of the sea-salt industry of north-east England', *Scottish Geographical Magazine*, 51 (1935)

(*d*) Building

A. Clifton-Taylor, *The pattern of English building*, new edn. (1972)

W. G. Hoskins, 'The rebuilding of rural England, 1570–1640', *Past and Present*, 4 (1953)

(*e*) Iron

T. S. Ashton, *Iron and steel in the Industrial Revolution*, 4th edn. (1968)

M. W. Flinn, 'The growth of the English iron industry, 1660–1760', *Econ. Hist. Rev.*, 11 (1958)

M. W. Flinn, 'Timber and the advance of technology: a reconsideration', *Annals of Science*, 15 (1959)

G. Hammersley, 'The charcoal iron industry and its fuel, 1540–1750', *Econ. Hist. Rev.*, 26 (1973)

B. L. C. Johnson, 'The Stour Valley iron industry in the late seventeenth century', *Trans. Worcs. Archaeol. Soc.* (new series), 27 (1950)

B. L. C. Johnson, 'The Foley partnerships: the iron industry at the end of the charcoal era', *Econ. Hist. Rev.*, 4 (1952)

B. L. C. Johnson, 'New light on the iron industry of the Forest of Dean', *Trans. Bristol and Glos. Archaeol. Soc.*, 72 (1953)

S. R. H. Jones, 'The development of needle manufacturing in the West Midlands before 1750', *Econ. Hist. Rev.*, XXXI (1978)

R. A. Mott, 'The Shropshire iron industry', *Trans. Shropshire Archaeol. Soc.*, 56 (1958)

R. A. Pelham, 'The migration of the iron industry towards Birmingham during the sixteenth century', *Trans. and Proceedings of the Birmingham Archaeol. Soc.*, 66 (1945–6)

H. R. Schubert, *History of the British iron and steel industry from c.450 B.C. to A.D. 1775* (1957)

E. Straker, *Wealden iron* (1931, reprinted 1969)

H. C. Tomlinson, 'Wealden gunfounding: an analysis of its demise in the eighteenth century', *Econ. Hist. Rev.*, 29 (1976)

(f) Coal

J. A. Bulley, '"To Mendip for Coal"—a study of the Somerset coalfield before 1830', *Proceedings of the Somerset Archaeological and Natural History Society*, 97 (1952)

D. C. Coleman, 'The coal industry: a rejoinder', *Econ. Hist. Rev.*, 30 (1977)

E. Kerridge, 'The coal industry in Tudor and Stuart England: a comment', *Econ. Hist. Rev.*, 30 (1977)

J. Langton, 'Coal output in South-West Lancashire, 1590–1799', *Econ. Hist. Rev.*, 25 (1972)

A. Moller, 'Coal-mining in the seventeenth century', *Trans. Royal Hist. Soc.*, 4th series, 8 (1925)

J. U. Nef, *The rise of the British coal industry*, 2 vols. (1932)

L. Stone, 'An Elizabethan coalmine', *Econ. Hist. Rev.*, 3 (1950)

E. R. Turner, 'English coal industry in the seventeenth and eighteenth centuries', *Amer. Hist. Rev.*, 27 (1921)

(g) Lead and tin

D. B. Barton, *A history of tin mining and smelting in Cornwall* (1967)

J. Hatcher, *English tin production and trade before 1550* (1973)

G. R. Lewis, *The stannaries: a study of the medieval tin miners of Cornwall and Devon* (1908)

A. Raistrick and B. Jennings, *A history of lead mining in the Pennines* (1965)

(h) Brass and copper

D. B. Barton, *A history of copper mining in Cornwall and Devon*, 2nd edn. (1968)

H. Hamilton, *The English brass and copper industries in 1800*, 2nd edn. (1967)

G. Hammersley, 'Technique or economy? The rise and decline of the early English copper industry, c.1550–1660', *Business History*, 15 (1973)

R. Jenkins, 'The copper works at Redbrook and at Bristol', *Trans. Bristol and Glos. Archaeol. Soc.*, 63 (1942)

F. J. Monkhouse, 'Some features of the historical geography of the German mining enterprise in Elizabethan Lakeland', *Geography*, 28 (1943)

J. A. Robey, 'The Ecton copper mines in the seventeenth century', *Bulletin of the Peak District Mines Historical Society*, 4 (1969)

(i) Glass

D. W. Crossley, 'The performance of the glass industry in sixteenth-century England', *Econ. Hist. Rev.*, 25 (1972)

E. S. Godfrey, *The development of English glassmaking 1560–1640* (1975)

G. H. Kenyon, *The glass industry of the Weald* (1967)

(j) Paper

D. C. Coleman, *The British paper industry 1495–1860. A study in industrial growth* (1958)

A. H. Shorter, *Paper making in the British Isles. An historical and geographical study* (1971)

(k) Shipbuilding

D. C. Coleman, 'Naval dockyards under the later Stuarts', *Econ. Hist. Rev.*, 6 (1953)

R. Davis, *The rise of the English shipping industry in the seventeenth and eighteenth centuries*, 2nd impression (1972)

Entrepreneurs and business

I. S. W. Blanchard, 'Seigneurial entrepreneurship: the bishops of Durham and the Weardale lead industry 1406–1529', *Business History*, 15 (1973)

P. Deane, 'Capital formation in Britain before the railway age', *Economic Development and Cultural Change*, 9 (1961)

M. W. Flinn, 'Sir Ambrose Crowley, ironmonger, 1658–1713', *Explorations in Entrepreneurial History*, (1953)

M. W. Flinn, 'The Lloyds in the early English iron industry', *Business History*, 2 (1959)

M. J. Galgano, 'Iron-mining in Restoration Furness: the case of Sir Thomas Preston', *Recusant History*, 13 (1976)

J. W. Gough, *The rise of the entrepreneur* (1969)

R. Grassby, 'The personal wealth of the business community in seventeenth century England', *Econ. Hist. Rev.*, 23 (1970)

H. J. Habakkuk, 'Economic functions of English landowners in the seventeenth and eighteenth centuries', *Explorations in Entrepreneurial History*, 6 (1953)

R. A. Pelham, 'The establishment of the Willoughby ironworks in north Warwickshire in the sixteenth century', *University of Birmingham Historical Journal*, 4 (1953–4)

S. Pollard, 'Fixed capital in the Industrial Revolution in Britain', *Journal of Economic History*, 24 (1964)

R. G. Schafer, 'Genesis and structure of the Foley "ironworks in partnership" of 1692', *Business History*, 13 (1) (1971)

R. S. Smith, 'Huntington Beaumont: adventurer in coalmines', *Renaissance and Modern Studies*, 11 (1967)

R. S. Smith, 'Sir Francis Willoughby's ironworks, 1570–1610', *Renaissance and Modern Studies*, 11 (1967), 90–114

L. Stone, *Family and fortune. Studies in aristocratic finance in the sixteenth and seventeenth centuries* (1973). See especially pp. 190–4, 'The Rielvaux Ironworks'.

Towns

General

C. Chalklin, 'The making of some new towns, c.1600–1720' in C. W. Chalklin and M. A. Havinden (eds.), *Rural change and urban growth 1500–1800* (1974)

P. Clark, *The early modern town: a reader* (1976)

P. Clark and P. Slack (eds.), *Crisis and order in English towns 1500–1700* (1972)

P. Clark and P. Slack, *English towns in transition 1500–1700* (1976)

P. Corfield, 'Urban development in England and Wales in the sixteenth and seventeenth centuries', being pp. 214–247 of D. C. Coleman and A. H. John (eds.) *Trade, government and economy in pre-industrial England* (1976)

A. Everitt, 'Urban growth 1570–1770', *The Local Historian* VIII (1968–9)

J. Patten, *English Towns 1500–1700* (1978)

J. Patten, 'Urban Life before the industrial revolution', *Geographical Magazine* XLIII (1970)

Some particular towns

K. A. Adey, 'Seventeenth-century Stafford: a county town in decline', *Midland History* II (1973–4), 152–167

A. B. Appleby, 'Nutrition and disease: the case of London 1550–1750', *Journal of Interdisciplinary History* VI (1975–6), 1–27

P. Corfield, 'A provincial capital in the late seventeenth century: the case of Norwich' in Clark and Slack (1972) *op. cit.*

A. D. Dyer, *The city of Worcester in the sixteenth century* (Leicester, 1973)

F. J. Fisher, 'The development of the London food market 1540–1650', *Econ. Hist. Rev.* 1st Series V (1934–5)

—'The development of London as a centre of conspicuous consumption in the sixteenth and seventeenth centuries'. *Trans. Roy. Hist. Soc.* 4th series, XXX (1948)

D. V. Glass, 'Socio-economic status and occupations in the city of London at the end of the seventeenth century', in (eds.) A. E. J. Hollaender and W. Kellaway, *Studies in London History* (1969)

J. W. F. Hill, *Tudor and Stuart Lincoln* (Cambridge, 1956)

W. G. Hoskins, *Industry, trade and people in Exeter 1688–1900* (2nd ed. Exeter, 1968)

W. J. MacCaffrey, *Exeter 1540–1640* (2nd ed. Cambridge, Mass. 1976)

W. E. Minchinton, 'Bristol: metropolis of the West in the eighteenth century', *Trans. Royal Hist. Soc.* 5th Series IV (1954)

D. Palliser, 'York under the Tudors: the trading life of the northern capital' in A. Everitt, *Perspectives in English Urban History* VIII (1973)

—'Epidemics in Tudor York', *Northern History* VIII (1973)

G. D. Ramsay, *The City of London in international politics at the accession of Elizabeth Tudor* (Manchester 1975).

H. B. Rodgers, 'The market area of Preston in the 16th and 17th centuries', *Geographical Studies* 111 (1965), 46–55

W. B. Stephens, *Seventeenth-century Exeter* (1958)

E. A. Wrigley, 'A simple model of London's role in changing English society and economy, 1650–1750', *Past and Present* 37 (1967)

Urban occupations

K. Charlton, 'The professions in sixteenth-century England', *Univ of Birmingham Hist. Jour.* 12 (1969), 20–4

D. Davis, *A history of shopping* (1968)

R. B. Dobson, 'Admission to the freedom of the City of York in the later Middle Ages', *Econ. Hist. Rev.* 26 (1973), 1–22

A. Everitt, 'The marketing of agricultural produce' in J. Thirsk, (ed.) *The agrarian history of England and Wales, Vol. IV, 1500–1640* (1967)

W. G. Hoskins, 'English provincial towns in the early sixteenth century', *Trans. Roy. Hist. Soc.* 5th series 6 (1956), 1–16

J. Patten, 'Village and town: an occupational study', *Agric. Hist. Rev.* 20 (1972)

J. Patten, 'Urban occupations in pre-industrial England', *Trans. Inst. Brit. Geogr.* NS.2 (1977), 296–313

J. F. Pound, 'The social and trade structure of Norwich 1525–1575', *Past and Present*, 34 (1966), 49–69

Urban internal social and economic structure

D. V. Glass, 'London's inhabitants within the walls', *London Rec. Soc. Publications*, 2 (1966)

—'Notes on the demography of London at the end of the seventeenth century', *Daedalus* 97 (1968), 581–92

M. Falkus, 'Lighting in the dark ages of English economic history: town streets before the industrial revolution' in D. C. Coleman and A. H. John, *Trade, government and economy in pre-industrial England* (1976)

J. Langton, 'Residential patterns in pre-industrial cities: some case studies from seventeenth-century Britain', *Trans. Inst. Brit. Geogr.*, 65 (1975), 7–87

—'Late medieval Gloucester: some data from a rental of 1455', *Trans. Inst. Brit. Geogr.*, NS.2 (1977), 259–77

J. F. Pound, 'An Elizabethan census of the poor', *University of Birmingham Hist. Jour.*, VIII (1962), 135–51

E. Ralph and M. E. Williams (eds.), 'The inhabitants of Bristol in 1696', *Bristol Record Soc. Publ.*, XXV (1968)

Rural-urban migration

E. J. Buchatzsch, 'Places of origin of a group of immigrants into Sheffield, 1624–1799', *Econ. Hist. Rev.*, 2nd Series, 2 (1949–50), 303–6

A. F. Butcher, 'The origins of Romney Freemen, 1433–1523', *Econ. Hist. Rev., XXVII* (1974), 16–27

P. Clark, 'The migrant in Kentish towns 1580–1640', pp. 117–63 of P. Clark and P. Slack (eds.), *Crisis and order in English towns 1500–1700* (1972)

D. Cressey, 'Occupation, migration and literacy in East London', *Local Pop. Studies*, 5 (1970), 53–60

A. D. Dyer, *The city of Worcester in the sixteenth century* (1973), esp. 180–6

C. I. Hammer, 'The mobility of skilled labour in late medieval England: some Oxford evidence', *Viertel jahrshrift für sozial und Wirtschaftsgeshcicte*, 63 Band, Heft 2 (1976)

D. Hollis (ed.), 'Calender of the Bristol apprentice book, 1532–1565', (Pt. 1, 1535–42), *Bristol Record Society*, XIV (1948), *introduction*

L. G. Matthews, 'London's immigrant apothecaries 1600–1800', *Medical History*, 18 (1974), 262–74

D. F. McKenzie, 'Apprenticeship in the Stationers Company 1550–1640', *The Library*, 5th series, 13 (1958), 292–8

A. L. Merson, (ed.) 'A calender of Southampton apprenticeship registers, 1609–1740', *Southampton Record Series*, 12 (1968), *introduction*

J. Patten, 'Rural-urban migration in pre-industrial England', *University of Oxford, School of Geography Research Paper 6* (1973)

J. Patten, 'Patterns of migration and movement of labour to the pre-industrial East Anglian towns', *Jour. Historical Geography*, 2 (1976) 111–29

R. A. Pelham, 'The immigrant population of Birmingham 1686–1726' *Trans. Birmingham Archaeol. Soc.*, LXI (1937), 45–82

S. R. Smith, 'The social and geographical origins of the London apprentices 1630–60', *Guildhall Miscellany*, IV (1973), 195–206

P. Spufford, 'Population mobility in pre-industrial England II: The magnet of the metropolis; III: Conclusion', *Genealogists' Magazine*, XVII (1974)

E. A. Wrigley, 'A simple model of London's role in changing English society and economy, 1650–1750', *Past and Present*, 37 (1967), 44–70

Transport and trade

Transport: general

H. J. Dyos and D. H. Aldcroft, *British transport: an economic survey from the seventeenth century to the twentieth* (1969)

W. T. Jackman, *The development of transportation in modern England*, 2nd edn. (1962)

J. Parkes, *Travel in England in the seventeenth century* (1925)

E. A. Pratt, *A history of inland transport and communication* (1925)

J. Thirsk and J. P. Cooper (eds.), *Seventeenth-century economic documents* (1972), *passim*

Transport: specific modes

W. Albert, *The turnpike road system in England, 1663–1840* (1972)

J. A. Chartres, 'Road carrying in England in the seventeenth-century: myth and reality', *Econ. Hist. Rev.*, 2nd Ser., XXX (1977)

J. Crofts, *Packhorse, waggon and post: land carriage and communications under the Tudors and Stuarts* (1967)

R. Davis, *The rise of the English shipping industry in the seventeenth and eighteenth centuries* (1962)

H. G. Fordham, 'The earliest tables of the highways of England and Wales 1541–1561', *Transactions Bibliographical Society.*, 2nd Ser., VIII (1927–8)

B. C. Jones, 'Westmorland pack-horse men in Southampton', *Transactions of the Cumberland and Westmorland Antiquarian and Archaeological Society*, LIX (1960)

M. J. T. Lewis, *Early wooden railways* (1970)

E. J. Pawson, *Transport and economy: the turnpike roads of eighteenth-century Britain* (1977)

G. Scott-Thomson, 'Roads in England and Wales in 1603', *Eng. Hist. Rev.*, XXXIII (1918)

W. B. Stephens, 'The Exeter Lighter Canal, 1566–1698', *Journal of Transport History*, 3 (1957–8)

S. and B. Webb, *The story of the King's Highway* (1913)

T. S. Willan, *River navigation in England, 1600–1750* (1936)

T. S. Willan, 'Yorkshire river navigation, 1600–1750,' *Geography*, XXII (1937)

T. S. Willan, 'The river navigation and trade of the Severn valley, 1600–1750', *Econ. Hist. Rev.*, 1st Ser. VIII (1937–8)

T. S. Willan, *The English coasting trade, 1600–1750* (1938)

Trade: internal

P. J. Bowden, *The wool trade in Tudor and Stuart England* (1962)

J. A. Chartres, *Internal trade in England, 1500–1700* (1977)

A. Everitt, 'The marketing of agricultural produce', in J. Thirsk (ed.), *The agrarian history of England and Wales*, vol. IV (1967)

A. Everitt, 'The English urban inn, 1560–1760', in A. Everitt (ed.), *Perspectives in English urban history* (1973)

F. J. Fisher, 'Development of the London food market, 1540–1640', *Econ. Hist. Rev.*, 1st Ser. V (1935)

N. S. B. Gras, *The evolution of the English corn market* (1915)

M. J. Hodgen, 'Fairs of Elizabethan England', *Econ. Geography*, 18 (1942)

H. B. Rodgers, 'The market area of Preston in the sixteenth and seventeenth centuries', *Geographical Studies*, 3 (1956)

A. P. Wadsworth and J. de L. Mann, *The cotton trade and industrial Lancashire, 1600–1780* (1931)

T. S. Willan, *The inland trade* (1976)

D. Woodward, *The trade of Elizabethan Chester* (1970)

Trade: overseas

R. Davis, *English overseas trade, 1500–1700* (1973)

F. J. Fisher, 'London's export trade in the early seventcenth century', *Econ. Hist. Rev.*, III (1950)

W. E. Minchinton (ed.), *The growth of English overseas trade in the seventeenth and eighteenth centuries* (1969)

G. D. Ramsay, *English overseas trade during the centuries of emergence* (1957)

L. Stone, 'Elizabethan overseas trade', *Econ. Hist. Rev.*, II (1949)

T. S. Willan, *Studies in Elizabethan foreign trade* (1959)

The distribution of taxable population and wealth in England during the early sixteenth century

JOHN SHEAIL

Senior Scientific Officer, Monks Wood Experimental Station (Nature Conservancy), Huntingdon

ABSTRACT. Lists of taxpayers were compiled during the lay subsidy surveys of 1524–25 and 1543–45. It is possible to map the distribution of taxpayers and the amounts of tax paid over the greater part of England, and these maps may be taken as a guide to some of the major elements in the distribution of population and wealth at that period. This paper examines the nature of the lay subsidy surveys, and discusses their limitations as source material. It is concluded that the surveys provide a framework into which the mass of more local evidence on the economy and society of Tudor England may be placed.

THERE is very little information on the distribution of population and wealth in the early sixteenth century because there were no national or regional censuses. Priests did not begin to keep parish registers until 1538 and many of these early records have been lost: for example, only half of the parishes in Huntingdonshire have registers going back as far as the sixteenth century.[1] As a result, historians and geographers have attempted to use taxation records which relate to the greater part of England and affected a relatively high proportion of the population. J. Cornwall, for example, took samples from the muster of 1522 and the lay subsidies of 1524 and 1525[2] and estimated a provisional population figure of 2·3 million.[3] Fiscal returns must be used very carefully in this type of social and economic study for, as G. R. Elton has noted, 'studies demanding systematic records are usually handicapped, either by loss of evidence or, more seriously, by the fact that the ages in question were not interested in the statistics which the modern historian wishes to extract'.[4] There is, however, no other source which is likely to help in studying the distribution of population and wealth over the greater part of the country in the early sixteenth century, and this paper will suggest ways of interpreting the taxation lists prepared for the lay subsidy returns of 1524–25 and 1543–45.

THE SOURCE MATERIAL

The subsidies were a form of taxation and they were levied in 1524–25 on each man's most important form of wealth, as defined by the Act,[5] namely personal property (goods), landed incomes and wages. The first category was very ill-defined but included coin, plate and debts owing to the taxpayer and excluded standing corn and personal attire. The second class of wealth was defined in the following way:

Fee Symple Fee Taile tyme of lyfe tyme of Yeres Execucion by Warde by Copye of

55

Court Roll or at Will, in any Castelles Honours manors londes tenements Rentes services hereditaments Annuyties fees corrodies or profittes.

The third category included wage-earners who earned at least £1 a year. Most tax surveyors did not go to the trouble of finding out how much this class earned because each man paid a poll-tax of 4 pence.[6] Where a man did not earn £1 or more in landed income or wages and did not own £2 or more in goods, he paid no tax at all.[7] It was clear to those who drew up the Act of Subsidy that three different forms of wealth were being taxed and that an assessment of £1 in goods was not comparable, in terms of real value, with £1 in what might be loosely called landed incomes. The rates of taxation were, therefore, adjusted so that men paid one-fortieth in tax on goods and one-twentieth on landed incomes. Men assessed for £20 and more in goods paid the same rate as those on landed incomes, namely one-twentieth, but wage-earners simply paid a poll-tax of 4 pence. In practice, most men were assessed on their goods. For example, in the hundred of Earsham, Norfolk, about 70 per cent of the taxpayers were taxed on their goods, which accounted for about 90 per cent of the tax paid in the hundred in 1525.[8]

The tax surveyors recorded only the major source of personal wealth because this alone was taxed. There is, therefore, no direct evidence to show what proportion of wealth went unrecorded in the subsidy surveys, but there is some indirect evidence which suggests that it was relatively small. The 1522 muster lists for Happing hundred, Norfolk, are extant and give information on both goods and landed incomes. About 90 per cent of the wealth recorded in the muster was assessed on goods, which suggests that a large proportion of the wealth of each man and vill was based on goods,[9] but there were some differences in the basis of the muster and subsidy surveys and the proportion probably varied from one part of the country to another.

The Act of Subsidy took into account the fact that many men held incomes and owned property in two or more vills. Accordingly, the wealth of each man, however dispersed, was assessed and then recorded in the lists of the vill where he

shall kepe his house or dwellynge, or where he then shalbe moost conversaunt abydyng or resyaunt or shall have his moost resorte

This meant that a man's name appeared only once in each year's subsidy returns, and there were some cases of taxpayers being crossed out of the taxation lists with a note in the margin that their assessments had been recorded in the lists of another vill. Unfortunately, most surveyors did not amend their lists in this way, and this kind of information is not given. They did not state what proportion of the wealth recorded in the lists was actually derived from the vill, or how much had been recorded in the lists of other vills.

The subsidy lists gave the name of each taxpayer, the source and value of his wealth, and the amount of money he owed in taxation. They did not usually contain any further information on the taxpayer because this was a tax survey, not a census. There was no need to list any children or housewives, and the names of some men were excluded because they paid no tax. Consequently, some households were represented by one taxpayer and others by two or more names in the survey and some households received no representation at all because no one was wealthy enough to contribute to the subsidy. The number of taxpayers cannot, therefore, be equated with the number of households in each vill.[10] This raises the question as to whether the lists can be used as a guide to the distribution of population and wealth at that date. For this to be possible, there must have been a constant relationship between the number of people listed and the real total population and wealth of each area.[11] This relationship is extremely difficult to check, but there are three obvious distortions which affect the interpretation of the subsidy returns.

First, by definition, the lay subsidy returns excluded religious persons and thereby gave a distorted impression of the total distribution pattern. It would be helpful if the lay subsidy material could be supplemented with data from a clerical subsidy, but the surveys were held at different times and upon different sets of criteria. It should be noted, however, that R. S. Schofield examined this form of distortion with respect to the 1512–16 subsidies, and found that clerical incomes reinforced, rather than modified, the over-all patterns.[12]

Secondly, it has already been noted that some other sections of the population were excluded. Children below the age of 16 years were exempt and women were not included unless they were acting as heads of household.[13] These people, and the men who were exempt on account of their poverty, were not named in the lists and so it is not possible to find out exactly what proportion of the total population passed unrecorded.

The third form of distortion relates to the way in which the lists were compiled. Two or more commissioners were responsible for implementing the subsidy surveys in each hundred and borough and they appointed surveyors and collectors of tax. Naturally, the nature of the lists reflected the way in which these groups of men interpreted the Act and carried out their work. There is evidence that the Exchequer found cases of misunderstanding and under-assessment. A memorial, or memorandum, was prepared in 1524 and sent out to the commissioners, but its text has not been discovered. From indirect evidence, it seems to have clarified the terms of the Act. There are two sets of lists in parts of Oxfordshire for the first year of the survey, 1524,[14] and it is possible that the second set was prepared after the commissioners had received and read the memorial. The same number of taxpayers appeared in the two lists and the richest and poorest sections experienced little change in their assessment. There is a note concerning the memorial in the survey of 1524 for Radlow hundred in Herefordshire.[15] The amount of tax had been set for £42, but on receipt of the memorial this figure was revised upwards to £53. It is not possible to find out whether other sets of commissioners changed their lists to the same extent, but some of them wrote notes explaining why a few assessments were lower than in the earlier muster of 1522. This was presumably intended to allay the suspicions of the Exchequer that they were being too lenient.

It is important to see whether there were significant differences in the character of the surveys held in 1524 and 1525. Table I compares the number of taxpayers in the extant returns of the two years: this examination is confined to hundreds and boroughs with complete lists in both 1524 and 1525.[16] It is concluded that the lists of 1525 contained 1·7 per cent fewer contributors. The surveys of individual hundreds and boroughs may be compared: the lists of the hundred of Pershore, Worcestershire, survive for both years and contain 1099 names in 1524 and twelve more names in 1525.[17] These two examples, at the small and large scale, suggest that there was little difference between the number of contributors. On the other hand, the lists of 1525 were not simply a copy of those of the previous year. In the hundred of Towcester, Northamptonshire, for example, there were 278 names in 1524 and 273 in 1525, but 47 men were listed only in the first survey and 42 in the second.[18] This suggests that surveyors were recording changes which were actually taking place in the intervening months. A few taxpayers died and their wives or heirs were listed in 1525. Some migrated into and out of the hundred, and others came of taxable age.

TABLE I

A comparison of the number of taxpayers in the lay subsidy returns of 1524 and 1525*

County	Number of taxpayers	
	1524	1525
Berkshire	3840	3933
Buckinghamshire	1913	1844
Cambridgeshire	2477	2711
Cornwall	1715	1677
Devonshire	8291	8619
Dorset	1222	1198
Essex	3361	3311
Gloucestershire	494	488
Hampshire	5563	5338
Herefordshire	611	580
Hertfordshire	2408	2376
Lancashire	789	827
Leicestershire	1571	1495
Lincolnshire	2339	2451
Norfolk	7484	7321
Northamptonshire	2669	2606
Oxfordshire	3472	3627
Rutland	226	206
Shropshire	881	645
Somerset	4105	3266
Staffordshire	875	909
Suffolk	6010	6274
Surrey	1126	1205
Sussex	3423	3399
Warwickshire	3978	3721
Wiltshire	1406	1332
Worcestershire	1099	1111
Yorkshire: North Riding	118	110
West Riding	2449	2017
Total	75 915	74 597

* Only the hundreds and boroughs with extant lists in both years are included in this Table.

There is little other documentation which can be used to check the relationship between numbers of people listed and absolute population but in a few parts of the country the lay subsidy returns can be compared with those of the muster of 1522.[19] About 37 per cent of the men included in the muster for Coventry were omitted in the later subsidy returns and a third of those in Exeter and Leicester.[20] On the other hand, there was a decline of only 10 per cent in the number of names in the lists for Happing hundred, Norfolk—the muster contained 746 names compared with 674 entries in the subsidy lists of 1525.[21] The muster for Happing included even the poorest adult males, who were described as being 'nullius valor'. It may be significant that there were 189 such men and only 86 of their names appeared in the 1525 subsidy, taxed for £1 in wages. These variations may reflect differences in the incidence of poverty in England at that time: the subsidy surveys may have measured not only variations in population density but also differences in the wealth of areas with an equally dense population. However, it is very difficult making comparisons between the

TABLE II

A comparison of the number of taxpayers in the lay subsidy
returns of 1524–25 and 1543–45*

County	Number of taxpayers	
	1524–25	1543–45
Berkshire	1391	1361
Buckinghamshire	915	1219
Cambridgeshire	3875	3203
Cornwall	3427	4242
Derbyshire	910	1077
Devonshire	13 403	13 986
Dorset	5319	5124
Essex	2472	2399
Gloucestershire	5957	7491
Hampshire	9265	8192
Hertfordshire	5835	5132
Kent	8828	6908
Lancashire	120	1236
Leicestershire	1512	1495
Lincolnshire	9846	11 076
Norfolk	7814	6811
Northamptonshire	3274	3150
Oxfordshire	3899	4024
Shropshire	642	1961
Somerset	2762	4263
Staffordshire	909	889
Suffolk	7156	6540
Surrey	2154	2359
Sussex	3594	3200
Wiltshire	4543	4240
Yorkshire: North Riding	242	1300
West Riding	1859	5411
Total	111 923	118 289

* Only the hundreds and boroughs with extant
lists in one year of each of these periods are included in
this Table.

muster and subsidies. For example, the muster of Happing can only be compared with the subsidy list of 1525 because that of the previous year, 1524, is not extant. During the intervening months migration had occurred, some men died and children reached the age of sixteen. It is interesting that although the muster should have included all men, irrespective of wealth, the list of 1525 contained 92 names absent from the earlier muster.

There were three later subsidy surveys, held in 1543, 1544 and 1545, which included in their lists men assessed for £1 and more in landed incomes and goods. Table II compares the returns of the 1540s with those of the 1520s.[22] There were only 5·69 per cent more entries in the later series of surveys, which might suggest that the two series were almost equally comprehensive. But there were many more taxpayers in Lancashire, Shropshire and Yorkshire in the 1540s. For example, the hundred of Leyland has 120 taxpayers in 1525 and 1236 in 1545; the number rose from 97 to 474 in the wapentake of Hallikeld.[23] These parts of England may have been under-assessed in the 1520s and if the totals for Lancashire, Shropshire and Yorkshire are excluded from Table II, there were less than 0·5 per cent more taxpayers in the surveyed areas in the 1540s. There is some evidence that the commissioners in the north of England organized their surveys of the 1520s in a different way from the rest of the country,[24] but there were also slight changes in the liability of each man to taxation in the surveys of the 1520s and 1540s. In the 1520s, men without wages and owning less than £2 in goods and men earning less than £1 and owning no goods, were exempt. In the 1540s, there was no wages liability and the goods minimum was reduced to £1.[25] These changes affected the liability of the poorer section of the community: servants, without any goods, might appear in the lists of the 1520s, but might be absent from those of the 1540s; squatters, who were too poor to be taxed for £2 in goods in the 1520s, might be included in the 1540s when the minimum fell to £1. As a result, counties with many servants but few extremely poor independent men would have fewer taxpayers in the 1540s, whereas those areas with few servants and many squatters would have more taxpayers. This would help to explain the rise in the number of taxpayers in the later series of surveys for Lancashire, Shropshire and Yorkshire: their returns were influenced by the relatively large number of very poor, non-wage-earning peasants. It may be noted that there was a small decline in the number of taxpayers in the 1540s in some counties of Lowland England, where there may have been a higher proportion of wage-earners. Finally, it may be significant that a relatively high proportion of wealth was in church hands in the north of England, particularly in monastic hands. Some of this came into the lay tax arena in 1543–45.[26]

The subsidies of 1524–25 were not imposed on the people of Northumberland, Cumberland, Durham, Westmorland and Cheshire, and the Cinque Ports and three other centres were similarly omitted. Parts of Herefordshire and Shropshire were also left out because they were still in Wales in the 1520s, although they were transferred to England by the time of the 1540s returns.[27] The rest of England contributed to the subsidies, but many of the taxation lists are missing.[28] The gaps in the coverage have occurred in two ways.
(1) Many documents have been badly stored, some have disappeared and others appear as a mass of rotted membrane.
(2) The documents belong to the Public Record Office, class E 179, and C. A. F. Meekings has observed that, 'Many items in this class are mere haphazard sorting accumulations or bundles of miscellanea. . . . For this and other reasons the official list to this class is notoriously fallible'.[29] Some of the membranes have been wrongly identified and although well over 1500 P.R.O. references have been searched there may still be some relevant subsidy membranes 'concealed' in the index.[30]

At the present state of knowledge, there is no county with a complete set of lists. Hampshire and Northamptonshire have a relatively good cover, but some vills have lost their returns for both 1524 and 1525. Most of the membranes for Bedfordshire and Herefordshire are missing and the gaps in the documentation have greatly reduced the value of the subsidies as source material in those areas. The tax surveyors did not write down the number of taxpayers in each vill: the historian and geographer must count for themselves and if the membranes are defective or missing there is no way of finding out how many names were once written in the lists.

THE PRESENTATION OF THE DATA[31]

There have, so far, been few attempts to plot the distribution of taxpayers and their recorded wealth[32] because it is so difficult to assemble the data and find suitable mapping units.

Although the taxation vills often had the same names as the present-day civil parishes, they probably had a different layout.[33] Their precise extent and composition are not known and so in this paper larger mapping units have been used which are made up of several modern civil parishes. These larger units represent, albeit imperfectly, the extent of the corresponding groups of vills and the boundaries coincide with the parish boundaries. The groups of

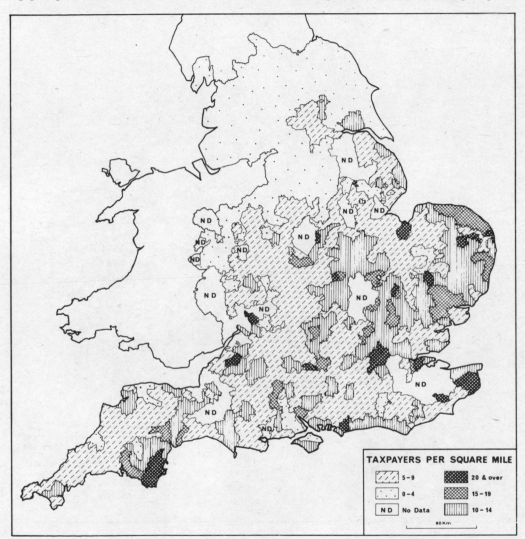

FIGURE I. The distribution of taxpayers as indicated in the extant returns of 1524–25

vills have been arranged so that they reflect in great measure the topography and regional character of each part of the country and so it should be possible to compare the number of taxpayers in areas such as the Cotswolds, Chilterns, Cannock Chase and Charnwood Forest.[34] The maps include the returns of both urban and rural settlements. It is usual to find that such centres as Canterbury, Chichester and Coventry are included in areas with

John Sheail

more than 19 taxpayers per square mile (2·59 km²) and paying over 49 shillings per square mile in taxation. It may be noted, however, that even if these centres had been excluded and mapped separately, many of these mapping units would have remained in the highest category of taxable population and wealth as indicated on the maps.

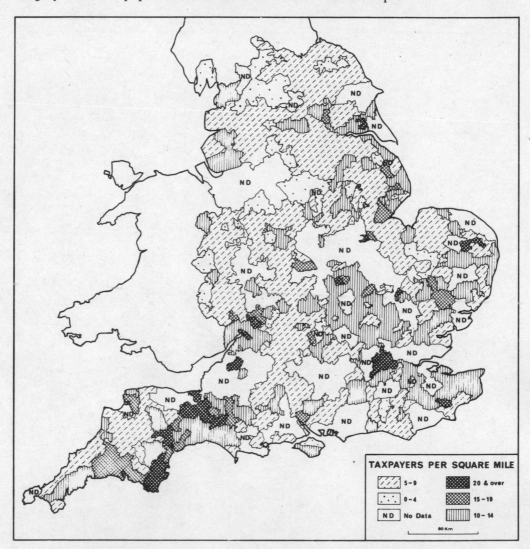

FIGURE 2. The distribution of taxpayers as indicated in the extant returns of 1543–45

Figure 1 shows the distribution of taxpayers as indicated in the extant returns of 1524–25. The map suggests the number of taxpayers per square mile in 1525 and where this information is not available the returns of 1524 have been used instead. In parts of Kent, Somerset and the Midlands, the documents of both years are so defective that the distribution patterns cannot be studied. For this reason, the subsidy returns of the 1540s have also been mapped and Figure 2 shows the distribution of taxpayers in 1543–45 for each part of the country where documents survive. Unfortunately, many lists have been lost or misplaced.

Figure 3 is a synthesis of the previous two maps. Where the returns of the 1520s and 1540s survive, the average number of taxpayers per square mile is shown but in many cases the returns of only one survey can be found and these have been used. The lists of the 1540s have been employed, wherever possible, for Lancashire, Shropshire and Yorkshire

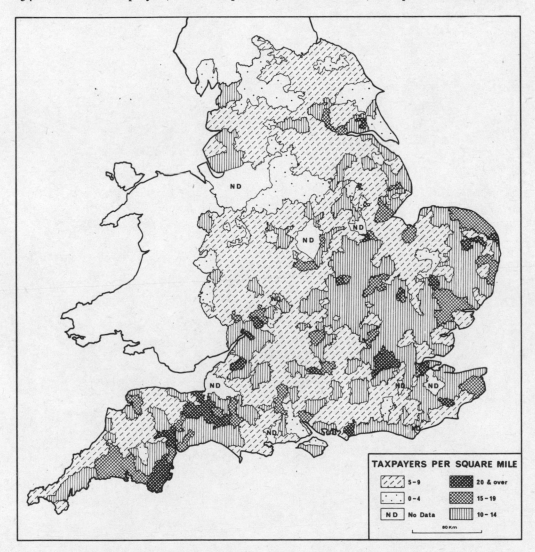

FIGURE 3. The distribution of taxpayers as indicated in the extant returns of the 1520s and 1540s: a synthesis

because of the difficulties outlined above. Cheshire was surveyed only in the 1540s, and the returns are so defective that they cannot be used. Both series have been lost in parts of Dorset, Kent, Leicestershire, Lincolnshire, Somerset and Surrey.

Figure 4 shows the amount of tax paid per square mile in 1524–25. It must be stressed that the map is based on the amount of money paid in taxation and not on the assessments of wealth. This is because incomes and capital wealth were taxed and their assessments, taken together, give a distorted picture of the actual distribution of wealth. The Act tried to resolve this problem by using different rates of taxation, and so the amounts of money

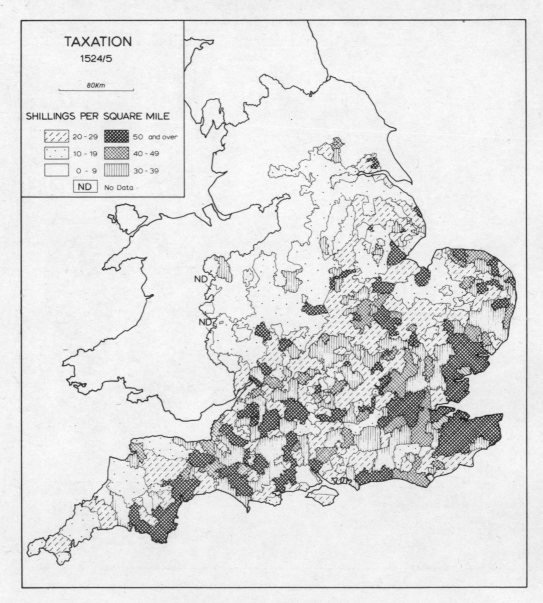

FIGURE 4. The amount of money paid in taxation in 1524–25

paid in taxation have been taken as the more reliable guide. Furthermore, the tax surveyors wrote down the amounts of tax to be paid by each vill, hundred and borough, whereas they did not normally add up the assessments and record these figures in the lists.[35]

THE DISTRIBUTION OF TAXABLE POPULATION AND WEALTH

The returns suggest that the east Midlands and East Anglia were more densely populated than the west Midlands and central southern England[36] but for most counties there was a range in the returns. In Hampshire, for example, there were 44 taxpayers per square mile in the Avon valley, about 30 around Alton and Winchester, and fewer than 20 taxpayers per square mile in the north-east. Parts of the coast were exceptionally prosperous and had large centres of population. The Thames estuary and south Devon had very high returns, and coasts of Lindsey, Norfolk and Sussex had higher returns than most places inland. The pattern in south Kent is obscured by the fact that the Cinque Ports were excluded from the lay subsidy.

The survey lists may be a guide to the relative size of settlements and the level of prosperity. There were 784 taxpayers in Canterbury, 523 in Cambridge, 431 in Oxford, 401 in Leicester, and 330 in Winchester in the 1520s, which suggests how the towns may have ranked in terms of total population. This kind of information can be supplemented with data on tax payments.[37] In 1524, the City of London contributed £8263 in tax, followed by Norwich which paid £749, Bristol (£465), Coventry (£463), Salisbury (£405), and Southwark (£387). Many towns paid a large part of their respective county's contribution—Norwich paid a sixth of Norfolk's tax. Wealth was often concentrated in towns and in very few hands. The towns associated with the textile industry, such as Lavenham, Long Melford, Nayland and Sudbury in Suffolk were very prosperous. In 1524, taxpayers in the four towns paid an average of 11 shillings each, whereas taxpayers in the remaining twenty-eight vills in the hundred of Babergh contributed an average of 3 shillings each, but even in these four towns, the bulk of the wealth was held by only a few people. About £180 in tax was paid at Lavenham: 164 taxpayers paid £9 and the remaining thirty-five people contributed £170.[38]

Although the subsidy returns are a guide to the spread of men and their wealth in the early sixteenth century, they do not give any information on the reasons for the distribution patterns. For example, very few lists identify the employment of the taxpayers.[39] In one or two cases, the tax surveyors found that men owned a great deal of property in more than one vill. For instance, five men owned goods in St Ives, Huntingdonshire, although they lived in other parts of the county and neighbouring Cambridgeshire.[40] This pattern of dispersed wealth could mean that regions quite distinctive topographically were economically and socially inter-dependent. The resources of the Fens, for example, were exploited by villages on the neighbouring uplands of Huntingdonshire, Cambridgeshire, Norfolk, Suffolk and Lincolnshire.[41]

Poll-taxes and lay subsidy returns have been extensively used by historians and geographers to study individual medieval settlements and the returns of the early sixteenth century are particularly important in this context. Most of the deserted medieval villages had been abandoned by that time and the subsidy surveys should confirm that changes had taken place. Table III shows the number of taxpayers recorded in each vill in the hundred of Rothwell, Northamptonshire, in 1525 and 1543. There were only eleven fewer taxpayers in 1543, and the ranking of the vills is broadly similar for both dates. K. J. Allison *et al.* have identified six deserted medieval villages in the hundred,[42] and it may be significant that there were very few taxpayers in these six vills in the 1520s and that five of the units were not identified in the 1543 returns.[43] Their taxpayers, if any, were listed with those of other vills in the 1540s.

TABLE III

The number of taxpayers in the hundred of Rothwell, Northamptonshire in 1525 and 1543

	Vills		Number of taxpayers	
			1525	1543
1	Rothwell		106	82
2	Desborough		58	40
3	Braybrooke		50	51
4	Kelmarsh		42	45
5	Rushton All Hallows		28	47 (with St Peter)
6	Farndon		28	30
7	Harrington		28	26
8	Maidwell		26	26
9	Oxendon, Great		26	33
10	Arthingworth		25	26
11	Marston Trussel		25	25
12	Sibbertoft		25	27
13	Clipston		24	34
14	Bowden, Little		23	30
15	Loddington		22	19
16	Orton		18	15
17	Haselbech		17	21
18	Thorpe Mallsworth		17	20
19	Draughton		15	14
20	Hothorpe	D.M.V.	13	16
21	Rushton St Peter		9	(with All Hallows)
22	Sulby	D.M.V.	7	—
23	Oxendon, Little	D.M.V.	3	—
24	Thorpe Underwood		2	—
25	Barford	D.M.V.	1	—
26	Glendon	D.M.V.	1	1
27	Newbottle	D.M.V.	0	—
Total			639	628

Note: D.M.V. indicates that the vill has been identified as containing the site of a deserted medieval village.

Subsidy surveys of the sixteenth and earlier centuries are a useful guide to changes which took place in the size and prosperity of settlements in the medieval period, but the evidence is frequently hard to interpret. For example, the omission of the name of a deserted village is not, by itself, evidence that desertion had taken place. The name of the deserted village of Abbotstone, Hampshire, is present in the 1334 returns, absent in both 1524 and 1525, but present again in the list of 1543. Some surveyors included the name of each hamlet and farmstead in their tax lists, whereas others included the taxpayers under the name of one substantial settlement in the locality.

The names of deserted settlements often only appear in the subsidy lists if a prosperous person was still living there. This was probably the reason why the name of Hundon, Lincolnshire, was given, as one taxpayer there was assessed for £20 in goods: if there had been only a shepherd, assessed for perhaps £1 in wages, his entry would probably have been included with those of a neighbouring settlement. There is a further difficulty in analysing the tax returns. It is never possible to say where the taxpayers lived in the vill. For example, Godwick in Norfolk has extant returns for 1525 and 1543: the five taxpayers in 1525 and the two men in 1543 may have lived on the site of the deserted village, or they may have occupied farms a long way from the former village centre, near the boundaries of the taxation unit. Wherever possible, other documentary evidence should be used to check and supplement the taxation material for, by itself, a tax list is not a sufficiently reliable indicator to the fortunes of individual medieval settlements.

The subsidy lists are very useful for studying the relative distribution of aliens and for comparing their number with taxpaying denizens. Aliens paid twice the normal rates of taxation and where they had no wealth at all they contributed a poll-tax of 8 pence. In some parts of the country it appears that both men and women paid this tax. Aliens are clearly distinguished in the subsidy lists and frequently their place of origin is given. They were common in London and Middlesex, and many were concentrated in Smithfield. There were above-average numbers of aliens in the lists of such ports as Kingston upon Hull and Bishops Lynn but, unfortunately, their distribution in many parts of the country cannot be studied owing to the loss of so many subsidy documents.

Although the surveys were held within one year of one another, it is extremely hard to trace cases of population migration. This is because the surveyors did not usually give any reasons for changes in the composition of the lists. Occasionally the name of a taxpayer occurs in a different vill, suggesting that he had moved house between the two surveys but it is difficult to track down many migrants in this way. The variety of Christian names was so small and so few extra details were given that it is usually impossible to identify people accurately in this way. To make matters worse, the documentation is frequently so defective that the lists of one year cannot be compared with those of another. There are few extensive areas of the country where complete sets of documents survive.

J. Cornwall, from studies mainly in Buckinghamshire and Rutland, has assumed that changes in the composition of the lists were largely the result of under-registration and that relatively little migration occurred between 1524 and 1525,[44] but T. H. Hollingsworth examined the same data and from a mathematical analysis concluded that the tax surveyors succeeded in listing all those liable for taxation and that 'death and migration were responsible for almost all the differences in the composition of the lists'.[45] There is one hundred where the surveyors gave reasons for the non-appearance of taxpayers in 1525.[46] In the hundred of Towcester, Northamptonshire, 47 of the 278 taxpayers in 1524 failed to appear in the survey of 1525 as 6 had died and 41 migrated to other hundreds. There were 91 wage-earners in the 1524 list, and one died and 31 migrated before the second list was prepared. The surveyors did not state why some names appeared in the 1525 list for the first time, but it is interesting to find that 28 of the 42 people who did so paid £1 in tax. There may have been some extremely mobile poor people in that part of Northamptonshire at that time.

Finally, it should be stressed that the subsidies were raised in only 5 years of the early sixteenth century, which means that the lists may portray an abnormal period in the life of a taxpayer or the history of a settlement. There is evidence that some places suffered from unusually bad weather in the 1520s and 1540s. Heavy rains in 1524 caused much flooding which ruined crops and encouraged disease among livestock. Taxpayers in the settlements along the River Witham and its tributaries in Lincolnshire complained that they had lost cattle and corn. In the hundreds of East Budleigh and Colyton, Devon, 3744 sheep, 39 horses, 30 cows, 15 bullocks and hogs, and 13 oxen were lost, leaving the farmers much poorer.

CONCLUSIONS

The Exchequer intended that the subsidy surveys should be compiled in a uniform way in each part of the country and that the lists should be audited and preserved in London. To a large extent, the Exchequer succeeded in its aims and today it is possible to study the regional distribution of population and wealth as indicated by the returns.

The picture of England in the subsidy returns is neither complete nor accurate in all its details, but it is probably safe to assume that the returns reflect some of the major elements in the distribution of population and wealth. The tax lists do not give undue emphasis to any one form of industry and treat town and countryside in a similar manner. In this respect, the subsidy surveys are unusual since most medieval sources relate to one industry or one part of the country. By using the surveys, it is possible to make general comparisons: for example, the textile centres of Suffolk and Norfolk can be studied in relation to the centres in the West Country. While the broad patterns indicated by these returns may be modified by subsequent research on more local evidence, the subsidy surveys provide a framework into which this local information can be placed.

ACKNOWLEDGEMENTS

The research for this paper was carried out during the period 1964–67, while the author was a Research Student in the Department of Geography, University College London. Professor H. C. Darby, Dr R. E. Glasscock and Mr G. R. Versey gave much help in the early stages of this work. The author thanks Professor M. W. Beresford and Dr R. S. Schofield for their comments on drafts of this paper, and Gillian M. Sheail for her many helpful suggestions. The maps were prepared by Mr P. Sheail.

NOTES

1. J. C. RUSSELL, *British medieval population* (1948); J. THIRSK, 'Sources of information on population, 1500–1760', *Amat. Hist.* 4 (1959), 131; J. CORNWALL, 'An Elizabethan census', *Rec. Bucks.* 16 (1953–6), 258–73

2. Only one survey was undertaken in each year. The subsidy lists of each vill in 1512–16 were not preserved by the Exchequer and are missing today. The subsidies of 1526 and 1527 included only a few of the taxpayers who contributed to those of the previous two years.

3. J. CORNWALL, 'English population in the early sixteenth century', *Econ. Hist. Rev.* 23 (1970), 32–44

4. G. R. ELTON, *England 1200–1640* (1969), 53–4

5. *Statutes of the Realm*, 14 & 15 Henry VIII, c. 16

6. The Act simply stated that everyone of the age of 16 years and above, 'and havyng none other substaunce wherby the same person shuld or ought to be set accordyng to this acte as is aforesaid at a higher or gretter some (should pay) four pence yerely duryng the said twoo yeres'.

7. For full details of the Tudor lay subsidies, see R. S. SCHOFIELD, 'Parliamentary lay taxation, 1485–1547', Unpubl. Ph.D. thesis, Univ. of Cambridge, 1963

8. Public Record Office (P.R.O.), E 179 150/281

9. P.R.O., E 36/25 & E 179 150/250

10. This point is not made clear in the paper by L. M. NICHOLLS, 'The lay subsidy of 1523: the reliability of the subsidy rolls as illustrated by Totnes and Dartmouth', *Bgham hist. J.* 9 (1964), 115. Miss Nicholls states that 'the lists give roughly the name of every householder who was living in the country in 1524'.

11. E. J. BUCKATZSCH, 'The geographical distribution of wealth in England, 1086–1843', *Econ. Hist. Rev.* 3 (1950–1), 180–202

12. R. S. SCHOFIELD, 'The geographical distribution of wealth in England, 1334–1649', *Econ. Hist. Rev.* 18 (1965), 483–510

13. *Statutes of the Realm*, 14 & 15 Henry VIII, c. 16

14. See, for example, P.R.O., E 179 161/173

15. P.R.O., E 179 117/88

16. J. SHEAIL, 'The regional distribution of wealth in England as indicated in the lay subsidy returns of 1524/5', Unpubl. Ph.D. thesis, Univ. of London, 1968. This contains a gazetteer giving the tax payments and number of contributors in 1524 and 1525 for each vill with extant returns. This paper is based on the data contained in the gazetteer.

17. P.R.O., E 179 200/132, 172 & 126

18. P.R.O., E 179 155/132 & 131

19. See, for example, J. CORNWALL, 'The people of Rutland in 1522', *Trans. Leicester. archaeol. hist. Soc.* 37 (1961–2), 7–28

20. W. G. HOSKINS, *Local history in England* (1959), 102–4; D. CHARMAN, 'Wealth and trade in Leicester in the early sixteenth century', *Trans. Leicester. archaeol. hist. Soc.* 15 (1949), 69–97

21. P.R.O., E 36/25 & E 179 150/250

22. The Table consists of the highest extant figure for taxpayers in 1524 and 1525, and 1543, 1544 and 1545.

23. P.R.O., E 179 130/80 & 86; E 179 212/100 & 103

24. The surveyors may not have prepared lists giving the name and contribution of each taxpayer in parts of the North and East Ridings of Yorkshire.

25. The value of the £ had also declined owing to inflation during the intervening 20 years.

26. I am most grateful to Dr R. S. Schofield for bringing this to my attention.

27. *Statutes of the Realm*, 14 & 15 Henry VIII, c. 16

28. Lay subsidy returns have been transcribed in: S. H. A. HERVEY, 'Suffolk in 1524', *Suffolk Green Books* 10 (1910); J. TAIT, 'Taxation in the Salford hundred, 1524–1802', *Chetham Soc.* 83 (1924); A. C. CHIBNELL and A. V. WOODMAN, 'Subsidy roll for the county of Buckinghamshire, anno 1524', *Bucks. Rec. Soc.* 8 (1950); J. C. CORNWALL, 'The lay subsidy rolls for the county of Sussex, 1524–5', *Sussex Rec. Soc.* 56 (1956–7)

29. C. A. F. MEEKINGS, *The hearth tax, 1662–1689, exhibition of records* (1962–3), 2

30. For example, part of the list for a hundred in Northamptonshire was indexed under a hundred in Cambridgeshire. A membrane for the hundred of Dunworth, Wiltshire, was found indexed under the wapentake of Ainsty, Yorkshire.

31. Imperial units have been used in order to allow comparison with other works on the distribution of population and wealth in medieval England, especially those by H. C. Darby *et al.* for the Domesday survey of 1086 and R. E. Glasscock for the 1334 subsidy returns. See also note 34.

32. For example: B. REYNOLDS, 'Late medieval Dorset', Unpubl. M.A. thesis, Univ. of London, 1958; C. T. SMITH, 'The Cambridge region: settlement and population' in *The Cambridge region* (ed. J. A. STEERS, 1965), 133–51

33. This has also been noted by J. CORNWALL, 'English county towns in the 1520s', *Econ. Hist. Rev.* 15 (1962–3), 60

34. The mapping units adopted in this paper were devised by H. C. DARBY *et al.* in compiling the maps showing the Domesday geography of England. See, for example, H. C. DARBY, *The Domesday geography of eastern England* (1952) and subsequent volumes. The units have also been adopted in plotting the distribution of taxation as recorded in the 1334 lay subsidy returns. See R. E. GLASSCOCK, 'The distribution of lay wealth in south-east England in the early fourteenth century', Unpubl. Ph.D. thesis, Univ. of London, 1963, and 'The distribution of wealth in East Anglia in the early fourteenth century', *Trans. Inst. Br. Geogr.* 32 (1963), 113–23

35. There are only two extant lists where the surveyors recorded the sum total of the assessed wealth in each vill. They were for New Windsor, Berkshire (E 179 73/130), and the hundred of Waltham, Hampshire (E 179 173/182).

36. Note, however, the difficulties in interpreting the returns from the north and west of England.

37. Also demonstrated by W. G. HOSKINS, 'English provincial towns in the early sixteenth century', *Trans. R. hist. Soc.* 6 (1956), 4

38. P.R.O., E 179 180/135

39. The occupations of many taxpayers were noted in the surveys of Bristol, Cambridge, Coventry and Northampton, and in the hundreds of Fareham and Titchfield, Hampshire.

40. P.R.O., E 179 122/91

41. J. THIRSK, 'Fenland farming in the sixteenth century', *Univ. of Leicester, Dept. of English Local History, Occas. Pap.* 3 (1965)

42. K. J. ALLISON, M. W. BERESFORD and J. G. HURST, 'The deserted villages of Northamptonshire', *Univ. of Leicester, Dept. of English Local History, Occas. Pap.* 18 (1966). The authors did not, however, use the 1520s' returns in identifying these six cases of desertion.

43. P.R.O., E 179 155/133 & 147; E 179 156/184

44. J. CORNWALL (1961–2), 24

45. T. H. HOLLINGSWORTH, *Historical demography* (1969), 42–52

46. P.R.O., E 179 155/132 & 131

RÉSUMÉ. *La distribution de la population imposable et de la richesse en Angleterre au debut du seizième siècle*. Des listes de contribuables étaient compilées pendant les études à propos de la subvention laïque à la période 1524 à 1525 et 1543 à 1545. Il est possible de faire une carte de la distribution des contribuables et les sommes d'impôt payées sur la plupart d'Angleterre et ces cartes donnent quelques indications sur la distribution de la population et de la richesse à cette époque. Dans ce rapport on examine la nature des études de la subvention laïque et discute leurs limitations comme matériaux de source. On peut déduire que les études fournissent un cadre ou on peut classer l'ensemble des connaissances concernant l'économie et la société régionales en Angleterre sous les Tudors.

FIG. 1. La distribution des contribuables comme indiqué surveint les declarations existantes de 1524 à 1525
FIG. 2. Comme Fig. 1, mais 1543 à 1545
FIG. 3. La distribution des contribuables comme indiqué surveint les declarations existantes des années 1520 à 1529 et 1540 à 1549: une synthèse
FIG. 4. Le montant d'argent payé comme impôt pendant l'année 1524 à 1525

ZUSAMMENFASSUNG. *Die Steurzahler- und Reichtumverteilung in England am Anfang des sechszehnten Jahrhunderts: eine Erklärung.* Während der ‚Lay Subsidy Surveys' von 1524–25 und 1543–45 wurden die Listen von den Steuerzahlern zusammengestellt. Es ist möglich, die Verteilung der Steuerzahler aufzuzeichnen, so wie auch die Gesamtbeträge der Steuer, die die Leute in den meisten Teilen Englands zahlten und diese Landkarten kann man auch benutzen, in das sie auf einigen der bedeutenden Bestandteile der Bevölkerung- und Reichtumverteilung jener Periode hinweisen. Diese Prüfungsarbeit untersucht den Inhalt von den ‚Lay Subsidy Surveys' und uberlegt dessen Begrenzungen als Quellenmaterial. Es wird beschlossen, dass die ‚Surveys' eine Gerippe leisten, worin man die Menge von etwas mehr örtlichen Beweisen setzen kann, die um die Wirtschaft und die Gesellschaft von Tudor England handeln.

ABB. 1. Die Verteilung der Steuerzahler an den 1524–25-vorhandenen Erklärungen angegeben
ABB. 2. Gleich Abb. 1, aber 1543–45
ABB. 3. Die Verteilung der Steuerzahler auf den 1520–29 und 1540–49-vorhandenen Erklärungen angegeben: eine Zusammensetzung
ABB. 4. Die Gesamtbeträge der Steuer, die in 1524–25 bezahlt wurden

Population distribution in Norfolk and Suffolk during the sixteenth and seventeenth centuries

JOHN PATTEN

ABSTRACT. Sources for the estimation of the distribution of English population in the sixteenth and seventeenth centuries usually survive for widely separated dates. Moreover, they were invariably not compiled for the direct purpose of counting people, but are taxation lists or religious surveys which record different portions of the population, and do not give the demographic detail of surviving parish registers. As such, they permit only the crudest estimation of growth rates, and are of most use in facilitating the fairly rapid plotting of distributions on a local, regional or national scale. Analysis of parish registers, when carried out to obtain broad estimates of vital trends and distributions, involves immense labour. Changing population distributions within Norfolk and Suffolk for both town and country are examined to illustrate the usefulness of the different sources, and a standardized method of approach to them is advanced, based on the use of estimates derived from inferred contemporary age structure. The two counties are shown to have experienced a relatively slow overall growth and to have had a stable population distribution throughout the two centuries. Population density seemed strongly related to agricultural activity, and the presence or absence of textile manufacturing. Towns, however, particularly the larger ones, were growing much faster than the countryside by the seventeenth century.

AT the beginning of the sixteenth century the population of England had probably not yet recovered to the level of the early fourteenth century, and the economy and towns had not yet fully regained prosperity after the nadir of the fifteenth century. But records giving both direct and indirect information on population were becoming ever more plentiful and detailed. By the end of the seventeenth century, after two hundred years of change in population, as well as in the economy and in society, the country was poised on the brink of great interrelated advances in agriculture, industry, trade and population that were to transform it. Yet still, remarkably little is known in detail about population movements during these important years of the modernization of the kingdom, despite marked advances in the analysis of parish registers by aggregative and nominative techniques.[1] The broad outline of successive advances and retreats in population is now reasonably firmly established.[2] But it will be many years before surviving parish registers will reveal accurate and detailed information[3] at a regional, rather than strictly local, scale about both population distributions and dynamics. Meanwhile, discussion of any aspect of the historical geography of this pre-industrial period will usually demand at least some information about population totals or distributions. Two English counties, Norfolk and Suffolk, are examined to illustrate the sources and methods available by which these may be achieved. Interesting in themselves as making up an area of high population and marked, if erratic, prosperity compared to much of pre-industrial England,[4] they also provide a good case study in the population geography of the times, the lessons from which may be applied to other parts of the country. The flavour of this examination may seem more in the tradition of old-style 'political arithmetic' as practised by Gregory King[5] and his contemporaries, than that of the new historical demography; yet such an approach is still necessary to provide both basic information and a framework for analysis, given the available sources.

SOURCES

The major sources for population study of the sixteenth and seventeenth centuries—excluding parish registers—are of two main types; lists compiled as records of fiscal and of religious administration. Government fiscal listings include the Lay Subsidies of 1524 and 1525, as well as those of the 1540s[6] reinforced by the Musters of Harness of 1522, where these survive;[7] the Hearth Taxes of 1662–1674;[8] the Poll Taxes taken in the later seventeenth century;[9] and the Tax on Births, Deaths, Marriages, Spinsters and Batchelors of 1695.[10] In the religious group, taken at the behest of Archbishop or Bishop, are the Religious Survey of 1563;[11] the Communicant Returns of 1603;[12] and the Compton 'Census' of 1676.[13] Between the two in type are the Protestation Returns of 1641, which recorded sworn loyalty to the King by men aged over 18.[14]

Of this variety not all survive, or survive in sufficient cover, to permit their use in making estimates for every part of Norfolk and Suffolk, as is also the case for most other English counties. The lay subsidies of the 1540s omit a number of those previously taxed, and thus recorded, in the subsidies of 1524/5, and are incomplete in their coverage of the two counties. The Poll Taxes and the exceptionally comprehensive Tax of 1695 survive only for a few local areas; the Religious Survey of 1563 not at all; the Protestation Returns only in some local copies. However, from those records that do survive it is possible to produce regional evidence, at various levels of accuracy, of totals and distributions of population for the 1520s (fiscal), for 1603 (religious) and for the later years of the seventeenth century (fiscal and religious). In addition, crude growth rates between these dates may be estimated and these can themselves be related to what is known of demographic trends during the period, trends which show a cumulative but uncertain overall upward movement, but one whose regional variations have yet to be studied in much depth.

APPROACHES TO ANALYSIS

These different lists do not give totals of population, for they represent only part of the community, usually adult and most often male, which may be recorded as mustered soldieries, taxpayers, communicants or 'households'. Moreover, they are not directly comparable with each other. The information in them is most useful when converted, by the application of a 'multiplier', to an estimate of total population, an approach common from King's time to today.[15] One conventional method has been, for example, to equate taxpayers in the lay subsidies of 1524 or 1525 with 'households' which are multiplied by a constant factor representing their supposed mean size to obtain an estimated figure. Immediate difficulties present themselves. Do taxpayers really represent heads of families, and therefore by implication households, or do the lists contain people who were not of this sort? What was a 'household', was it nuclear or extended; how many children, how many servants did the typical household contain at different dates? Is it possible to equate households with families; are the two the same?[16] Laslett has made an important study of this problem of household size, based largely on post-1650 censuses and from which he offers precise and logical meanings for the terms 'household' and 'family' in the light of twentieth-century experience, since for earlier centuries '. . . nothing like a definition of the family or household (has survived)'.[17] Both this study of original listings, and a further examination of information from printed works,[18] has revealed the typical size of these 'blocks' to be around 4·75 persons. It remains, however, that only in the case of apparent direct, or probable indirect, enumeration of 'households' or 'families' such as the 1563 Religious Survey or the Hearth Taxes, can such an approach be used with safety. An alternative method would simply focus attention on trying to get comparable figures by, for example, using the raw numbers of households or families.[19] Smith held that: 'There are, indeed, advantages in counting the household as the basic unit of population until the nineteenth century, since it avoids the intractable problem of finding suitable multipliers.'[20] This challenging suggestion suffers from the problem of equating listed totals of various sorts with heads of households—whatever that term meant. Of the sources cited above, perhaps only the Religious Survey of 1563 seems definitely to refer to 'families' alone. Equally, it is not possible to compare estimates directly with those drawn from other sources listing taxpayers, communicants, and thus different sectors of the population.

An alternative standardized approach to most sixteenth- and seventeenth-century population sources is one that avoids the 'intractable problem' of household multipliers. By treating diverse, but intrinsically quite similar, sorts of information drawn from lists made for different purposes in exactly the same way, any error consequent on the method, if not the source, should be constant. The Lay Subsidies, the Communicant Returns and the Compton Census all represent adult population, above the age of about 16; usually males alone in the first case, males and females in the second two. Whether or not those enumerated represent 'households' or 'families' is not accurately discernible; that they are adults is, in each case, without doubt. Adult males and females have to be assumed to be approximately equal in number. In order to estimate the proportion of the population under 16 years of age, reference may be made both to contemporary estimates[21] and to life tables. These life tables may be models based on countries which, it is suspected, resemble in type the characteristics of Britain in the sixteenth and seventeenth century.[22] Life tables are derived from empirical data of present-day populations to show typical age structures given different life expectations. For pre-industrial England this has been estimated at a mean of about 40 years:[23] it must be noted, however, that 'the widest relative range of variation is observed between the first and the fifteenth year of age: it is particularly wide in the age group 1–4'.[24] The conclusion drawn from this examination, given such life expectation, is that the proportion of children in the total population was about 40 per cent. The standardized method adopted in this paper is, therefore, the estimation of population totals by adding to total adults drawn from these various sources a percentage which represents the proportion of children. The problems introduced by the differing characteristics of the sources themselves, rather than by the general method, will be examined as the picture of the population distribution in the two counties over the two centuries is developed. In this, it should be realized, regional variation in population structure must have occurred, even in such a relatively small area.

Population in the two counties is shown in two forms, by isopleth maps in order to illustrate population distribution itself, and by proportional circles to demonstrate urban populations. The former sort of map was constructed from figures for individual parishes, which were plotted and built up from this 'raw' framework into isopleth regional maps. Two difficulties always arise in this process in an historical context. First, parish boundaries and acreages were not accurately surveyed until the nineteenth century, from when the framework used here perforce dates. Parish extents in the sixteenth and seventeenth centuries depended rather on ancient custom than on parliamentary sanction, and as such they were ill-defined. Second, although most parishes in Norfolk and Suffolk were fairly small, up to 5000 acres or so (a few of the fenland parishes reaching 10 000 acres or more), and contained only one settlement, this was not always the case. In larger parishes parts of the population may have lived in quite substantial hamlets. Although usually these are all included with the main settlements' figures in the lists, it is only occasionally that detailed information is afforded. Wymondham, for example, a substantial town in a large parish is described in the Hearth Tax returns as 'cum membris' and these are returned; Earsham in Norfolk is, in the same return, divided into the main settlements and the 'outshifts'.[25] This mapping method is perhaps likely to be more accurate than those used hitherto on similar population data, such as that by Smith on Cambridgeshire or Sheail for the whole of

TABLE I

Norfolk and Suffolk, estimated population

	1520s	Per cent change	1603	Per cent change	1670s
Norfolk	112 000	27	143 000	2	181 000
Suffolk	90 000	20	108 000	15	125 000
Total	202 000	24	252 000	21	306 000
		Total increase 1520s–1670s in Norfolk		61%	
		in Suffolk		38%	
		Counties combined		51%	

the country. Smith[26] divided the county into three kilometre squares, and used these as the mapping units, but this approach suffers from the disadvantage that parishes often straddle the edges of such squares; Sheail,[27] on the other hand, used units the size of hundreds as the mapping unit, but these units—being of some size—may include considerable variations within them, which are generalized by the overall density value for each one. On the other hand, with over one thousand parishes in the two counties, chorochromatic mapping using individual parishes as the base units would produce far too complicated a picture.

POPULATION DISTRIBUTIONS

Whilst in the sixteenth and seventeenth centuries there were quite marked changes in the population of the two counties, the actual rate of growth was not great. It was probably highest in the middle and later sixteenth century than in the seventeenth, when it became more erratic and uncertain. It may well have been levelling off entirely towards the end of that century. Overall, a population growth curve for the whole period would probably approximate to a straight line (sloping upwards), thus implying a decreasing rate of growth, as Eversley has pointed out.[28] Estimated population totals (Table I) show that an increase in population of about one-half over those at the beginning of the sixteenth century had taken place by the 1670s. But the individual rate of growth of some of the large towns in the area was far outpacing this by the end of the seventeenth century (Table II). Such urban growth, in conditions of very high mortality, could only have been made possible by immigration, on a large scale, of country-dwellers to the towns.

Population in the 1520s

The years at the end of the first quarter of the sixteenth century are the first for which more than local estimates of population may be made in Norfolk and Suffolk since the time of the Poll Taxes of the 1370s. They were also years when sustained population growth was gaining momentum again in the area, as it was generally in the rest of the country. Town population must certainly have fallen during the fifteenth century, but it is probable that urban wealth comprised a far greater proportion of total wealth in 1524/5 than at the time of the taking of the equivalent subsidies in 1334.[29] They almost certainly—depending on what definition of 'town' is used—held a greater proportion of total population than in 1377. Russell's general estimate for 1377 of about 10 per cent may be too low for East Anglia, but by the 1520s at least 20 per cent lived in towns in Norfolk and Suffolk.[30] The full subsidy listings of that decade cover nearly all of England, and give a standard measurement of the distribution of people and wealth. The situation revealed by numbers of taxpayers alone in 1524/5 demonstrates that the two counties, together with parts of the West Country, possessed some of the highest densities of population in England. There was a relatively high yield from the lower levels of taxpayers; distributions of these would suggest a

TABLE II
The towns of East Anglia 1520–1670s (rounded figures)

	Population 1524/5	Per cent change	Population 1603	Per cent change	Population 1670	Overall per cent change
Norwich N	8 000	37	11 000 (?)	81	20 000 (X)	150
Kings Lynn N	4 500 (?)	33	6 000 (?)	50	9 000 (?)	100
Gt Yarmouth N	4 000 (?)	37	5 500 (?)	81	10 000 (X)	150
Bury St Edmunds	3 550	26	4 500	37	6 200	74
Ipswich S	3 100	61	5 000 (?)	58	7 900	154
Wymondham N	1 450	10	1 600	93	3 100	113
Hadleigh S	1 500	16	1 750 (?)	20	2 100	40
Beccles S	1 200	−8	1 100	59	1 750	45
Sudbury S	1 200	12	1 350	48	2 000	66
Dunwich S	1 150	−26	850	−64	300	−73
Little Walsingham N	1 100 (X)	−27	800 (?)	6	850	−22
Aylsham N	1 100	−36	700 (X)	92	1 350	22
Lavenham S	1 050	14	1 200	25	1 500	42
Long Melford S	1 000	15	1 150	56	1 750	75
Woodbridge S	950	15	1 100	31	1 450	52
North Walsham N	800	12	900	77	1 600 (X)	100
Diss N	800	−12	700	114	1 500	87
Lowestoft	750	33	1 000	0	1 000	33
Thetford N	700	28	900 (?)	33	1 200	71
Attleborough	700	7	750	40	1 050	50
Mildenhall S	700	42	1 000	90	1 900	171
Aldeburgh S	700	85	1 300 (X)	−50	650 (X)	−7
Bungay S	650	61	1 050	14	1 200	84
Southwold S	650	38	900 (?)	50	1 350	107
E. Dereham N	600	83	1 100	36	1 500	150
Swaffham N	600	41	850	23	1 050	75
Stoke-by-Nayland S	600	—	—	—	—	—
Framlingham S	550	36	750	33	1 000	81
Nayland S	525	57	825	—	—	—
Debenham S	500	0	500	0	500	0
Stowmarket S	500	60	800	75	1 400	180
Eye S	500	0	500	70	850	70
Harleston N	400	75	700 (?)	21	850	112
Fakenham N	400	25	500	45	725	81
Needham Market S	400	37	550 (?)	27	700	75
Downham Market N	350 (X)	0	350 (X)	185	1 000	185
Wickham Market S	350	50	525	4	550	57
Loddon N	325	23	400	75	700	115
Holt N	325	23	400	50	600	84
Woolpit S	325	23	400	6	425	30
Ixworth S	300	66	500	10	550	83
Burnham Market N	275	−9	250	40	350	27
Halesworth S	250	140	600	66	1 000	300
Gorleston S	250	—	—	—	550	120
Cromer N	225	133	525	−71	150 (X)	−33
Saxmundham S	200	0	200 (X)	212	625	212
Watton N	175	71	300 (?)	50	450	157
Wells N	—	—	1 300	15	1 500	—
Foulsham N	—	—	500	30	650	—
TOTAL	50 225		65 425		98 375	

Note: (?) = Estimated figure from partial source. (X) = Figure from doubtful source. N = Norfolk. S = Suffolk.

denser and (per capita) probably wealthier population than average. The lay subsidies recording taxpayers which give this evidence are mostly to be found in the returns to the Exchequer contained in class E 179. in the Public Records, but while some have been published in different forms, the burden of work of their collation has been carried out by Sheail, who has provided a comprehensive gazetteer.[31] Some doubt has been cast on how accurately figures of taxpayers may be converted to total populations. Sheail indeed wrote '. . . it is impossible to invoke a single quotient to the number of taxpayers in the vill of 1524/5, and thereby find the number of inhabitants. The time for a correlation of the density of taxpayers with the distribution of population is premature'.[32] This assertion, however, is based solely on a criticism of attempts to equate taxpayers with households, one which stresses rightly that little was known of the total numbers of households within each community. Whilst agreeing with this view, the application of the method outlined above does enable estimates of population to be made by treating these taxpayers as the adults that they undoubtedly were, rather than the heads of households that they might have been. Indeed, only in this way can full use of this information on population, available after such a great hiatus, be made.

Despite the considerable work done on the subsidies, both unpublished and published,[33] close examination of them is needed to justify these contentions. The assessors grouped wealth under three headings in these listings: land, goods and wages. They were thus certainly the most comprehensive of Tudor taxes, including for the only time the 'wage-earning classes', those recorded as getting but twenty shillings a year. These subsidies of 1524/5 were unique for their inclusion of daily and weekly wage earners. These paid 4d in tax on their assessment of £1. 'The wage earner was asked to contribute the sum of 4d to the subsidy. It was a poll tax levied on all those above the age of fifteen. . . .'[34] Yet the very poorest, below even this level, were omitted entirely; their numbers, particularly in towns, may have been high. However, all males of any substance should have been enumerated, including living-in servants. For example, in a Muster Return of 1522 for Bures in Babergh Hundred, Suffolk, 24 men were enrolled as 'servants of Sir William Waldegrave'. The same 24 appeared in the 1524 lay subsidy list together, described as 'servants, every one of them in wages by year'.[35] On the other hand, women were most infrequently mentioned, usually only when they were the head of a business. This was so in the case, for example, of Alice, widow of the great clothier, Thomas Spring of Lavenham.[36] In Suffolk, Babergh Hundred returned 35 women, in every case termed widows; Blything Hundred returns mentioned eleven women, but did not describe them; in the county as a whole, one in which some 17 000 taxpayers are enumerated, less than 3 per cent were women.

Of the two subsidy lists for Norfolk and Suffolk, about 75 per cent of the total combined names were present in the 1524 returns and 70 per cent in those for 1525. This allows compensating factors of 25 per cent and 30 per cent to be applied to the 1524 and 1525 returns respectively, in order to take account of those not enumerated in both years. This of course ignores death, maturation, changes of financial circumstance and, most important, migration between the two dates. The problems of handling the raw material are considerable indeed. On a regional scale, however, such factors may be disregarded for the intervening year or so; indeed, similar proportions have been found for other parts of the country.[37] Adult females are presumed to be equal to adult males; the greatest problem remains the exclusion of those in the poor classes. The lay subsidies themselves give no hint as to their number. Reliance for any estimate of these must be put entirely on the Musters of Harness of 1522, which were self-assessed records of ability to contribute to, or fight in, a threatened war.

Often those exempt because of poverty are recorded: Muster returns giving this information survive for Great Yarmouth and three Norfolk hundreds, West Flegg, Happing and Tunstead,[38] as well as Babergh Hundred in Suffolk.[39] These give a good indication of conditions in settlements ranging from tiny hamlets to a substantial port. An analysis has revealed that those assessed as poor in 1522, and not subsequently appearing in the subsidies, represented about 10 per cent of the combined recorded names in the lay subsidies of 1524 and 1525.[40] A few were to be taxed

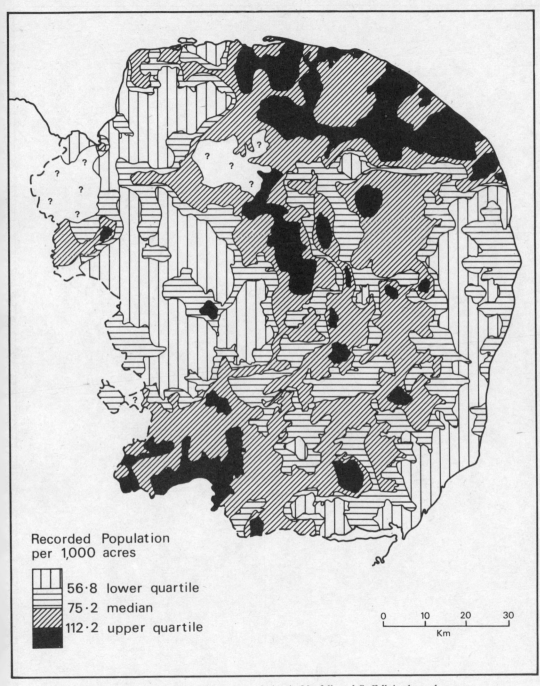

Recorded Population
per 1,000 acres

56·8 lower quartile
75·2 median
112·2 upper quartile

0   10   20   30
Km

FIGURE 1. Distribution of estimated population in Norfolk and Suffolk in the early 1520s

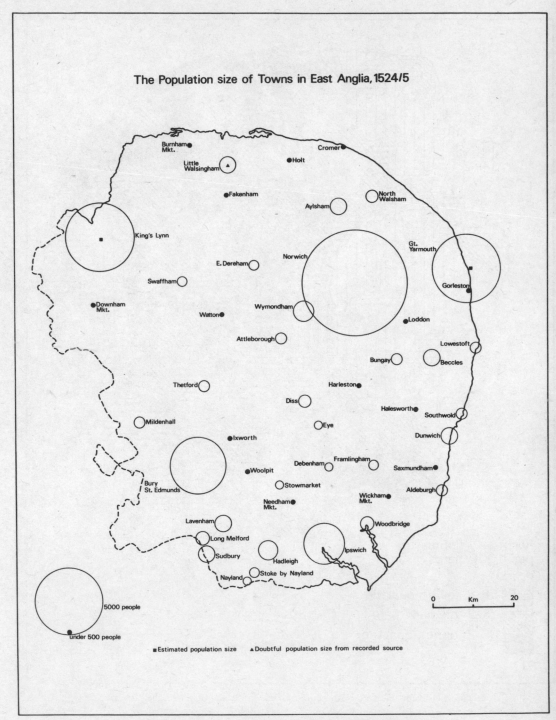

The Population size of Towns in East Anglia, 1524/5

Burnham Mkt.
Little Walsingham
Cromer
Holt
Fakenham
Aylsham
North Walsham
King's Lynn
Gt. Yarmouth
E. Dereham
Norwich
Swaffham
Gorleston
Downham Mkt.
Watton
Wymondham
Loddon
Attleborough
Lowestoft
Bungay
Beccles
Thetford
Harleston
Diss
Halesworth
Southwold
Mildenhall
Eye
Dunwich
Ixworth
Debenham
Framlingham
Saxmundham
Woolpit
Stowmarket
Aldeburgh
Bury St. Edmunds
Needham Mkt.
Wickham Mkt.
Lavenham
Woodbridge
Long Melford
Sudbury
Ipswich
Hadleigh
Nayland
Stoke by Nayland

0   Km   20

5000 people

under 500 people

■ Estimated population size   ▲ Doubtful population size from recorded source

FIGURE 2. Population size of towns in Norfolk and Suffolk in the early 1520s

in 1524, however. In the Norfolk village of North Walsham, 25 people are described as *nullus valor*, yet some confusion existed even in this simple recording in the muster, for some had '20s' added to their name. In the Suffolk village of Polsted, thirteen people were recorded as of no value in 1522, whilst 30 twenty-shilling payers appeared in the 1524 lists; of these, two, a weaver and a carpenter, had previously been numbered amongst the poor in the Muster. Despite such anomalies, for those hundreds for which no muster survives this figure of 10 per cent has been applied on the regional scale. Thus the estimated figures of total population, on which the distribution of population (Fig. 1) and town size (Fig. 2) in the 1520s is based, have been obtained throughout by taking the figures from the more comprehensive 1524 lists, adding 20 per cent compared to that of 1525 to compensate for omissions in it, with a further figure for poor omissions based on the 1522 Muster, an average of 10 per cent. Females are then taken to be equal in number to males; and 40 per cent added to this figure to allow for the approximate proportion of children under 16 years of age, the usual tax-paying age. This method, then, differs from the approach of simply multiplying totals of taxpayers (together with those presumed omitted as exempt from payment) by a factor such as 4·0 or 4·5, which purports to represent typical household size in the early sixteenth century, about which we know so little. In addition, it must always be remembered, the subsidies recorded taxpayers and the number of those who were actually 'householders' is difficult, if not impossible, to discern. The act setting up the subsidy makes no mention of 'heads of households', for the taxation was based on wealth and not family status. Indeed, as Sheail has written: 'The surveys cannot be used in an enumeration of the households in each vill—they are instead a list of most of the men over the age of fifteen in each taxation unit'.[41] Earlier writers have produced no figures for these two counties with which those utilized here can be compared; equally, although it would be interesting to do an exercise on the Norfolk and Suffolk subsidies using multipliers such as 4·5 for comparative purposes, the considerable doubts as to what proportion of those listed were householders would perhaps make this meaningless.

Based on these calculations, therefore, Figure 1 demonstrates that, in this densely populated region of England,[42] there were none the less strong intraregional variations in population density. These, indeed, were to prove consistent throughout the sixteenth and seventeenth centuries. The area was dominated by a belt of fairly dense population, mostly of over 75 persons per 1000 acres (the median value), running roughly north–south through the region. To east and west, however, were large areas of relatively low population density. The lowest densities in north-west Norfolk, for example, are attributable to the poorly drained nature of the marshes and fens which have a generally low-density 'fenland' economy still based—in a pre-Vermuyden age—on wild fowling, fishing, reed-gathering and some pasturing: on the other hand, congested communities could be found locally within the fenland. These low densities in north Norfolk were on what were then the 'poor sands', a relative desert of warrens and sheep runs which was not to flower until the age of improvement of the eighteenth century. Towns like Downham Market on the fen edge, or Thetford amidst the sandy brecklands of west Norfolk and Suffolk, stand out strongly in such areas of low density by comparison. A similar area of infertile sands ran south behind the Suffolk coast, part of the hinterland of declining ports, such as Dunwich or Orford, long past their trading prime.

Areas of richer farming land in north-east and central Norfolk stand out in contrast: so do the two great country textile-making areas, Worstead and its surrounding villages, to the northeast of Norwich, spinning for that great city's manufacture and producing their own worsted cloths[43] and the great broadcloth area of south-western Suffolk[44] along the Stour valley. This area, centred on towns like Sudbury, Long Melford and Lavenham, had spread into the surrounding villages also, and contained some of the wealthiest and most densely populated hundreds in

England, most notably Babergh.[45] These were the areas of highest density, above 110 people per 1000 acres. Intermediate in density between these two are areas such as the heavier clay lands of east Norfolk, or the 'wood-pasture' region of central 'high' Suffolk[46] with its mixed pastoral and spinning economies.

The places of greatest concentration were, of course, the towns. Norwich, second city of the kingdom, then contained 4 per cent of Norfolk's population and 6 per cent of that of the whole area. It was the region's greatest centre, performing a role within its region rather similar to that which London was beginning to play within the whole kingdom. Between 20 and 25 per cent of the population of the two counties lived in towns. Norwich (Table II) had a population of at least 8000 and was clearly dominant over the group of county towns and ports below it: Ipswich and Bury St Edmunds, Kings Lynn and Great Yarmouth. These had populations of only half as big at most, 3000–4000. Many of the more important local marketing centres, textiles centres or ports, like Wymondham, Long Melford or Woodbridge were around 1000 in size. But most of the small towns, 'market towns' in truth perhaps only on market day, were a few hundred or so in size. Places like Ixworth or Woolpit, both in Suffolk, with populations of only 300 or 400 were what Camden termed 'little mercat towns'.[47] But no place in the two counties, except perhaps some of the isolated Breckland parishes, were very far from some kind of town.

Population in 1603

Little opportunity presents itself to examine population distributions throughout the two counties between the 1520s and the year 1603. Returns of 'households' made in 1563 for religious purposes are completely lacking for the Diocese of Norwich, which covered the whole area. The subsidies of the 1540s are less comprehensive than those of 1524/5, and thus, while providing perfectly acceptable measures of the relative distribution of wealth, are less reliable for estimates of population. For it seems that the effort of surveying and collecting money from the wage earner did not produce worthwhile amounts of money and thus, 'in the otherwise very full returns of the subsidy of 1543/5, the wage earner disappears from the lists'.[48] And the wage earner made up, like the poor, a considerable proportion of the population. The returns of communicants taken in 1603 do, however, afford an opportunity to look at population, at the end of a period of apparently considerable, if erratic, demographic growth during the middle and later years of the sixteenth century. As in the case of similar movements in the thirteenth century, this largely petered out and levelled off in response to a complex of factors during the course of the seventeenth century. Both the exact nature and interaction of these forces remain as yet ill defined in any detail. The end of this period of population growth was marked by famine and want, though nothing in comparison with the ravages of medieval famines and the Black Death. Poor crop yields persisted throughout the 1590s; recurrent outbreaks of plague wrought havoc, especially in 1602 and 1603 in East Anglia. These broke out repeatedly, though largely locally, culminating in the terrible year of 1666.[49]

The Communicant returns of 1603, whilst permitting an adequate description of the population of Norfolk and Suffolk, suffer from a number of drawbacks as a source. The most important of these, without doubt, is that, in their replies to the enquiry directed to them by the Archbishop of Canterbury on numbers of male and female communicants, recusants and dissenters ('they that do not receive') in their parishes, the clergy's answers are often 'rounded'; 72 per cent of those in the Norwich Archdeaconry are in this form; 53 per cent in the Sudbury Archdeaconry; and 38 per cent in Suffolk Archdeaconry, immediately casting doubts on their accuracy. This has also been found for similar lists in France, and earlier religious surveys in other parts of England.[50] In addition, the returns do not survive in original form at all for the fourth archdeaconry, that of Norfolk. But in practice about 70 per cent of them may be retrieved from

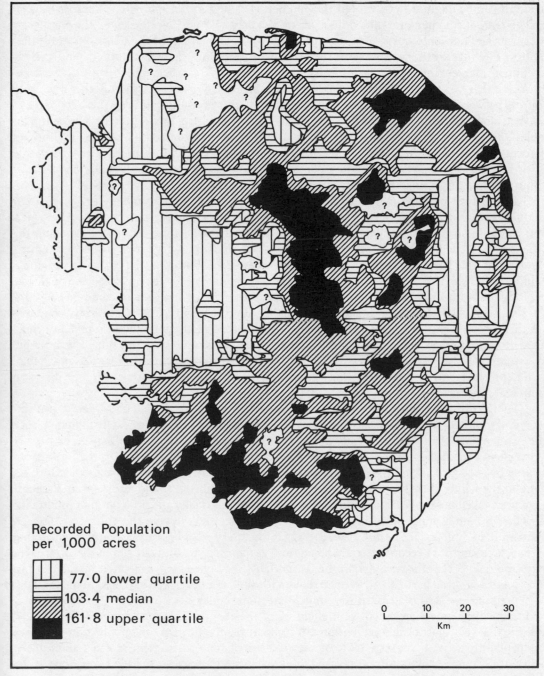

Recorded Population
per 1,000 acres

77·0 lower quartile
103·4 median
161·8 upper quartile

0   10   20   30
Km

FIGURE 3. Distribution of estimated population in Norfolk and Suffolk in 1603

the constant references in Blomefield's 'Norfolk' to 'the number of communicants returned in 1603' (or some similar formulae) of the various parishes,[51] indicating that the author had access to the originals which are now lost. Only relatively small areas in Norfolk, and in Suffolk, cannot thus be accounted for (Fig. 3). Nevertheless, the figure must be approached with reservation.

Many incumbents must have treated the enquiry as calling for an estimate, rather than for an exact count, of communicants and others. Many also may have under-represented the numbers of recusants and nonconformists in an attempt to present a good picture of the religious state of their livings. Hollingsworth has discussed the frequency of 'round figures' returned, and the un-likelihood of recusants and nonconformists being correctly returned, but despite these draw-backs felt that '. . . the totals may be close to the truth'.[52] Thus, in the absence of other large-scale sources between the early and mid sixteenth and the later seventeenth centuries these returns can-not be dismissed lightly. For Norfolk and Suffolk,[53] as elsewhere, these directly represent adult males and females, and may be converted to estimates of total population by the addition of a percentage (see above) representing approximate numbers of children under 16 years of age. They are thus one stage nearer reality compared to the lay subsidies, in actually enumerating adult people (and, ostensibly at least, all of them).

The critical problem in this context remains whether 15 or 16 years of age was that of communion, as it was of tax-paying in the lay subsidies. It would seem that the average age of first communion, and thus appearance in such a survey as that of 1603, was indeed at about this age. This was higher than in pre-Reformation times, but one which was to become normal throughout the later sixteenth and all of the seventeenth centuries. In 1583, for example, Middleton, Bishop of St Davids, laid down that 'no notorious offender, wrong-doer, malicious person, infant under fourteen years . . . shall be admitted by an minister to communicate', but by 1598 Archbiship Bancroft was enquiring whether those of 16 years and more receive commun-ion three times a year.[54] Sixteen seems to have become the age of communion, separating child-hood from adulthood, and to have been typically used in documents of the time. For example, in lists prepared in the later sixteenth century of Flemish immigrants at Norwich and King's Lynn for the Church authorities, those above and below this age are carefully and distinctly enumerated.[55]

The returns themselves are suspect on yet one further ground, that they were taken in a period of violent plague outbreaks[56] and thus could represent a year of peculiarly high mortality. How much this might affect distributions is difficult to judge, for Archbishop Whitgift had written to all the Bishops of his province of Canterbury in June 1603, requiring the information desired by the new King on the religious state of his realm. The returns were in the hands of the King in the winter of that year;[57] this timing is in all respects vital as the returns would seem to have been taken during the late summer and early autumn, usually the peak period of mortality. Parishes in both counties show high mortality in their registers during the course of 1603. At Southwold in Suffolk, for example, the registers during the period between 1602 (from when they first survive) and 1611 recorded 429 baptisms and as many as 792 burials; 373 of the latter being in 1603 alone.[58] The effects of the plague on mortality may have been mitigated by the fact that 1603 was a very good harvest year,[59] even though it would not have been gathered in until August or September, perhaps too late to have much effect on the levels of individual susceptibility to infection. The reservations about the reliability of the 1603 returns are important, but do not indicate that they must be ignored entirely. A comparison of figures of total population estimates, independently derived from a sample of the registers of nine parishes in Norfolk and Suffolk, with those from the communicant returns showed figures quite close to each other in order for all but two of them.[60] These figures give at least some added confidence in consideration of the estimates of population distribution (Fig. 3) and of town size (Fig. 4, Table II) which plot changes in population since the 1520s.

By 1603 estimated population had grown by some 24 per cent overall (Table I). This figure undoubtedly concealed many fluctuations taking place in the sixteenth century; Norfolk had grown by a greater proportion than Suffolk; the crude overall growth rate for both counties

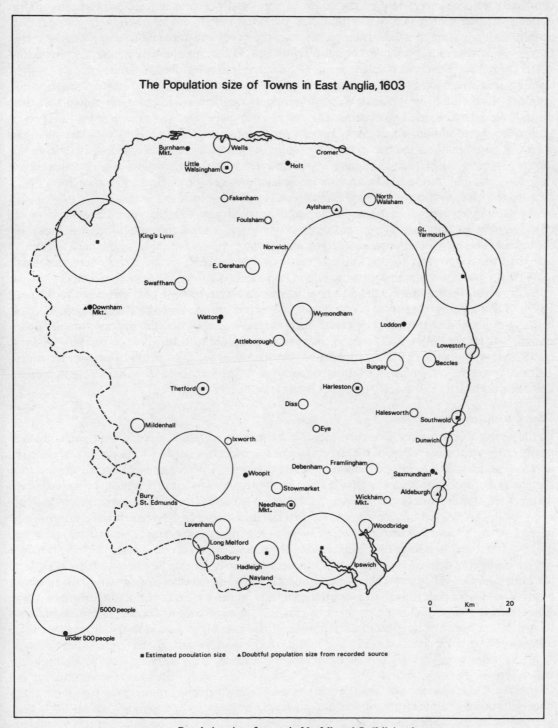

The Population size of Towns in East Anglia, 1603

Burnham Mkt.
Wells
Cromer
Little Walsingham
Holt
Fakenham
North Walsham
Aylsham
Foulsham
Gt. Yarmouth
King's Lynn
Norwich
E. Dereham
Swaffham
Downham Mkt.
Watton
Wymondham
Loddon
Attleborough
Lowestoft
Beccles
Bungay
Harleston
Thetford
Diss
Halesworth
Southwold
Mildenhall
Eye
Dunwich
Ixworth
Debenham
Framlingham
Woopit
Saxmundham
Stowmarket
Aldeburgh
Bury St. Edmunds
Wickham Mkt.
Needham Mkt.
Woodbridge
Lavenham
Long Melford
Sudbury
Hadleigh
Ipswich
Nayland

0   Km   20

5000 people

under 500 people

■ Estimated population size   ▲ Doubtful population size from recorded source

FIGURE 4. Population size of towns in Norfolk and Suffolk in 1603

combined was, however, only of the order of one-third per cent a year. No radical shift in population distribution occurred within this period (Fig. 3); indeed there was considerable stability in the nature of the distribution between the 1520s and 1603. However, a small growth in relative density is noticeable in central Norfolk and Suffolk, particularly in a sector stretching south from East Dereham over the border of the two counties beyond Diss; this was a rich farming area which contrasted strongly in density with, for example, the thinly peopled Suffolk sandlings to the east. Sir Thomas Wilson, writing of England at around 1600, noted that this central area was very rich, and exclaimed against the numbers of its gentry with money to spend; such were the conditions about 'Windhame' (Wymondham, Norfolk) and many other places.[61] A belt of parishes along the Stour valley in southern Suffolk similarly seemed to experience an increase in density which may well have been connected with the broadcloth manufactures there, then at, or passing, their peak. In a period immediately before the marked emigration from these areas to the New World,[62] such speculations deserve detailed local examination.

Just as there were more people in the 'rural' areas, so also were the towns larger and more crowded (Fig. 4). Just over 25 per cent lived in them now, a small increase in the proportion in the 1520s. The increase in population for towns in the period was nearly 30 per cent, a greater rate than the 23 per cent for the two counties as a whole (Tables I and II). Indeed the mean increase for those towns with a growing population reached nearly 40 per cent. Some towns had in fact, for various reasons, declined in population; Dunwich because of the erosion by the sea, Little Walsingham because of its decline as a pilgrimage centre after the Reformation, Beccles because of some disastrous fires. Despite such exceptions, however, the general rate of urban growth was marked. Above all Norwich was growing rapidly to at least 12 000 in 1603, when it contained 7 per cent of Norfolk's population. On the other hand, no smaller towns experienced any great growth rate, the major county towns and ports grew at about the same rate as Norwich, and the port of Ipswich, indeed, probably even faster during the period.

Population in the 1670s

In the 1670s, we have a better opportunity to examine the overall magnitude of population than at any other time in the course of the sixteenth and seventeenth centuries. The Compton 'Census' of 1676 which records information on the total numbers of communicants, recusants and dissenters for each parish, in a similar fashion to the returns of 1603, gives quite comprehensive information. Where it does not survive, the Hearth Taxes of 1662–74, and particularly those of 1674 itself, can be used to supplement—as well as check—figures derived from the information in the Compton Census. These lists record those paying, and those exempt from paying, chimney money, and thus by implication households. More, and more accurate, parish registers enable checks on figures derived from these two sources to be obtained, neither of which are complete for both counties. Thus up to three independently derived estimates of population for any one parish can be obtained, and the figures produced from all three sources at the time are close. This was probably a time of slowing population growth compared with the erratic spurts of the sixteenth century or the more sustained explosion of the later eighteenth century. It was certainly a stable demographic situation compared to the volatile demographic times around 1600.

The Compton 'Census', one of the most important contemporary ecclesiastical enquiries, was taken by Bishop Compton of London under the direction of Sheldon, the Archbishop of Canterbury. The Salt manuscript copy[63] of these returns which gives numbers of communicants, nonconformists and recusants differs, in fact, from the exact form apparently asked for in the original letter from Sheldon to Compton.[64] This required not only dissenters and recusants to be enumerated but also 'What number of persons, or at least families, are by common account . . . within each parish . . .' to be stated. In effect, as may be seen from the Salt copy and from some surviving original certificates,[65] it was communicants instead that were usually recorded. There is no reason to suspect that women of communicant age were omitted, as wives, relations or servants. They would seem to be carefully enumerated, for in other contemporary religious returns, such as lists of recusants or conventicle rolls, women are often mentioned individually, and female servants charged with attending conventicles.[66] As the century passed, religious control tightened and so did recording. Norfolk and Suffolk, although not noted as recusant counties, were rife with dissenters. But these seem to have been well surveyed and recorded in the Compton Census, the problem of 'round' numbers becoming relatively insignificant. The returns survive for the Norwich, Norfolk and Sudbury, but not Suffolk, archdeaconries of the diocese of Norwich. They represent recorded male and female adults over 16 years of age; they may thus be treated in exactly the same way as the earlier lay subsidies and communicant returns, 40 per cent being added as a standardized figure to the combined total of communicants for each parish to account for children. Evidence exists for a figure of this kind at about the same time, in the Petty Sessional Division of Wingham, Kent,[67] for example.

In the case of the Sudbury archdeaconry, for which the Compton returns do not survive, and also in order to act as a check on figures estimated from it elsewhere, the Hearth Taxes have been used.[68] The administrative procedure of the taking of these taxes has been fully examined elsewhere;[69] the major problem with their use for many counties,[70] including Norfolk and Suffolk, is that surviving enrolled returns do not necessarily include those exempt from paying the tax.[71] These in practice may be obtained from the original certificates, where they survive.[72] Totals of taxpayers are thus obtainable, though they do not necessarily represent most adult male taxpayers, as the lay subsidies did. On the contrary, they consist only of those paying for the number of chimneys in their 'household', for which they were responsible: what proportion of the total adult population these taxpayers represent is simply not open even to estimation.

Any kind of estimate of total population from the Hearth Tax to supplement the data from the Compton Census may not, therefore, be made according to the standardized method suggested here for dealing with diverse sources which share the common characteristic of recording adults; instead a multiplier, in this case of 4.75, is used on each household to represent mean household size.[73] Whilst the most complete roll for Norfolk, that of 1674,[74] is used, many parishes enrolled on it are illegible or missing owing to the damaged state of the document itself and these have had to be consolidated by references to earlier taxes going back as far as eight years to 1666. Obvious inconsistencies must result from the use of data from such widely spaced years.[75] However, they have had to be used to achieve some estimate where data from the Compton Census are not available. As in the case of the 1603 returns, a check has been obtained from a sample of parish registers, fifteen in number, which give close estimates to those derived from the two main sources.[76] The two combined truly give us '... the only picture we have of the incidence and distribution of population ... at a time when the agrarian changes of the Tudor and the Elizabethan age had reached a stage of equilibrium and before the silent expansion of the eighteenth century';[77] a silent expansion which was, it is true, to affect these two counties less than many more industrialized regions.

Certainly the rise in overall total population between 1603 and the 1670s (Table I) was only a little less, at 21 per cent, than in the slightly longer period between the 1520s and 1603, when the increase had been 24 per cent. Norfolk once more experienced a greater percentage increase of 26 per cent compared to 15 per cent in the case of Suffolk. But the overall crude annual percentage increase of about one-third of one per cent a year was the same in the seventeenth century as it had been in the sixteenth century. Over the whole period, indeed, a total of only about 50 per cent population growth took place. These relatively low rates of total and annual population growth, even in their (demographically) crude generality, bear witness to the uncer-

John Patten

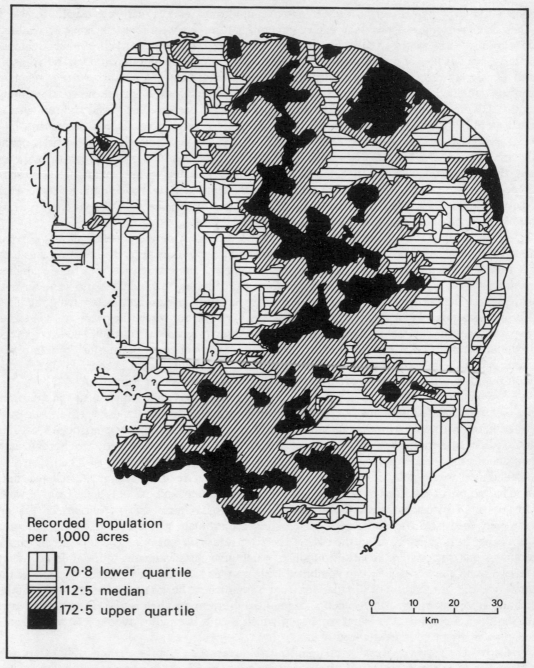

Recorded Population
per 1,000 acres

70·8 lower quartile
112·5 median
172·5 upper quartile

0   10   20   30
Km

FIGURE 5. Distribution of estimated population in Norfolk and Suffolk in the 1670s

tainty of population at the time, with its general advances and sudden, neo–Malthusian falls.
Population was indeed falling in at least some East Anglian parishes in the last quarter of the
seventeenth century.[78] But, once again, marked stability in population distributions in the two
counties in the 1670s (Fig. 5) was apparent, compared with earlier years (Figs 1, 3). The central

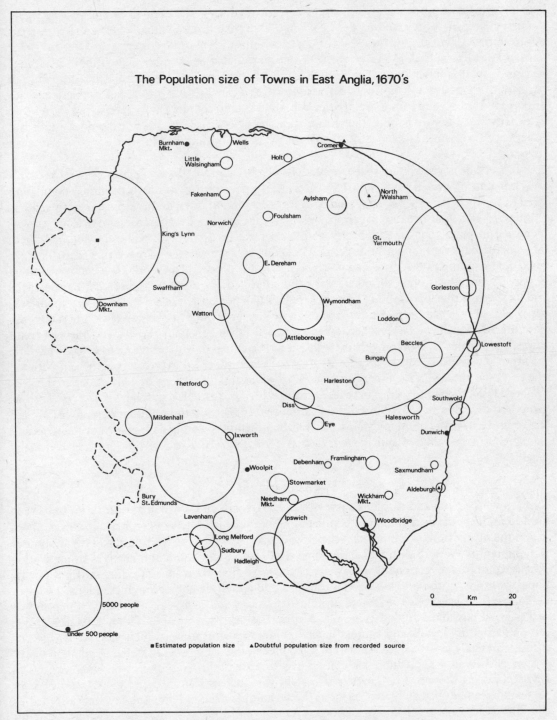

The Population size of Towns in East Anglia, 1670's

Burnham Mkt.
Wells
Little Walsingham
Holt
Cromer
Fakenham
Aylsham
North Walsham
Norwich
Foulsham
King's Lynn
Gt. Yarmouth
E. Dereham
Gorleston
Swaffham
Wymondham
Downham Mkt.
Watton
Loddon
Attleborough
Beccles
Lowestoft
Bungay
Thetford
Harleston
Southwold
Mildenhall
Diss
Halesworth
Ixworth
Eye
Dunwich
Debenham
Framlingham
Woolpit
Saxmundham
Stowmarket
Bury St. Edmunds
Needham Mkt.
Wickham Mkt.
Aldeburgh
Lavenham
Ipswich
Woodbridge
Long Melford
Sudbury
Hadleigh

5000 people
under 500 people

0   Km   20

■ Estimated population size   ▲ Doubtful population size from recorded source

FIGURE 6. Population size of towns in Norfolk and Suffolk in the 1670s

belt of high-density population was even more marked and well defined in contrast to thinly populated sectors to west and east. The changes in agricultural practice which were to revolutionize farming on some of these lighter soils, except on the sandiest brecks, had yet to gather pace in Norfolk. Indeed, the value of the lower quartile had fallen quite perceptibly since 1603; increases, in this latter period of relative standstill of population, seemed generally likely in parishes of already established high density. North and north-east Norfolk, rich arable areas with important weaving and spinning activities in both town and country, had experienced an increase in density since 1603. On the other hand, some parishes in south and south-west Suffolk had experienced a decline of density of population; this area's cloth production was now well past its peak.

It was the increase in urban population which was most marked, however.[79] Despite a constant rate of overall population increase, nearly one-third of the two counties' population lived in towns by the 1670s, compared with less than one-quarter in the early sixteenth century (Tables I, II). The pace of urban growth was quickening; by the coarsest measure, towns increased in population size by nearly 50 per cent between 1603–70, while the countryside at large increased by only about 11 per cent. Marked in-migration must have fed this growth, under prevailing conditions of high urban mortality.[80] In this process, Norwich's role continued to be dominant, for its share of Norfolk's total population had increased to 11 per cent by the 1670s and its share of the population of the whole region to 6 per cent. Thus it was twice as important, relatively, than it had been in the 1520s, both to the county and the region (Fig. 6). Whilst the size interrelationships of the other towns remained fairly constant, there was a marked trend towards a greater rate of growth of larger towns compared with lesser market centres. The (arbitrarily chosen) largest twenty towns by size in fact increased by nearly 55 per cent between 1603 and the 1670s. On the other hand, the smallest twenty or so grew by only about 20 per cent (Table II). These were being outpaced presumably because of a number of factors, such as growth in the scale and complexity of the larger towns' manufactures and service provision; and the improvement of communications that was lengthening possible daily journeys to towns and the spread of distributive and other trades into villages which had hitherto relied on near-by small towns.

CONCLUSION

Until now, the fiscal and religious surveys of the sixteenth and seventeenth centuries have been used to indicate the distribution of population either in small tracts of countryside and in towns or, on the other hand, at a more superficial level over the whole of the country. This study uses the different surveys to distinguish, in some detail, the distribution and changes in population over a region, moreover one that was one of the most important in pre-industrial England. Its population during these two centuries, despite undoubted demographic fluctuations, has been demonstrated to be relatively stable in its distributions and densities, a stability which in fact makes at all possible a study based on the 'comparative statics' adopted here. This description of population in Norfolk and Suffolk indeed points to a situation in which marked change was restricted largely to urban growth within a region experiencing broadly stable population distribution and limited population increase. To what extent this was typical of other regions of England during these two centuries remains unclear, and rests on further regional studies. How such studies might be conducted, as far as the techniques used to refine the raw data afforded by the different lists are concerned, of course remains to be seen. It may be concluded that the analysis and mapping of the different classes of those surveyed—taxpayers, communicants or whatever—give only a relative and potentially confusing picture, while on the other hand their conversion by different techniques to estimated approximate totals are full of pitfalls. No one method is without them. But that standardized approach suggested here does in each case, whether using subsidy or communicant lists, begin by treating the contents of each list as what *was* apparently recorded—adult males over 16, adult males and females over 16—and not as what *may* have been recorded, such as heads of households. The problems of even obtaining a simple picture of population distribution during the sixteenth and seventeenth centuries are considerable, however, and this must be realized before attempts are made to explain population change, or use population evidence as part of an explanation of change in the geography of the time.

ACKNOWLEDGEMENTS

The author is grateful to C. T. Smith and E. A. Wrigley for their guidance in the early stages of preparation of this study, and also to R. S. Schofield for his advice. He is equally indebted to F. V. Emery for commenting on a final draft, and making valuable suggestions. Any deficiencies remaining are the responsibility of the author. This paper was completed whilst the author was on sabbatical leave from the University of Oxford.

NOTES

1. See, e.g., WRIGLEY, E. A. (ed.) (1966) *An introduction to English historical demography* (London)

2. CLARKSON, L. A. (1971) *The pre-industrial economy in England 1500–1700*, pp. 25–32; CHAMBERS, J. D. (1972) *Population, economy and society in pre-industrial England*, pp. 9–32 (London)

3. KIRBY, D. A. (1972) 'Population density and land values in County Durham during the mid seventeenth century', *Trans. Inst. Br. Geogr.* 57, p. 87

4. SHEAIL, J. (1972) 'The distribution of taxable population and wealth in England during the early sixteenth century', *Trans. Inst. Br. Geogr.* 55, 111–25

5. GLASS, D. V. (1965) 'Two papers on Gregory King', in GLASS, D. V. and EVERSLEY, D. E. C. (eds) *Population in history*, 159–220

6. SCHOFIELD, R. S. (1963) 'Parliamentary lay taxation, 1485–1547', unpubl. Ph.D. thesis, Univ. of Cambridge; SHEAIL, J. (1968) 'The regional distribution of wealth in England as indicated in the 1524/5 lay subsidy returns', unpubl. Ph.D. thesis, Univ. of London

7. CORNWALL, J. (1965) 'A Tudor domesday: the musters of 1522', *J. Soc. Archiv.* 111, 19–24

8. MARSHALL, L. M. (1936) 'The levying of the hearth tax, 1662–1688', *Engl. hist. Rev.* 51, 628–46; MEEKINGS, C. A. F. (1951) *Dorset hearth taxes, 1662–1674*, VII–XXIII (Dorchester); STYLES, P. (1957) 'Hearth tax returns', *Warwick County Rec.* 1, introd.; PATTEN, J. (1971) 'The hearth taxes, 1662–1689', *Local Popul. Stud.* 7, 14–27

9. SCHOFIELD, R. S. (1970) 'Comment', *Local Popul. Stud.* 4, 61–2

10. GLASS, D. V. (1968) 'Notes on the demography of London at the end of the seventeenth century', *Daedalus* 14, 581–92

11. FOSTER, C. W. (ed.) (1926) 'The state of the church', *Lincoln Rec. Soc.* 23, 441–4

12. e.g. JESSOP, A. (ed.) (1888) 'The condition of the Archdeaconry of Norwich in 1603', *Norfolk Archaeol.* 10, 1–7

13. WHITEMAN, A. *The Compton census* (forthcoming); I am grateful to Miss Whiteman for her advice.

14. e.g. KIRBY, op. cit., pp. 87–9

15. GLASS (1965) op. cit.; KIRBY, op. cit.

16. LASLETT, P. and HARRISON, W. (1963) 'Clayworth and Cogenhoe' in BELL, H. E. and OLLARD, R. C. (eds), *Historical essays, 1600–1750*, 157–84 (London); LASLETT, P. (1965) *The world we have lost*, p. 64 (London); idem. (1970) 'The comparative history of household and family', *J. Soc. Hist.*, 75–87; idem. (ed.) (1972) with the assistance of WALL, R., *Household and family in past time*, pp. 24–8, 86 (Cambridge)

17. LASLETT, P. (1969) 'Size and structure of the household in England over three centuries, Pt. 1', *Popul. Stud.*, 201–2

18. WALL, R. (1972) 'Mean household size in England from printed sources' in LASLETT, P. (ed.) *Household and Family in past time*, 159–203 (Cambridge)

19. SMITH, C. T. (1965) *V. C. H. Leicestershire* 111, 143–4; see also THIRSK, J. (1959) 'Sources of information on population, 1500–1760' *Amat. Hist.* 4, 129–33 and 182–4; and MUNBY, L. (1963) 'Hertfordshire population statistics, 1563–1801', *Herts. Local Hist. Council*, p. 15

20. SMITH, C. T. (1965) 'The Cambridge region: population' in STEERS, J. A. (ed.) *The Cambridge region*, p. 137 (Cambridge)

21. BARNETT, G. E. (1936) *Two tracts by Gregory King* (Baltimore); GLASS (1965) op. cit.

22. e.g. U.N.O. (1953) *The determinants and consequences of population trends*, pp. 1–5 (New York); idem. (1955) *Age and sex patterns of mortality* (New York); idem. (1968) *The concept of a stable population: application to the study of countries with incomplete demographic statistics*, p. 7 (New York)

23. GLASS, D. V. (1950) 'Gregory King's estimates of population in England and Wales, 1695', *Popul. Stud.* 3, 338–74; COLEMAN, D. C. (1965) 'Labour in the English economy of the seventeenth century', *Econ. Hist. Rev.* 8, p. 284; WRIGLEY, E. A. (1968) 'Mortality in pre-industiral England', *Daedalus*, p. 576

24. U.N.O. (1955) op. cit., p. 3; SCHOFIELD, R. (1971) 'Comment', *Local Popul. Stud.* 6, 61–5

25. P.R.O., E. 179. 154/697

26. SMITH (1965) op. cit., p. 138

27. SHEAIL (1968) op. cit., pp. 82–9

28. EVERSLEY, D. E. C. (1966) 'Appendix B' in WRIGLEY, E. A. (ed.) *An introduction to English historical demography*, p. 266 (London)

29. GLASSOCK, R. E. (1963) 'The distribution of lay wealth in south-east England in the early fourteenth century', unpubl. Ph.D. thesis, Univ. of London; and idem. (1968) 'The distribution of wealth in East Anglia in the early fourteenth century', *Trans. Inst. Br. Geogr.* 44 ,113–23

30. RUSSELL, J. C. (1960) 'The metropolitan city region in the middle ages', *J. Reg. Sci.* 2, p. 60; PATTEN, J. (1972) 'The urban structure of East Anglia during the sixteenth and seventeenth centuries', unpubl. Ph.D. thesis, Univ. of Cambridge. Those places referred to as towns in Norfolk and Suffolk in the couse of this study are defined in that thesis.

31. SHEAIL (1968) op. cit.; I am most grateful to Dr Sheail for his generosity in allowing me to draw on his unpublished gazetteer (1968) for population mapping.

32. Idem. (1968) pp. 128–30.

33. SCHOFIELD (1963) op. cit.; SHEAIL (1968) op. cit.; CHARMAN, D. (1949) 'Wealth and trade in Leicester in the early sixteenth century', *Trans. Leics. Archaeol. Soc.* 25; CHIBNELL, A. C. and WOODMAN, A. V. (1950) 'Subsidy roll for the county of Buckingham, anno 1524', *Bucks. Rec. Soc.* 8; CORNWALL, J. (1956–7) 'The lay subsidy rolls for the county of Sussex, 1524–25', *Sussex Rec. Soc.* 56; SALZMAN, L. F. (1960) (1961) 'Early taxation in Sussex', *Sussex Archaeol. Collns* 98, 29–43 and 99, 1–19; NICHOLLS, L. M. (1964) 'The lay subsidy of 1523: the reliability of the subsidy rolls as illustrated by Totnes and Dartmouth', *Birmingham Hist. Jl* 9

34. SHEAIL (1968) op. cit., p. 33

35. Ipswich Public Library, Suffolk Collns, 942. 64(3); HERVEY, S. H. A. (1910) 'Suffolk in 1524', *Suffolk Green Books* 10, p. 19

36. McCLENAGHAN, B. (1924) *The Springs of Lavenham* (Ipswich)

37. SHEAIL (1968) op. cit.; CORNWALL, J. (1962) 'English country towns in the fifteen-twenties', *Econ. Hist. Rev.* 15, 54–69; idem., (1961–2) 'The people of Rutland in 1522', *Trans. Leics. Archaeol. Soc.* 38, 7–28

38. P.R.O., E36/25.

39. Ibid.

40. PATTEN, J. (1972) 'Village and town', *Agric. Hist. Rev.* 20, 4–7; idem. (1972), unpubl. thesis

41. SHEAIL (1968) op. cit., p. 46

42. Ibid.

43. ALLISON, K. J. (1960) 'The Norfolk worsted industry in the sixteenth and seventeenth centuries', *Yorks. Bull. Econ. Soc. Res.* 12

44. MITCHELL, J. B. (1954) *Historical Geography*, pp. 222–53 (London)

45. PATTEN (1972) 'Village and town', op. cit.

46. THIRSK, J. (ed.) (1967) *The agrarian history of England and Wales, IV, 1500–1640*, pp. 46–9 (Cambridge)

47. CAMDEN, W. (1639) *Britannia*, pp. 459–483 (London); cf. Norwich, see POUND, J. F. (1966) 'The social and trade structure of Norwich, 1525–1575', *Past and Present* 34; and other larger Norfolk and Suffolk towns, PATTEN (1972) unpubl. thesis, op. cit.

48. SHEAIL (1968) op. cit., p. 37; see also RAMSAY, G. D. (1954) 'Two sixteenth century taxation lists, 1547 and 1576', *Wilts. Archaeol. Nat. Hist. Soc. Rec. Branch* 10

49. CREIGHTON, C. (1965) *History of epidemics in Britain* (London); HOLLINGSWORTH, M. and T. H. (1971) 'Plague mortality rates by age and size in the parish of St. Botolph's Without, Bishopsgate, London, 1603', *Popul. Stud.*, 131–46

50. GOUBERT, P. (1965) 'Recent theories and research in French population between 1500 and 1700' in GLASS, D. V. and EVERSLEY, D. E. C. (eds) *Population in History*, p. 459, stresses a similar problem of 'round numbers' in the Easter lists of communicants in catholic France; see also CORNWALL, J. (1959) 'An Elizabethan census', *Rec. of Bucks.* 16, 258–73

51. BLOMEFIELD, F. (1805) Norfolk, *An essay towards a topographical history . . .* 12 vols., *passim* (London); I am much indebted to Miss A. Whiteman for indicating this source.

52. HOLLINGSWORTH, T. H. (1969) *Historical demography*, pp. 80–5 (London)

53. The originals are in the B.M., Harl. MS. They are transcribed by JESSOP, A. (ed.) (1888) 'The condition of the Archdeaconry of Norwich in 1603', *Norfolk Archaeol.* 10, 1–49, 166–84; idem. (1888) (1903) 'The condition of the Archdeaconries of Suffolk and Sudbury in the year 1603', *Proc. Suffolk Inst. Archaeol.* 6, 361–400 and 11, 1–46; for the Norfolk Archdeaconry, BLOMEFIELD (1805) op. cit.

54. KENNEDY, W. P. M. (1924) *Elizabethan episcopal administration*, Vol. 3, pp. 146, 307 (London)

55. RYE, W. (1887) 'The Dutch refugees in Norwich', *Norfolk Antiq. Misc.* 3, 189, 243–5

56. CREIGHTON (1965) op. cit.

57. JESSOP (1888) op. cit., pp. 1–17

58. From figures in the possession of the Cambridge Group for the History of Population and Social Structure, 20, Silver Street, Cambridge; I am most grateful to them for making these, and other figures from parish registers cited in this study, freely available.

59. HOSKINS, W. G. (1964) 'Harvest fluctuations and English economic history, 1480–1619', *Agric. Hist. Rev.* 3, p. 39; APPLEBY, A. B. (1973) 'Disease or famine? Mortality in Cumberland and Westmorland, 1580–1640', *Econ. Hist. Rev.* 26, 403–32

60. PATTEN (1972) unpubl. thesis, op. cit., pp. 49–53

61. WILSON, T. (1936) 'The state of England anno do. 1600' *Camden Soc. Publ.* 52, p. 12

62. TYSACK, N. C. P. (1952) 'Migration from East Anglia to the New World before 1600', unpubl. Ph.D. thesis, Univ. of London, pp. 189 *et seq.*

63. William Salt Library, Stafford, Salt MS 33; see also RICHARDS, T. (1927) 'The religious census of 1676', *Cymmrdn, Soc. Publ. Suppl.*, 7–11; DYMOND, D. P. (1966) 'Suffolk and the Compton census of 1676', *Suffolk Rev.* 3, 103–18; GUILDFORD, E. L. (1924) 'Nottinghamshire in 1676', *Trans. Thoroton Soc.* 28, 106–13; LANGLEY, A. S. (1920) 'A religious census of 1676 A.D.', *Lincs. Notes and Queries* 16, 33–51. Other communicant 'censuses' of the period, such as that of 1688, seem to survive at best only in summary form; see DALRYMPLE, J. (1773) *Memoirs of Great Britain and Ireland*, Vol. 2, pp. 11–15 (London and Edinburgh) and HOLLINGSWORTH (1969) op. cit., pp. 81–8

64. CARDWELL, E. (1839) *Documentary annals of the reformed church of England*, Vol. 2, pp. 288–91 (London)

65. DYMOND (1966) op. cit., p. 103; but see ANON. (1973) 'The Compton Census—Peterborough', *Local Popul. Stud.* 10, 71–4.

66. CHALKLIN, C. W. (1960) 'The Compton census of 1676', *Kent Rec.*, p. 156

67. Ibid., p. 157

68. For Suffolk, HERVEY, S. H. A. (1905) *Suffolk Green Books*, 11 and P.R.O. E 179/345; For Norfolk, P.R.O., E 179 154/697, E 179 153/42, E 179 253/45, E 179/336, 337 and 338

69. MARSHALL, MEEKINGS, STYLES, PATTEN (1971) op. cit. (note 8)

70. It is not the case, as KIRBY has contended, op. cit., p. 87, that in all Hearth Tax returns post-1663 both taxable *and* untaxable were always enumerated.

71. PATTEN (1971) op. cit., pp. 18–22

72. For Suffolk P.R.O., E 179/35; and for Norfolk P.R.O. E 179/336, 7 and 8

73. PATTEN (1972) unpubl. thesis, pp. 62–9 and Appendix 1

74. P.R.O., E 179 154/697.

75. Such as from migration, see MEIRION-JONES, G. E. (1971) 'The use of Hearth Tax Returns and vernacular architecture', *Trans. Inst. Br. Geogr.* 53, p. 147; cf. other local studies, MEEKINGS, C. A. F. (1940) 'Surrey hearth tax, 1664', *Surrey Rec. Soc.* 17; SOGNER, S. (1963) 'Aspects of the demographic situation in 17 parishes in Shropshire, 1711–1760', *Popul. Stud.* 17, 126–46

76. PATTEN (1972) unpubl. thesis, pp. 57–61

77. PARRY, O. M. (1953) 'The hearth tax in Merioneth', *J. Merioneth Hist. Rec. Soc.* 11, p. 17

78. E.g. GRACE, F. R. (1970) 'The population of East Bergholt, Suffolk, 1653–1836', *Suffolk Rev.* 3, 260–72

79. RIPLEY, P. (1972) 'The parish register evidence for the population of Gloucester', *Trans. Bristol and Glos. Archaeol. Soc.* 91, 199–206

80. PATTEN, J. (1973) 'Rural-urban migration in pre-industrial England', *Sch. of Geogr., Univ. of Oxford, Res. Pap.* 6

Probate inventories and the geography of livestock farming: a study of east Worcestershire, 1540–1750

J. A. YELLING

Lecturer in Geography, Birkbeck College, University of London

ABSTRACT. Probate inventories often record the livestock and sometimes the crops possessed by individual farmers in early-modern England. The paper shows how this material can be used to provide a simple quantitative account of two main aspects of the geography of livestock farming, namely, the relative importance of livestock compared with crops, and the distribution of the various livestock types. A general theoretical discussion is linked to a study of the documents relating to east Worcestershire. Inventories for four periods, 1540–99, 1600–60, 1670–99 and 1700–50 are treated separately, and the results compared by means of simple indices. The documents for each period are analysed within a framework of small regions and, from this, larger distinctions can be recognized. In particular, the products of a champion area in the south can be contrasted with those of a mainly enclosed area to the north. The former district retained a relatively stable and basically arable economy throughout the study period. Relative to the north it placed less emphasis on cattle and oxen, more on sheep and horses. The mainly enclosed district, although initially strongly pastoral, became more crop-orientated as time progressed, and its choice of livestock also became increasingly similar to that of the south. These changes were associated with the general intensification of English agriculture in the early-modern period.

PROBATE inventories have been a major source for research on the agriculture of early-modern England ever since their use was first popularized by W. G. Hoskins.[1] Their chief advantage is that they list the crops and livestock of individual farmers in a manner which normally allows some simple quantitative assessment of types of farm production. They also exist in large numbers and, for many parts of the country, give a continuous record of farming practice extending over more than two centuries. Individual inventories, however, vary considerably in quality, some being much more detailed than others. The printed documents for Oxfordshire give a sample of the various types.[2] Another drawback is that the amount of documentation available changes greatly from one area to another. Some indication of this is provided by A. J. Camp's revised edition of *Wills and their whereabouts* (1963), but it is only a preliminary guide. General accounts and criticism of probate inventories as source material have been given by O. Ashmore, F. W. Steers, J. Thirsk and J. West.[3]

The present paper attempts to show how a large collection of inventories can be used in a geographical study of livestock farming. It relates specifically to east Worcestershire, an area which, as delimited in Figure 1, contains about 91 500 ha.[4] The Worcester Record Office houses some 6250 inventories made between 1540 and 1750 which are relevant to the study. The paper describes methods of processing this information, dealing first with matters of general policy, such as the number of inventories to be used, and the employment of periodic and regional divisions. Later sections are concerned with methods of

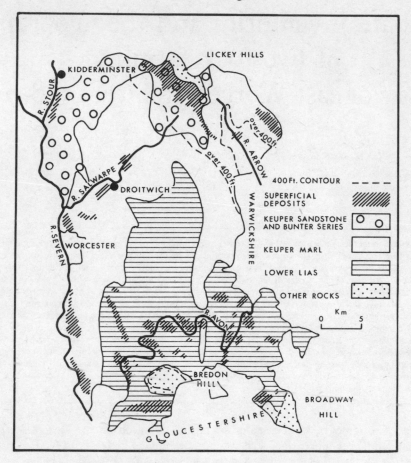

FIGURE I. East Worcestershire: physical and location map

treating the entries in the documents dealing with the relative importance of livestock and crops, and with the distribution of livestock types.

Each individual inventory records the position on one particular farm at one particular point in a single farming year. While this in itself can be a major asset, the documents have to be used in bulk to form a reasonable basis for statistical generalization. They are normally arranged in groups according to their date, which is specified by year and usually by day and month, and according to the location of the farm, which is specified by parish. Joan Thirsk, for instance, in her treatment of Lincolnshire inventories made between 1530 and 1700, began by dividing the county into four large regions, and then sampled a sufficient number of the inventories available for each region in four specific periods.[5] This general approach has been followed by most other workers. It has the advantage of simplicity, allowing easy comparison of the distributions of different farm products, and facilitating the study of regional trends from one period to another. On the other hand it assumes *a priori* that an area such as the Lincolnshire Marshland was a true region from the point of view of agricultural production with known boundaries which remained fixed from one period to another. This disadvantage can, however, be overcome to a large extent by adopting a general strategy which allows the use of many small regions. In this way, although each particular region may be established *a priori*, the results for these small units can be used to identify larger divisions in an empirical manner. It is thus the synthetic method of regionalization, rather than the analytical, which is appropriate for inventory studies.

In the present case two steps have been taken which together permit a greater emphasis on regional differentiation. First, the entire body of inventories has been used rather than a sample. Secondly, the inventories have been grouped within four long periods, namely 1540–99, 1600–60, 1670–99 and 1700–50. There is a 10-year gap in the inventory record between 1660 and 1670, which means that the third period is shorter than the others, but fortunately the number of inventories available per year at this time is larger than the norm. In comparison, the four periods used by Thirsk varied in length from 70 years (1530–99) to a decade (1630–9, 1660–9 and 1690–9). The adoption of long periods is not of course in itself a positive advantage, rather the contrary, but it does permit the use of small regions. In the first instance, east Worcestershire was divided into fourteen parts with a mean size of 6500 ha compared with the 171 000 ha of Thirsk's regions. A second net of five regions (mean size 18 300 ha) was also formed, through a process of amalgamation, to meet the requirements of certain methods for which only a few inventories were suitable. However, all the data were later re-worked within the framework of the five-region net, and this has been used in preference whenever the loss of detail is regarded as acceptable.[6]

Discussion of the actual location of the basic regions needs to be accompanied by some short description of the study area. East Worcestershire lies between the Cotswolds and the Birmingham plateau, and is bounded on one side by the Severn and on the other by Warwickshire. It consists mainly of a clay plain formed from Lower Lias and Keuper Marl, although the fringes of the plateau intrude in the north-east, and there is a small district of light soils overlying Bunter and Keuper sandstone in the north-west (Fig. 1). Unlike Lincolnshire, the region cannot be easily divided into physiographic units convenient for inventory analysis. In the early modern period, however, there was a marked regional differentiation in degree of enclosure which must have affected the geography of farm production. The 'South' was mainly champion country, but, in the north and along the Severn valley, enclosures were much more extensive, so that these districts were described by contemporary writers as 'woodland'. Open field was least prominent in the north-east.[7] This distinction between champion country and woodland was considered too important to ignore, and the boundary between the two was demarcated as the first step in the regional division of the area (Fig. 2). The two districts were then divided into what are in effect sub-regions, although of course each is independent in terms of results. Such regions had to be of roughly similar size and to consist of a grouping of contiguous parishes. Within these limitations, the choice of boundaries was made following an inspection of the inventories parish by parish, so that the principle of synthetic regionalization was applied in a loose fashion even at this level. The amalgamation of regions to form the five-region net was carried out after many results had already been obtained on the fourteen-region basis. The resulting disposition of the two regional nets is shown in Figure 2.

THE RELATIVE IMPORTANCE OF LIVESTOCK

Turning specifically to the livestock entries in the inventories, attention may first be given to the relative importance of livestock in regional farm production. This is of particular

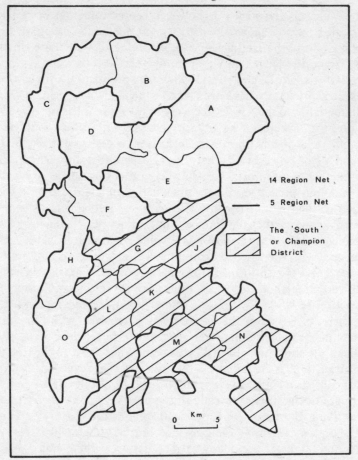

14 Region Net

5 Region Net

The 'South' or Champion District

FIGURE 2. East Worcestershire: regional divisions used in the probate inventory analysis

interest since the closer integration of livestock and crop farming was a major feature of agricultural improvement in the early-modern period.[8] It must have altered the balance of regional output; indeed, this was noticed by contemporaries such as Walter Blythe who remarked on the increased growth of crops in former pastoral areas including north Warwickshire and Worcestershire.[9] It is difficult, however, for modern scholars to identify such trends from independent statistics. The traditional source has been the land-use data given in surveys and terriers, but this is not easy to interpret since it makes little allowance for the value of common waste, for varying fallow intervals or for temporary grass. It also generally relates to only a few individual parishes at widely scattered dates. This makes it worthwhile to try to assess the relative importance of livestock from inventory material although it, too, is not really well-suited for the purpose. Most documents record the value of crops and livestock, the numbers of livestock by type and sometimes the area under tillage crops. They do not record either the area of grassland or the total area of the holding, and this makes any sophisticated analysis impossible. Nevertheless, crop and livestock output can be compared in various ways to give a crude indication of regional economies which is useful for comparative purposes. Here, also, the inventory material has the great merit of covering wide territories and long chronological spans.

The first approach which may be adopted is to compare the value assigned to livestock in the inventories with that given to the arable crops. It has already been employed by G. Kenyon[10] in his study of Kirdford and, on a regional scale, by W. H. Long[11], in his account of the Yorkshire inventories for 1688–9. The latter was able successfully to identify major regional characteristics such as the high reliance on corn in the Wolds. In the present study the index used will be the percentage of the value of livestock listed to the total value of livestock and crops, including hay. One difference from Long's method is that only the August, September and October inventories are used in an attempt to minimize inevitable seasonal variations in stocks of grain and hay.[12] Moreover, although smaller regions are employed, the inventories are grouped within long periods, and the results for different periods are compared. This raises a major problem in the use of the 'value method', which is that it makes no allowance for changing prices. The first part of the study period in particular was marked by inflation in which the prices for arable products increased more rapidly than for livestock. Using the decade 1540–9 as a base, the price index for arable crops had risen to 440 by 1640–9, compared with 410 for cattle and 324 for sheep.[13] This certainly makes it difficult to establish any precise chronology of relative movements between the crop and livestock sectors. But, within the context of an admittedly crude set of statistics, it should not seriously distort either the regional distinctions within one period or the major relative changes in regional values from one period to another.

A second approach is to make use of the record of livestock numbers. M. A. Havinden in his paper on Oxfordshire[14] noted that the median numbers of cattle and sheep recorded in inventories both increased considerably between the periods 1580–1640 and 1660–1730, and saw in this evidence of a swing to livestock. While this may be true, it is a dangerous assumption to make in the absence of any information about the size of holdings to which the inventories refer. A safer method is to employ only those documents which record both livestock numbers and cropped acreage, and to relate the two figures. Such inventories are relatively few, since they must be taken in the summer months when all the crops grown in a particular harvest year would be on the ground. Livestock numbers are best expressed in terms of stock equivalents, and the index used here is that of livestock units per thousand cropped acres. The actual units allocated to the various stock classes were as follows: oxen, bullocks and steers 1·2, other cattle including young stock 0·8, horses and colts 1·0, sheep and lambs 0·1, swine 0·1.[15] Because of the small number of useful inventories, this 'stock unit' method can only be employed within the five-region net, and even then insufficient data are available for one region after 1540–99.[16] The value method which can use the finer fourteen-region net seems more reliable, but an alternative method is most valuable, particularly one which is not directly affected by relative price movements over time.

Ultimately, the value of these methods has to be assessed by examining actual results for specific areas. Those for east Worcestershire are illustrated in Figures 3 to 5, and attention may first be turned to the geographical pattern which prevailed in the sixteenth century.[17] Here both methods bring out the major regional distinction between the woodland district, which appears to have been strongly pastoral in character, and the champion South where crops were of greater importance. Both methods also demonstrate that live-

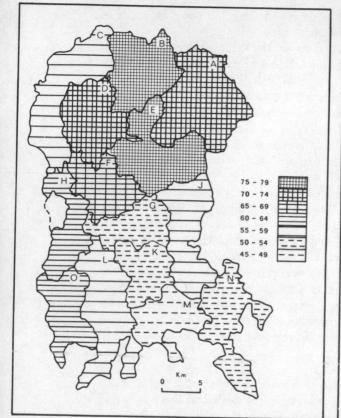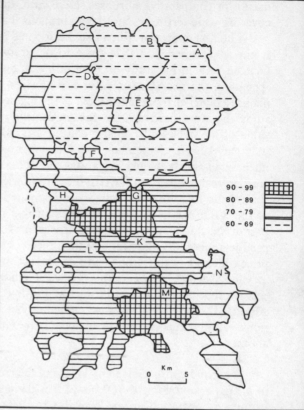

FIGURE 3. East Worcestershire: proportion of stock values to total stock and crop values (August—October). *Left*—basic results 1540–99; *right*—index numbers 1700–50 (1540–99 = 100). *Source*: probate inventories

stock were particularly dominant in the north-east, on the plateau and its fringes, which was also the most enclosed district. There was a lesser emphasis on livestock in the lower area around Droitwich and along the Severn valley. The 'value method' also indicates that the lighter soils of the extreme north-west produced a greater reliance on crop products, but this is not shown within the wider regional groupings necessary for the 'stock unit' method. In the champion district, physical conditions and farming structure were more uniform and the ratio of crops to livestock was fairly similar over most of its surface. However, region J and particularly region L, bordering the lower Severn valley, seem to have been characterized by a greater reliance on livestock than was normal in the district as a whole.

These results, then, indicate that geographical changes in the relative balance of crops and livestock within one period can be reconstructed with fair precision. It will be evident from the preceding discussion, however, that chronological trends are more difficult to establish. Nevertheless, the overall pattern of change between 1540–99 and 1700–50 can be clearly discerned, and is illustrated here by using index numbers obtained from the 'stock value' results (Fig. 3), and by comparison of the 'stock unit' maps for the two periods

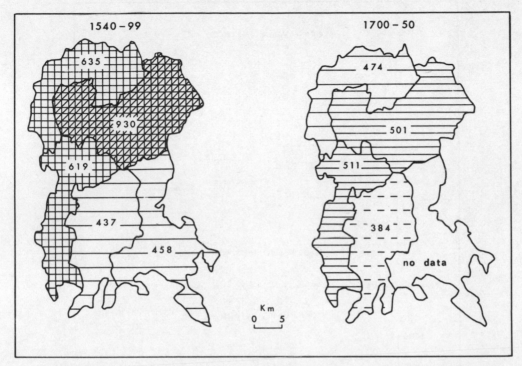

FIGURE 4. East Worcestershire: livestock units per thousand acres of tillage crops. *Source*: probate inventories

(Fig. 4). There seems little doubt that there was a general and significant fall in the relative importance of livestock, and that this fall was particularly concentrated in the most pastoral areas. Undoubtedly, the north-east showed the greatest decline, but crops had become much more important throughout the woodland zone except in the lower Severn valley (region O). Since the champion district was more stable in its land use, there was a major reduction in the regional differences observable in the sixteenth century. These general trends can be supported by land-use data drawn from surveys and terriers and by other documentary evidence.[18] They also correspond with the course of prices and confirm Blythe's observations about the increased growth of crops in the woodland districts.

The main difficulties occur when greater precision is sought about the timing of these shifts between the livestock and crop sectors. The results for each period are depicted in Figure 5, using the five-region net, and it is apparent that in this respect the two methods do not produce entirely similar patterns. The 'value' method places the main movement towards crop production in the early part of the study period, when apparently not only was there a pronounced fall in the relative value of livestock in the woodland district, but a significant reduction in the South as well. By contrast, the 'stock unit' method concentrates the bulk of the fall in the latter part of the study period, and even shows a shift towards livestock in two regions between 1540–99 and 1600–60. This does not give much scope for any firm interpretations. My own view is that, whereas the relative order of the regions in any period is best demonstrated by the 'value' approach, the 'stock unit' method ought to give the most satisfactory indication of general long-term trends.

J. A. Yelling

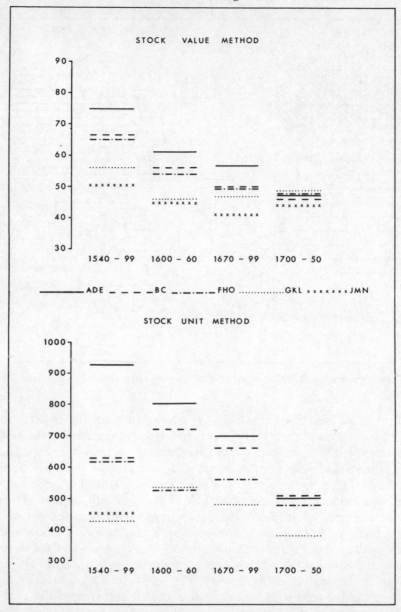

FIGURE 5. East Worcestershire: periodic changes in the relative importance of livestock 1540–1750. *Source*: probate inventories

THE DISTRIBUTION OF LIVESTOCK TYPES

Although most inventory studies have dealt with livestock as well as crops, they have rarely been concerned with the distribution of livestock types *per se*. The main topic of interest has been the average number of the various types kept per farm, this being normally expressed in the form of the median. Without knowledge of the size of the farms concerned, such figures can only give a rough indication of regional distributions, and cannot of course be used for further statistical calculations. Mean figures, such as were used by Long[19] for Yorkshire are more amenable but, even so, the relative importance of the various types is not readily appreciable from these alone. In research relating to later periods, stock equivalents are normally used for comparative purposes, and these, expressed in percentages, will be the main method employed in the present study.[20] This is not, of course, to say that the number of livestock per farm, and their combination on farms, is not of considerable interest and importance. But for geographical purposes it is desirable that the regional patterns of distribution should be first established.

Fortunately, the livestock entries in the inventories are normally more detailed than those for crops, the most common type being of the form 'x oxen £y'. The chief difficulty which these entries present in a regional study concerns the treatment of young stock. It is generally agreed that sheep and swine cannot be consistently separated from their young. In the Worcester inventories it is possible to distinguish young cattle and horses in most documents, certainly for the earlier periods, but if they are not specifically mentioned one cannot be sure that they were really absent. In the present study I have combined young stock with the adults for the basic calculations, following the practice of Thirsk and other workers who have dealt with a long series of inventories. But figures for young stock have also been calculated separately so that these can be used where desirable.[21] It may also be noted that the inventory entries do not say much about the use for which the animals were kept; whether, for instance, oxen were for draught, meat or both. Combined with a lack of information on markets this limits the degree to which recorded livestock distributions can be explained, and thus also makes it more difficult to establish their reliability.

Apart from changes by region and by period, the relative importance of livestock types can also be expected to vary according to the season and to the size of farms. Seasonal changes are difficult to calculate when other factors such as the size and precise location of the farms cannot be accurately determined. It is generally agreed, however, that draught animals would vary least in number and sheep most, being fewer in winter. Since the present study is not concerned with seasonal variations in themselves, inventories from all months of the year have been used. In view of the number of documents available it seems unlikely that the variation in seasonal distribution of inventories from one region/period group to another would be sufficient to cause serious distortion of the results. The effect of farm size in determining stock choice seems, however, too important to leave out of account, especially as the average size varied regionally and rose considerably during the course of the study period.[22] There are several ways in which inventories give an impression of the size of farm to which they relate; the problem is to find a criterion that can be expressed numerically. Here, calculation in terms of stock equivalents provides a most useful clue, since the total number of livestock units per farm can be established. It is not a very good yardstick since its relation to the area of the farm must obviously vary according to land use. Nevertheless, it does give a rough indication of which were the larger and smaller farms, and the arbitrary figure of fifteen stock units will be used to separate them. It is suggested that the actual results will show that this is a meaningful division within the context of the present study.

Horses and oxen

Table I gives an analysis of the total stock units recorded in each period in terms of stock

J. A. Yelling

type and major regions. The results, however, will be discussed in two parts, dealing first with the oxen and horses. Bullocks and steers have been included with the oxen since they were also worked, had the same regional distribution and disappear from the documents at the same time.[23] But the youngest stock destined for draught work cannot be separately distinguished in the inventories and have to be included with 'cattle' in the statistics. Nevertheless, oxen, bullocks and steers may usefully be compared with horses and colts since their functions overlapped in many spheres, particularly in work at the plough. The competition between the two is shown in the complementary nature of their distributions, and in the eventual abandonment of oxen in favour of horses in all regions.

TABLE I

Distribution of livestock types, 1540–1750

| | Oxen | Percent total stock units | | | | Total stock units |
		Horses	Cattle	Sheep	Swine	
1540–99						
E. Worcs.	22	17	43	14	4	21 945
Woodland	25	15	44	12	4	14 248
Champion	17	20	41	18	4	7 697
1600–60						
E. Worcs.	8	20	51	17	4	15 504
Woodland	12	18	51	16	3	9 807
Champion	3	24	51	18	4	5 697
1670–99						
E. Worcs.	3	24	52	18	3	13 545
Woodland	3	23	53	17	3	7 934
Champion	2	26	50	20	3	5 611
1700–50						
E. Worcs.	2	27	48	20	3	20 334
Woodland	2	27	49	19	3	12 429
Champion	2	27	48	22	2	7 905

Note: Figures for oxen include bullocks and steers. Those for other classes include young stock.

In the sixteenth century, oxen were slightly more numerous than horses taking east Worcestershire as a whole, but they predominated in the woodland district, while horses were more important in the South (Table I). This is shown in more detail in Figure 6 which directly compares the two classes using the five-region net and distinguishes between larger and smaller farms. Oxen were most important on the larger farms, while the smaller farms found horses more useful, probably because of their greater versatility. But on both large and small farms the ox became gradually more favoured as one moved across the study region from the south-east towards the north-west. This same pattern of regional differentiation was retained in the period 1600–60 but, by then, oxen predominated only on the large farms of the extreme north-west (region BC), and they were rare in the South (Table I). The decline in the use of oxen had been in progress during the late sixteenth century, and probably began earlier. It continued into the seventeenth century, until by 1670–99 oxen were rare in all regions. During this period the proportion of horses to the total stock units naturally became higher even from one district to another, and by 1700–50

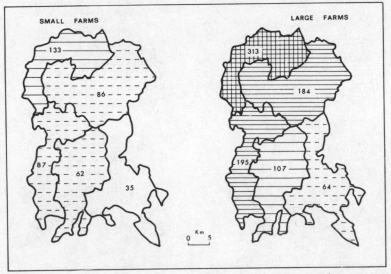

FIGURE 6. East Worcestershire: number of oxen, bullocks and steers per 100 horses (in livestock units) 1540–99. *Source*: probate inventories

showed only small regional variation. This also reflected the more even regional balance of crops and livestock at this time.

The distribution of horses and oxen reflected regional differences in farming conditions. In the champion district, horses could be tethered on leys within the common fields, and fed on beans which were a major product of the region's four-course field system.[24] The speed of the horse would also be an advantage in an intensive arable economy. In the north and west, there was an abundance of pasture closes in which oxen could be fed. They could be easily kept on for fattening after their working lives, especially on the larger farms. The importance of the ox as a source of meat is indicated by the substantial fall between 1540–99 and 1600–60 in the percentage of the total stock units represented by oxen and horses combined, a fall which is unlikely to have been brought about by any increase in tractive efficiency (Table I). However, in east Worcestershire, such economic factors cannot entirely explain the observed distributions in draught animals, since the noticeable tendency for oxen to increase in importance towards the north-west only partly correlates with the division between champion and woodland. Indeed, oxen were most favoured on the light sandstone soils of region BC which was also one of the most arable parts of the woodland zone. It is possible, however, that this situation was produced as a stage in a diffusion process, and that the abandonment of oxen involved a change in fashion which spread across the area from the south-east. The very speed of the movement would seem to support this, since the associated economic changes were slower to take effect.

Sheep and cattle

In contrast to the transient nature of the ox and horse distributions in sixteenth-century Worcestershire, the geographical pattern of sheep and cattle farming bears the appearance of maturity (Table I, Fig. 7). It was retained in broad outline throughout the early modern period, and is similar to that revealed by the early Agricultural Returns. The most striking

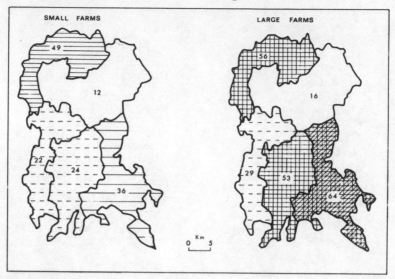

FIGURE 7. East Worcestershire: number of sheep per 100 cattle (in livestock units) 1540–99. *Source*: probate
inventories

feature is the association between sheep farming and the presence of arable land. Sheep
were also favoured on the common wastes, particularly those of a sandy nature. Their
numbers were therefore greatest on the Triassic sandstone and in the champion district,
especially the extreme south-east. It is noticeable, too, that sheep were relatively more
important on the larger farms, which again is an expected occurrence. But it is surprising to
find that the difference in stock composition between large and small farms was much
greater in the South than in the woodland district. No satisfactory explanation has been
suggested for this, but it will be interesting to see whether the phenomenon recurs in other
similar areas.

It is clear, however, that east Worcestershire was predominantly cattle country. In the
period 1540–99, this class constituted 43 per cent of the total stock units recorded in the
inventories compared with 14 per cent for sheep (Table I). Later, both these figures rose,
reaching 52 per cent and 18 per cent respectively in 1670–99, although in the case of cattle
this was partly a technical adjustment following the abandonment of oxen. If one compares
these figures with those produced by Long[25] for Yorkshire regions in 1688–9 (converting
his figures into stock equivalents), it appears that east Worcestershire kept a rather similar
proportion of sheep to Holderness (17 per cent), Cleveland (15 per cent) and the Plain of
York (14 per cent), but fell considerably below the proportion kept on the Wolds (36 per
cent). Figures of this order were only reached in limited parts of the study area, namely in
regions C (32 per cent) and N (31 per cent). Between 1660–70 and 1700–50 the proportion
of sheep continued to rise in east Worcestershire, while that of cattle fell slightly. In the
final period, then, the proportion of sheep to cattle was 28 per cent higher than it had been
in 1540–99.

In view of the crude nature of the inventory statistics, such a moderate rise in the
importance of sheep relative to cattle is not easy to define closely in regional or chronological terms. Nevertheless, certain changes of a logical nature may be detected both among

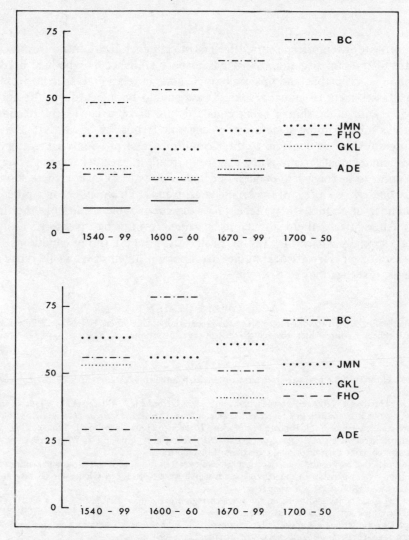

FIGURE 8. East Worcestershire: periodic changes in the number of sheep per 100 cattle (in livestock units) 1540–1750. *Upper*—small farms; *lower*—large farms. *Source*: probate inventories

the larger and smaller farms (Fig. 8). Between 1540–99 and 1600–60, conditions were much influenced by the decline in the numbers of oxen. Both sheep and cattle increased their proportion of the total stock units, but in the South the increase was mainly confined to cattle, whereas in the north and west sheep were most favoured. Here the probable increase in numbers of cattle kept for meat was counter-balanced by a fall in the number of young stock which had formerly been bred for the plough. In addition, the increased area under tillage was creating an environment more favourable for sheep. In subsequent periods the proportion of cattle to total stock units remained stable or fell slightly, whereas sheep continued their advance in all regions. This was especially noticeable in the more pastoral districts of the woodland zone, and on the smaller farms rather than the larger.

REVIEW

Whenever probate inventories are used for statistical generalization, the results can only approximate to the real situation. What has to be established is whether the degree of approximation is acceptable, and this can only be done in relation to specific problems and from critical assessment of actual results. These should be logical from the agricultural point of view and, other things being equal, should show a consistent relationship to factors such as soils, farming structure and economic trends. In broad outline the results for east Worcestershire do conform to these conditions, and provide a satisfactory general view of the main regional variations and long-term trends in livestock farming. They do not, however, appear to be consistent enough in detail to provide a basis for more sophisticated analysis, particularly with regard to chronological trends. This may become possible when a larger number of results are available following comparable studies of other inventory collections. Alternatively, there is much to be gained from using inventories as individual documents, especially where they can be related to specific farming conditions. It is one of the functions of general statistical studies to pinpoint problems that would repay detailed, but laborious, investigations of that type.

ACKNOWLEDGEMENT

The author thanks Dr E. M. Yates for his advice in the preparation of this paper. He also gratefully acknowledges a grant from Birkbeck College which covered the cost of the illustrations.

NOTES

1. W. G. HOSKINS, 'The Leicestershire farmer in the sixteenth century', *Essays in Leicestershire history* (1950), 123–83

2. M. A. HAVINDEN, 'Household and farm inventories in Oxfordshire', *R. Commn hist. Manuscripts* 10 (1965).

3. O. ASHMORE, 'Inventories as a source of local history: II. Farmers', *Amateur Hist.* 4 (1960), 186–95; F. W. STEERS, 'Short guides to records: 3. Probate inventories', *History* 47 (1962), 287–90; J. THIRSK, 'The content and sources of English agrarian history after 1500', *Agric. Hist. Rev.* 3 (1955), 66–79; J. WEST, *Village records* (1962), 92–131. This also contains a list of printed collections of inventories

4. It includes that part of the modern county which lies east of the Severn and Stour and south of the City of Birmingham. But certain parishes in the extreme south which were formerly in Gloucester Diocese are excluded.

5. J. THIRSK, *English peasant farming* (1957)

6. In most cases tables and maps on the fourteen-region basis are available in J. A. YELLING, 'Open field, enclosure and farm production in east Worcestershire 1540–1870', Unpubl. Ph.D. thesis, Univ. of Birmingham (1966)

7. Enclosure conditions are more fully described in J. A. YELLING, 'Common land and enclosure in east Worcestershire 1540–1870', *Trans. Inst. Br. Geogr.* 45 (1968), 157–68

8. E. KERRIDGE, *The agricultural revolution* (1967), 181–221

9. W. BLYTHE, *The English improver improved* (3rd. Imp. London, 1652) 83

10. G. KENYON, 'Kirdford inventories 1611–1776,' *Sussex archaeol. Collns* 93 (1955), 78–157

11. W. H. LONG, 'Regional farming in seventeenth-century Yorkshire', *Agric. Hist. Rev.* 8 (1960), 103–24

12. There are some other differences from Long's approach; for instance, he included farm gear in his calculations, but this was a relatively small item.

13. These calculations are derived from figures in J. THIRSK, (ed.), *The agrarian history of England and Wales: IV. 1540–1640* (1967), 857–8

14. M. A. HAVINDEN, 'Agricultural progress in open field Oxfordshire', *Agric. Hist. Rev.* 9 (1961), 73–83

15. These stock equivalents have been adapted from those used in modern studies on a necessarily arbitrary basis. They are broadly similar to those used by G. KENYON, op. cit. 103

16. The median numbers of inventories used in the regional groupings were as follows: Stock Value Method (14 regions)—1540–99: 15; 1600–60: 17; 1670–99: 17; 1700–50: 20; Stock Unit Method—1540–99; 19; 1600–60: 25; 1670–99: 23; 1700–50: 36

17. Tabulated results of the inventory analysis are given in J. A. YELLING, op. cit. (1966), 216–26

18. J. A. YELLING, op. cit. (1966), 281–4

19. W. H. LONG, op. cit. 106

20. The livestock units allocated to the various stock classes are described in the previous section.

21. When young stock were calculated separately the stock equivalents were revised as follows: Adult cattle 1·0, young stock 0·5; horses 1·2, young stock 0·8.

22. J. A. YELLING, op. cit. (1966), 151–96

23. Bullocks and steers were less frequently recorded than oxen; in 1540–1600, the latter made up 67 per cent of the total of these three types.

24. J. A. YELLING, 'The combination and rotation of crops in east Worcestershire 1540–1660', *Agric. Hist.* 17 (1969), 24–43

25. W. H. LONG, op. cit., 106

RÉSUMÉ. *Les inventaires de succession et la géographie pastorale : une étude de la partie orientale du comté de Worcestershire entre 1540 et 1750.* Très souvent les inventaires de succession énuméraient les bestiaux (et quelquefois les produits agricoles) possédés par les exploitants agricoles au début de l'époque moderne en Angleterre. Cet article montre qu'on peut utiliser cette documentation pour étudier, d'une façon quantitative, les deux éléments les plus importants de la géographie pastorale, c'est-à-dire l'importance relative des bestiaux, en comparaison avec la production végétale, et la répartition de toutes les espèces animales. Après un commentaire générale et théorique, on présente les résultats d'une analyse de la documentation pour le Worcestershire oriental. Les inventaires sont étudiés pour quatre périodes individuelles (1540–99, 1600–60, 1670–99 et 1700–50) et ces résultats sont mis en comparaison. Les documents pour chaque période sont regroupés en petites régions pour faciliter l'analyse. À une autre échelle, on peut distinguer des régions synthétiques plus grandes. Les produits de la « campagne » méridionale contrastent avec ceux de la région bocagère du nord du Worcestershire. La première partie, au sud du comté, se caractérisait par une économie céréalière pendant toute la période étudiée. Les espèces bovines y étaient moins importantes mais les ovins et equins plus importants que dans le nord. Le bocage, fortement pastoral pendant le 16ᵉ siècle, devenait plus céréalier à travers les siècles suivants. Les combinaisons des espèces animales trouvées dans les deux parties du comté devenaient de plus en plus semblables. Ces modifications furent associées à une tendance d'intensifier la production agricole en Angleterre au début de l'époque moderne.

FIG. 1. Worcestershire oriental: carte d'orientation et du milieu naturel

FIG. 2. Worcestershire oriental: petites régions employées pendant l'analyse des inventaires de succession

FIG. 3. Worcestershire oriental: proportion des valeurs de bétail comparée aux combinaisons des valeurs de bétail et des produits végétaux (août à octobre). *À gauche*—resultats de base 1540–99; *à droit*—indices 1700 à 1750 (1540–99 = 100)

FIG. 4. Worcestershire oriental: unités de bétail pour chaque surface de 1000 acres (*c.* 400 ha) cultivés, d'après les inventaires de succession

FIG. 5. Worcestershire oriental: variations dans l'importance relative du bétail 1540–1750, d'après les inventaires de succession

FIG. 6. Worcestershire oriental: nombre de bovins et d'équins pour chaque centaine de chevaux (en unités de betail) 1540 à 1599, d'après les inventaires de succession

FIG. 7. Worcestershire oriental: nombre d'ovins pour chaque centaine de bovins (en unités de betail) 1540 à 1599, d'après les inventaires de succession

FIG. 8. Worcestershire oriental: variations dans le nombre d'ovins pour chaque centaine de bovins (en unités de betail) 1540 à 1750. *En haut*—petites exploitations; *au bas*—grandes exploitations, d'après les inventaires de succession

ZUSAMMENFASSUNG. *Testimentarische Aufstellungen (Probate inventories) and die Verteilung der Viehzucht : eine Untersuchung über das östliche Worcestershire zwischen 1540 und 1750.* Testimentarische Aufstellungen geben oft eine Übersicht über die Viehbestände, die die einzelnen Bauern in der frühen Neuzeit in England besassen und manchmal über die Flächen, die mit verschiedenen Feldfrüchten bebaut wurden. Der vorliegende Artikel zeigt, wie dieses Material benutzt werden kann, um ein einfaches quantitatives Bild erstens der Wichtigkeit der Viehzucht im Verhältnis zum Ackerbau zu geben und zweitens der Verteilung der einzelnen Vieharten. Eine allgemeine theoretische Erörterung ist mit einer Untersuchung der schriftlichen Quellen über das östliche Worcestershire verbunden. Aufstellungen für die vier Zeitspannen 1540–99, 1600–60, 1670–99 und 1700–50 werden getrennt behandelt und die Ergebnisse verglichen mit Hilfe einfacher Indizes. Die Quellen jeder Periode werden analysiert innerhalb eines Rahmens von kleinen Teilgebieten; hierdurch können Unterschiede auf räumlich höhere Ebene erkannt werden; z.B. die Produkte des offenen Ackerbaugebietes im Süden werden mit denen des Gebietes mit allgemeiner Verkoppelung im Norden verglichen. Im Süden herrschte eine verhaltnismassig gleichbleibende Ackerbau-Wirtschaft während der zwei Jahrhunderte, die diese Untersuchung behandelt. Im Vergleich zum Norden waren Ochsen und Rindvieh weniger wichtig; man legte mehr Wert auf Schafe und Pferde. Das verkoppelte Gebiet im Norden war ursprünglich sehr auf Viehzucht ausgerichtet; langsam aber wurde der Ackerbau wichtiger und die gewählten Vieharten wurden ähnlich denen, die im Süden gehalten wurden. Diese Veränderungen in der Wirtschaftsstruktur verdeutlichen die allgemeine Intensivierung der englischen Landwirtschaft in der frühen Neuzeit.

ABB. 1. Das östliche Worcestershire: physische Geographie und Orientierungskarte

ABB. 2. Das östliche Worcestershire: Teilräume, die für die Analyse der testimentarischen Aufstellungen benutzt wurden

ABB. 3. Das östliche Worcestershire: Verhaltnis des Viehwerts zum Gesamtwert von Vieh und Feldfrüchten (August—Oktober). *Links*—absoluter Wert 1540–99; *Rechts*—Indizes für 1700–50 (1540–99 = 100). *Quelle*: testimentarische Aufstellungen

ABB. 4. Das östliche Worcestershire: Grossvieheinheiten pro 1000 acres (*c.* 400 ha) Feldfrüchte. *Quelle*: testimentarische Aufstellungen

ABB. 5. Das östliche Worcestershire: Veränderungen in der relativen Wichtigkeit der Viehzucht 1540–1750. *Quelle*: testimentarische Aufstellungen

ABB. 6. Das östliche Worcestershire: Ochsen, Jungvieh und Stiere pro 100 Pferde. *Quelle*: testimentarische Aufstellungen

ABB. 7. Das östliche Worcestershire: Schafe pro 100 Stück Rindvieh, 1540–99. *Quelle*: testimentarische Aufstellungen

ABB. 8. Das östliche Worcestershire: Veränderungen in der Zahl der Schafe pro 100 Stück Rindvieh (1540–1750). *Oben*—kleine Höfe; *Unten*—grosse Höfe. *Quelle*: testimentarische Aufstellungen

The Combination and Rotation of Crops in East Worcestershire, 1540–1660

By JAMES YELLING

STUDIES of English agriculture in the early modern period have always been much concerned with the nature of common-field farming and the economic significance of enclosure. But the methods of approach have varied, and the last decade has seen a noticeable increase in local studies which utilize the existence of a close and well-defined pattern of farming regions. One purpose of such research is to define open field and enclosed territory more precisely so that each may be studied in some degree of isolation. It is also possible to examine the response of the various systems to specific physical and economic conditions. What might be termed 'the method of regional testing' will no doubt be even more widely employed now that Dr Thirsk's general survey of English agricultural regions has been completed.[1] In the present paper it is used to examine one particular aspect of farming, the production of tillage crops, under the contrasting conditions of champion and woodland country.

The area chosen for study is that of Worcestershire, east of the Severn.[2] This district was divided quite distinctly between two farming regions which were similar to the better-known Arden and Feldon of adjacent Warwickshire. One part, which will be called the 'South', was village territory lying principally in open field,[3] and most of its townships were eventually enclosed by Act. In the other part, the 'North and West', settlement was much more dispersed and common field was never as extensive. By 1540 it had already been subject to a considerable degree of piecemeal enclosure, especially in the north-east, and enclosures of open field by Act were of small importance.

The approximate boundary between these champion and woodland regions is indicated on Fig. I. The map also shows that East Worcestershire contains an interesting variety of physical conditions. The bulk of the area is a clay plain formed from Lower Lias and Keuper Marl, but terrace deposits give rise to soils of lighter character along the river valleys, especially those of the Severn and Avon. North of Worcester itself a more extensive area of light soils

[1] 'The Farming Regions of England' in J. Thirsk (ed.), *The Agrarian History of England and Wales, IV, 1500–1640*, 1967, pp. 1–109.

[2] The modern county boundary is used except in the south where parishes formerly in Gloucester county and diocese are excluded. Few probate inventories survive for these parishes.

[3] Enclosure conditions in East Worcestershire are described more fully in J. A. Yelling, 'Open Field, Enclosure, and Farm Production in East Worcestershire', Ph.D. thesis, Birmingham, 1966.

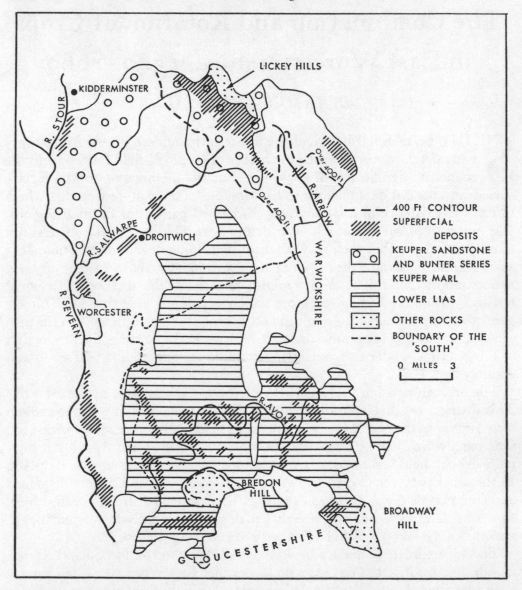

FIG. I

THE STUDY AREA

is based on the outcrop of Bunter and Keuper sandstones, whilst in the north-east higher land associated with the fringes of the Birmingham Plateau introduces a further complicating factor.

The study begins with an overall survey of crop distributions and combinations. This is obtained by statistical comparison of the acreage entries in probate inventories, aggregated by area and period in the manner successfully adopted by Thirsk, Long, and others.[1] Such a general view serves two main purposes: (i) it provides quantitative material for comparison with other periods and districts; (ii) it provides a framework for more detailed study and suggests themes for further investigation. These are then taken up in the second and main part of the paper (Sections II–V) which uses inventories in a more flexible manner in conjunction with material derived from surveys and terriers.

I

Probate inventories are now sufficiently well known as source material not to require any extended treatment from the methodological point of view. It may be remarked, however, that their use in regional statistical studies is subject to two sorts of error: (i) that arising from the small number of inventories which supply full quantitative information; and (ii) that arising from periodic and regional variations in farming types. These two factors have to be balanced against one another, but in practice nearly all studies have involved small numbers of inventories relating to relatively large areas of uniform physical character. In the present case, though the approach is similar, the emphasis is placed on the use of relatively small areas, and for this purpose the whole body of available inventories was searched.[2] East Worcestershire itself comprises only 226,000 acres[3]—less than the Lincolnshire Fens or Yorkshire Wolds—and this is divided into seven regions. The boundaries of the regions were determined by preliminary inspection of the inventories parish by parish.[4] Two periodic divisions are used, namely 1540–99, and 1600–60.

The inventory entries show that in East Worcestershire as a whole barley was the most important crop in the sixteenth century, occupying about 26 per cent of the total crop acreage.[5] It was closely rivalled by wheat (22 per cent), whilst pulses (19 per cent), rye (17 per cent), and oats (10–11 per cent) were the other major crops. Muncorn, vetches, and dredge were also mentioned, but only in small amounts. These overall totals, however, conceal the existence of strong contrasts in the pattern of crop production between one part of East

[1] J. Thirsk, *English Peasant Farming*, 1957; W. H. Long, 'Regional Farming in Seventeenth Century Yorkshire', A.H.R., VIII, 1960, pp. 103–14.

[2] The Worcester Diocesan inventories are housed in the Worcester County Record Office (=WRO).

[3] Excluding the former Gloucestershire parishes.

[4] Even so, some important local variations in cropping practice are bound to be concealed if quantitative data alone is used. These variations are described in the more detailed sections which follow.

[5] These figures have been adjusted by weighting the crop proportions found in each region according to its total crop acreage recorded in the 1867 Agricultural Returns. Whilst this is in many ways unsatisfactory, it does help to eliminate error caused by biased regional 'sampling', and produces trends in cropping practice which accord with those found within the individual regions. The crude figures are also given in Tables I and II.

Worcestershire and another—a feature emphasized by the virtual absence of each of the major crops from at least one of the regional divisions employed (Table I, Fig. II).

TABLE I

REGIONAL CROP STATISTICS, 1540–99

Wh=Wheat, *Mu*=Muncorn, *Ba*=Barley,
Pu=Pulse, *Dr*=Dredge, *Ve*=Vetches, *Ma*=Maltcorn

Area		Wh	Mu	Rye	Ba	Oats	Pu	Dr	Ve	Other	Total
ABE†	acres	5	—	35	3	35½	—	3½	—	8(*Ma*)	90
	%	6	—	39	3	39	—	4	—	9	
C	acres	—	—	31	27½	2	—	1	4		65½
	%	—	—	47	42	3	—	2	6		
DF†	acres	55	10½	5	23	10	77	1	—	15½(*Ma*)	197
	%	28	5	3	12	5	39	½	—	8	
GJ	acres	121½	2	—	122½	1	105½	—	—		352½
	%	34	½	—	35	½	30	—	—		
KL	acres	115½	7½	20	148	4	93	—	—		388
	%	30	2	5	38	1	24	—	—		
HO	acres	77½	16	79½	145½	2	90½	—	—		411
	%	19	4	19	35	½	22	—	—		
MN	acres	166	—	2	158	—	117	—	—		443
	%	37	—	½	36	—	26	—	—		
Total	acres	540½	36	172½	627	54½	483	5½	4	23½	1,947
	%	28	2	9	32	3	25	—	—	1	
Adj. Totals* %											
N. and W.		12	2	30	19	18	13	2	1	3	
South		34	1	1	36	2	27				
Total		22	2	17	27	10	19	1	2	1	

* These totals are adjusted according to the total crop acreage recorded in each area in 1867.

† Without maltcorn the percentages were: ABE—wheat 6; rye 43; barley 4; oats 43; dredge 4; DF—wheat 30; muncorn 6; rye 3; barley 13; oats 5; pulse 42.

In the case of the winter crops a relatively simple pattern of substitution seems to have occurred. Wheat dominated the south, and rye the extreme north and west, whilst muncorn achieved some importance in the transitional

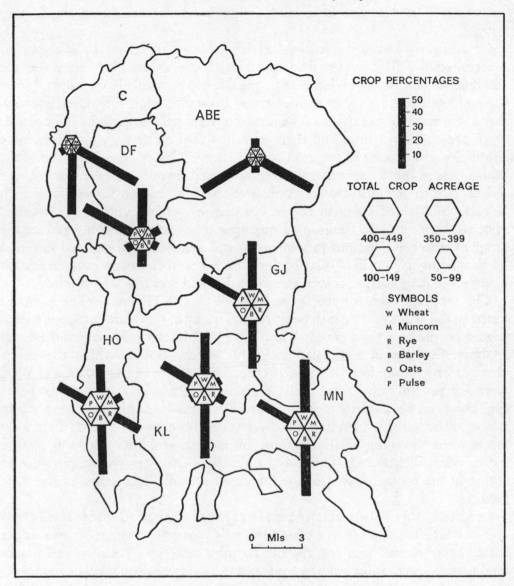

Fig. II

CROP DISTRIBUTIONS, 1540–1599

zone. There is the expected strong correlation between the use of rye and the presence of light soils—on the sandstone outcrop and Severn terraces—whilst the higher relief of the north-east seems also to have favoured this crop. The most widespread of the spring crops was barley, which was important everywhere except in the north-east, where it was largely replaced by oats. Pulses were also virtually absent from this district and also from the sandstone outcrop, whilst oats was little grown outside its stronghold on the plateau fringes.

Certain easily recognizable physical factors seem, therefore, to be the major determinants of all these distributions. Indeed, it is reasonable to allow that the significance of physical variations for land use has probably been reduced since the sixteenth century by improved crops and cultivation practices. Even so, there is much else to explain. The clear-cut regional distinctions in choice of crops are still surprising, and there is also within many regions a noticeable simplicity and balance in the crop combinations. This is especially true of the South, where the three constituent regions each favoured wheat, barley, and pulses, and in significantly equal proportions. The reason for many of such features undoubtedly lies in the mechanism by which crops and rotational systems were selected. Communal organization or tradition could reduce the range of crop combinations in local areas, and so accentuate regional variation by producing a 'step-like' distributional change rather than a gradual one. It is hoped to demonstrate this in the more detailed sections which follow.

The crop statistics for the second period (Table II) are similar in broad terms to those of the sixteenth century, and many of the minor changes represented no doubt arise through 'sampling error' in the material available for analysis. Stability is especially noticeable in the South, whilst the major changes which were to revolutionize cropping practice in the North and West were not yet fully under way. The beginnings of two important adjustments can, however, be discerned. In some areas rye was beginning to give place to wheat, although this trend was not yet very pronounced. Again, the spring crops were becoming relatively more important, and oats and pulses were more widely distributed. This was a reflection of the growing importance of arable in the economy, and of the increased use of tillage crops in livestock feeding.[1]

In spite of this, it is generally true to say that the period under review was one in which the market was biased towards pastoral products. It was under these circumstances that contrasts in farming between champion and woodland districts were most pronounced, and the study of crop statistics immediately helps to make it clear that this was not a simple matter of 'advanced' or 'backward' farming, but of two specialist systems. The champion region possessed a crop combination which was suitable to a mainly arable economy. Conversely, the choice of crops in the woodland district resulted not only from the relative absence of high-yielding arable soils, but also from the pre-

---

[1] The relative importance of livestock and crops in East Worcestershire at this time is described in J. A. Yelling, *op. cit.*, pp. 205–35. Spring crops were also becoming more important in Leicestershire during this period.—W. G. Hoskins, 'The Leicestershire Farmer in the Seventeenth Century', *Agric. Hist.*, 25, 1951, pp. 11–14.

dominant interest in livestock farming which reduced the incentive to improve crop rotations or to overcome physical deficiencies through beneficial cultivation practices.

II

Cropping systems are easiest to study in the South where communal organization was strongest. In consequence, survey evidence is of more value in this district, and may be used to supplement information derived from the inven-

TABLE II

REGIONAL CROP STATISTICS, 1600–60

Abbreviations as in Table I

Area		Wh	Mu	Rye	Ba	Oats	Pu	Dr	Ve	Other	Total
ABE	acres	14	1½	72	10	133	5½	—	—		236
	%	6	½	31	4	56	2	—	—		
C	acres	—	1	67½	29	17½	11½	4	1½		131
	%	—	1	52	22	13	9	3	1		
DF	acres	26½	20	—	23½	4	62½	—	—	7(Ma)	143½
	%	19	14	—	16	3	43	—	—	5	
GJ	acres	52	1½	1	60½	2	62½	—	2		181½
	%	29	1	½	33	1	35	—	—		
KL	acres	115½	7½	20	148	4	93	—	1		389
	%	30	2	5	38	1	24	—	—		
HO	acres	59	5	15	87	7	85½	—	—		258½
	%	23	2	6	34	3	33	—	—		
MN	acres	23½	—	7	24	—	29	—	—		83½
	%	28	—	9	29	—	35	—	—		
Total	acres	290½	36½	182½	382	167½	349	4	4½	7	1,423
	%	20	3	13	27	12	25				
Adj. Totals* %											
N. and W.		11	4	25	16	28	18				
South		28	2	5	27	—	33				
Total		18	3	16	24	15	24	0·4	0·3	0·6	

* These totals are adjusted according to the total crop acreage recorded in each area in 1867.

tories. For 1584–5 there are sixteen terriers of glebe holdings[1] in the South which describe in some way the layout of common field arable, and, of these, eight mention the existence of four fields. Most are very simple in style; for example, at Flyford Flavell there was recorded, "One yardland containing by estimation 40 acres or thereabouts, lying in the four fields of Flyford Flavell aforesaid by eight or ten acres in every field." In addition, twenty terriers deal with common arable either for 1616 or for 1634–5, and, of these, eight again describe four fields. The existence of such four-field layouts clearly correlates with the crop combinations noted from the inventories, namely wheat, barley, and pulses in roughly equal proportions. To these three crops may now be added a fallow to make up the fourth shift in the rotation.

Large numbers of terriers, however, refer only to furlongs, or sometimes use a mixture of field and furlong names. The exact significance of this cannot be proved, but it is unlikely to mean that the four-course system was absent. Most of the townships involved are known from documentary sources to have possessed a four-field layout at some other time within the study period. But there is no clear pattern of historical development. Usually, an early terrier listing land only by furlongs is followed by a later example giving both fields and furlongs, but in some cases the sequence is reversed. The most important evidence, however, comes from inventories, examined parish by parish. For despite the small numbers of returns available, four-course cropping characteristics may be recognized for the vast majority of Southern townships.

Some examples of inventories for particular parishes are given in Table III. These returns, of course, highlight the differences which occurred between farms, but on the whole the regularity of their crop combinations is impressive. In most cases the irregularities which do occur are within the limits compatible with the normal layout of holdings, even in those parishes, such as Church Honeybourne, which were to be enclosed before the period of Parliamentary awards. In these examples the wheat and barley shifts were more or less equal; only slight differences are observable between their acreages, giving a bias sometimes to the one and sometimes to the other crop. The acreage in the pulse shift, however, was not infrequently out of line with that of the other two, and, unlike the minor irregularities just mentioned, this seems to have arisen from cropping practice, and not from the layout of holdings. Indeed, in these cases the acreage sown in the pulse field often represented about half the amounts in the other two fields, as at Bretforton in the two inventories for 1558 tabulated below. This feature was widespread in the South, and continued into the early eighteenth century, but only in a minority of the returns for any particular parish. It is probable that the land not sown with pulses

[1] These terriers are contained in WRO 2358 and 2735. They are described in more detail in J. A. Yelling, *op. cit.*, pp. 329–35.

was left uncropped, but it is just possible that grass seeds were sown with the preceding barley crop, producing a one-year ley which passed unrecorded in the inventories. If such grassland existed, however, it could not be correlated with the 'leys' mentioned in surveys which were of a much more permanent nature.

TABLE III

INVENTORIES FOR SOUTHERN PARISHES

L=Lands. Other abbreviations as in Table I.
Other figures in acres.

The symbols * and † mean that the acreages given apply to all the crop types indicated

	Wh	Mu	Rye	Ba	Oats	Pu	Ve	Total
Bretforton								
1557/112‡	18			20		3		41
1558/442	10		2	10		6		28
1558/498	26			26		12		64
1598/61d	24*		*	32		26†	†	82
Church Honeybourne								
1557/109	13			11		11		35
1592/28	18			20		15		53
North Piddle								
1597/72	2L			1		1		
1618/383	2L			4L		3L		9L
1619/62	1			1		1		3
1623/5	20			20*	*	20		60
1640/195	29L			27L		27L*	*	83L
Bishampton								
1615/172	2			2		3		7
1616/263h	3			4		3		10
1619/35b	2¼			2½		2		6¾
1620/9	5*		*	7		6½		18½
1623/35	24*	*		18†	†	17		59
1642/50	10			7*	*	7		24

‡ The inventories are referenced by number within each year, i.e. 1560/1 denotes the first inventory in the collection for 1560.

These occasional shortfalls in the acreage under pulses may in fact be a lingering reflection of the manner in which the four-field system was originally introduced. It seems likely that it developed from the two-field system by 'hitching' part of the fallow field for pulses. Certainly, many townships in the

South possessed two-field systems in the thirteenth and fourteenth centuries; for example, Upton Snodsbury, which had four-course cropping by the end of the sixteenth century and four fields in 1771.[1] The glebe terrier of Naunton Beauchamp (1585) makes the derivation even more explicit. It mentions 24 acres of arable in North Field (46 lands) and South Field (41 lands) and continues "which said two fields are divided into four parts or fields according to the course of husbandry for three crops of corn to be had and taken thereof and for the fourth to lie yearly fallow." Two other townships—Bishampton and Peopleton—persisted in two-field nomenclature in their glebe terriers,[2] but from the inventories it seems most likely that they followed the four-course cropping pattern (Table III).

The transition from two fields to four fields in the South therefore seems to have been completed by about the middle of the sixteenth century. This means that it occurred rather earlier than the general dates given by Gray who remarked that "a four-field system making its appearance in the English Midlands in the sixteenth and early seventeenth centuries, was employed more and more in the course of the latter century and in the early eighteenth."[3] It also means that it must have occurred some time between 1350 and 1550, when elsewhere there was widespread conversion of arable to pasture, and when the desertion of villages was at its height. In the face of the same market pressures, it looks as though the villagers of the South chose instead to retain their arable system and to improve its efficiency.

III

In contrast to the uniformity of the champion district, the North and West possessed several distinct cropping systems, and these may be dealt with in turn. Conditions were most closely similar to those of the South around Droitwich (Area DF), and the major crops were the same, although grown in different proportions. Here, too, a considerable amount of common field was still present in the study period, especially in the southern part, and, although there were also many piecemeal closes, these were probably used mainly for pasture. Even in 1777, although only 49 per cent of the improved land in Himbleton lay in common, this included 78 per cent of the arable; similar figures are available for neighbouring Tibberton at the same date.[4] Two centuries earlier, when the proportion of closes was probably not so great, and the market less favourable to arable products, the correlation between enclosure and pasture would have been even more pronounced.

[1] Birmingham Reference Library, Calendar of Manuscripts relating to Worcestershire in the Shrewsbury (Talbot) Collection of the British Museum, Worcs. M16; WRO 1861.
[2] Glebe Terriers—Bishampton, 1616, 1670, 1714; Peopleton, 1585, 1616.
[3] H. L. Gray, *English Field Systems*, 1915, Reprint 1959, p. 136.
[4] WRO 1691/14; 1691/32.

The distribution of common arable was in itself, however, often complex. The surveys and terriers fall mainly into two groups. The first type, of which Himbleton, Salwarpe, and Rushock[1] provide examples, mentions a large number of small fields. The glebe at Himbleton, for instance, in 1616 included lands in six fields—Ladiaker (4), Inning (9), Mill (9), Stocking (3), Blackpit (8), and Hill (12 and 2 layes). It is known from later evidence that such a distribution was not peculiar to the glebe, that all the arable lay in one township, and that the fields were not always separated from each other by enclosures. Such features, however, may account for some of the irregularities in other terriers. In contrast, certain surveys seem to refer to a three-field allocation of land. Examples of this type relate to Hadsor, Bredicot, Westwood, and Huddington[2] where the fields were Shatherlong (36 acres), Badney or Windmill (20 acres), and Hill (30 acres). All these townships are small, but their field descriptions are of added significance in that they are the only ones in this district which might conceivably correspond with a regular rotation practice.

In view of the presence of piecemeal closes and some complex field divisions, the entries in the inventories appear surprisingly regular. In several parishes to the south of Droitwich, including Himbleton (Table IV), the acreage of pulses frequently equates with the acreage of winter cereals and barley combined. These same parishes also followed the practice, not found elsewhere, of grouping the winter cereal and barley acreages in many of the inventories. This cropping regularity was undoubtedly followed in the common fields, since in many parishes most of the arable lay open at this time, and the Oddingley inventory 1625/239 specifically mentions that both wheat and barley were growing in the common field there known as Old Field.[3] It may be added, too, that the rotation wheat or barley, pulses, fallow, was frequently found in Leicestershire common fields during this period.[4]

Another cropping regularity can be recognized in the parishes of Salwarpe, Elmley Lovett, and Rushock. There, the acreage under winter cereals was roughly equal to that of all the spring crops (Table IV). Again, this certainly reflects a common-field rotation. Indeed the Salwarpe inventory 1603/13 names the fields involved. In Copcote Field there were 5 acres of rye, in Postell Field 1 acre of barley, and 4 acres of oats, and in Little Field 6 kine and 3

[1] Himbleton, Glebe Terrier 1616, WRO 1691/14; Salwarpe, Glebe Terrier 1617; Elmley Lovett, Glebe Terriers 1585, 1635.

[2] Hadsor, Glebe Terrier 1585, Bredicot Glebe Terrier (no date); Parliamentary Survey—T. Cave and R. Wilson, *The Parliamentary Surveys of the Lands and Possessions of the Dean and Chapter of Worcester, c. 1649,* 1924, pp. 14–17; Westwood, PRO E 315/400; Huddington, PRO E 317, Worcs. 6.

[3] Old Field is mentioned as a common field in the Calendar of Shrewsbury (Talbot) MSS., *op. cit.,* Worcs. K 37 (1619).

[4] W. G. Hoskins, *op. cit.,* p. 11.

James Yelling

calves. In most cases, however, the chief crops continued to be wheat or rye, and pulses, as in the parishes mentioned in the last paragraph. Compared with these latter parishes there was simply a slight shift in production from pulses to winter cereals. This shift was, in fact, part of a general trend from spring to winter crops which was encountered in moving northwards in East Worcestershire to more pastoral districts with grass feeding. In the South winter cereals accounted for one-third of crop production. To the south and west of Droitwich this proportion rose probably to about 40 per cent, and further north-east to one-half.

TABLE IV

THE DROITWICH DISTRICT

Abbreviations as in Table I; symbols and references as in Table III.

	Hard Corn	Lent Corn	Wh	Mu	Rye	Ba	Oats	Pu	Other	Total
Himbleton										
1555/43			10*		*	4		15		29
1556/113			14		2	5		12½		33½
1557/156			4		3	2½	4*	8	*(Ma)	21½
1560/40			13	4		8		22*	*(Ve)	47
1561/92a			6			2		5		13
1563/93			8*			*		10		18
1570/317						1		1		2
1587/65a			13*			*		14		27
1623/186			4*		*	7		6		17
1628/139			1*			*		1		2
1633/175			10*			*		8		18
1634/121				3*		*		6		9
1643/37			1½			7		9		17½
1649/92			24*	*		*		21		45
Elmley Lovett										
1582/20c	5	5								10
1619/25	5	12								17
1622/68			13*		*	4	†	9†	†(Ve)	26
1630/154		8	9*		*					17
1639/15	12	12								24
Salwarpe										
1558/848	6							8*	3½(Ma) *(Ve)	17½
1560/60	10	11								21
1594/84			14*	*	*	†	†	16†	†(Ve)	30
1601/181				2		3	*	4*	2(Ma)	11
1603/83					5	1	4*		*(Ve)	10

The main problem in dealing with common-field agriculture in this district lies, therefore, not so much with the pattern of production, which seems reasonably clear, but with the methods of field management in those townships where complex divisions were recorded. Collective management must have persisted in at least some spheres, since common pasture stints are recorded in glebe terriers, and one can only assume that most fields were grouped for rotation either on the basis of the entire township or in sectors. The other main problem is to assess the impact of piecemeal enclosure on production, and this is extremely difficult because one cannot be sure that any township lay wholly enclosed during this period, and there was certainly no sharp boundary beyond which farms with a large enclosed sector could be recognized from their crop combinations. It appears from later evidence,[1] however, that the general result of enclosure was to break down the pre-existing symmetry of production, and to emphasize spring crops to a greater extent. But no township can be said with certainty to have been dominated by this type of cropping pattern within the study period.

IV

The next district to be considered is the Severn Valley, beginning with the section north of Worcester where almost all the arable was located on light or very light soils. Here common field was still present in many parishes before 1660, but was of very varying importance. It was probably of greatest extent in Ombersley where piecemeal closes were relatively few in 1605, and mainly in the outer parts of the parish, whilst the central part definitely possessed a three-field system.[2] Three fields are also mentioned in a glebe terrier (1585) of Churchill near Kidderminster, which lay on sandstone soils immediately to the north of the present study region. Again, a court roll of Hartlebury (1649)[3] was concerned with regulating common pasture in the "campos siligenos" and "campos hordeos" of Charlton and Torton hamlets. In short, where large amounts of common field remained they were almost certainly cropped in a three-course pattern, and examination of individual inventories must be concerned to reveal the details of this practice, and to see if it dominated crop production as a whole.

The inventories of the two largest parishes, Chaddesley Corbett and Ombersley, have been selected for more detailed study (Table V). It is noticeable that during the study period the crop choice changed more radically in these parishes than in those previously encountered. In both cases, however, the sixteenth-century entries relate mainly to rye and barley, a feature which is equally true if one looks beyond the acreage statistics to the far larger number

---

[1] J. A. Yelling, *op. cit.*, p. 381.   [2] WRO 3190/29.
[3] Court Roll, 5 April 1649, WRO 2636 (92373).

of inventories which recorded their crops in some other way. In Chaddesley pulses and wheat were not specifically mentioned in an inventory until 1627, but oats and pulses were quite common in the second quarter of the seven-

TABLE V

THE SEVERN DISTRICT

L=Lands. Other abbreviations as in Table I; symbols and references as in Table III.

	Winter Crops	Spring Crops	Wh	Mu	Rye	Ba	Oats	Pu	Other	Total
Chaddesley Corbett										
1545/23					16	16				32
1598/53		6			8					14
1598/54		3½			3					6½
1601/47					5	1				6
1614/226					8	5	3			16
1624/24					3				4(Dr)	7
1627/25	4					3¾	½	1	1½(Ve)	10¾
1627/142				1			2			3
1644/90					3	*	4	7*		14
Ombersley										
1568/64					6	13*	*		*(Ve)	19
1593/31					8	9				17
1614/70					2	1			3L(Ve)	
1614/204	6	6								12
1619/16					10		2	3		
1620/70	3	3								6
1625/130	4					1	4			9
1625/198					23	13	4	3		43
1638/129			*		8*	6		6†	†(Ve)	20
1641/115					5		1	3		9
(1656) 794/33			16*		*	16†		†		32
Severn Stoke										
1565/51					8	5		1		14
1574/30					6	4				10
1574/73					7	5		3		15
1587/91	30					16	*	22*	*(Ve)	68
1589/52					7½	6½	1	1		16
1596/34			7*		*	2		10		19
1603/76					4	7		1½		12½
1614/10			4*		10*	5		8		27
1643/100				2		2		2		6
1643/103			7*		*	5	1	4		17

teenth century. At Ombersley, too, wheat was not recorded until 1626, but half the sixteenth-century inventories mentioned pulses, and these together with oats were normal crops after 1600.

A key feature in these returns is the presence or absence of balance between the acreages of spring and winter crops. During the sixteenth century, when rye and barley dominated, such a regularity does in fact occur in many inventories. Taken in conjunction with the survey evidence already recorded, including that relating to Ombersley itself, this strongly suggests that the current common-field rotation in this district was rye, barley, fallow. The next point to determine is what happened to this balance when oats and pulses became increasingly popular. Here, some contrast is noticeable, more especially after 1620, between Ombersley where regularity was preserved, and Chaddesley Corbett where it was not. The small number of inventories involved, however, make it necessary to go beyond the boundaries of the study period in order to reinforce this point.

INVENTORY CROP ACREAGES

	Chaddesley Corbett		Ombersley	
	winter	*spring*	*winter*	*spring*
Pre-1620	40	$34\frac{1}{2}$	32	35
1620–50	11	$23\frac{3}{4}$	59	60
1660–99	$59\frac{3}{4}$	133	$65\frac{1}{2}$	$57\frac{1}{2}$
1700–50	53	108	102	$153\frac{1}{2}$

It seems reasonable to suppose that the balance between winter and spring crops at Ombersley, found throughout the seventeenth century, was connected with the strong survival of common field in that parish. The degree of enclosure was small in 1605, and although piecemeal enclosure developed strongly after the Civil War, a substantial amount of open land was still present in 1695.[1] Only after this date did spring crops attain the ascendancy. This means that pulses and oats were introduced into the common fields in the barley shift, which is theoretically logical, and in accord with the evidence of individual inventories. In effect, it brought common field practice in Ombersley very close to that of adjacent Elmley Lovett and Salwarpe (Table IV). The change may well be connected with the introduction of horses as plough animals instead of the oxen which predominated in the sixteenth century.

At Chaddesley Corbett, the proportion of spring crops—no more than half before 1620—was never less than two-thirds thereafter. This parish was cer-

[1] PRO E 134, 5W. & M., Mich., 54.

tainly wholly enclosed in 1745,[1] and in 1635 the vicarage had "five fields of arable, all which contain three score and twelve acres." It is likely, therefore, that the cropping practice observed after 1620 related mainly to enclosed arable; thus there was some contrast with the production in common fields in the same district. Whether common land was present in any quantity in Chaddesley Corbett before 1620 is a matter for speculation, but it seems a strong possibility.

Lastly, the crop region delimited to the south of Worcester on Fig. II can be shown by more detailed analysis to consist of two distinct parts. To the east most parishes followed the practice of the South, their arable being mainly open and cropped according to the four-course arrangement. Only the parishes actually bordering the Severn, where much of the arable was located on light terrace soils, followed a distinctive practice similar to that of the Severn district north of Worcester. Severn Stoke is an example (Table V). The crop choice appears similar to that further north except that pulses were more common and oats less so. From the reasoning of the last paragraph, most of the arable in the seventeenth century would seem to have been enclosed, because spring crops dominate. On the other hand, in the sixteenth century the arable, even if enclosed, was cropped according to the prevailing common-field pattern.

v

The final region, the north-east, was the most enclosed part of East Worcestershire, and predominantly pastoral in character. Although subject to continuing piecemeal enclosure, some common field persisted around most of the main nucleations, but these lay far apart. Although collective management still continued in some cases, there is no evidence of any regular common-field divisions during the study period. One solitary piece of evidence points to the previous existence of a three-field system.[2] In any event, closes must soon have come to dominate the arable in most parishes as crop production rose from 1540 onwards.

The early inventories for Bromsgrove and Tardebigge (Table VI) show that rye and oats were the main crops in this district with barley playing a lesser role. At Bromsgrove rye remained virtually unchallenged by wheat before 1650, and the main change was the gradual adoption of pulses. The inventory record is not satisfactory before 1600, but after this date spring crops certainly predominated. Wheat was much more important at Tardebigge where the presence of common field in substantial quantities also seems more likely. There were certainly farms in the north-east during the sixteenth century where most of the arable lay in common field—the glebe at Belbroughton in

[1] WRO 844.   [2] At Shurnock (Feckenham) in 1237.—H. L. Gray, *op. cit.*, p. 504.

TABLE VI

THE NORTH-EAST

Fl=Flax, *de*=days earth (i.e. work). Other abbreviations as in Table I; symbols as in Table III.

	Winter	Spring	Wh	Rye	Ba	Oats	Pu	Other	Total
Tardebigge									
1560/85				3de	*	4de	*		7de
1563/35				4	1	5			10
1587/31				6		5			11
1591/74			9*	*	8	6			23
1603/113			2	11		19			32
1641/12			1		4*	2	*		7
1642/28			6			4		1(*Fl*)	11
Bromsgrove									
1552/95				1				1(*Dr*)	2
1552/98				1		1			2
1567/85				1de	1de				
1569/34				18		20		8(*Ma*)	46
1602/56				5		21			26
1603/44				14		42			56
1614/164				14	4				18
1616/17				2½	*	5½*		*(*Ve*)	8
1616/29				7	3	5			15
1617/1				2		3½	½		6
1625/103				5		4	2		11
1628/142	4				16				20
1642/63				2	3	5½*		*(*Ve*)	10½
1644/21					3	3	3		9
1646/83					½	3			3½
1648/40				6		6			12
Feckenham									
1592/80	10			2½	6	*	18*		36½
1632/20			9*	*	1½	7	7		24½
(1634) 821/3874			3		2	*	6*		11
1646/52					3	2½	1		6½
Stoke Prior									
1552/94	7de	2de							9de
1576/1	7				£1	*	6*		
1593/5d	12	6							18
1624/6					3	2	4		9
1638/162			16*	*	2	13†	†		31
Hanbury									
1579/304			29*	*	†		34†		63

1585 is one example. Although there is no proof, it may well be that the cropping pattern on such common land was similar to that suggested in the early inventories for Tardebigge, namely, one shift of rye, one of oats with a little barley, and a third fallow. Such an arrangement would be similar to that practised immediately to the west, except that oats was substituted for barley because of the higher altitude and wetter climate of the plateau region.

The inventories show that the parishes of Feckenham, Hanbury, and Stoke Prior possessed crop combinations which were rather distinct from those of the rest of the north-east. All those places lay off the plateau itself, just to the south, and grew less oats in favour of pulses, whilst wheat was also more prominent (Table VI). Unfortunately, there are not enough inventories to describe the pattern in more detail, but the three-course framework found elsewhere in the North and West is discernible. In many ways the choice of crops appears similar to that of the Droitwich district, but the entries show a greater degree of irregularity.

VI

The cropping arrangements revealed by these more detailed investigations are conveniently summarized in Fig. III. Perhaps the most surprising feature is the extent to which farms in many parts of the North and West followed regular cropping systems similar to those of their neighbours. In most cases these systems were the ones used in the common fields, and the regularity prevailed despite the frequent presence of piecemeal closes and complex field divisions. Especially in the early part of the study period, when pastoral products received most attention, the bulk of the arable in many parishes lay open, and in others farms with a mixture of open and enclosed land may have continued to use the normal rotation of the district in which they lay. This does not mean that cropping practice was inflexible. Indeed, it is clear that the communal system was capable of accommodating marked changes in crop combinations within limited areas where physical or economic conditions required these. If the probable rye–oats–fallow of the north-east is allowed, there were at least five different regional cropping systems in East Worcestershire's common fields.

There is also no reason to believe that common-field practice remained static for a very long time in the face of decisive economic trends. In the study period arable products were becoming more profitable, and in the North and West oxen were being replaced by horses. The economy of the South was already well-suited to take advantage of these new conditions. In the North and West, too, many districts used a wide variety of crops with some choice within the principal shifts. It was the two-crop districts of the mid-sixteenth century which underwent most alteration in cropping practice before 1650, including,

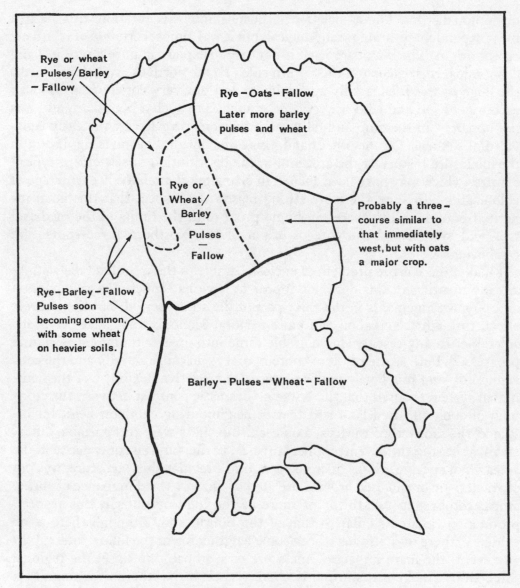

**Rye or wheat
— Pulses/Barley
— Fallow**

Rye — Oats — Fallow

**Later more barley
pulses and wheat**

**Rye or
Wheat/
Barley
—
Pulses
—
Fallow**

**Probably a three-
course similar to
that immediately
west, but with oats
a major crop.**

**Rye — Barley — Fallow
Pulses soon
becoming common,
with some wheat
on heavier soils.**

Barley — Pulses — Wheat — Fallow

FIG. III

TENTATIVE MAP OF DOMINANT CROPPING TYPES

on common-field land, the introduction of a wider range of crops into the Spring Field. It may be added that, since the economy of the medieval period was by no means static, none of the rotations prevalent in the sixteenth century can be regarded as necessarily of great antiquity.

A more stable element appears in the boundary between four-course and three-course cropping, which more or less coincided with the edge of the champion district. This association of the most intensive rotation with the area most dependent on arable seems logical, but it was almost certainly of relatively recent origin. The boundary itself is not easy to explain in purely physical and economic terms, except on the Severn side. To the north the coincidence with the edge of the Lias is only approximate and not very convincing. Modern accounts of soil and land use[1] give no emphasis to such a boundary, and it is not apparent in the crop and fallow distributions revealed by the early Agricultural Returns. On the other hand, this same line of division is significant in the enclosure history of the area and in the distribution of settlement types,[2] features which may have been shaped in character at a relatively early stage of colonization. In sum, there are strong reasons to suspect that this is an inherited boundary, but there can be no proof until the limits of the medieval two-field system and the date of origin of the Northern three-course are established.

Finally, there is the problem of enclosed arable in the woodland district. As already mentioned, this does not appear to have had much direct impact on cropping arrangements in the early part of the study period, but the indirect effect, through the creation of a more pastoral economy, may have been considerable. In any case, enclosed arable came into greater prominence as time progressed, both as the result of contemporary enclosure activity and the conversion of land previously under pasture. The relative flexibility of the communal system ensured that there was no dramatic contrast between the cropping of such enclosed land and that of neighbouring common field; for instance, the same crops were used on each. But there were recognizable differences, at least in the seventeenth century. In particular, the equivalence in the acreages of specific groups of crops, denoting a regular shift structure, was not characteristic of enclosed ground. Related to this was the dominance of spring crops, comprising two-thirds or more of the total output. In this respect, production became similar to that of the South, and, although there is no evidence, there may also have been some lengthening in the fallow interval. In any event, the main impact of enclosure was probably to upset the regional three-shift arrangements formerly characteristic of Northern cropping. This meant the rejection of an aspect of communal cropping which seems to owe more to historical inheritance than to current needs.

[1] For example K. M. Buchanan, *The Land of Britain, Part 68, Worcestershire*, 1944.
[2] J. A. Yelling, *op. cit.*, pp. 23–63.

The mechanics of innovation:
clover cultivation in Wales before 1750

Frank Emery

Welsh agriculturists were more responsive to the introduction of new crops in the seventeenth and early eighteenth centuries than is generally assumed. In particular, they appreciated the nutritious fodder that could be provided for their livestock by the sown grasses, notably clover, sainfoin and perennial rye grass. These legumes were tried on Welsh estates at least as early as 1668. The initial mechanics of innovation are explored: what were the processes by which knowledge was gained, distributed, tested and used in the decision-making of those who first cultivated the grasses? On the Trevor estates the stages of adoption included the inception of trial plots of sainfoin; observation and enquiry with several English growers; assessment of soils and seeds; parallel experiments at two sites; close reference to the printed word about the crop, in papers of instruction and books. Welsh initiators also followed patterns of imitation, in some cases based on clover cultivation already established in Wales, in others on the classic model of Herefordshire. The scale of adoption is indicated by data from every Welsh county, and for landowners and farmers at different levels of operation. The literature of improved agriculture was directly influential, as were the ties of family kinship, language and religion among adopters. The working of a three-step flow of communication is suggested.

The time is ripe to show that Welsh agriculture was more responsive to the introduction of new crops in the seventeenth and early eighteenth centuries than is generally assumed, even by Welsh historians.[1] Such arguments have become common enough in recent years for the "agricultural revolution" in England, the advent of basic improvements in farming being shown to substantially pre-date the middle decades of the eighteenth century.[2] In advancing a similar case for Wales, this study will concentrate on what a Welsh agriculturist, as early as the 1690s, did not hesitate to refer to as "Clover and other Adventitious Grasses". It cannot be denied that such new fodder crops were of primary value to Welsh farmers then as now, and they have been the spearhead of agricultural progress in other environments in more recent times, for instance with the adoption of *Trifolium subterranum* in South Australia since 1945.[3] There is a lineage of Welsh adoption going back to some time before 1668 in the case of these nutritious legumes, in particular clover (*Trifolium pratense*), sainfoin (*Onobrychis sativa*) and perennial rye grass (*Lolium perenne*). In Wales they enjoyed as precocious an origin as for any English

---

[1] See (for instance) David Howell, Pembrokeshire gentry in the eighteenth century, pp. 158–85 of Tudor Barnes and Nigel Yates (Eds), *Carmarthenshire studies* (Carmarthen 1974), particularly 171–4

[2] E. L. Jones, *Agriculture and the industrial revolution* (Oxford 1974) 3–7, 23–99

[3] Michael Williams, *The making of the South Australian landscape* (London 1974) 311–21. The merits of subterranean clover were understood and publicised before 1912, but it was not adopted for nearly a quarter of a century

county where the sown grasses were taken up, and so far this is unsuspected. It is often stated that the new legumes were diffused widely and rapidly through England from the 1650s onwards, but hitherto their progress has not been plotted specifically from the archival sources for a defined area. Information about them is elusive, admittedly, and sometimes difficult to interpret, but even the printed summaries of tithe disputes in the Court of Exchequer have scarcely been tapped. The aim of this paper is to isolate the initial mechanics of the innovation, that is to say the processes by which knowledge of the new grasses was gained, distributed, tested and used as a basis for decision-making by those who first cultivated them. It is planned to go on to analyse the community of Welsh adopters, rich and poor, and the spatial diffusion of clover, in the fifth volume of *An agrarian history of England and Wales*, which will cover the period from 1640 to 1750.

Early chronology

A pointer to the earliness of clover cultivation may be found, by way of introduction, in the Welsh language. The agrarian vocabularies of all the Welsh speech-areas were rich and varied, but it is also true that Welsh has absorbed new farming words without inhibition. *Meillion* is the native term for the natural clovers, but the English word was borrowed as *clofer* for the sown grass. *Clofer* is first recorded in print in a Welsh book published in 1762, and *cloferau* (the verb "to clover") in another of 1769.[1] It is easy to show that the word was in use long before that: Owen Thomas, who lived near Denbigh in North Wales, wrote his journal in Welsh and observed for July 1748 that *digon o wair a chlofer a thegwch iw drin*— "there is plenty of hay and clover in fair growth".[2] So by 1748 we find this earliest acceptance of *clofer* in everyday use, and the crop must have been a familiar item of Welsh husbandry. Significantly, red clover is still known in Welsh as *clofer coch Seisnig*, that is to say, "English red clover", much as the English agriculturists in their turn would write of "Dutch red clover".

As befits a nation known for its obsession with pedigrees, the Welsh lineage in clover cultivation is not only long but impeccable as to its origins. There was recently discovered a letter written by Sir Richard Weston in February 1651, at a time when the first edition of his *Discours of husbandrie* was running out of print.[3] The book was the first of many to champion "use of the Clover-seed". Weston's letter dealt with the difficulties of threshing clover-seed, recommended a London seedsman, and gave instructions to sow ten pounds of seed per acre upon barley already harrowed: "This is after you intend to lay it up wholly for grasse." The person to whom he gave this advice may now be identified as John Lloyd of Forest Glyncothi, an estate near Brechfa (see Fig. 1) in Carmarthenshire.[4] Lloyd had become Weston's neighbour in Surrey by his marriage with the widow of James Zouch, whose estate was near Woking; Lloyd and his wife came of the same Pembrokeshire stock, and he was made baronet in 1662. It is very likely that John

[1] *Geiriadur Prifysgol Cymru, cyfrol* 1 (Cardiff 1950–67). (This is the standard *Dictionary of the Welsh language*)

[2] E. D. Jones, Llyfrau cofion a chyfrifon Owen Thomas, 1729–1775 *The National Library of Wales Journal* 16 (1969) 148

[3] A. R. Michell, Sir Richard Weston and the spread of clover cultivation *Agricultural History Review* 22 (1974) 160–1

[4] *Complete baronetage* (Exeter 1903) 246. Brechfa is located on Fig. 1, which also shows the location in Wales of other places mentioned in this paper

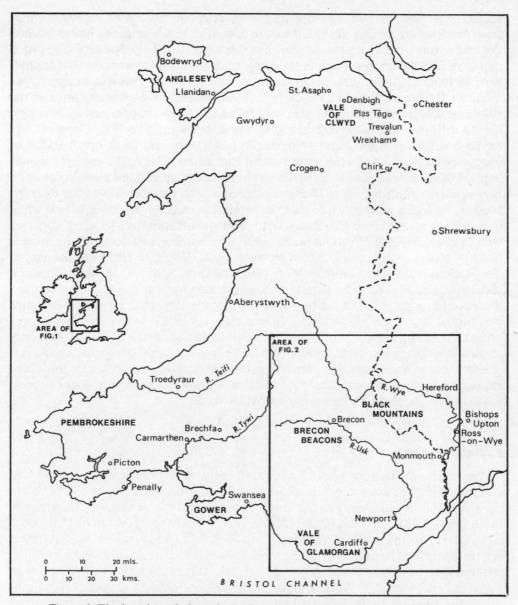

Figure 1. The location of places in Wales and the borders, mentioned in the text.

Lloyd made it his business to find out about clover on behalf of someone living in Carmarthenshire or Pembrokeshire. Nor is it impossible that he wanted the information for his own estate at Forest. Family letters show that he was planting trees and designing walks there in 1654, while by 1665 his brother (who managed the property for him) was claiming recompense for his "layings out towards ye Improvement of this land".[1]

Besides Weston, the other acclaimed pioneer of "the Clover Husbandry" is Andrew Yarranton. He was the author of the first book purely and simply on the

[1] N.L.W. (National Library of Wales) Ms. 18983F 729,730

subject, *The improvement improved, by a second edition of the great improvement of lands by clover*, appearing in 1663. If we are to believe him, Yarranton had published the first edition earlier that same year, but it is highly unlikely that he did so; such duplicity was common enough in the book trade. He is important on two counts: first, he lived at Astley, near Kidderminster, and it is clear that due in part to his initiative the clover husbandry became well established in Worcestershire and the adjoining county of Herefordshire in the 1660s and 1670s. They formed a key region for the diffusion of clover, and their geographical proximity to Wales, particularly to the counties of Brecon and Monmouth, put a premium on the probability of contagious diffusion.[1] In the second place, Yarranton gives us the earliest account in print of the mechanics of this particular innovation, in *England's improvement by sea and land*, published in 1677. By comparison with the idealism of Sir Richard Weston, he had a more down-to-earth appreciation of the problems involved when introducing a new crop. His idea was to send quantities of clover-seed, together with printed sheets of directions on the method of sowing, to a dealer at the market town of Ross-on-Wye. From him they were available free of charge to farmers in the Archenfield "sands district" of Herefordshire. Only if the new practice succeeded and proved to be as profitable as claimed for it in the literature (no less than doubling the value of land), would the farmers then have to pay seven pence per pound for their clover-seed. "There was no other way", in Yarranton's uncompromising words, "to force that Husbandry upon the People." His only known Welsh connection is a letter to a colliery owner in Glamorgan, characteristically about improving the river navigation for selling coal to sea.[2] But there are equally early and more detailed revelations of how the process of innovation in fodder crops went on, emanating from Wales itself.

Experimentation

An exact and thorough-going policy of early experimentation with sainfoin comes to light in the correspondence of Sir John Trevor, whose royal offices before the Civil War added greatly to the family fortune, and whose son was Secretary of State in the 1660s. Sir John inherited Plas Têg in 1630 and Trevalun in 1638, both estates lying to the north of Wrexham. He lived in London, so his agents' letters are full of routine business, of buying land, leasing it for twenty-one years, marling, covenants to burn (or "Denshire") the land, take three corn crops from it and then put it down to grass.[3] Against this background of efficiency, and at a time of depressed corn prices, in 1668 we first read about sainfoin. It was to figure in the letters right down to Sir John's death in 1673 at the age of ninety-two, somewhat older than might be expected for such an innovator. The merits of sainfoin were already set out in the later editions of Walter Blith's book, *The English improver improved*, in the 1650s. It was best suited to thin, dry soils, lasting longer than clover; thickly sown with spring corn, or on its own in autumn, it could be mown as hay for two years, then grazed. Sainfoin was especially recommended for dairy cattle and fattening sheep, and as these were integral parts of farming in the border

[1] E. L. Jones, *op. cit.*, introduces some of the facts in his second chapter, Agricultural conditions and changes in Herefordshire, 1660–1815, especially 48–50
[2] N.L.W., Ms. 19148B; see M. Wight, A letter from Andrew Yarranton *Transactions of the Worcestershire Archaeological Society* 1 (1965–7) 79–80
[3] Clwyd Record Office (Hawarden), D/G 3272, 18, 24; 3274, 25, 28; 3275, 10, 11, 25

lands of Flint and Denbigh, the crop was obviously attractive to Sir John.[1] His agent at Trevalun was asked to find out "the best information" about sainfoin, and it is clear from his report (10th October 1668) that some sainfoin was already growing at Trevalun.

As Roger Kenrick, the agent, rode from London back to North Wales, he was advised to visit an innkeeper on the road between Uxbridge and Aylesbury, only to find that he was growing cinquefoil. Fresh enquiries then took him to an estate near Chertsey in Surrey, where the bailiff showed him their fields of sainfoin. Next he stopped at Woodstock (Oxfordshire), and inspected a hundred acres of sainfoin that Mr Huxley had sown on thin *stonebrash* soils. When Kenrick compared the crops he had seen, he concluded: "the Ground (for sainfoin) ought to be not the worse sort of land. I thinke oure Ground is as fitt for it as thers." Huxley sold the seed and gave away "the printed page" of directions for sowing it; he promised to supply in 1669, sending it by road to Gloucester, where Sir John could have it taken by boat up the Severn to Shrewsbury, and so to Trevalun. Such a journey implies there was no supply of sainfoin seed nearer home.[2]

By mid-April 1669 thirty-two bushels of seed were sown thickly over eight acres, with barley and oats, as stated in the directions. In the summer of 1670 Kenrick blamed bad seed, both English and French, for a thin crop, asking Sir John to send the fresher seed already used in trial plots. The 1671 sowing rose to sixty bushels, and he experimented with an autumn sowing of sainfoin alone. At Sir John's other estate, the Plas Têg agent was also trying it after barley, rye and buckwheat, although confessing to "not having had any experience in yt waye of improvement". Sir John was determined to enlighten him, and in addition to the paper of directions that he had used already, sent a new book that answered the objections to growing sainfoin. The letters show it to have been a twenty-page pamphlet, *St. Foine Improved . . . written by a Person of Honour lately deceased*, published in 1671. Its author (hitherto in doubt) may be identified as Nathaniel Fiennes, who died in December 1669 at his estate in the Wiltshire chalklands.[3] Inspired by this, the Plas Têg agent also began to experiment: he tried sainfoin on land that had been burnt, concluding (unlike Kenrick) that it preferred more barren ground, without all the preparations recommended for it. He was dissatisfied with the 1673 crop, weaker and paler than in 1672, and Kenrick was pessimistic about sainfoin at Trevalun: "the land and the Clymet is not Right", and he advised Sir John to discontinue. But his master refused to give up, perhaps because he knew that "it did not prosper" with an old political rival, Thomas Myddelton, who was also experimenting with sainfoin locally at Chirk.

The various stages in Trevor's adoption of a new legume are at the outset impressive for their refinement and deliberation. They include the initiation of trial plots of sainfoin; observation and enquiry with several English adopters; assessment of the characteristics of soils and seeds, in aiming at optimisation; parallel experiments on two estates; and reference to the printed word about the crop, in papers of instructions and books.

[1] Frank Emery, The farming regions of Wales, pp. 113–160 of Joan Thirsk (Ed.), *The agrarian history of England and Wales, volume* **IV**, *1500–1640* (Cambridge 1967) especially 131–2

[2] The details of sainfoin cultivation in this paragraph and the next are based on a series of letters in C.R.O., D/G 3277–8

[3] The argument for this identification rests on the relationship between comments made in the printed text and in the Trevor letter, and will be published shortly in *The Agricultural History Review*. (Nathaniel was father of Celia Fiennes)

Imitation: internal sources

A different order of initiative, on two counts, may be traced in the actions of Watkin Owen. No great landowner, he was steward of the largest estate in the Vale of Conwy, again in North Wales, There are accounts by him dating from 1684, a few years after the Gwydyr estate passed by marriage of the last Wynn heiress to Lord Willoughby.[1] The chronology of changing ownership of such properties, with the fresh policies of management that may then be introduced, is potentially of great bearing on innovation. A second difference from Sir John Trevor's method is that Owen soon set out to imitate the cultivation of sown grasses, but by following the model of adopters already growing them in North Wales. He started with perennial rye grass, writing to discover where seed might be bought, and how to sow it. The reply is dated 22nd January 1691. Owen's informant lived at Deganwy and explained that (like his neighbour Robert Wynne of Bodyscallen) he had obtained seed from Banbury: "The way we got it was wn. my son went to Oxford, ye horses return'd empty home, carryed it; we had two sorts of it, the one had very near halfe Trefoyle seed mixt & ye other had none, the fformer is ye better, sweeter & thicker grass."[2] Banbury being a cattle-market then much visited by Welsh drovers, who took cattle by road to the English graziers, we should accept that knowledge of the fodder crops (as with much else) could reach Wales very readily through the medium of these drovers or *porthmyn*. Owen also filed the instructions for rye grass as given in an advertisement published by a London grass seedsman, Francis Weston, who sold all the legumes "for ye Improvement of lands, with Directions in print".[3]

A striking feature of Watkin Owen's notes, both on rye grass and clover, is that he wrote them as addenda to his copy of the best-known book on farming published in the later seventeenth century—*Systema agriculturae: the mystery of husbandry discovered*, by John Worlidge. Owen had a copy of the re-issue of the fourth edition, 1698, bearing his signature and "May 1698".[4] He had about forty blank pages bound in after Worlidge's text, for his own addenda; Worlidge of course had a section "Of Several new Species of Hay or Grass", dealing mainly with clover, sainfoin and lucerne. Good though his reputation was as an accurate author, Owen preferred to consult a local adopter with practical experience of growing clover. He was given full details by Edward Roberts of Crogen, in Merionethshire, dated November 1700.[5] The clover-seed was bought at Shrewsbury, and sixty pounds were sown in a field that was well manured, fallowed, sown with barley, and harrowed; "then ye clover seed was sowed carefully as turnipp seed is usually sowed", and harrowed again. After the barley was harvested, the field was securely fenced and cattle kept off it throughout the winter; the following summer "ye clover grass was mowed and a great cropp had thereon", with plenty of aftermath when the hay was cleared; these yields were repeated the next year. Roberts offered other advice, and while it is not yet certain that Watkin Owen followed suit with clover cultivation at Gwydyr, he was thoroughly well informed about it.

[1] N.L.W., Ms. 9719E. In 1687 Owen completed a rental of the full estate in the counties of Caernarvon, Denbigh and Merioneth: N.L.W., Ms. 6414D
[2] N.L.W., Ms. 5977D, *Addenda* 70
[3] *Ibid.* 69
[4] This is N.L.W., Ms. 5977D. On Worlidge, see G. E. Fussell, *The old English farming books 1523 to 1730* (London 1947) 56, 68–72, 95–6; the publishing history of Worlidge's book is more complicated than Fussell suggests
[5] N.L.W., Ms. 5977D, *Addenda* 66

Imitation: external sources

Another situation, where the Welsh adopter surely did grow clover and rye grass, reveals a smallish landowner basing his practice on knowledge gained from a classic source in the English borderlands. Edward Wynne inherited in 1709 his demesne of 650 acres of mixed farming in Anglesey, and from the outset he regularly dressed his arable with sea-sand, lime and farmyard manure. He alternated his crops with laying down to grass: "it's no good Husbandry to run the Land ground out of heart".[1] As Chancellor of the diocese of Hereford, he had every opportunity of being *au fait* with progressive agriculture in Herefordshire, and his own business-like approach to farming made it likely that he would copy some of its practices. Accordingly in December 1717 he ordered a quantity of clover-seed from Ross-on-Wye, asking John Tudor (by his name, not only Welsh, but from Anglesey) to consult with another Ross man to guarantee good quality. Tudor replied on 30th December that "the clover markets are not come yet", i.e. seed would be stocked near to the spring sowings: shades of Yarranton and his clover agent at Ross.[2]

Wynne modelled his entire system at Bodewryd on that of John Hullett, a tenant farmer of 300 acres at Bishop's Upton: this was only a few miles from Ross, in the core area of clover husbandry. He had a comprehensive summary of Hullett's method, costs, yields and profits in his ledgers, and followed the rotation in every respect, except that he had to lime and manure more often than Hullett's once in six years.[3] The rotation ran: wheat; barley; peas and beans; barley and clover; mowing clover; grazing clover, "and so begins again with wheat". His earliest purchase of clover-seed in North Wales was in March 1720, at Wrexham market when selling cattle.[4] He complained in 1725 that it cost ninepence per pound at Hereford, "so will be very dear at Wrexham", but it was bought there at fivepence; in 1727 it was down to threepence, and in 1729 he bought 240 pounds of clover-seed at Wrexham.[5] By then he was sowing a mixture of clover and rye grass, which the books advocated on sour, wet ground, such as Wynne had on parts of his property. From the 1730s until shortly before his death in 1753, he bought some of his seed at Chester, and the threefold sequence of purchasing first at Ross, then at Wrexham, and finally at Chester must reflect the spreading interest taken in clover.[6]

Wynne's imitation must be placed in the still wider context of the printed literature on improved farming. His notebooks show his knowledge of some of the most influential authors, for instance Richard Bradley: he copied at length from *A compleat body of husbandry* (1727), possibly because Bradley was strong on costing. He also used *The duty of a steward to his lord*, by Edward Laurence, in the second edition of 1731, which gave prominence to the sown grasses, enclosure and consolidation of land. Another discriminating choice was *The country gentleman's vade mecum* (1717), by Giles Jacob.[7] Wynne did not own these books, but borrowed copies and extracted the information he wanted, and a close relationship

[1] University College of North Wales (Bangor), Ms. Penrhos i 360
[2] U.C.N.W., Ms. Penrhos v 588
[3] N.L.W., Bodewryd Ms. 63E. Hullett sowed ten pounds of clover seed per acre, and one-and-a-half bushels of rye grass seed per acre
[4] U.C.N.W., Ms. Penrhos v 255
[5] U.C.N.W., Ms. Penrhos i 524A, 868
[6] N.L.W., Bodewryd Ms. 56F, 61E, 65B
[7] N.L.W., Bodewryd Ms. 61E, 63E, 64F, 66D, 68B

is struck here between a progressive agriculturist and the printed literature. It is in this light we may appreciate Wynne's other innovations, such as the cultivation of potatoes (by 1728) and turnips (by 1737).[1] His influence also reached his wife's estate in the Vale of Clwyd, fifty miles from Anglesey. A tenant there agreed to sow fields with barley, oats and 180 pounds of clover in 1737, again in 1739 (with 200 pounds) and in 1740. The landlord carried the costs of sowing and harrowing the clover-seed, which was provided; Wynne already did that at Bodewryd by 1727, and such allowances were a usual and good means of encouraging tenants to adopt the grasses.[2]

Idea agriculturae

Wynne was not a solitary innovator. Anglesey was a productive, go-ahead region of mixed farming, with a higher proportion of resident landlords of smallish estates than was usual in North Wales.[3] For this reason alone, its mean information field was potentially diverse and efficient. No better measure of this could be found than in a book entitled *Idea agriculturae, an essay on the theory and practice of husbandry . . . principally relating to the Isle of Anglesey*. The author was Henry Rowlands, who belonged to a native landowning family; he was rector of Llanidan, a talented naturalist and historian; two other books were written by him. Rowlands worked on *Idea agriculturae* during the 1690s, finishing it by 1704.[4] Quite ignored by Fussell and other commentators, it nonetheless presents a scientific approach to farming; one manuscript version of the *Idea*, for instance, has the earliest soils map for any part of Wales, and possibly only the second sketch-map to show soils in Britain.[5] Rowlands also argued, at this early date, for the establishment of an agricultural society in his county.[6]

The book is built around a vigorous argument for improved agriculture, stressing three non-traditional composts: shelly sand, first used in Anglesey in the 1640s; white marl, first tried in the 1650s, Rowlands having interviewed its innovator; and liming, which dated from the 1660s with lime burnt on the island. A prominent place is also given to a section "Of Clover, and other Adventitious Grasses". Rowlands writes about these as if they were perfectly familiar to his readers, and entirely from the local angle.[7] For a clover ley, he says, there was no need to dung the fields first, simply sow it with the spring corn; he even uses the traditional Anglesey units of measurement for it. A double cut of clover could normally be guaranteed for two or three years; it was the best feed for store cattle before they left the farm, at a time when they had to swim to the mainland before being driven to the English markets. Dairy cows thrived on it in the spring, and it quickly built up weak stock or working animals. Such merits made clover ideally

[1] N.L.W., Bodewryd Ms. 54E, 57E

[2] N.L.W., Bodewryd Ms. 384; U.C.N.W., Penrhos Ms. i 362, iii 190

[3] A. H. Dodd, *A history of Caernarvonshire, 1284-1900* (Caernarvon 1968) 199–200. Dodd draws a contrast between Anglesey and Caernarvonshire, where many landowners were absentees

[4] The book was not published until 1764, in Dublin

[5] N.L.W., Church of Wales Ms. B/Misc. Vols/16

[6] He made it a general proposal that societies of gentlemen should be formed "in several parts of the county they live in", also admitting "such of their neighbouring farmers as are known to be men of sense and veracity". They should meet regularly each summer to make trials and experiments, keeping a running record of results: *Idea agriculturae* lv–vi

[7] *Idea agriculturae* 170–6, 183–92

suited to the needs of Welsh farmers in general, and Rowlands' book proclaims (in a way that the standard sources rarely do) that clover was well known in Anglesey by 1700. "Hay seeds", probably threshed from native grasses, were also sown, and as early as 1703 John Owen of Penrhos had "the seed of all the ray grass etc" on land that he leased out.[1] Elsewhere in Anglesey, the diary of William Bulkeley shows him buying clover-seed at Wrexham fair (1737), sowing it mixed with "our country hay seed"; a Holyhead resident summarised (in one of his books, 1746) the method of growing a mixture of clover and rye grass; at Bodorgan clover, rye grass and "hay seed" were cultivated in 1755–6.[2]

Scale and incidence of adoption

Wales was an alien environment, in a conceptual sense, long after the Act of Union with England, and certainly so in the later seventeenth century, as nowadays it finds itself implicitly beyond the range of some debates in agrarian history.[3] Its differences lay not so much in distance from London, its upland terrain or its sparse population (it was hardly more disadvantaged than northern England in those respects), but rather in its native language, society and culture. Despite these potential barriers to innovation, adoption and diffusion, all parts of Wales were remarkably open to the cultivation of the new grasses after 1650. In total, the data supporting this conclusion are convincing, varied, and derive from every Welsh county, but they may be illustrated briefly at three levels; hierarchical, general and personal. The first source is so called because it derives from the accounts, surveys and letters drafted by landowners and the stewards of their estates, the dominant group in rural society and its economy; also the two other levels of data have increasingly wider connotations. In fact, since the estate records were relatively plentiful and tend to survive in the archives, there is an inherent risk they might distort our judgment in favour of this most affluent group, to which after all, belonged the innovative gallery of John Lloyd, Sir John Trevor, Watkin Owen and Edward Wynne.

To neutralise the risk, the reality of the situation (so remote from the free barbecues and telephone calls used in simulating the patterns of pump irrigation in twentieth-century Colorado,)[4] was that innovation could begin on the demesne or "home farm" of an estate, and then the adoption be guided by the landlord as he encouraged his tentants through the mechanisms of allowances or clauses in their leases. Diffusion by contagion would then take place as a third stage, among tenants of other estates where the innovation had not struck at all, and among independent freeholders. Many of the North Wales landowners in fact shared in this process: at Erddig (Denbighshire) clover was first grown in 1709, the steward deciding to sow it immediately after harrowing the barley: "This is a better way than to sow the clover when barley is two or three inches high, which is the common custom of this country. That can only damage the growing barley and also the

[1] U.C.N.W., Ms. Penrhos ii 720
[2] U.C.N.W., Ms. Henblas A18, Ms. Bodorgan 1326–7; *A natural history of Ireland in three parts* (Dublin 1726), a copy at the National Library of Wales with the signature of John Jones, Cefncoed
[3] See (for instance) Eric Kerridge, *The agricultural revolution* (London 1969), where the author does not venture beyond Offa's Dyke
[4] L. W. Bowden, The diffusion of the decision to irrigate *University of Chicago, Research Paper* 97 (Chicago 1965)

ground is then too dry to produce good clover." His reference to "the common custom of this country" is eloquent of the North Walians' familiarity with the crop as early as 1709, and both clover and rye grass were grown on the Erddig estate between 1721 and 1747.[1] The Mostyns bought "Trefoil seed" (1723), and tried their luck with lucerne (1731); clover-seed was purchased at Wrexham for their tenants in Denbighshire and Flintshire, down to 1751, and a similar story (including rye grass) can be pieced together for other estates at Lleweni, Nannau, and St Asaph.[2] Turning to South Wales, at this hierarchical level, we may note in 1697 John Parry, archdeacon of Cardigan, writing to Edward Lhuyd at Oxford asking him to send a quantity of sainfoin: Parry wished to try it on his property at Troed-yr-aur, and sought "direction how to use the land it is to be sown in and what manner of soil it requires". He would take some good clover-seed as an alternative, although clearly he could get clover elsewhere if need be.[3] In Pembrokeshire, one of the Phillipses of Picton was improving a farm at Penally in 1708, "hayinge this yeare sowed above 200 weight of Clover seed, and doe resolve next yeare to try St foine".[4] In Glamorgan, the Mansels of Margam were spending freely on clover-seed by 1712; the restrictive coventants in a lease (1742) of a Gower farm included one requiring the tenant to sow ten pounds of clover-seed for each bushel of barley, etc., "with every fourth crop of corn".[5] Another lease (1743) from the Vale of Glamorgan asked the tenant to agree to have only two fields under the plough during the final year of an eleven-year lease. Of those two fields, one was "to be sufficiently sown with clover by him", the other by the landlord, who took the clover crop after the tenant's corn was harvested. Trefoil and clover-seed were bought for estates near Cardiff (1745–50), some of it obtained from Bristol.[6]

Just two examples will be given of the second set of data, which is of a general nature in that it is not derived from the more affluent innovators. One is the record of customs in the Port Books for Cardiff and its creeks, during the 1690s: cargoes of clover, trefoil and rye grass seed were shipped from Minehead across the Bristol Channel to Aberthaw, imported for a range of purchasers in the Vale of Glamorgan.[7] Then there are the parish replies to questionnaires sent through Wales by Edward Lhuyd, replete with first-hand comment on agriculture. One of his best correspondents told him (1697) "in divers parts of Swansea hundred there are much Clover grass & seed", but more telling still was the Monmouthshire reply (one of only five surviving from that county): "by sowing clover, greater numbers of cattle are of late bred and fed than was formerly".[8] This echoes with uncanny accuracy the independent testimony of John Aubrey for adjoining parts of Herefordshire: "they are fallen into the vein of clover, and those which kept no kine before now keep some 12, some 20".[9]

At the personal level, most information is yielded by the wills and inventories of movable goods owned by individual farmers when they died. So far, clover is

[1] C.R.O., D/E 361, 363, 373, 539, 547
[2] U.C.N.W., Mostyn Ms. 5508, 6431–2, 6486, Mostyn Letters IX 14; Kinmel Ms. 1675; Nannau Ms. 3629–30; General Collection 7134, 7137; D/GA 782
[3] Bodleian Library, Oxford, Ashmole Ms. 1817a, 74, letter dated 16th February 1697
[4] N.L.W., Picton Castle Ms. 1457
[5] N.L.W., Penrice and Margam Ms. 1760, 3381
[6] Glamorgan Record Office, Nicholl of Merthyr Mawr Ms. D/DN 230–1; D/D MBN 64, 67, 68
[7] Moelwyn I. Williams, The economic and social history of Glamorgan, 1660–1760, pp. 311–73 of Glanmor Williams (Ed.), *Glamorgan county history* 4 (Cardiff 1974), especially 336–7
[8] Bodleian, Carte Ms. 108 27a; Rupert H. Morris (Ed.), *Parochialia*, etc. (London 1911) 3, 39
[9] Bodleian, Aubrey Ms. 2, 152

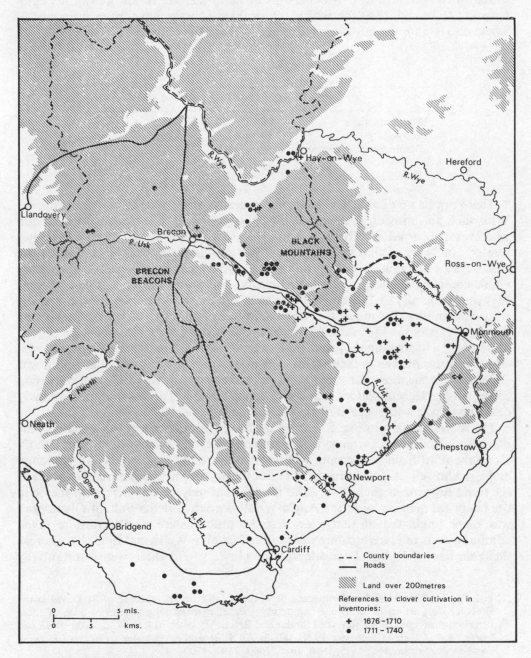

Figure 2. Early adopters of clover in south-eastern Wales. The map covers the counties of Brecon and Monmouth, and most of Glamorgan (omitting the deanery of Gower in west Glamorgan). It locates each farmer (139 in all) whose inventory contains some reference to clover: data from National Library of Wales, Probate Mss. Llandaf and St David's, archdeaconry of Brecon, 1675, 1680, 1685, 1690, 1695, 1700–40. The choice of 1710 as a break-point is simply to give two equal phases in the period studied. Roads are taken from Morden's maps in the 1695 edition of Camden's *Britannia*.

found in the inventories of 139 persons in south-eastern Wales, at various dates
between 1676 and 1740 for which the probate sources have been examined.[1]
These clover adopters are mapped in Fig. 2, from the data in Table 1.

TABLE 1

	1676–1710	1711–1740
Monmouthshire	28	54
Breconshire	10	37
Glamorgan (less Gower)	1	9
Total	39	100 clover adopters

There can be no doubt that clover was under-recorded in the Welsh inventories.
With such an innovation, there was no obligation to give it a separate valuation
wherever it occurred, and instead it would be hidden in the farmer's "Hay and other
fodder", or "Hay of all sorts". In view of this, and the fact that will-makers in any
case were a small minority, the group of 139 cultivators by no means comprises the
whole company of those who adopted clover. An important point is that whereas
they were generally well-to-do, they represent a fair cross-section of the will-making
rural community.[2] Among the one hundred inventories first collected from the
diocesan papers for Llandaf and for the archdeaconry of Brecon, 24 were gentry,
38 yeomen, 5 husbandmen, 4 were tradesmen of various kinds and 12 were widows;
17 were unspecified as to their status. The mean value of their personal wealth was
£136; that of the most numerous sub-group, the yeomen, was £92; but more than
25 per cent of the cultivators were worth less than £38. It seems that from an early
date clover was within reach of the small farmers.

The spatial pattern in Fig. 2 shows a profusion of adopters in the lowland areas
of prosperous mixed farming in Monmouthshire and Breconshire, particularly
along the road from Monmouth to Brecon and around centres like Abergavenny
and Crickhowell. It is tempting to interpret this as simply another manifestation of
the trend towards anglicisation, valid though that may be as a persistent theme in
the historical geography of the Anglo-Welsh border. But the Vale of Glamorgan
was more anglicised at that time than Monmouthshire or Breconshire (even
adjoining parts of Herefordshire were still bilingual in Welsh and English), whereas
the Vale has fewer and later adopters of clover.[3] All three were substantially

[1] N.L.W., Probate Mss. for the diocese of Llandaf, and (in the diocese of St David's) the
Breconshire portion of Brecon archdeaconry, were searched: the territorial base of these
jurisdictions (consistory counts of Llandaf and Brecon) is given in J. S. W. Gibson, *Wills and
where to find them* (Chichester 1974) 180–2. All wills and inventories from the following
bundles were examined: 1675, 1680, 1685, 1690, 1695, 1700–40

[2] It is calculated that one man in 12, and one woman in 50, died leaving enough goods to merit
a will and inventory: J. A. Johnston, The Vale of Evesham, 1702–8: the evidence from
probate inventories and wills *Vale of Evesham Historical Society*, Research Papers 4 (1973)
85–96. Clover did not appear in 101 inventories from this region, nor in those studied by
D. G. Vaisey, *Probate inventories of Lichfield and district, 1568–1680* (Staffordshire Record
Society 1969); of the latter 75 per cent date from 1660–80

[3] Something of the background to this situation is given by W. T. R. Pryce, Migration and the
evolution of culture areas: cultural and linguistic frontiers in north-east Wales, 1750 and 1851
Transactions of the Institute of British Geographers 65 (1975) 79–107; Brian Ll. James, The
Welsh language in the Vale of Glamorgan *Morgannwg* 16 (1972) 16–36

landscapes of enclosed fields, and their differences lay rather in the dairying–corn system of the Vale of Glamorgan offering less scope for clover than the store cattle–sheep–corn farming in the other regions, which readily followed the Herefordshire model.[1] There were also important social differences: religious dissent is one facet of these by the late seventeenth century, with a large number of Nonconformist congregations flourishing in the counties of Monmouth and Brecon (adding a special set of social linkages), whereas very few were founded in the more manorialized Vale of Glamorgan.[2] This may also have a bearing on the peculiarly cellular sub-patterns that existed within Monmouthshire and Breconshire, whereby a particular locality shows much higher than average densities of clover adoption, both chronologically over a longer time span, and in the diversity of status of its several cultivators.

Conclusions

The new legumes were definitely being adopted in Wales from the middle decades of the seventeenth century. Landowners and farmers at different scales of operation became involved with the sown grasses. As with the English tobacco-growers, even the small farmer was not slow to take up innovations when they suited his economic and social circumstances, and too much may have been made of "the ignorance and stubborness of peasants" in this context.[3] The clover cultivators also endorse and justify the complaint, voiced as late as 1815, that "Strangers who have never seen Wales consider it as something like Siberia, and form very low estimates of its produce".[4]

The Welsh innovators suffered no special constraints in terms of accessibility and information. Seed for clover and sainfoin was readily bought at, and carried from, eight different sources of supply in England and one in Wales. The farmers also soon discovered how to furnish their own seed, as shown by the inventory of a Monmouthshire yeoman (1701): "Clover and hay and Clover seed unthreshed, £5."[5] The literature of improved farming was directly influential, as seen in the readings and writings of Owen, Wynne and Rowlands, and a profitable start has been made to exploring the contents of landowners' libraries for such books at this period. Finally, the social relationships between ties of family kinship among the adopters, their linguistic facilities in Welsh and English, and their religious beliefs, call for testing in a sufficient number of individual cases. For instance, it may seem more probable that Nonconformist farmers (such as the many yeomen in the early Monmouthshire and Breconshire congregations), would follow the exhortations of Puritan writers like Richard Baxter to honour God by making their land more

[1] Emery, *op. cit*. 132–5

[2] R. Tudor Jones, The older dissent of Swansea and Brecon, pp. 117–141 of Owain W. Jones and David Walker (Eds), *Swansea and Brecon historical essays* (Llandybie 1974); Thomas Richard, The religious census of 1676 *Transactions of the Honourable Society of Cymmrodorion* **1925–6** 52–96; E. T. Davies, Glanmor Williams and Gomer Roberts, Religion and education in Glamorgan, 1660–1775, pp. 431–533 of Glanmor Williams (Ed.) *op. cit*.

[3] Joan Thirsk, New crops and their diffusion: tobacco-growing in seventeenth century England, pp. 76–103 in C. W. Chalklin and M. A. Havinden (Eds) *Rural change and urban growth 1500–1800. Essays in English regional history in honour of W. G. Hoskins* (London 1974)

[4] Walter Davies, *General view of the agriculture and domestic economy of South Wales* **1** (London 1815) 462

[5] N.L.W., Probate Mss., Llandaf: inventory of John Rosser, Bryngwyn, 31st December 1701

productive. On the other hand, innovators like Edward Wynne and Henry Rowlands were Anglican clergymen.

In technologically advanced societies today, the mechanics of innovation may appear as a two-step flow of communication.[1] Information with the mass media is diffused universally, but is accepted only by the opinion leaders, who then diffuse it to their followers and influence them to accept it. This flow typically distorts or loses information in various ways; the quantity possessed by the followers may increase through time infinitely or to a limit, or remain constant, or decrease to a limit.[2] Given that mass media were unknown in the later seventeenth century, may we detect an alternative process at work, particularly in the way the new grasses succeeded as innovations? The Welsh evidence suggests that a three-step flow of communication was in operation:

(i) Information was accepted by the opinion leaders (who were relatively fewer and firmly established at the top of a social hierarchy), according to a wide range of personal choices and contacts. The most specific of these was their knowledge of, and ability to understand, the printed literature of improved farming.

(ii) Their followers were more formalized as tenants on the estates of opinion leaders, and could be firmly guided towards acceptance through the institutional framework of estate management, as in allowances, conditions and restrictive clauses in their leases.

(iii) There was then sufficient scope for the information to spread farther to other potential opinion leaders (using such linkages as kinship, administrative or religious ties), and to their followers. In addition, it could reach others outside the leaseholding system, especially the independent freeholders who in any case were better placed to generate a contagious form of diffusion. Only at that stage is it reasonable to assume the kind of face-to-face contact that would justify recognition of a mean information field.[3]

School of Geography
University of Oxford

[1] L. A. Brown and K. R. Cox, Empirical regularities in the diffusion of innovation *Annals of the Association of American Geographers* **61** (1971) 551–9. See John R. Tarrant, *Agricultural geography* (London 1974) for a review of related ideas in agricultural location theory, especially 48–67

[2] W. Norton, Description and analysis of the two step flow of communication in an innovation diffusion process *South African Geographical Journal* **57** (1975) 46–50

[3] This paper is based on a lecture given at the Annual Conference of the British Agricultural History Society, 8th April 1975. In his work on the Welsh archival sources, the author is indebted for much help and advice from Eiluned Rees, Daniel Huws, Gwyn Walters, Emrys Williams, Stephen Porter, David Howell and Ronald Lloyd. He is also grateful to Penny Timms for drawing the maps

Patterns of migration and movement of labour to three pre-industrial East Anglian towns

John Patten

The very population growth of most pre-industrial English towns of any size depended on considerable immigration: certainly their economic well-being was equally dependent on continuous influxes of labour to fill urban manufacturing, trading and service occupations. Rates of immigration will always be impossible to quantify exactly, but without doubt no town of any standing—from London downwards—could for long have grown in size, or prospered economically, without such influxes of newcomers.

Three East Anglian towns, the great provincial capital of Norwich, and the seaports of Great Yarmouth and Ipswich, are discussed in order to examine migration patterns to towns of different sizes and economic roles within a regional framework. Registers of apprentices enrolled in them are the sources which are used. These sources are the only surviving for the sixteenth and seventeenth centuries for any town in East Anglia which give a relatively coherent picture of geographical patterns of migration. Apprentices were but one group amongst all those moving to towns in search of work it is true, but they were a substantial one; then, as today, younger people formed a majority in the migrant sector of society.

Migration appeared generally to have been densest from the immediate surroundings of these towns; from other, smaller towns in the region; and from areas with which they had a special link, such as similar manufacturing interests. It could also be marked from areas of high population and low agricultural or manufacturing opportunities. The migratory "pull" and attraction of the bigger Norwich, throughout the two centuries examined, was more marked than that of Great Yarmouth or Ipswich—both within East Anglia, and indeed all England. For northern and western upland England indeed supplied a good number of immigrants to the economically buoyant and attractive Norwich, while long range coastal migration was an important component of the total movement of apprentices to the two ports.

Immigration undoubtedly contributed a great deal to both the demographic and economic health of towns in pre-industrial England. Actual rates of immigration will always remain hard to quantify exactly. The fact, however, that most towns of any standing could not really have grown in size, or have prospered, without such influxes of newcomers must now be regarded as established.[1] Little as yet is

[1] See e.g. E. A. Wrigley A simple model of London's rôle in changing English society and economy, 1650–1750 *Past and Present* 37 (1967) 44–70; P. Clark, The migrant in Kentish towns 1580–1640, pp. 117–163 of P. Clark and P. Slack (Eds), *Crisis and order in English towns 1500–1700* (1972); J. Patten, Rural–urban migration in pre-industrial England, University of Oxford *School of Geography Research Paper* 6 (1973); P. Spufford, Population mobility in pre-industrial England: I, The pattern of migration *Genealogists' Magazine* XVII (1973); S. N. Smith, The London apprentices as seventeenth century adolescents *Past and Present* 61 (1973) 149–161; S. N. Smith, The social and geographical origins of the London apprentices 1630–60 *Guildhall Miscellany* IV (1973) 195–206; A. F. Butcher, The origins of Romney Freemen, 1433–1523 *Economic History Review* 2nd Ser. XXVII (1974) 16–27; P. A. Slack, Vagrants and vagrancy in England, 1598–1664 *Economic History Review* 2nd Ser. XXVII (1974) 360–79

known, compared for example with the nineteenth century,[1] of patterns of movement then from country to town. Yet a variety of sources—from deposition books to settlement papers—exist to allow migration in pre-industrial times to be examined. In East Anglia, for example, a series of apprentice indentures survive for Norwich and Great Yarmouth in Norfolk, and Ipswich in Suffolk, for the sixteenth and seventeenth centuries: the evidence they contain permits an examination of the overall picture of movement of this sort of migrant to towns of different sizes, and different economic activities, purely at a macro-scale. More detailed explanatory discussion of why apparently apprentices chose to move, and what their migratory careers were, requires the amassing of a large sample of individual biographies, as much as that can be done; in the light of this, the study presented here pretends to provide no more than a descriptive framework.

Norwich, great provincial city and capital of its region, had perhaps 12,000 people at the middle of the sixteenth century, reaching a population of nearly 30,000[2] by the end of the seventeenth century; centre of the Norfolk worsted manufacture,[3] which for much of the period acted as a barometer of the city's changing economic fortunes, in its variety of shops and services offered[4] it aped the capital's style, if not its scale. Great Yarmouth and Ipswich by comparison were both smaller, regionally less important, and had their fortunes tied quite closely to the sea. Great Yarmouth, around 5,000 in size at the middle of the sixteenth century had reached only 10,000 or more by the end of the next; Ipswich, perhaps 4,000 and around 8,000 at the same dates. The former town had few noted manufactures, though it acted as an outlet for the export overseas of Norwich's textiles, and those of the villages around Worsted in north-east Norfolk. Important concerns were, on the other hand, with the North Sea herring fisheries; with trade across it, and to the Baltic and Iceland; and with associated activities like shipbuilding, and its allied trades. It was also an important stopping-off point on the coastal trade in sea coal, as was Ipswich. This Suffolk port, and capital of the eastern division of its county, had a rich agricultural and textile manufacturing hinterland;[5] it supplied dairy produce for the capital, though the export of

[1] e.g. D. Friedlander and R. J. Roshier, A study of internal migration in England and Wales, 1851–1951: geographical patterns of internal migration *Population Studies* **XIX** (1966) 239–79

[2] Population figures used for Norwich, Great Yarmouth and Ipswich are from J. H. C. Patten, The urban structure of East Anglia in the sixteenth and seventeenth centuries (unpubl. Ph.D. thesis, Univ. of Cambridge 1972)

[3] K. J. Allison, The Norfolk worsted industry in the sixteenth and seventeenth century *Yorkshire Bulletin of Economic and Social Research* **12** (1960) 77–83, and **13** (1961) 61–77

[4] e.g. J. F. Pound, The social and trade structure of Norwich, 1525–1575 *Past and Present* **34** (1966) 49–69

[5] J. Thirsk (Ed.), *The agrarian history of England and Wales, IV, 1500–1640* (Cambridge 1967) 40–9

broadcloth from the declining manufacture of the Stour valley[1] became less important after the end of the sixteenth century. Its position as an important coasting port, deeply involved in the eastern carrying trade to and from Newcastle and London, was similarly in decline in the seventeenth century,[2] "eaten up" by London, though its fortunes remained relatively wedded to the sea throughout.

Sources

Altogether, as might be expected, these three towns proved to be "magnets" of various strengths for young migrant labour from different directions. As far as is known, no further full series of indentures exists for any other town in this region. Nearly 6,000 apprenticeship indentures exist for Norwich, largely in the middle and later sixteenth, and seventeenth centuries.[3] The number is very much smaller for Great Yarmouth and Ipswich, and they survive for a shorter period in each case. In Great Yarmouth nearly 500 were taken between the 1560s and 1660s;[4] the series is apparently deficient for a number of years during Elizabeth's reign. Only some 370 exist for Ipswich, taken between 1596 and 1651.[5] Small proportions of the total populations of the last two towns it is true, although enough to demonstrate overall patterns, in a similar fashion to those given by the 1,200 depositions used by Clark for a study of migration to three Kentish towns over the sixty-year period, 1580–1640.[6] The disparities in the numbers of apprentices enrolled, as well as the different lengths of time over which the series for the three towns extend, affect their direct comparability. This is the case even though immigration could be expected to have been much less marked anyway to the two smaller ports; they did not have any noted manufacturing interests to provide employment opportunities on the scale of Norwich's textiles, for instance.

In their best, and most useful form, apprentice indentures give the name, occupation and place of residence of the apprentice's father; the name of the apprentice himself or more rarely herself; and the name and occupation of his prospective master. Not every indenture necessarily contains all, or even a large part, of this information. The regulation of labour was of national,[7] as well as of local concern. Of the three East Anglian towns considered here, only the regulations governing entry to the trades of Norwich have been subjected to any kind of

[1] e.g. J. B. Mitchell, *Historical geography* (1954) 249–50

[2] e.g. D. Defoe, *A tour through the whole island of Great Britain I* (London 1927) 40–5; W. B. Stephens, The cloth exports of the provincial ports, 1600–1640 *Economic History Review* 2nd Ser. **XXII** (1969) 228–48

[3] W. M. Rising and P. Millican, Apprentices indentured at Norwich 1510–1752 *Norfolk Record Society* **XXIX** (1959); P. Millican (Ed.), *The Register of the Freemen of Norwich 1548–1713* (Norwich 1934) Appendix

[4] Norfolk and Norwich Record Office (hereafter *N.N.R.O.*) C.4/258–C.4/357; *N.N.R.O.* Great Yarmouth Corporation Assembly Books 1614–1637

[5] Ipswich and East Suffolk Record Office, A.IX.4. These indentures are calendered in Ms J. Glyde, Ipswich Reference Library, 942/64 (Ip.929–4)

[6] Clark, *op. cit.* 120–2

[7] F. Unwin, *Industrial organisation in the sixteenth and seventeenth centuries* (1st publ. Oxford 1904; repr. 1957) 117–20; O. J. Dunlop, *English apprenticeship and child labour* (1912); M. G. Davies, *The enforcement of English apprenticeship 1563–1642* (Harvard 1956)

[8] Millican, *op. cit.* **XVI–XX**; Rising and Millican, *op. cit.* xi–xiv; W. Hudson and J. Tingay, *The records of the City of Norwich*, **II** (1910) *passim*

detailed examination.[8] Such control, it must always be remembered, was not solely a matter of the prevention of what was thought of as "unfair" competition between those engaged in the same craft within the same town, but was also intended to control what was thought of as equally unfair competition from the surrounding countryside from whence so many eventual urban apprentices came. Such rural dwellers might have all the advantages of land holding and its revenues during times of slump in demand for craft manufactures, yet had none of the burdens of urban fees and dues, or civic responsibility, often so costly. The Statute of 1563 seems to have been specifically aimed against, amongst other activities thought of as abuses, countrymen taking craft apprentices; this was taking "divers men's living into one man's hands".[1] The Statute also limited apprenticeship in most skilled crafts, including weaving, to the sons of freeholders of land worth above £2 a year. This was increased to £3 a year for those going into apprenticeship in a corporate town—such as were Norwich, Great Yarmouth and Ipswich. It is not clear how far it was enforced in this context, and therefore what effect it may have had on apprenticeship generally.

The information contained in apprenticeship indentures does in some cases allow the place of origin of individuals coming from outside the town of eventual indenture to be stated, and thus general geographical patterns of migration to be constructed. Equally, when both father's and prospective master's occupations are given something can be found out about the occupational mobility of the boys, going perhaps from the house of a yeoman to that of a merchant. A great mass of criss-crossing spatial and occupational movements is apparent. It is difficult to estimate the exact proportion of apprentices in any of the towns at any one time. But within the overall body of indentured apprentices migrants played an important role. They made up about a third of all those indentured in Norwich; and over a half of those in both Great Yarmouth and Ipswich. Any use of the evidence of these indentures must always be tempered by the realisation that the already small numerical sample is representative only of apprentice migration, which was, however, probably quite likely to be permanent; it is certainly not representative of characteristically more temporary movements as may be recorded in depositions[2] or in settlements. On the other hand, apprentices being young, and presumably both economically and socially motivated, were likely to be part of one notably mobile sector of the population; or at least the "non-vagrant" sector. The most mobile section of the population today is undoubtedly comprised of the young adult; the same was most likely of pre-industrial England. Spufford suggests that the most mobile age group in the seventeenth century was that between fifteen years of age and marriage, particularly for living-in servants.[3] The one fact about migration which seems definitely established is that it is age-selective.[4] Reservations felt about drawing any general conclusions from such information may thus be tempered by the knowledge that apprentices were likely to be not unrepresentative of at least those economically active migrants staying for any length of time in their new place of residence.

[1] Unwin, *op, cit*. 138; R. H. Tawney and E. Power (Eds), *Tudor economic documents* I (1935) 339

[2] Clark, *op. cit.*

[3] P. Spufford, Population movement in seventeenth century England *Local Population Studies* 4 (1970) 41–50

[4] Friedlander and Roshier, *op. cit.* 246

Patterns of migration

Patterns of short and long range migration must be carefully separated in the case of each town, the one being an important component of the overall and interrelated everyday economic system, the other largely comprising a few highly defined streams, representing contact between the three towns and certain parts of the rest of England, predominantly to the north. As such it is the *description* of patterns of migration within East Anglia which presents the biggest problem if the great mass of information is to be reduced to a semblance of order. The description of patterns of migration into East Anglia is, of course, a much more straight-forward matter. In order to define and examine patterns of migration using the evidence available in apprentice indentures, maps illustrating the relative density of migrants within Norfolk and Suffolk going to each of the three towns were constructed. Information on the place of residence of immigrant apprentices is always available in a point form, viz. "... of Wymondham", "... of Beccles", etc. The home town or village is usually specified but nothing more; the actual place of residence of the migrant within what could be a quite large parish is almost never stated.[1] Such locational information is thus approximate. Given this, simple plotting of the places of origin of migrants to whichever town is under consider-ation, by the use of dots on a map, would tell something, but not enough, of the patterns of migration. For it would omit consideration of the actual numbers of migrants coming from each place, and equally omit any consideration of how important a fraction of population migrants might be. The relative density of migration needs to be examined to provide a more realistic framework. Density is thus defined as the number of migrants divided by the estimated approximate population of the home village or town, so providing a more meaningful descrip-tion of patterns of migration than simple place of origin data. This ratio of density of migrants for each place—in practice the main settlement of each parish—forms the basic information subsequently mapped. Approximate information on popula-tion was derived, for each period, from sources such as lay subsidies, different communicant "censuses" and hearth-taxes; this is described elsewhere.[2] Regular distribution of population within each parish's total area had to be assumed, as no more detailed information survives.

The labour of converting these to a density distribution map by conventional cartographic methods would be lengthy. In fact so lengthy as to make the whole exercise seem not worthwhile—as a consideration of the great volume of work required in plotting the location, and calculating the density, for the over 450 villages and towns which sent migrant apprentices to Norwich at one time or another, readily shows. The recent development of computer graphics, by which the speedy machine drawing of such maps is facilitated, allows these practical problems to be overcome; in addition, they are more accurate than the most experienced cartographer could attempt. A SYMAP V computer mapping programme[3] was used in this case, one which requires no more information than,

[1] J. H. F. Brabney, *The comprehensive gazetteer of England and Wales* (Edinburgh and Dublin 1911) gives, **V**, 37, some 690 ecclesiastical parishes for Norfolk (678 places are recorded in the Lay Subsidies of 1524–5) and for Suffolk, **VI**, 125, some 510 ecclesiastical parishes (505 places are recorded in the Lay Subsidies of 1524–5)

[2] Patten, Urban structure of East Anglia *op. cit.* 12–71

[3] See, e.g. K. E. Rosing, Computer graphics (unpubl. Ph.D. thesis, Univ. of London 1970) 39–58; see also K. E. Rosing and P. A. Wood, *Character of a conurbation. A computer atlas of Birmingham and the Black Country* (1971)

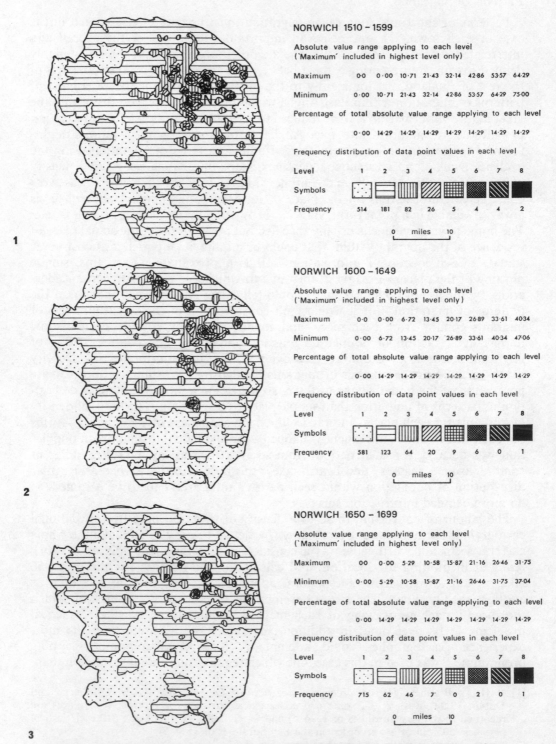

Figure 1. Migrant apprentices to Norwich, 1510–1599. *Figure 2*. Migrant apprentices to Norwich, 1600–1649. *Figure 3*. Migrant apprentices to Norwich, 1650–1699.

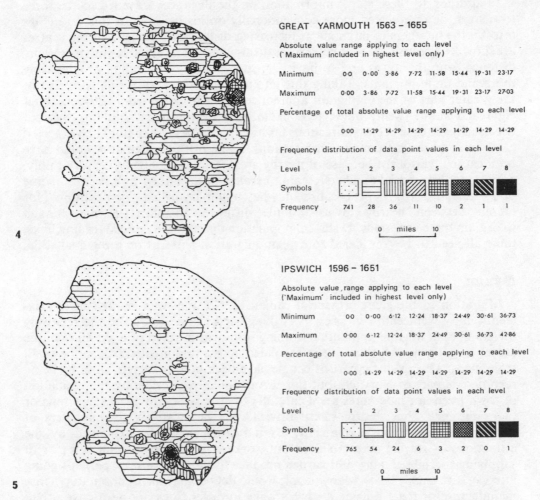

4

GREAT YARMOUTH 1563 – 1655

Absolute value range applying to each level
(`Maximum´ included in highest level only)

Minimum	0·0	0·00	3·86	7·72	11·58	15·44	19·31	23·17
Maximum	0·00	3·86	7·72	11·58	15·44	19·31	23·17	27·03

Percentage of total absolute value range applying to each level

0·00   14·29   14·29   14·29   14·29   14·29   14·29   14·29

Frequency distribution of data point values in each level

Level	1	2	3	4	5	6	7	8
Symbols								
Frequency	741	28	36	11	10	2	1	1

0   miles   10

5

IPSWICH 1596 – 1651

Absolute value range applying to each level
(`Maximum´ included in highest level only)

Minimum	0·0	0·00	6·12	12·24	18·37	24·49	30·61	36·73
Maximum	0·00	6·12	12·24	18·37	24·49	30·61	36·73	42·86

Percentage of total absolute value range applying to each level

0·00   14·29   14·29   14·29   14·29   14·29   14·29   14·29

Frequency distribution of data point values in each level

Level	1	2	3	4	5	6	7	8
Symbols								
Frequency	765	54	24	6	3	2	0	1

0   miles   10

Figure 4. Migrant apprentices to Great Yarmouth, 1563–1655. *Figure 5*. Migrant apprentices to Ipswich, 1596–1651.

variously, an exact location of each place as specified by mapping coordinates, the numbers of migrants in any period and the estimated population in any period. It makes no statistical demands on the data. The ratio of migrants to total population was therefore used in each case to present the average condition for each parish for which it was being calculated; the point for which information was available, in practice the most important settlement of each parish, was taken to be the *centroid*, or average point in each parish for the computation of conventional isopleth maps. This in effect simply represents in a spatial sense the same sort of reasoning whereby an average value is acceptable in statistical computations. Every place in the two counties not sending any recorded apprentices had also to be taken into account in the program, being assigned a nil-value, so that the correct interpolations in constructing the density isopleth maps could be made. From the patterns mapped, which are in effect like three-dimensional surfaces with the "peaks" of highest density standing up like icing on a cake, differences in migration fields can be examined (Figs 1 to 5).

In addition to these maps, information on the distances travelled to the three towns can be represented more conventionally on histograms. In this case (Figs 6 to 8), the numbers of migrants at increasing distances from each of the centres are shown. Of course, the four mile bands themselves increase in area with increasing distance from the towns and so have a greater chance of including progressively more and more migrants. Taking this into account, although for all three towns the greater part of the immigrant apprentices seem to come from between about eight and about twenty miles, it is made clear by the maps that this was not necessarily the case in every direction; far more, or far less, than might be expected came in some cases from certain directions. Some of this irregularity could have been caused, variously, because of nearby areas being very highly, or very thinly, populated; by especial numbers coming because of a marked link between some of them and a town; or because of what might be called "competition" for labour between nearby towns. Simple distance, therefore, is not enough to explain these variations. Distance, population distribution, special trading links, these all need to be considered to explain migration patterns on a regional scale.

Norwich

Migration to the great provincial capital of Norwich was marked in the sixteenth and seventeenth centuries. A striking aspect appeared to be the relatively low number of migrant apprentices coming from within seven or eight miles of the centre (Fig. 6), though these are interpolated across to a great extent in the small scale maps. This might in part of course have been due to villages close by being recorded as part of Norwich, but this seems unlikely, considering the regulation of town freedom; indentures seem carefully to specify nearby places at a mile or two's distance, thus "Eaton-next-Norwich".[1] The relatively low numbers of apprentices moving in permanently from nearby might be explained by the attractions of staying as established out-workers for urban manufacture; or of supplying specialised dairy and garden produce to the city; or even perhaps going into work on a daily basis. Many people would deliberately have chosen to practise manufacture or trade outside a town's walls in order to escape restrictive urban regulations on quality of manufacture or size of enterprise, and to avoid the burdens of contribution to poor relief, and other urban dues, while on the other hand benefitting from nearness to markets and other outlets. Certainly this kind of suburban expansion caused concern to many town governments. On more than one occasion Norwich corporation, or those weavers of influence in it, complained about manufacturing outside the town and asked that it should be brought at least under the same rigorous quality controls their workforce laboured under.[2] This was seen as a problem around London to a much greater extent of course.[3] A further major characteristic of the pattern of migration was that, whilst the density of migrants declined with distance fairly evenly from Norwich in most directions, this was not the case towards Great Yarmouth, just over twenty miles to the east. Far fewer places from the Great Yarmouth direction sent apprentices relative to other areas at an approximately equal distance from Norwich, a fact

[1] Rising and Millican, *op. cit. passim*

[2] e.g. Calendar of State Papers Domestic (hereafter C.S.P.D.) Jas. I, CLVII (1623) 34; M. Campbell, *The English Yeomen under Elizabeth and the early Stuarts* (New Haven 1942) 159

[3] J. R. Kellet, The breakdown of Gild and Corporation control over the handicraft and retail trades in London *Economic History Review* 2nd Ser. X (1958) 381–94

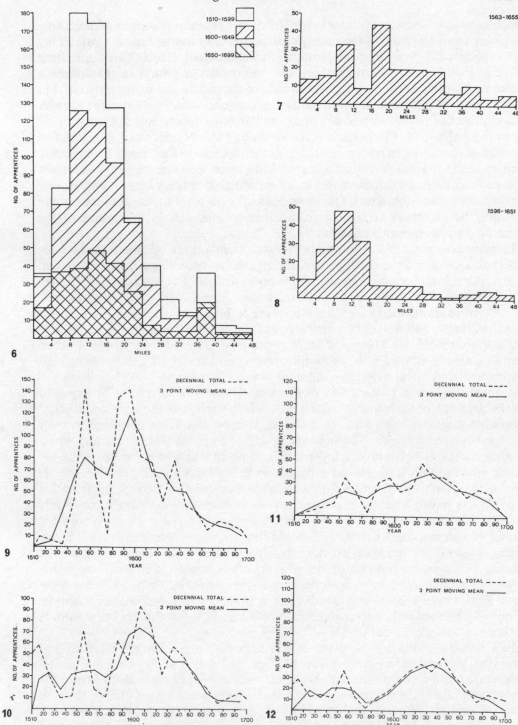

Figure 6. Migrant apprentices to Norwich. *Figure 7.* Migrant apprentices to Great Yarmouth. *Figure 8.* Migrant apprentices to Ipswich. *Figure 9.* Decennial enrolment of migrant apprentices to Norwich, non-textile trades. *Figure 10.* Decennial enrolment of migrant apprentices to Norwich, textile trades. *Figure 11.* Decennial enrolment of indigenous apprentices to Norwich, non-textile trades. *Figure 12.* Decennial enrolment of indigenous apprentices to Norwich, textile trades.

which cannot be explained away by reference to the low population undoubtedly obtaining in some (only) of the poorly drained parishes in this region. Presumably this reflected the very marked local migration field of Great Yarmouth itself (see e.g. Figs 1 to 4); a pattern that was particularly apparent in the sixteenth century. Yarmouth seems, in this context, to have had its own restricted but definite field of influence, from which few apprentices went to Norwich; it never sent apprentices to Norwich in any number relative to its size, nor indeed received many from that city. Further away, the sandy and thinly populated Breckland to the west and south-west sent a small number of apprentices as might be expected, relative to other areas at similar distance. Villages of the extreme west of Norfolk sent almost none at all; otherwise the migration field of Norwich extended over most of the two counties with few exceptions. Yet only about ten apprentices can definitely be identified as coming from Essex to Norwich in the course of the sixteenth and seventeenth centuries.[1]

In contrast, numbers of migrants, greater than otherwise might have been expected, came from the north-east of the city, the textile villages around Worsted in particular, and this can be much more easily explained. For it was to be expected, as connexions of the two were close through their interrelated spinning and textile manufactures. Particularly high densities were to be found also in the rich arable area to the south and west of Norwich around large market towns like Wymondham and Attleborough. Sir Thomas Wilson, writing of England around 1600, noted that this area was very rich, exclaiming over the number of gentry there with money to spend. Such were the conditions about "Windhame" (Wymondham).[2] Of course, migration was marked from most other towns, as might be expected on the grounds of their greater size alone, which increased the simple statistical chance of migrants being sent. In addition, it must also have been due to their greater connectivity with Norwich via markets, fairs and other trading links. Chance meetings between employer and prospective employee, or perhaps his father, must always have played a large role in setting up such actual contacts; knowledge about opportunities, or what the opportunities were thought to be, must always have played an important part in migration. We are only very rarely likely to get much information on exactly why people chose to move; indeed studies of contemporary societies in developing countries demonstrate that many migrants cannot, surprisingly, exactly identify why they chose to move, other than because of vague aspirations of betterment, often based on inadequate knowledge.[3] This may often have been the case in pre-industrial England.[4] But most other East Anglian towns sent numbers of apprentices to Norwich; for example, 27 out of 30 places with market rights in Norfolk in fact did, and about two-thirds of those in Suffolk, 22 out of 32.

Few notable changes took place in this general pattern in the sixteenth and seventeenth centuries, as comparison of Figs 1, 2 and 3 show; the first period which takes into account the relatively small number of apprentices enrolled in the first years of the sixteenth century is thus some thirty years longer than in the case of the second two fifty-year periods. The "negative area" towards Great Yarmouth became less marked in the early seventeenth century, while on the other hand more

[1] Patten, Urban structure of East Anglia *op. cit.* 274–5

[2] Sir T. Wilson, The State of England Anno. Dom. 1600 *Camden Society* **LII** (1936) 12

[3] A. K. Speare, A cost-benefit model of rural to urban migration in Taiwan *Population Studies* **XXV** (1971) 117–30

[4] Clark, *op. cit.*

apprentices seemed then to come from the agricultural areas of north-central Norfolk—the "poor sands" of the day. It is difficult to advance any definite suggestions as to why this should be in these two cases. The apparent increase during the seventeenth century from the crowded, wood pasture, region of central high Suffolk is perhaps more easily attributed to population pressure there[1] in a time when employment opportunities in spinning for the declining Suffolk broadcloth industry must have been lessening.[2] Even the Norwich weavers were turning more and more away from such sources of spun yarn towards those of areas like Westmorland.[3] Overall then the strictly geographical pattern of migration to Norwich from within the confines of East Anglia was marked by general stability over two centuries. Those concerned with rural/urban migration in other countries and other periods have found tremendous continuity in migration patterns also. Hägerstrand, studying migration patterns over a hundred years in Sweden, stressed that there was a striking lack of variation in both distances and directions involved,[4] emphasising ". . . the stability of the rural migration field and the element of continuity in its changes"[5] and that,

> "if our opinion is correct, that the migration field is to be considered as a feedback process of historical continuity, the conclusion must be that it would be in vain to look for a deterministic theory connecting migration and distance, be it measured by km, cost or 'intervening opportunities'. The best we can hope for is a roughly adequate description of particular empirical materials". [6]

Certainly this was the case with the movement of apprentices to towns within East Anglia: for the tendency for relatively fewer migrants than might be expected to come from within eight miles of Norwich to that city was noted also for the later eighteenth century from evidence contained in the more numerous settlement papers. Between 1754 and 1788 for example the largest proportion of that class of migrants came from between ten and twenty-nine miles, strikingly similar to the pattern of apprentice migration in the sixteenth and seventeenth centuries.[7]

A small number of apprentices came from further afield (see Table 1). Many English counties sent at least one or two: some apprentices even came from London to Norwich, in addition to the great number of Norwich folk who must have gone in the opposite direction. This indeed points to Norwich's stature at the time; the number of people who went from London to get their training elsewhere must have been much less than those who streamed to the capital in ever increasing numbers. The only case of any special long range link seeming to develop was with Yorkshire, especially the West Riding, and other north-western counties apparently experiencing population pressure, like Lancashire (mostly from north of the Ribble), Westmorland and Cumberland. Indeed, a part of the migration to Norwich from these counties seems to have developed due to special links with

[1] Thirsk, *op. cit.; idem* Industries in the countryside in F. J. Fisher (Ed.), *The economic and social history of Tudor and Stuart England* (1961)

[2] N. C. P. Tyack, Migration from East Anglia to the New World before 1660 (unpubl. Ph.D. thesis, Univ. of London 1951)

[3] A. E. Bland, P. A. Brown and R. H. Tawney (Eds), *English economic documents* (1914) 484–5; C. Wilson, *England's apprenticeship* (1965) 77–191

[4] T. Hägerstrand, *Innovation and diffusion* (Chicago 1967) 167

[5] T. Hägerstrand, Migration and area: A survey of Swedish migration fields *Lund Studies in Geography* Series B, **13** (1957) 77

[6] *Ibid.* 150

[7] I am indebted to Mr C. Pond of Queen's College, Cambridge, for this and other information on eighteenth-century settlements, *personal communication*

TABLE 1

Counties sending apprentices to Norwich

County	No.	County	No.
Yorkshire	157	Warwickshire	3
Lincolnshire	49	Nottinghamshire	3
Lancashire	31	Middlesex	2
Leicestershire	22	Cornwall	2
Westmorland	20	Worcestershire	2
Cambridgeshire	19	Shropshire	2
(London	15)	Northamptonshire	2
Cumberland	8	Isle of Ely	2
Durham	7	Berkshire	1
Essex	7	Denbigh	1
Cheshire	7	Gloucestershire	1
Kent	6	Oxfordshire	1
Huntingdonshire	5	Buckinghamshire	1
Northumberland	4	Hampshire	1
Derbyshire	4	(Berwick-on-Tweed	1)
Staffordshire	4	(Rotterdam	1)
Hertfordshire	4	(Amsterdam	1)
Bedfordshire	4		

the textile trade. On the other hand, some of the movement into other trades and occupations from Yorkshire may just have been a reflection of that county's size, greater than other English counties; equally neither that county[1] nor Cumberland, Westmorland and Lancashire were particularly prosperous agricultural regions.[2]

The effects on the city of all three sorts of apprentices, those born in Norwich, those coming from within its region or those from other parts of the country, must have varied from year to year.[3] Certainly the enrolments for that city fluctuated quite widely from year to year in some cases (see Figs 9 to 12). Quite a large sector of Norwich's recorded apprentices came from elsewhere, for about a third (1932 : 5835) of all those indentured were immigrants and many must have continued to be mobile after they had served their apprenticeship. Indeed, of all apprentices—indigenous and migrant—as yet only about 17 per cent (995 : 5835) can definitely be said to have remained in the city at the end of their term, these being those who later took up their freedom.[4] Others of course may have stayed on as unrecorded journeymen, but it is certain that many must have moved on in a fashion very rarely recorded then,[5] and only recently much discussed now.[6] And they were equally occupationally mobile. Occupational information is given for about 95 per cent (5550 : 5835) of all apprentices in Norwich; in the case of migrants about 90 per cent of those for whom the necessary information is recorded (1238 : 1932) went to different jobs from those that their fathers were employed in.

[1] Thirsk, *Agrarian history op. cit.*
[2] Some apprentices from these parts certainly seemed to have returned to their home dales with newfound skills: see a letter, *Agricultural History Review* XVI (1968) 84, and Patten, Urban structure of East Anglia *op. cit.* 338–41
[3] Other important long range flows both into and out of the region—such as the Fleming and French immigrations or the East Anglian emigration to the New World—cannot be examined here
[4] Calendered in Millican, *op. cit.*
[5] e.g. R. Gough, *Antiquities and memoirs of the Parish of Myddle . . .* (Shrewsbury 1875)
[6] Clark, *op. cit.*

Certainly the course of temporal trends of enrollment may at least indicate, though without much precision, something of the impact of apprenticeship on the city, as well as of the city on apprenticeship. Throughout the sixteenth and seventeenth centuries a lot of the economic activity of Norwich was concerned with and therefore its prosperity dependent, on the manufacture of textiles.[1] At first largely the traditional worsteds, and then the new draperies. The draw of the textile and allied trades was marked then. Forty-eight per cent of apprentices who came to Norwich during this period, and who cannot be definitely traced as staying in the city, entered the worstead weaving and allied trades (2252 : 4605), and 15 per cent (762 : 4605) tailoring; the proportions of those entering these two trades who stayed more permanently, at least long enough to take up their freedom, was 28 per cent (271 : 945) and 18 per cent (172 : 945). This dominance of textiles is most marked. However, the decennial entry of apprentices in the worsted weaving trades fluctuated widely (see Figs 10 and 12). The peaks and troughs of enrolment represented there, present even when the more marked changes have been smoothed out by the use of a three point moving mean, seem to echo to a large extent various changes in the prosperity of the textile trades themselves, though also must have been much influenced by general population trends and the effects of plagues. This even without taking the impact of the Flemish into account. The textile trades, as Allison demonstrated, certainly were not in very good heart at the beginning of the sixteenth century. On the other hand, the fairly high numbers recorded as entering apprenticeship agreements between 1510 and 1520 probably indicates no more than the effects of reaction to legislation on crafts, and the registration of apprentices, introduced in 1511 after previous laxity in this respect.[2] Enrolments fell off once more in the 1530s and again in the 1560s and 1570s and the 1620s and 1630s. These trends in enrollment seem to follow the cyclical depressions of the English manufacture brought about variously by the changing terms of foreign trade and the interruption of war. The slump in the 1550s and 1560s probably followed the crisis in Antwerp in 1551; a slump well known to older commentators on the economic affairs of the day.[3] Manufacturers concerned with the new draperies suffered badly again particularly at the end of the first quarter of the seventeenth century.[4] And the trends of apprenticeship enrollments thus seemed broadly to reflect trends in the prosperity of the textile manufactures of the city. This is followed whether indigenous, East Anglian or longer distance immigrant apprentices are considered. Numbers fell off towards the end of the seventeenth century, but this may well have simply followed some decline in administrative control over enrolment rather than any decline in the trade itself, not yet setting in.[5]

Enrollment of apprentices to all other trades followed roughly parallel to these movements (see Figs 9 and 11); it is of course impossible to do anything more than

[1] Allison, *op. cit.*; D. C. Coleman, An innovation and its diffusion. The new draperies *Economic History Review* 2nd Ser. **XXII** (1969) 417–29

[2] Allison, *op. cit.*

[3] Blomefield, **III** 382

[4] e.g. Wilson, *op. cit.* 69–79; B. E. Supple, *Commercial crisis and change in England 1600–1642* (Cambridge 1959) *passim*

[5] e.g. M. F. Lloyd-Pritchard, The decline of Norwich *Economic History Review* 2nd Ser. **III** (1950–1) 371–7; P. Corfield, A provincial capital in the late seventeenth century: the case of Norwich in P. Clark and P. Slack (Eds), *Crisis and order in English towns 1500–1700* (1972)

to suggest that the general decline in the economy of the whole city, consequent on poor conditions obtaining in the textile trade from time to time, may help to explain this. These apprentices certainly entered a broad spectrum of trades and services, about 105 in all.[1] It would be naive to propose that these graphs are finely adjusted to a number of economic, demographic, or even simple administrative factors—they instead broadly reflected their influence. Periodic inaccuracies in recording, fluctuations in prosperity, times of population pressure or replacement after plagues, all must be taken into account. It would, for example, be dangerous in the extreme to expect to be able to accurately reflect the demographic history of Norwich or any other town from figures of entry of apprentices or freemen.[2]

Great Yarmouth

Being smaller, Great Yarmouth had a much more restricted migration field than Norwich, but it was a thriving sea-port, exporting, *inter alia*, some Norwich cloth as well as being a base for the herring fleet and scene of the great Herring Fairs.[3] It thus particularly attracted immigrants entering into maritime and mercantile trades. One hundred and twenty-one villages and towns in Norfolk and Suffolk sent migrants to Great Yarmouth at some time or another. As might be expected, a majority of these apprentices came from near-by. The most marked characteristic of its East Anglian migration field was that (see Fig. 4) there was a notable density of migrant apprentices coming from ten or twelve miles around the town, which then fell off sharply westwards as Norwich's influence presumably became stronger; this was what might be called the seaport's own local "apprentice-shed", the area of local movement to the nearest town centre which was nothing out of the ordinary in pre-industrial England, which most English towns must have experienced, for which every day "mobility" is perhaps a better term than migration.[4] Almost all of the rest came from within central and eastern Norfolk and Suffolk; the town's "pull" or attractiveness to migrants extended only about half way across East Anglia compared to Norwich which attracted people from all over the region. In contrast to Norwich migration was much more marked from coastal parishes and towns, and relatively much less from inland market and other towns. Only eight out of thirty market towns in Norfolk and seven out of thirty-two from Suffolk sent apprentices to Great Yarmouth, and these were all to the east of the region, near the port itself. Thus, although even Norwich itself, together with some other smaller towns like North Walsham and Holt to the north-west and Beccles, Bungay, and Diss to the south-west, of Great Yarmouth, sent a number of apprentices, the burden from inland came from nearby rural parishes particularly to the north-west. Some of these were in the marshy areas of the broads, parishes like Bastwick and Martham; others were in a belt around Worsted and Coltishall which were engaged in textile manufacture, and also

[1] Patten, Urban structure of East Anglia *op. cit.* 334–6, 342–5
[2] As Bartlett seems to suggest for York, see J. N. Bartlett, The expansion and decline of York in the later Middle Ages *Economic History Review* 2nd Ser. **XII** (1959) 17–33; but see also R. B. Dobson, Admissions to the Freedom of the city of York in the later Middle Ages *Economic History Review* 2nd Ser. **XXVI** (1973) 1–22
[3] See e.g. D. Defoe, *A tour through the whole island of Great Britain*, I (1927) 66–7; N. J. Williams, The maritime trade of the East Anglian ports, 1550–90 (Unpubl. D.Phil. thesis, Univ. of Oxford 1952) 72 *et seq.*
[4] Patten, Rural–urban migration *op. cit.* 23–5

notably sent apprentices to Norwich. These areas were quite densely populated and in times of slump such areas of rural textile and spinning outwork may have been hard-hit. Very few apprentices came from the thinly peopled area of the Suffolk Sandlings, to the south of the town.

It is the coastal pattern of migration which is most marked, however. Apprentices travelled to Yarmouth from many of the coastal areas of Norfolk and Suffolk, from as far as Kings Lynn around the coast to Ipswich. That this should be so is not surprising considering the coasting trade in this busy and prosperous region, and much movement must thus be accounted for. Most notable for instance are high densities from the north and north-eastern fishing and coastal trading ports of Cley, Sheringham and particularly Cromer, as well as Lowestoft to the south. Some movement may have been due to the extreme poverty of coastal parishes, encouraging migration. Reports in the course of the sixteenth and seventeenth centuries repeatedly emphasised their poverty. The area was one of by-employment in slack periods of the farming and fishing year, for the knitting of stockings in particular.[1] In 1568 for example the "poor inhabitants" of the coasts of Norfolk in parishes like Siderstrand, Overstrand, Trimingham and Repps, which sent a number of apprentices to Great Yarmouth, petitioned the Queen for renewal of the concession which allowed them to export fish free of duty.[2] Nearly seventy years later there were complaints to the farmers of Customs against the merchant adventurers for refusing to trade in the stockings of the area because of their low quality.[3] And it was certainly the sea connexion which also led to the one marked longer distance stream of migrant apprentices going to Great Yarmouth (see Table 2) as in the case of Norwich. These again came from the north, but in this case from the coastal parts of Yorkshire, Durham and Northumberland. The evident connexion between Yarmouth and these areas via the coastal coal and associated carrying trades would presumably have led to the setting up of this link. Others came from as far around the coast in the opposite direction as Dorset. These last represent movements the reasons for which cannot even be hinted at in a macro-scale study such as this, without detailed examination of the histories of individual migrants, the evidence for which may be often missing.

The number of apprentices enrolled at Great Yarmouth in the years 1563–1669, some 487 in all, was low at the beginning and end of the period, about 20 a decade or so, but reached a peak in the 1610s, 1620s and 1630s. It is difficult to suggest any

TABLE 2

Counties sending apprentices to Great Yarmouth

County	No.	County	No.
Yorkshire	21	Cheshire	2
Northumberland	15	Essex	1
Durham	11	Middlesex	1
Lincolnshire	6	Nottinghamshire	1
Dorset	6	Northamptonshire	1
Kent	4	Herefordshire	1
Sussex	3	Scotland	1
Westmorland	2	(London	2)

[1] Thirsk, *Agrarian history op. cit.* 46
[2] *C.S.P.D.* **XLVIII** (1568) 83
[3] *C.S.P.D.* **CCLXXXVI** (1635) 37

particular reason for this other than administrative. Occupational mobility was high, of immigrants some 90 per cent (194 : 207) entered jobs different from their fathers. Although they entered a wide range of trades, 53 in all, the dominance of the sea trades is apparent. The occupations entered by most, 464, are known. Thirty per cent (143 : 464) became mariners, 17 per cent apprenticed to merchants (81 : 464) and 11 per   cent (54 : 464) to shipbuilders and services, ranging from shipwrights to anchor-smiths and compass makers. Twenty-five were also apprenticed to the cooper's trade. The dominance of these sea trades in the overall occupational structure of the town was marked, around 60 per cent. The allied activities of seafaring, trading and shipbuilding played a part in Yarmouth's economy as marked as that played by the worsted and textile trades in Norwich, which accounted for some 55 per cent of all trades entered there. By comparison with Norwich, however, over the whole period only two apprentices in Great Yarmouth were indentured to weavers, further confirmation of the stranglehold Norwich had on the urban manufacture of worsteds, for textiles produced in Great Yarmouth or Kings Lynn had to be sent to that city for finishing.[1]

The influence of the sea seems to have been all penetrating, and many of the work people of Great Yarmouth ostensibly engaged in other trades, in fact may have spent some of their time involved in activities associated with it.[2] For example, one apprentice put to a cooper in Great Yarmouth was to be sent on one sea voyage a year; another was apprenticed to a tailor, but if he proved "unfit or unwilling" he was to be put to sea.[3] The trading activities of the port were highly organised, an apprentice from Mundham in Suffolk, for example, being indentured to a merchant of Great Yarmouth in 1612 "to keep books and accounts, after the manner of merchandise called debtor and creditor";[4] the links with Holland and the Low Countries in the "North Sea community", were also marked. Apprentices were to "learn the Dutch and French language" by being sent to reside in Holland for a year,[5] and (presumably) to conduct business for their masters abroad. Apparently much business in the Low Countries was conducted on behalf of the English merchants by factors or apprentices.[6] This certainly appears to have been the case, for example, with the young man apprenticed to a hosier in 1627, who was to be "maintained half the year in Holland".[7]

Ipswich

The Suffolk port of Ipswich, "capital" also of the eastern division of that county, had on this evidence at least a restricted migration field compared even to Great Yarmouth, which was not much larger than it (Figs 4 and 5). Seventy-two of the ninety places in East Anglia which sent migrant apprentices to Ipswich were in Suffolk, and these mostly in the eastern part of that county. A notable density occurred around the port itself, falling off in intensity in most directions to the eastern and coastal parts of the county, while numbers came from the market towns to the north, like Stowmarket and Needham Market. Any migration from

[1] Allison, pt 1, *op. cit.* 74
[2] J. Patten, Freemen and apprentices *Local Historian* **9** (1971) 232
[3] *N.N.R.O.* C19/6, f.35
[4] *N.N.R.O.* C4/305, m.25
[5] *N.N.R.O.* C19/5, f.226
[6] Ramsay, *op. cit.* 18–19
[7] *N.N.R.O.* C19/6, f.53

beyond the Norfolk/Suffolk border seems also to have come from market towns like Wymondham or East Dereham in the central and southern parts of Norfolk. Twelve out of thirty-one market towns in Suffolk sent apprentices to Ipswich but only seven out of thirty from Norfolk. The area of notable population density in the cloth-weaving regions of the Stour Valley to the North-west of Ipswich also sent a number, although few came from Bury St Edmunds and its immediate area. That town, for which few sources on migration survive as far as is known, presumably had its own, and equally marked, local migration field. Ipswich's migration field was very local[1] and presumably it was similar in this respect to other east coast ports nearer London; Colchester[2] in the eighteenth century seemed to get most of the migrants from under fifteen miles, for example, as settlement papers reveal and the picture is very similar for Maldon.[3] In comparison to Great Yarmouth the number from, for example, East Anglian coastal parishes was also much lower being restricted to the Kings Lynn area and the Suffolk coast between Aldburgh and Lowestoft. None came from Great Yarmouth, or the Norfolk coast in between, and surprisingly few came from nearby Essex, most of these being from Colchester and Maldon.

Once more some apprentices came from a long distance, a number from the North East coast, particularly Northumberland (see Table 3). The enrolment of apprentices reached peaks in the 1600s and 1630s, during the short period of

TABLE 3

Counties sending apprentices to Ipswich

County	No.	County	No.
Essex	17	Sussex	2
Northumberland	11	Wiltshire	2
Yorkshire	5	Bedfordshire	1
Cambridgeshire	3	Devon	1
Durham	2	Rutland	1
Kent	2	Shropshire	1
Leicestershire	2	Westmorland	1

1596–1651 for which indentures survive, but as is the case with the similar fluctuations for Great Yarmouth, no particular weight can be given to these. But, like Great Yarmouth, the sea dominated those occupations entered, about twenty-five types in all. Of the 319 apprentices for whom occupational information is recorded 62 per cent (199) became mariners and 12 per cent (40) entered the shipbuilding trades, yet only a bare 1 per cent (4) were apprenticed to those called "merchants". Whether this is a reflection of the town's trading position in the earlier seventeenth century, already "eaten-up" by London, or simply a reflection of local usage, "mariner" being interchangeable with "merchant", it is difficult to discern. Certainly the port of Ipswich appears to have been in general depression during the seventeenth century.[4] Many people called "mariners" may have been those concerned largely with the simple carrying of small broken lots of different sizes to

[1] Dr Reed suggests a radius of about fifteen miles in the seventeenth century, see M. Reed, Ipswich in the seventeenth century (Unpubl. Ph.D. thesis, Univ. of Leicester 1973) 96
[2] ex Mr C. Pond
[3] W. J. Petchey, The Borough of Maldon, Essex, 1500–1688 (unpubl. Ph.D. thesis, Univ. of Leicester 1972) 77–114
[4] A. S. E. Jones, The port of Ipswich *Suffolk Review* 3 (1968) 247–9

different ports and creeks in the coastal trade. How much of the coal trade was in Ipswich's hands by the seventeenth century is not known. Both cloth and dairy products were exported through the port.[1] Otherwise new apprentices entered a variety of urban trades and services,[2] and occupational mobility was high, over 90 per cent (154 : 164) of migrants going into new jobs. It would be interesting to compare Ipswich, as well as Norwich. and Great Yarmouth, with other smaller towns in East Anglia with respect to migration. As many questions are posed by an examination of apprentice indentures as are answered, particularly the fascinating problem of the actual mechanism by which a migratory movement set off. Presumably it was personal contact brought about by trade which induced the son of one Yorkshire Badger to be apprenticed to an Ipswich Oatmeal maker in 1601.

Conclusion

The discussion of the migration patterns to these three East Anglian towns has been essentially descriptive. The very brief description of the enrolment and trades of apprentices is based on traditional and simple methods of counting and cross tabulating. which reveal equally simple facts about urban trade structures most briefly summarised here, although evidence of extreme occupational mobility is revealing. The description of migration patterns, however, is based on the less traditional but in fact equally simple method of computer mapping. As such, both approaches obviously suggest more questions than are answered, and leave much open to speculation. For example, there were many immigrants to Norwich from the cloth-weaving villages to its north-east. Many of these went into textile trades. But there is no more evidence than this to suggest there was therefore a *definite* link between the two, brought about by the textile manufacture. The nut of migration is not so easily cracked. It is also difficult to compare local patterns in other regions in this way as yet. But it is certainly the case that the East Anglian picture is likely to be repeated in other regions. On a regional scale the larger Norwich, as might be expected, attracted more apprentices over a wider area, both within the region and in the rest of England, than the smaller Great Yarmouth and Ipswich, even though these had their long range contacts. On a national scale, in comparison, London would have attracted the greatest number of migrants of course, but it would be wrong to discount such movement to very much smaller places.[3] Certainly movement to places the size of all three East Anglian towns was far from rare. It was common enough to Bristol, the great provincial centre of the west at the time, to which besides marked numbers of local migrants came many from the north-west of England, especially Westmorland.[4] It was common enough to a smaller port like Southampton,[5] which apparently had a much more restricted migration field, like Ipswich's with some marked local coastal connexions. Inland towns of a similar size to Great Yarmouth

[1] Stephens, *op. cit.*; Tyack, *op. cit.*; Thirsk, *op. cit.*
[2] Patten, Urban structure of East Anglia *op. cit.* 357–8
[3] As Mr Spufford seems to do, *op. cit.* 44 and 48
[4] D. Hollis (Ed.), Calender of the Bristol apprentice book, 1532–1565 (Pt 1, 1535–42) *Bristol Record Society* **XIV** (1948)
[5] A. L. Merson (Ed.), A calender of Southampton apprenticeship registers, 1609–1740 *Southampton Record Series* **12** (1968)

and Ipswich like York[1] or the smaller Worcester and Leicester[2] experienced similar local migration patterns, and some longer range links; a whole interrelated network existed to some tiny towns in Kent.[3] London's pull covered the whole country; below it, provincial cities, county towns and market towns probably had their own hierarchy of migration fields decreasing in size as the size of the towns and their economic importance also decreased, although there were exceptions; Oxford, for example, with its nationally famous university, seemed to attract immigrants from a distance disproportionately further than its size would suggest in the sixteenth century, numbers of them from the northern and western parts of England.[4] Migration to them was not necessarily direct and could have involved intermediate stages between, for example, a remote north-western Norfolk marshland parish and the city of Norwich, taking in smaller towns en route. No direct evidence exists for this in apprentice indentures, it would have probably involved journeymen and adults rather more than apprentices bound for their first job; deposition books give evidence of this in plenty.[5] But, besides the aimless and hopeless movements of the destitute and vagrant, migration of a more permanent kind, as evinced by the evidence of apprentice registers, seems generally to have been densest from the immediate area of a town, from other smaller towns in the region and from areas with which they had a special link, such as similar manufacturing interests; it could also be marked from areas of high population and low agricultural or manufacturing opportunities, or those with which there was a link in landownership. Apprentices were of course only one group, a fluctuating one at that, amongst overall labour migration but an examination of their migration to these three East Anglian towns suggests much of the pattern and dynamics of migration of pre-industrial England.[6]

School of Geography, Oxford

[1] D. M. Palliser, Some aspects of the social and economic history of York in the sixteenth century (unpubl. D.Phil. thesis, Univ. of Oxford 1968) 66–76, and map in end pocket

[2] A. D. Dyer, The city of Worcester in the sixteenth century (Unpubl. Ph.D. thesis, Univ. of Birmingham 1966) 304–10, 490; *idem. The city of Worcester in the sixteenth century* (Leicester 1973) 169, 180–96; R. A. Jenkins and C. T. Smith, Social and administrative history, 1660–1835, pp. 153–200 of *Victoria County History of Leicester* IV esp. 193–4

[3] Clark, *op. cit.*

[4] C. I. Hammer, The mobility of skilled labour to Oxford *personal communication to author*

[5] e.g. J. Cornwall, Evidence of population mobility in the seventeenth century *Bulletin Institute Historical Research* XL (1967) 143–52; Clark, *op. cit.*

[6] I am most grateful to Dr J. Thirsk and Dr P. Slack for their kindness in reading early drafts of this paper. Any deficiencies of fact or interpretation remain the responsibility of the author of course

Residential patterns in pre-industrial cities: some case studies from seventeenth-century Britain

JOHN LANGTON

Lecturer in Geography, University of Liverpool

ABSTRACT. The models of pre-nineteenth-century cities formulated by Sjoberg and Vance are compared. The two writers postulated different kinds of social ecology because they based their deductions about spatial patterns upon different social structures, and this difference, in turn, resulted from their use of different economic variables as sociological determinants. An analysis of the hearth tax returns for three British cities, and of data produced by linking these returns with the admissions lists of freemen in Newcastle, shows that neither of their models replicates what happened in these cities. In Newcastle, a merchant oligarchy existed, dominating a particular residential-cum-economic area, and the gild organization of crafts was reflected in the spatial zoning of occupational groups. Although some parts of Newcastle were occupationally mixed, this probably did not represent the emergence of 'class zoning'.

IN the literature of urban geography, little space is devoted to pre-nineteenth-century cities. When the subject is discussed it is usually treated with a bland lack of controversy: textbooks, and monographs and papers on historical and modern cities are alike in their exclusive and uncritical presentation of Sjoberg's generalizations about what he termed the 'pre-industrial city'.[1] The reasons for this situation are not, of course, hard to find. Until recently, this was the only set of generalizations available, and the continents in which much of the recent work in urban social geography has been done have no great fund of pre-nineteenth-century urban experience. The current preoccupation of urban social geographers with techniques of analysis which require large arrays of data, and with theories which link urbanism with industrialization or modernization, and thus define the pre-nineteenth-century city out of consideration, also contribute to this end. Moreover, the ease with which the processes which destroyed the 'pre-industrial city' can be thought of as synonymous with those which created the modern city has contributed to the development of the concept of 'ecological transition', and this fusion seems only to have bolstered the confidence of urban geographers in Sjoberg's monolithic ideas about the nature of cities before the transition occurred.[2] The result is a general agreement that urban society was segregated by wealth or status, with the rich and powerful living near to the centre and the poor and powerless on the periphery of cities before industrialization, or modernization. Afterwards, class-based segregation became manifest, and the social geography of cities, in terms of these two gross categories, was reversed.

It is time to question forcefully the basis of this certitude about the early stage of this sequence. Such questioning has been begun by Vance,[3] who recently introduced a welcome note of controversy into the geographical literature. It can be taken a stage further by examining the differences between the conclusions of Sjoberg and Vance, and the reasons for their differences. This should help to bring more sharply into focus the fact that there is not, yet, any set of acceptable generalizations about the social geography of pre-nineteenth-century cities. An attempt to relate the assumptions and conclusions of Sjoberg and Vance to a reasonably sound body of empirical evidence is also necessary, not only because of their differences, but also because each of them employed a methodology in which the formulation and verification of hypotheses were inextricably mixed, so that neither can really be said to have tested his own conclusions.

Such a compound exercise should at least indicate that attempts to generalize and explain the complexity of the social geographies of pre-nineteenth-century cities are enmeshed in some fundamental difficulties: it might too contribute, across the bridge of the ecological transition, something which is relevant to the major preoccupations of contemporary urban geographers.

SJOBERG'S IDEAS

The pre-industrial city

Sjoberg postulated that social order ultimately flowed from technology. He dichotomized the sweep of technical progress into pre-industrial and industrial periods, the change occurring when inanimate sources of energy were used to power tools.[4] Before this, society was 'feudal', comprising an élite, which was small, and much larger lower-class and outcast groups.[5] Functionally, the feudal city was dominated by religious, political, administrative and social (i.e. educational, ceremonial and entertainment) activities and the élite achieved its dominance by controlling these functions.[6] Economic activities were, of course, present, but they were of much lower status, and even wealthy merchants were excluded from the élite because a 'preoccupation with money-making and other mundane pursuits ran counter to the religious-philosophical value system of the dominant group',[7] whose authority was entrenched in traditional and absolute criteria which were often founded upon religious codes of practice and doctrine.

It was the spatial expression of this marked social cleavage between the élite and the remainder of society which produced the geographical hallmark of the pre-industrial city—its wealthy and exclusive central core. This was surrounded by a much larger area over which status diminished outwards, the poor living beneath and beyond the walls.[8]

The élite group was not attracted to the centre of the city because it was an economic focus, a place of business and exchange. Such functions may have been performed in the centre, but they were subservient to the administrative, religious, political, ceremonial and educational activities which were also carried on there, and it was to these non-materialistic attractions that the élite responded in its residential choice. This response produced an exclusive, high-status core. Tight segregation was further encouraged by primitive transport technology, bad road surfaces, a street system designed more for house access than intra-city travel, the physical repulsiveness of the garbage-strewn, poorly built and crowded non-central area, and the tightly knit structure of élite society, which was often reinforced by bonds of kinship and intermarriage. 'The highly valued residence, then, [was] where full advantage [could] be taken of the city's strategic facilities; in turn, these latter [had] come to be tightly bunched for the convenience of the élite'.[9]

Over the remainder of the city there were 'certain minor differences according to ethnic, occupational and family ties'.[10] Foreign and minority religious groups were alienated from feudal society and lived in spatially segregated quarters. Occupational zoning was the product of poor transport facilities, coupled with the external economies to be derived from spatial association by handicraftsmen-retailers, and reinforced by social organizations such as gilds, which fostered both the spatial propinquity and the group cohesion of members.[11] The lowest status groups of all lived on the outskirts of the city 'through the efforts of the élite to minimize contact with them'.[12] This group included those employed in malodorous jobs, such as tanners and butchers, as well as those who formed what Engels called the 'surplus army' of urban labour, 'which [kept] body and soul together by begging, stealing, street sweeping, collecting manure, pushing hand-carts, driving donkeys, peddling or performing occasional small jobs'.[13] As Jones [14] has vividly demonstrated, it was intermittency of work which produced a large army of this type, and in Sjoberg's city, where the major functions were subject to seasonal cycles, and where the élite might follow these cycles in periodic urban residence, this army would be a large one. Indeed, Sjoberg considered that the possibility of adding part-time agricultural earnings to the fluctuating income derived from urban occupations was a supplementary factor in the location of the houses of the poor in the outer areas of the city.[15]

The pre-capitalist city

Vance based his social order not on the technology used in production, but on the means of organizing production. Because the emergence of capitalism caused this to change before the Industrial Revolution, so did the prevailing social order change, and so, too, did the residential patterns which were based upon it. Capitalism brought with it a fundamental alteration in attitudes to land holding: in capitalist society 'men no longer held, they owned' land, and this change in attitude ushered in the emergence of the capitalist city at 'some time in the sixteenth century'.[16]

Vance's pre-capitalist society was, like that of the pre-industrial city, characterized by its recognition of immutable proportion and order, based on traditional, absolute and non-material criteria. And, in medieval times, 'city air made men free'. These two aspects of medieval urban life were interlaced in the evaluation of urban land plots according to the social intercourse it was possible to derive from a residence upon them, rather than in terms of the monetary rental income that they might produce. This attitude to urban land, the recognition of the need to regulate behaviour to achieve immutable order, and the needs of an urban economic base of craft production for local or regional hinterlands became embodied in, and exemplified by, the gilds. The gild was the archetypal social institution and structure of the pre-capitalist urban economy. City freedom, necessary before a craft could be practised, the holding of burgages, participation in city government and gild membership were inextricably entwined: the last was at once the avenue of access to, and the reason for, the possession of city land and the freedom it conferred.

Gild membership merely required, besides the profession of Christianity, the possession of the requisite skills and the right to burgage property, and as this often existed in minute parcels its ownership was not limited to the rich. The membership of any gild in a city provided the same opportunities, rights, duties and privileges. The result of this free access to institutions, which conferred equal rights and opportunities, was 'a society governing itself and establishing standards on what come rather close to our current notion of "one-man-one-vote" . . . there is little question that medieval urban life was popular rather than patrician. So long as a man was an artisan of accomplishment, a responsible citizen, and a defender of the commonwealth and faith, he might enjoy true participation in civil control'.[17] Gilds were, then, instruments of access to participation in civic life and exemplars of the completely enmeshed relationships between economic and social organization and functioning in the pre-capitalist city. Not surprisingly, 'gild associations were among the most powerful forces shaping the morphology of the medieval town'.[18]

Indeed, the social geography of the pre-capitalist city was dominated by the gild system: because he based his model of social structure on economic organization the gild became, for Vance, the pre-eminent ecological agency in the city, whereas for Sjoberg it was only a minor contributor to the secondary details of social geographical patterns. Because 'a man used rather than possessed land, his valuation of it was a functional rather than a capitalist one. In such a context, locations were not relative, but absolute; to exist within a gild area was necessary for the proper practice of a trade and for the receipt of the social benificence of the organization. In a true sense the value of land in the Middle Ages was the value of social association', and the places of residence and occupation, coextensive in handicraft technology, were located close to those of other members of the same gild.[19]

The distribution of these occupational zones had no rationale in terms of intra-urban locational economics. They were located by 'occupational accident rather than by rent-paying ability'.[20] Within them, because house, workshop, shop and store rooms were situated in the same building, because burgage plots were narrow, the better to spread precious street frontage, and because the master, his family, journeymen, apprentices and servants lived under the same roof, 'the residential structure of the medieval town was chiefly vertical', with the shops on the ground floor, the master's family quarters on the floor above, and, higher still, the rooms of the journeymen, apprentices and servants and the store rooms.[21] The result was occupational zoning and social class mixing; the city was 'many centred' in distinct craft quarters, each with its own shops, workplaces and full social spectrum.[22] 'Class organization of city space was not so obvious as it is in urban areas today'.[23]

These social geographical patterns can all be deduced from the existence of a social order in which status was not based on wealth; where the means of production were owned by, and the selling was done by, the producers; and where the producers were organized into institutions which regulated trade and through which the city was governed, with no social distinctions within and between the gilds, in which each apprentice and journeyman had the opportunity of becoming a master and all masters, of whatever gild, were freemen, participating equally in the civic control of 'a popular rather than patrician society'.[24] But Vance introduced an incompatible element into this urban society in a few statements scattered through his argument. He stated that 'for the most part . . . towns were crowned . . . by some form of patriciate created from the leading citizens of the place itself'.[25] This patriciate was recruited, unlike that of the pre-industrial city, from the merchant gild, and the members of this gild occupied the city centre for economic reasons: 'admittedly, the borders of the square might hold higher business potential than the back streets . . . for the gild merchant'.[26] Thus a small group, which was pre-eminent in status and wealth, lived in the centre of the city, and responded to economic criteria in the choice of its place of residence, expressing its preference, presumably, by bidding high rents for central locations. This situation is completely unconformable with the basic model of a 'one-man-one-vote' pre-capitalist city where there were no differences in wealth and status between gilds and where occupational zones were not based on economic criteria. This 'merchant city' really represents the germ of a completely different model of social order and economic geography from that of the pre-capitalist city.

The treatment of the poor is even more cursory than the treatment of the merchants. They have little place in the pre-capitalist city of craft gildsmen. Only one reference is made to them: 'outside [the ordered existence of the medieval town] lurked the proletariat subject to riot and contention'.[27] Engels's 'reserve army' must, of course, exist in any city. But it can be surmised that it would be larger in a city dominated by a merchant patriciate than in an egalitarian gild city. Where a group which was economically and socially dominant based its power on wealth, and where conspicuous consumption would thus be *de rigueur*, and where seasonal and extreme climatic factors would profoundly affect the business activity of the patriciate and the employment it provided—where, that is, menial and intermittent occupations were relatively common—conditions were more propitious for the emergence of a large 'reserve army' than in a craft gild city serving a local hinterland. Whereas such a social stratum formed an integral part of Sjoberg's pre-industrial urban social structure, and that of the 'merchant city', it falls, as Vance admits, outside the social order from which his main deductions about the social geography of the pre-capitalist city are made. As to how numerous they were, or where they lived within the city, in the vertically zoned areas or elsewhere, his basic model makes no suggestions since the poor, like the merchants, are mentioned only in *ad hoc* references.

The capitalist city

The demise of the pre-capitalist city occurred in the sixteenth century. Thenceforth, men owned rather than held property. Ownership became divorced from use, and 'a class of capitalists arose that had little to do directly with the production and trading activities of the town, or with the conduct of its government'.[28] The new dominant group was not, then, the equivalent or lineal successor of the patriciate of the pre-capitalist merchant city, and its existence contrasted even more markedly, of course, with the social order on which the pure form of pre-capitalist city was based.

As the accumulation of capital by individuals became not only morally acceptable, but the criterion of social status and power, so did competition for urban land plots grow, and their evaluation was now in terms of their yield as capital. These factors, in turn, entailed the occupation of land plots by that use which could yield the highest rent. The gilds, embodiments of protectionism, communalism and permanent structural order, were anachronistic to the new social ethos, and they declined. 'Once the basis upon which medieval social life was anchored had been modified, it was totally abandoned',[29] and with it went any influence which tended towards the evaluation of urban land plots in terms of their social ascription. Housing and workplaces became separate as the cement of craft organization dissolved because each use had different rent-paying propensities on particular plots. Within the residential districts, zoned by occupation whilst craft organization and its social accoutrements prevailed, class zoning became newly apparent, with rent-paying ability forming the index and arbiter of class ascription. Because house size was positively linked with price and price with builders' profits, the provision of housing through the market occasioned a shortage of cheap newly built small houses. At the same time, fashions were changing and these changes were reflected in new house styles. With the outward incremental growth of the built-up area, the currently most fashionable houses were inevitably concentrated on the periphery of the city. As a result, the wealthy moved out and the poor occupied the old-central area housing stock that they vacated. Thus evolved a social geographical pattern which was radically different from Vance's gild city of socially mixed occupational zones, and the inverse of his merchant city and Sjoberg's pre-industrial city: wealth was concentrated on the periphery, poverty in the centre.

CHANGE AND THE CITY

The statements of both Sjoberg and Vance are basically 'ideal type' models in which a sequence of economic development is predicated as the determinant of social structure and the nature of social change. Sets of archetypal social functional relationships are ascribed to stages in the sequence, and these entail certain kinds of residential distribution patterns, which change as the economic structure and attitudes of society change. Their models differ fundamentally simply because they abstracted different aspects from the complex matrix of economic relationships to act as the prime movers of their causal sequences, and this, in turn, led them to focus attention upon different aspects of the sociology of the pre-nineteenth-century urban world. After his definition of technology as the primal economic variable, Sjoberg could recognize only one major economic discontinuity of sufficient magnitude to engender fundamental social change, and that social discontinuity which seemed most commensurate in scale and correlative in time was the destruction of feudalism and the emergence of industrial-urban society. The stability and nature of the pre-industrial city is, then, analytically dependent upon the economic categorization used in the model.

But the way that production was organized did change before the Industrial Revolution, so that, given the economic variable upon which it was based, Vance's pre-nineteenth-century city must change before the late eighteenth century. However, the fact that this aspect of economic life was continuously, if gradually, changing in the towns of Western Europe from late medieval times made the calibration of stages in the sequence difficult. The pre-capitalist city presented relatively few problems in this respect because a social institution which was clearly linked with economic production and which had clearly recognizable geographical ramifications could be recognized in the gild. But the stage produced by the emergence of capitalism is much more difficult to handle. Capitalist organization and attitudes cannot be encapsulated in an archetypal social structure. Their impact on urban social geography is, as a result, less amenable to rigorous codification than either pre-industrial technology, with its correlatives of a rigid social dichotomy and immutable and absolute social values, or pre-capitalist production, with its gilds. Because there is no possibility of hypothesizing an archetypal social order from which to make ecological deductions, the links between the economic variable and residential patterns are more difficult to distinguish, and Vance was, in fact, forced to treat the capitalist city in terms of reflections upon how the geographical consequences of the development and general espousal of this new morality could be observed in a rather biased sample of passages from George's description of seventeenth-century London.[30]

None the less, although the incorporation of changes in the mode of production involved analytical difficulties, it does seem to accord with other influential theories on the links between economic activity and the structure and mores of society.[31] Moreover, the social changes of Vance's capitalist period represent what sociologists have defined as a fundamental element of social modernization, the transition from *Gemeinschaft* to *Gesellschaft*,[32] and he is not alone in recognizing such changes in European urban society of this period. According to Wrigley, many of those characteristics ascribed to the influence of industrialization by Sjoberg were already becoming evident well before the Industrial Revolution, and he proposes a distinction between modernization and industrialization, in social terms, as a result.[33] But whether these social changes had any recognizable impact on urban residential patterns, or whether they affected, in any really marked way, those sociological parameters which specifically influence residential choice, are questions which sociologists and historians had never addressed before Vance's rather idiosyncratic interpretation of a discursive account of seventeenth-century London.[34]

It is quite clear, then, that there is considerable room for fundamental disagreement about the nature of the pre-nineteenth-century city, in Western Europe at least: a firm foundation does not exist from which to launch generalizations about an ecological transition. It is equally clear that these disagreements cannot be completely resolved by 'testing' the two models against empirical evidence. They are 'ideal types' in the sense given to the term by Weber, and such simplifications are meant to convey the quintessential characteristics of a theoretically polar situation, not to replicate reality. Nevertheless, it is possible to probe empirically the questions that the differences raise. These are not simply about where the rich and poor members of society lived and whether there was a change in the spatial distribution of wealth and poverty before the nineteenth century. The more fundamental questions with which both models seek to grapple concern the structure of urban society, the links between this structure and the economic base of cities, and the way that it was reflected in patterns of residential choice. A search for empirical answers to these questions will not only help to evaluate the models of Sjoberg and Vance as representations and explanations of pre-nineteenth-century patterns of urban social geography but also, and perhaps more important, it will provide some soundly based factual information to supplement knowledge which has to date been mainly based upon deduction about why people chose particular kinds of neighbours in pre-nineteenth-century cities.

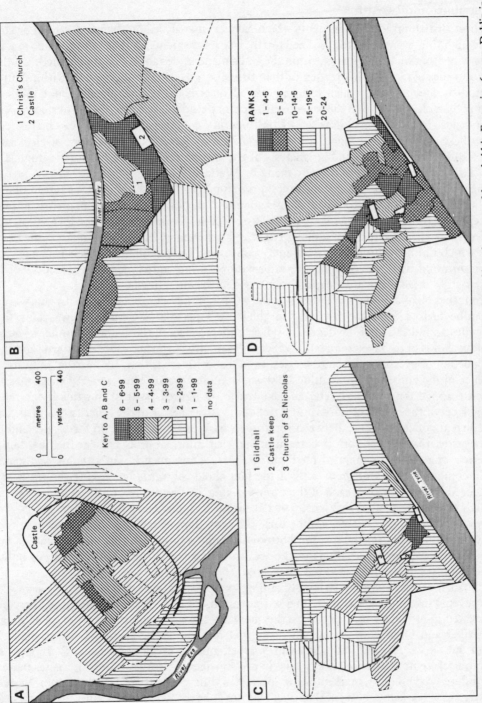

FIGURE 1. The distribution of wealth in some seventeenth-century British cities. A-C: average numbers of hearths per taxed household in Exeter in 1671-72, Dublin in 1671, and Newcastle in 1665, respectively. D: the ranks of Newcastle wards in 1665 on an index combining the average number of hearths per house, the percentage of tax payers in each ward, and the percentage of houses with six or more hearths

SOME EMPIRICAL EVIDENCE

The distribution of wealth

The earliest British taxation assessments which have been analysed on the ward, parish or street level at which they were collected are the Hearth Tax Assessments of 1662–66 and 1669–74, and the Survey of London's inhabitants within the walls made under an Act of 1694. There are thus, as yet, no studies of the distribution of wealth in British towns which fall definitely within Vance's pre-capitalist category, and which can be referred directly to his statements about the social geography of such towns. Even the seventeenth-century studies are by no means perfectly suited for the purpose in hand. Only Glass's work on London[35] contains a map which can be related to the hypotheses of Vance and Sjoberg, but this can be supplemented by the work of Hoskins on Exeter,[36] Butlin on Dublin,[37] and an analysis of the transcription of the Newcastle upon Tyne Hearth Tax Assessment Return of 1665 made by Welford.[38]

These tax returns provide information on the number of hearths and stoves in each household whose owner was liable to the tax, and sometimes, too, of the exempted poor.[39] It is generally accepted that these data provide a reasonable reflection of the size of the houses of a town and of the wealth of their occupants,[40] although inns and tenemented buildings had large numbers of hearths which did not reflect their occupants' wealth, and the possibility of their existence must be borne in mind when interpreting the information.[41] The households were usually listed by ward, parish or street, which were quite numerous in the large towns.

From these lists a number of indexes of the wealth of the households in the various wards of a city can be devised. First, the percentage of the households in each ward which was liable to the tax provides an indication of the degree of poverty there; second, the average number of hearths in the households of the taxed population reflects the wealth of the non-poor of a ward; and third, the proportion of exceptionally large houses, say those with more than six hearths, indicates the prevalence of the houses of the wealthiest citizens of all in a ward. The second of these measures has been mapped for Dublin, Exeter and Newcastle in figures 1A–1C.[42] But this index reflects only one facet of the wealth of wards and is not obviously superior to the other two, and although the coefficients of concordance between the three variables are high at 0·80 for Exeter and 0·89 for Newcastle, there is not perfect correlation, so that information is present in the other two data series which is not contained on Figures 1A–1C. Consequently, an attempt was made to derive a compound index of the wealth of the households of wards by ranking the sums of the ranks scored by each ward on each of the three variables.[43] These ranks of the summed ranks for Newcastle wards are plotted in Figure 1D. Because it includes more information which is descriptive of the indicated variable, and because the procedure of ranking obliterates some exceptionally large differences at the top and bottom of the interval scales, this map provides a much clearer general pattern of variations in the wealth of wards than that which portrays only the average numbers of hearths per taxed household.

But all four maps display strikingly similar patterns. In all cases houses of various sizes were unevenly distributed, and quite marked peaks existed in each city. In all three, these peaks were located in proximity to the castle, either between the castle and the main place of worship, as in Exeter and Dublin, or, as in Newcastle, between the castle keep and the gildhall. This location did not correspond with the main 'market square', or place of business. Indeed, such topographical 'centres' did not always exist in pre-nineteenth-century cities. In Exeter there was none, different commodity markets being located in different parts of the town;[44] in Newcastle there were nine markets, and six of them were located, like the twice-yearly fairs, in a single central market place of overwhelming predominance (see Fig. 2).[45] But this main market area, which comprised Mordon Tower ward, was filled with relatively small, poor households, and ranked

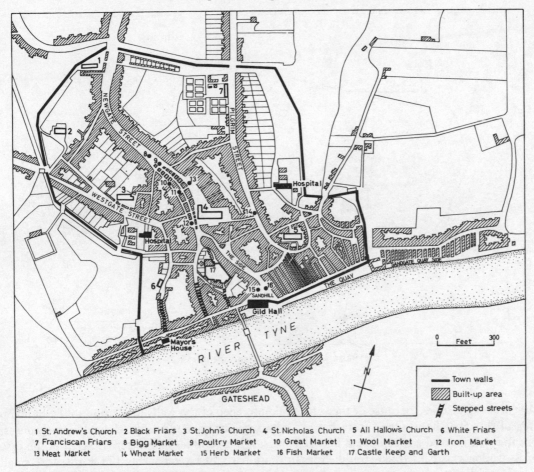

1 St. Andrew's Church   2 Black Friars   3 St. John's Church   4 St. Nicholas Church   5 All Hallow's Church   6 White Friars
7 Franciscan Friars   8 Bigg Market   9 Poultry Market   10 Great Market   11 Wool Market   12 Iron Market
13 Meat Market   14 Wheat Market   15 Herb Market   16 Fish Market   17 Castle Keep and Garth

FIGURE 2. Newcastle in 1745, showing the built-up area, streets, main buildings and markets. Although there had been growth since 1665, the basic lineaments of the town and the locations of the markets and major buildings were substantially the same then

twentieth out of the 24 wards on the compound index of wealth. Although two wards which fringed this central market area, Newgate and Stank Tower (see Fig. 3 for the locations of wards), ranked 2·5 and 4·5 on the compound index of wealth, other market-edge wards were of low rank, and generally the wards with the largest houses and least poverty were not in this economically central part of the city, but well to the south of it on the high bank across which the castle was linked to the riverfront and bridge-head by steep narrow lanes, some of which were stepped (see Fig. 2).[46] Figure 1D demonstrates how wealthy areas radiated out from this core towards the main gates, especially in the south, along the main thoroughfares of the city.[47]

In Newcastle, then, it seems to have been a combination of main road frontage and the 'strategic facilities' of castle, parish church, gildhall and riverfront which fixed the location of the highest status areas. In Exeter and Dublin, which were not so important as ports, the riverfront did not have the same influence, and there it was where the castle, cathedral/parish church and main road frontage combined that the highest status areas were found.

These patterns ostensibly go a considerable way to corroborate Sjoberg's hypotheses. So, too, does the prevalence of a sharp decline in wealth away from the peaks towards the walls or the

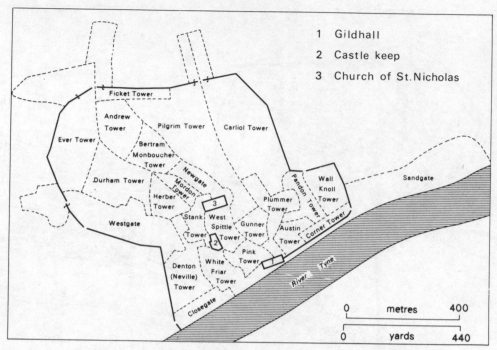

1 Gildhall
2 Castle keep
3 Church of St.Nicholas

FICKET TOWER
Andrew Tower
Pilgrim Tower
Carliol Tower
Ever Tower
Bertram Monboucher Tower
Newgate
Durham Tower
Mordon Tower
Herber Tower
Plummer Tower
Pandon Tower
Wall Knoll Tower
Sandgate
Stank Tower
West Spittle Tower
Gunner Tower
Austin Tower
Corner Tower
Westgate
Pink Tower
Denton (Neville) Tower
White Friar Tower
Closegate
River Tyne

0   metres   400
0   yards   440

FIGURE 3. The wards of Newcastle in 1665

outskirts of the cities. Because of the short circumference of the walls in relation to the built-up area of the city, the whole of intra-mural Dublin was characterized by relatively large houses, but the wall marked a sharp break between areas of high and less high status except in the case of St Audon's parish, which straddled it. In those parts of Exeter where the wards were small enough to allow a pattern to emerge, the size of houses decreased away from the core area of the city towards the wall and beyond, and in Newcastle, where the intra-mural area was large and the wards numerous, an almost completely Sjoberg-like pattern was apparent—except where the skewing effect of river frontage operated in the south—with the most remote wards inside and outside the walls being the poorest areas of the city. An entirely similar pattern is portrayed by the map of London prepared from the 1695 data by Glass, who concluded that 'London was an area with a fairly distinctive pre-industrial topography. The proportions of upper status households were higher in the centre, and the lower status households showed the greatest relative frequency on the periphery and in many of the parishes without the walls'.[48] Thus, three of the five largest English cities of the late seventeenth century, and Dublin, which was second to London in size in the British Isles as a whole, all displayed patterns of wealth distribution similar to those postulated by Sjoberg.

By this time Vance's capitalist city ought to have been in evidence, but the maps demonstrate clearly that the wealthy had not yet moved in significant numbers, if at all, to newer and more spacious peripheral areas. They did not, however, live in the most densely populated areas of all, in Newcastle at least. There, the Spearman rank correlation coefficient between the density of households and the compound index of wealth of wards was +0·03, so that high status was correlated with neither high nor low densities, and the spatial patterns of wealth and population density were equally regular, but completely different (compare Figs. 1D and 4).

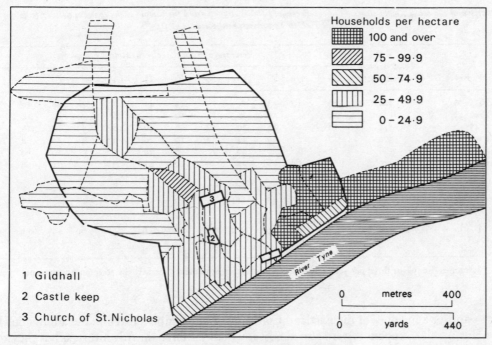

FIGURE 4. Household densities in Newcastle in 1665

Just as there was no indication of the existence of the capitalist city in late seventeenth-century Newcastle, neither was there any sign of the pre-capitalist city. With wealth and status spread within occupational groups which were spatially segregated and located willy-nilly over the city, a randomly variegated, rather than spatially concentrated, pattern of wealth distribution would have occurred. In the mercantile variant, the patrician group was concentrated around the market area. Neither of these patterns existed. Clearly Sjoberg's pre-industrial city model provides a much better approximation of the patterns of wealth distribution which actually existed in four of the largest British cities in the late seventeenth century.

The structure of society

Was the sociological order which underlay these patterns congruent with that of Sjoberg's model? Did an élite which was largely divorced from the economic functioning of the city dominate its government and occupy the high status core, surrounded by occupationally specialized gild areas and, beyond them, the 'outcasts' and 'poor'—non-gildsmen in unincorporated or malodorous occupations?

Because of the complex and voluminous nature of the Freemen's and Company rolls of seventeenth-century cities, and the labour involved in processing them, these questions will be pursued through an analysis of Newcastle only.

Information on the distribution of power within this urban society can be derived from lists of mayors,[49] accounts of inter-gild strife[50] and descriptions of the functions and composition of the Companies of Hostmen[51] and Merchant Adventurers.[52] Occupational data can be gathered from a number of sources. The admissions lists of the Merchant Adventurers[53] record whether a member was a mercer, draper, or boothman—the three constituent 'mysteries' of the Com-

TABLE I

A comparison of the occupational structure of the Freeman's Rolls, 1635–64 and the sample of occupations derived from the Rolls via the Hearth Tax Assessment Returns of 1665

Years	Total freeman Admissions*	Percentage of total per occupational group											
		A_1	A_2	A	B_1	B_2	B_3	B	C_1	C_2	C_3	C_4	C
1635–39	320	19	4	23	14	12	15	41	6	4	18	10	35
1640–44	172	14	4	18	24	13	10	47	8	3	11	14	35
1645–49	374	18	4	22	19	13	8	40	8	5	11	14	38
1650–54	300	17	2	19	24	14	10	48	9	6	10	8	33
1655–59	386	20	6	26	20	10	8	39	8	5	10	12	35
1660–64	350	21	5	26	22	9	10	41	7	7	11	9	33
1635–64 (a)	2,202	18	4	22	21	12	10	43	8	5	12	11	35
In taxed sample (b)	627	36	7	43	11	10	6	27	7	4	9	10	30
$\left(\dfrac{b}{a}\right)$	0·29	2·00	1·83	1·95	0·52	0·83	0·60	0·63	0·88	0·80	0·75	0·91	0·86

* Excludes the two or three per year whose occupations were not entered, mainly the recipients of personal freedom.

pany[54]—and/or a member of the Eastland Company. The members listed in the admissions lists of the Hostmen's Company[55] were also almost invariably Merchant Adventurers, but they dealt largely in coal and had the additional right to 'host' strangers.[56]

There were thus apparently four or five distinct occupational associations within the merchant community. But by the late seventeenth century these were not all functionally distinct. The three constituent mysteries of the Merchant Adventurer's Company had little significance except as avenues of access to the larger association, and the activities of members of the separate sub-groups apparently differed little. Moreover, after *c.* 1630 almost all Merchant Adventurers were members of the Eastland Company, so that it is not possible to distinguish from the surviving records between those who traded nationally and those who traded internationally. Consequently, the single occupational group of 'merchant' must be used to accommodate all Merchant Adventurers except hostmen, whose control of the coal trade still remained current.

The occupations of those who were not merchants (as well as those who were) can be identified in the lists of admissions of freemen.[57] These lists comprise two kinds of record, the Gild Books and the Register. The former have survived only for the period 1645–53. They record the proceedings at the three Gild Days held each year, when an apprentice who had served his time and entered his name had it called through his gild. If no objections were made to the name of an apprentice called on three consecutive Gild Days, then he became a freeman and and could have his name inscribed on the Register of Freemen. Not all suitors at the Gild Days were made freemen as objections were quite numerous, and not all new freemen had their names immediately recorded in the Register, so that the latter provides a less complete and less chronologically exact record of the mercantile and craft affiliations of the inhabitants than the Gild Books. However, the original Register, or nearly contemporary transcriptions of it, survive for almost every year from the 1580s, giving comparable records over the whole period during which the inhabitants of the town in 1665 would have been admitted to practise their trades there. Of course, these registers do not provide full details of the occupations of all the inhabitants, but only of those belonging to gilds, and not even all gildsmen were necessarily entered. On the other hand, they do not merely record gild affiliations, because 63 different occupations were recorded by an average of 73 people per year, so that the Register does provide a reasonably full, if not perfectly accurate, record of the occupations practised by those who belonged to neither the lowest nor the very highest strata of society, and who alone had the right to be involved in the government of the town.

The occupations given in the registers were classified according to the scheme given in detail in the Appendix. There are three main categories; merchants and those giving personal services (category A), those in shipping and service trades (category B), and manufacturers (category C). These categories are split into nine sub-groups which contain the more than 50 recorded occupations or combinations of associated occupations, and those who became mayor. The percentages of the total registered entries in each category and sub-group for each five-year period 1635–64 are given in Table I, which shows that there was relatively little change in the proportions employed in each group of occupations over this period and provides a reasonably unbiased sample of the occupational structure of the gild membership of the town in the mid seventeenth century.

The admissions list of the Merchant Adventurers and the Register were searched from 1634–70 for the occupations of those who were taxed in 1665, and therefore named on Welford's list. Of these 1472 inhabitants the occupations of 41 per cent can be established with reasonable certainty, and a further 10 per cent can be placed in an 'uncertain' class, where the occupation may have been one of a number in the same sub-group or category.[58] This is a large sample of occupations, representing 25 or 30 per cent of the total taxed and untaxed working population in 1665. But it must be used with especial caution, because it is biased in two ways.

First, it does not truly replicate the occupational structure of the town as delineated in the Register of Freemen. A rough comparison between the occupational structure of the Register and that of the taxed population of 1665 whose occupations are traceable is provided in Table I, which gives the ratios of the percentages in each occupational category and sub-group in the two sets of data. The table shows that the merchant and personal service groups are both considerably over-represented in the taxed sample; a result, presumably, of the non-registration of merchant freemen, the non-admission of those in personal service occupations, which did not all have gilds, and the relatively high proportion of these groups who were wealthy enough to be liable to tax, and who are therefore named on Welford's list. The shipping sub-group is least well represented in the taxed sample, the low figure for the sub-group as a whole being almost entirely due to the massive under-representation of the master mariners, for whom the ratio between the percentage of entries on the Register 1635–64 and the percentage in the taxed sample of 1665 was only 0·48. The second kind of bias in the taxed sample is the variation in the proportions of the taxed populations of wards whose occupations are known, ranging from over 90 per cent in Pink Tower ward to only 32 per cent in Herber Tower ward.

Both of these kinds of bias in the sample of 1665 will affect the significance of correlations between occupations and wealth on a ward basis, and they mean that maps of occupational distributions by ward must be interpreted with some caution. None the less, even when treated with the appropriate reservations, these data can still yield information on the questions posed earlier about the social and occupational structure of the town and the ways in which they were related to the geography of wealth.

A wealthy urban residential group which was not directly connected with the economic functioning of the city undoubtedly existed, but its members lived in Westgate and the northern part of Denton Tower wards, peripheral to the wealthy core of the city (compare Figs. 1D and 3).[59] All the indications are, too, that this group did not exert much influence in the government of the city: the merchant community was clearly dominant in both wealth and municipal power.

The wealth of the merchants is clearly demonstrable. The Spearman rank correlation

TABLE II

The average number of hearths per house of those in the
occupational sub-groups in 1665

Occupational sub-group*	Size of sample	Average hearths per house
A1	228	5·0
A2	42	3·9
B1	70	2·6
B2	62	2·9
B3	37	1·8
C1	44	1·5
C2	23	2·6
C3	59	2·2
C4	62	2·1

* The composition of these sub-groups is given in the Appendix.

coefficient between scores on the compound index of wealth and the proportions of the taxed populations of wards that were merchants was $+0·87$, whilst the correlation between wealth and the proportions of ward populations who were freemen of any kind was only $+0·56$. These statistics suggest that the merchants formed a wealthy élite within the community of freemen, and this suggestion is fully corroborated by the relative size of the merchants' houses compared with those of other occupational groups (see Table II). The merchants had, too, a tight grip on the government offices of the city. Of the 31 mayors who held office between 1637 and 1684, four lived outside the town—two seem to have had no city residence—and only four were not members of at least one of the merchant companies. This pre-eminent municipal position of the merchants was guaranteed by charter; only they were allowed to buy and sell purely for profit in the town, and their gild had firm control over the election of all the town officers, a control which it maintained in the face of intermittent craft-gild opposition until well into the eighteenth century.[60]

There was, then, neither a non-economically active urban élite nor a one-man-one-vote system of government. Moreover, distinctions in wealth and power were not limited to this simple dichotomy between the merchants and the rest. The merchant community was a large one, comprising about 20 per cent of the total freeman community, and sharp stratification developed within it. By the seventeenth century the members of the Company of Hostmen had attained dominance. They were wealthier than the remainder of the merchant group, with an average of 5·7 hearths per house compared with 4·3, and it was within this small clique, which never provided more than 4 per cent of the total freemen's registrations in any five-year period from 1635–64, that municipal control resided. Of the 31 mayors who held office between 1637 and 1684, 22 were Hostmen. Thirteen were governors of the Hostmen's Company, and only three men who held this office between 1637 and 1684 did not also hold the mayoralty within that period. This supreme status of the leading Hostmen was also reflected in the size of their houses, with the mayors/governors averaging 8·4 hearths per house (see Table III).

Below the merchant community, the craft gilds were similarly differentiated in wealth and power. The only gilds recognized by the Merchant Adventurers, during a period of theoretical leniency, for the purpose of qualifying for admission to their company, were the 'twelve principal mysteries of the town' which had existed as corporate groups since 1342.[61] This status classification still had meaning in 1665. The nine non-mercantile trades of the twelve had the right to

TABLE III

The average number of hearths per house of members of occupations with more than ten representatives in the sample of 1665

Occupation	Sub-group	Size of sample	Average hearths per house
Mayors	A1	26	8·4
Hostmen	A1	53	5·7
Other merchants	A1	149	4·3
Bakers	B2	25	3·2
Master mariners	B1	14	3·1
Mariners	B1	23	3·0
Barber-surgeons	A2	27	2·5
Joiners	C2	12	2·5
Cordwainers	C4	27	2·4
Weavers	C3	11	2·2
Shipwrights	B1	30	2·0
Butchers	B2	22	2·0
Coopers	C2	11	2·0
Tailors	C3	26	2·0
Tanners	C4	20	2·0
House-carpenters	B3	13	1·6
Blacksmiths	C1	28	1·4

limited participation in elections and had a meeting place in the same building, 'called now Bannet Chessy Friars', whilst the fifteen 'by-crafts' had even more circumscribed municipal rights and 'every one of them hath their meeting-houses in the towers of the wall'.[62]

These inter-craft differences are also reflected in the house size data (see Tables II and III). The victualling trades (B2) were the wealthiest non-merchant group on the evidence of hearth figures, followed by the shipping (B1) and woodworking (C2) trades. At the bottom came the building (B3) and metalworking (C1) trades, whose practitioners had, on average, less than two hearths in their houses. These sub-group averages conceal some quite large house sizes in particular occupations which have been grouped with poorer ones; the master mariners, bakers and mariners averaged more hearths per house than the barber-surgeons, who were placed in the wealthy A2 sub-group (see Table III), and so did the fullers, feltmakers and skinners, who do not appear on Table III because there were less than ten of them in the 1665 sample.

Other inhabitants, unpossessed of the freedom of the city, formed a much larger social stratum below these taxed craftsmen. Those untaxed in 1665 made up 43 per cent of the population of the city. The vast majority had one hearth in their houses, the rest only two.[63] Some of their number were undoubtedly poorer members of the ancient mysteries and by-crafts.[64] A much larger proportion was probably composed of members of incorporated crafts such as cook, collier, carrier, porter and keelman who seem rarely to have been admitted to the freedom of the city. Certainly, it is likely that the massive 79 per cent of the inhabitants of Sandgate ward who were untaxed, comprising 510 heads of households, were keelmen and seamen, for 'without this gate [are] many houses, and populous, all along the waterside; where ship-wrights, seamen, and keelmen most live, that are employed about the ships and keels'.[65] A further proportion of the 'poor', and the one to which this assignation is most appropriate, would be composed of Engels's 'reserve army of city labour', an army about which little information has survived.

The relationship between social structure and the distribution of wealth

Such a finely structured hierarchical society could have been related to the well-patterned distribution of wealth in a number of ways. Two possible extremes exist: either marked occupational concentrations could have occurred, as suggested by Sjoberg and Vance, with the spatial pattern of wealth reflecting the marked differences in the wealth of the various occupational groups; or a more 'modern', 'class-zoned' structure could have existed, with those of equal wealth and status living in close proximity irrespective of their occupations. This situation is in many ways similar to that envisaged by Vance for the capitalist city, although its grounding in a merchant-dominated society and its spatial expression in a wealthy central area are not, of course, congruent with that, or any other, stage of his model.

The location quotients of the occupational categories and sub-groups were calculated in an attempt to discover the extent to which the first of these possible extremes existed. A location quotient, according to whether it is greater or less than 1·0, indicates whether a ward contained more or fewer in a particular occupational group than would be expected on the basis of its population[66] and the number in the occupational group in the city as a whole. The quotients for wards in which there were less than five in an occupational group were ignored and, after an examination of the frequency distribution of the quotients for all the wards for all the occupations, values of 1·3 and 2·0 were used to indicate the existence of 'significant' and 'marked' occupational specialization in wards. The quotients for the three occupational categories are plotted in Figure 5A, which demonstrates the existence of two quite separate occupational sectors, separated by an almost continuous belt of wards with lower quotients in all three occupational categories, and therefore mixed occupational structures. These mercantile and manufacturing sectors correspond with those described in a topography of Newcastle written in 1649. The first, centred in the south-west, contained other mercantile 'strategic facilities' besides the gildhall,[67] and the second, centred on Mordon Tower ward, contained the main market, 'where all sorts of artificers have shops and houses', and the meeting house of the nine ancient mysteries of the town.[68]

Finer levels of occupational specialization by area became apparent when the location quotients for the nine occupational sub-groups were calculated and plotted. Figure 5B shows even more clearly than Figure 5A that the wards with concentrations of merchants were situated in the south-west, and that the eastern outlier of the aggregate category A pattern was, in fact, the location of a marked concentration of personal service tradesmen, primarily barber-surgeons. The houses of the highest status group, the mayors and hostmen, were not completely localized in the south-west, but spread over the whole inverted 'T' shape of the high status housing zone (compare Figs. 5B and 1D). The reasons for the failure of this group to be tightly embedded within the quarter of the mercantile community of which they formed the élite can only be surmised: it is possible that the availability of very large houses was related to main street frontage, 'pulling out' this highest status group of all from the otherwise clearly pervasive pattern of mercantile concentration.[69]

Figure 5C shows that the service sub-groups were similarly concentrated, the failure of these spatial patterns to occur on Figure 5A resulting from the heterogeneity of the occupations aggregated into category B. A pronounced service sector existed in the south-eastern part of the city. Inland from the personal service area were quite separate victualling and shipping quarters which overlapped in the interstitial ward of Pandon Tower. This statistically derived conclusion is also borne out to some extent by topographical evidence: 'east of the town is Sandgate . . . where ship-wrights, seamen and keelmen most live', and 'most butchers dwell' in the street which marked the boundary between Plummer Tower and Austin Tower wards.[70]

The tendency for occupational sub-groups to be concentrated and segregated was apparent also in the manufacturing trades, although in this case the contiguity of wards which contained concentrations of particular sub-groups of occupations, representing the existence of craft 'quarters', was not so pronounced as in the service trades. The degree of segregation was quite

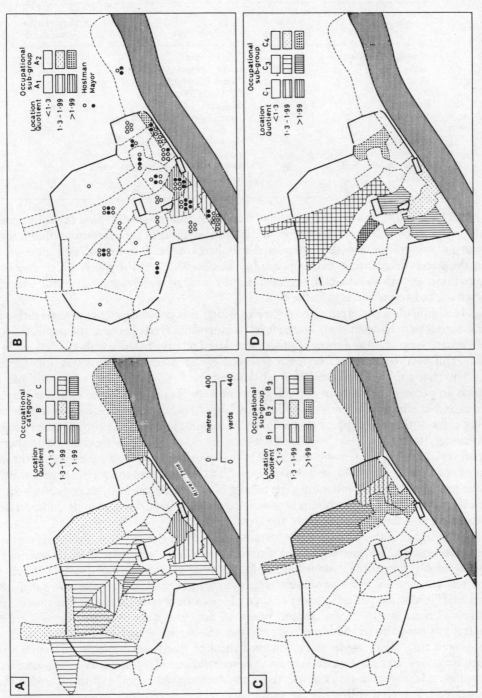

FIGURE 5. Occupational groupings in Newcastle in 1665. Occupational sub-group C2 (woodworkers) did not record any location quotients greater than 1·29

TABLE IV

The localized crafts of Newcastle in 1665

Craft	Total membership	Wards	% of total in named wards
Slater and bricklayer	8	Carliol Tower	75
Baker	25	Austin Tower and Pandon Tower	52
Butcher	22	Plummer Tower, Gunner Tower and Austin Tower	50
Shipwright	30	Sandgate	50
Barber-surgeon	27	Corner Tower, Wall Knoll Tower, and Austin Tower	48
Blacksmith	28	Mordon Tower, Pilgrim Tower and Carliol Tower	48
Master mariner and mariner	37	Wall Knoll Tower, Sandgate and Pandon Tower	46
			43

high; only Mordon Tower ward contained marked concentrations of more than one occupational sub-group, and only Pilgrim Tower ward contained significant concentrations of different manufacturing sub-groups. Loosely articulated metalworking and leatherworking quarters existed, but the woodworkers were 'over-represented' in no ward, and the wards which contained concentrations of textiles and clothing manufacturers were widely separated and located in the merchant and service sectors of the city.

It is difficult to determine the degree to which this concentration and segregation of economic activities percolated down to the level of individual crafts because the populations of some wards were very small and those of others very large relative to the numbers involved in any one trade, and ward boundaries frequently followed or cut streets, so that it was possible for actual concentrations to be 'dispersed' between a number of wards. Table IV shows those crafts in which 40 per cent or more of the practitioners were localized in three or fewer neighbouring wards and in which numbers were sufficiently large to render percentage statements meaningful. Only eight of the crafts appear on the table. Although the reason for the absence of some of the remainder is that they had too few members, in other cases, particularly in leatherworking, woodworking and clothing and textiles, it is that the practitioners were dispersed through non-contiguous wards. Table IV shows with great clarity that it was the service trades which tended to be most localized, corroborating the results of the statistical analysis of the sub-group data: all the service crafts in which numbers were reasonably large were strongly concentrated in the victualling and shipping quarters of the city.

An analysis of the sample of 1665 demonstrates quite clearly, then, that occupational groups were concentrated and segregated to a significant extent in Newcastle, finer distinctions existing within broad mercantile, victualling, shipping and manufacturing quarters. Each of these quarters contained its own particular 'strategic facilities' and, where relevant, specialized retail outlets. If it was not, perhaps, 'many centred', Newcastle was definitely 'four sectored': certainly, there was not a single 'centre' around which all activities were organized as they are around a central business district. This tendency towards the spatial grouping of craft activities must not be exaggerated. Some trades were scattered through many wards, some through a few widely separated ones, and some wards contained concentrations of a few trades which were in no ways affinitive. Moreover, in no case was there absolute concentration and in all trades there were 'stragglers', scattered willy-nilly across the city.

None the less, even though these qualifications are necessary, strong tendencies towards occupational grouping did exist. What is more, these groupings were quite clearly related to the

distribution pattern of house sizes. The wealthiest wards, in the south-west, scored high location quotients for the wealthiest trades, whilst the poorest wards were characterized by high
location quotients for the poorest trades or low quotients for all trades and therefore a greater
than 'expected' preponderance of non-freemen. It can be concluded, then, that there was some
tendency towards the first of the possible extreme relationships between social structure and the
geography of wealth that was defined earlier.

But, as the location pattern of mayors' and hostmen's houses hinted, the situation was not
quite so simple as these correlations between the residential status of areas and the wealth of
occupational groupings suggest. Newgate, Gunner Tower and Bertram Monboucher Tower
wards, for example, ranked 2·5, 4·5 and 6·5 on the compound index of wealth, but did not score
high location quotients in any sub-group of trades, whilst Stank Tower ward, in which only the
relatively poor leatherworkers were over-represented, ranked 4·5 in wealth. The results of a two-
way analysis of variance of the average size of houses classified by wards and the nine occupational sub-groups further demonstrates this complexity.[71] Although there was significant
variation, at the 0·1 level of probability, of hearth size classified by occupational sub-group
independent of variation in the ward means, there was also signficant variation in the ward means
independent of variation in the occupational means at the same level of probability. Clearly, in
addition to the tendency for the wealth of wards to vary according to the wealth of localized
occupational groups, there was also a tendency for other wards to be wealthy or otherwise irrespective of their occupational make-up.

The degree and disposition of this 'class-zoning' is portrayed in Figures 6A–D. These show
the number of standard deviations that the average numbers of hearths in the houses of members
of each occupational sub-group in each ward lay from the over-all average numbers of hearths
for the members of the occupational sub-groups. They thus show where the houses of practitioners of each trade were larger and smaller than the average for their trade. Of course, one
would not expect each occupational sub-group to have the same average house-size in each ward.
Some random variation must occur, especially between sample means such as these, and perhaps
little can be read into the differences which lay between, say, −1·0σ and +1·0σ. Nevertheless,
the differences between the averages for certain wards and the city-wide averages were so great,
and the wards which recorded high positive and negative deviations were so consistent across
occupational sub-groups, that a certain degree of 'class-zoning' is strongly indicated.

The pattern of positive and negative deviations from the mean house-size of occupational
category A corresponded with the pattern of location quotients for that group. Generally,
although there were detailed exceptions, the wards where merchants were 'over-represented'
were also those where their houses were larger than average, and vice versa (see Fig 6A). The service trades displayed a similar tendency. The wealthiest members of this category, the victuallers,
had houses which were larger than their sub-group average in the area where their houses were
most concentrated, and away from this core area their houses became smaller with an almost
regular progression. But in the wards where the shipping and building trades were concentrated
the houses of the members of these generally poorer trades were on the whole smaller than the
sub-group means, with a transition zone in Pandon Tower ward where the victualling and
shipping quarters overlapped.

This reversal, with areas of the greatest concentration of a trade containing members with
houses smaller than the average for their trade, was even more marked in the manufacturing
crafts (see Fig. 6C). Some of the manufacturing wards of the city, such as Mordon Tower,
Pilgrim Tower, Denton Tower and Pandon Tower, registered negative deviations from the
average house-size of manufacturing tradesmen, and the positive deviations in these trades
occurred in the southern, mercantile, area of the city. The patterns for the three occupational

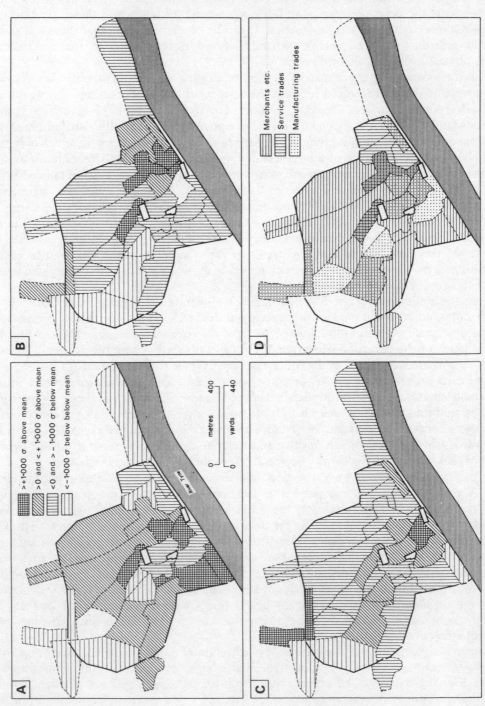

FIGURE 6. Deviations from the average household sizes of occupational groups, by ward, in Newcastle in 1665. The key on 5A refers to Figures 5A–5C. 5A: Merchants. 5B: Service Trades. 5C: Manufacturing Trades. 5D: wards which registered positive deviations from the mean number of hearths per house for the three occupational categories. There were no service tradesmen in Pink Tower ward

categories are mapped together on Figure 6D, which shows that the areas of highest residential status were as closely correlated with areas where the houses of the members of various occupational sub-groups were consistently wealthier than the average for their craft as they were with areas where wealthier occupational sub-groups were concentrated.

It seems, then, that the core areas of the wealthier trades contained the wealthier members of those trades and, in addition, 'creamed off' the wealthiest practitioners of crafts whose members were generally poorer.[72] Furthermore, the core areas of poorer trades contained only the less wealthy members of those trades and the poorest practitioners of crafts which were generally wealthier. However, this reinforcement of patterns based on occupational zoning was not the only way in which 'class zoning' operated. Certain wards existed, notably Newgate, near the market, which contained larger-than-average houses in all three occupational categories but high location quotients in none of them (compare Figs 6D and 5A–D), and others, notably Ever Tower in the north-west, had smaller-than-average houses in all three craft categories and no concentration of any poorer trade. In these wards, perhaps, true 'class-zoning', rather than the hybridized form which prevailed in other wards, occurred. But, in diametrical opposition to Vance's class-zoned capitalist city, the poorer wards were peripheral and the wealthier ones central.

DISCUSSION AND CONCLUSION

Conclusions about the general applicability of the models of Sjoberg and Vance obviously cannot be drawn from evidence about the society and economy of one city and about the distribution of wealth in three others. At its widest, the scope of the following conclusions will comprise the larger British cities of the seventeenth century. Indeed, Newcastle was in some ways distinct even within this small set. The lucrative control of London's coal supply provided a stronger base for the power of its merchant oligarchy than existed elsewhere, and the intimacy of its influence on London's welfare, plus its importance as a military strong-point, prompted more-than-usual interference from central government in its internal affairs. None the less, like most of the other larger British cities of the period, Newcastle was a port, governed by a small oligarchy, with an occupational structure reflecting the dominance of trade and craft industry in its economic base. In the context of residential patterns, these congruencies are sufficiently fundamental to ensure that conclusions based upon Newcastle data will have more than purely local significance. But a definition of the exact scope of these conclusions is not of great importance to the main objective of this study, which is simply to examine how far the models of Sjoberg and Vance are representative of the conditions which actually obtained in a particular city to which they should be applicable. A specification of the full set of cities to which any discrepancies that are found here are relevant must obviously await detailed work on cities of different sizes in different places at different times.

Predictably, the social geography of Newcastle in the mid seventeenth century was more complicated than any of the archetypes of Sjoberg or Vance. But it was not just more complicated: it was fundamentally different. Newcastle was not a feudal pre-industrial city, nor was it a pre-capitalist or a capitalist city. A merchant clique was pre-eminent in wealth and municipal power. Its social dominance was expressed geographically in the existence of a mercantile quarter in that part of the city where its economic purposes were best served and where the institutions through which it dominated the city were located. In addition, the city possessed other regularly patterned occupational districts which were in some areas reinforced by 'class zoning', and in others countervailed by it. If the city must be fitted into the schemes of Vance and Sjoberg, then it could be said to represent some hybrid of the mercantile pre-capitalist and the capitalist cities. Vance's stress upon the importance of economic power and relationships as ecological determinants within the city undoubtedly gets nearer to the truth of the matter than Sjoberg's feudal social order, in which the dominance of an élite group was derived from non-economic and extra-urban sources.[73]

Indeed, it might seem possible to read the evidence in ways which go much further towards corroborating Vance's ideas about the emergence of capitalist cities—an expectation which is also produced by the changes, spear-headed in the cities, which were demonstrably occurring in English society in general at that time. It could, for example, be hypothesized that the occupational-cum-wealth spatial groupings of Newcastle really reflected affinities based upon wealth and 'class' rather than the occupational congruencies which underlay them. Or, it could be hypothesized that the partial scattering of occupational groups into areas of similarities in wealth represented the beginnings of 'class-based' residential zones and the break-up of craft areas.

Neither of these hypotheses can be sustained. They require the existence of analytical chimera and ignore social and economic reality. Whether or not 'capitalism' had developed in Newcastle and engendered the crystallization of 'class' affinities cannot be demonstrated because these terms cannot be defined in ways which make their empirical existence demonstrable. Moreover, it is at least arguable that the first does not necessarily entail the second,[74] and that 'social class' is an intellectual device which has little relevance to seventeenth-century English society.[75] But it can be unequivocally demonstrated that economically and socially functional groups based on occupations still existed. The craft gilds and the companies of Hostmen and Merchant Adventurers had not yet become functionally hollow avenues of access into an urban society of equal opportunity and an urban economy of free competition. The gilds and companies had power over their members in seventeenth-century Newcastle; their members still acted in concert through them, and still had their municipal rights defined by their affiliations with them.[76] It would be unreasonable to suggest, in the face of this, and given the congruence of workplace and home in a craft economy, that the spatial groupings of people following the same occupations did not have their rationale in the practice of those occupations.

It is true that the evidence shows that these occupational groupings were neither absolutely firm in outline nor all-embracing in membership. It is also true that persons of dissimilar occupations lived mixed up together in certain parts of the city. But this situation may merely signify that the numbers practising particular trades had grown beyond the capacities of the areas in which their members were mainly concentrated. Certainly, the economy of the city was growing after the Civil War according to the evidence of admissions to freedom (see Table I), and the occupational concentrations were all located in crowded and completely built-up parts of the city (compare Figs. 2 and 5). If this was so, the additional craftsmen would have to find houses wherever they were available. Little is known of the seventeenth-century housing market, but it can be surmised that the options would not be legion, and that the customer would have to base his choice, or the specification of his commission to the builder, on the size of his particular household-cum-workforce. The degree of 'class-zoning' that was apparent might signify no more than this—that the economy of the city was growing. It is certainly not necessary to postulate the existence of 'class' affiliations based upon wealth to explain it. Indeed, it is as reasonable to argue that the growth in the numbers of craftsmen caused dispersal and a consequent weakening of occupational group ties, and that it was therefore a precursor and not a result of the development of other kinds of social associations.

One is left with the conclusions that pre-industrial cities did not necessarily exist before the Industrial Revolution, and that pre-capitalist cities could flourish in a capitalist era. They indicate the inadequacy of the models of Vance and Sjoberg. Sjoberg ignored the social and economic changes which occurred in Western Europe, and particularly in its cities, between medieval times and the Industrial Revolution. Vance accommodated them, but his model is inadequate in its mediation of the development of capitalism through a change in the attitude towards land holding to affect the social geography of cities. More proximate determinants of land plot assignment practices existed. The relationships between workplace and home, in functional and spatial terms;[77] the size and composition of households, and the nature of the housing and land markets are all more intimately related to the structure of society and the reasons why residential choices are made. The first two are vitally important components of the *Gemeinschaft* social structural relationships of pre-modern urban society: in a large part they were what made it pre-modern.[78] The third is the only possible mechanism for transmitting social changes into changed residential patterns. Questions about these aspects of pre-nineteenth-century cities and about how they changed in response to economic changes must be addressed and answered before the distinctiveness of these cities can be understood. Only after such understanding has been gained will it be possible to formulate a reasonable and reliable set of generalizations about the social geography of cities before the 'ecological transition', and to comprehend what, exactly, that transition comprised.

ACKNOWLEDGEMENT

Thanks are due to the University of Liverpool for a contribution towards the cost of illustrations.

NOTES

1. SJOBERG, G. (1960) *The pre-industrial city, past and present* (Glencoe, Ill.)

2. SCHNORE, L. F. (1965) 'On the spatial structure of cities in the two Americas' in HAUSER, P. M. and SCHNORE, L. F. (eds) *The study of urbanization*, 347–98 (New York). Schnore considered that the patterns of wealthy centre and poor periphery, which he found in Latin American cities, and poor centre and wealthy periphery, which characterizes North American cities, were 'both special cases more adequately subsumed under a more general theory of residential land uses in urban areas'. His work, and that of Sjoberg whose conclusions he quotes, form the basis of the meagre treatment of pre-nineteenth-century cities given in the two major recent textbooks of urban social geography by Johnston and Herbert. JOHNSTON, R. J. (1971) *Urban residential patterns* (London) and HERBERT, D. T. (1972) *Urban geography: a social perspective* (Newton Abbot)

3. VANCE JR., J. E. (1971) 'Land assignment in pre-capitalist, capitalist and post-capitalist cities', *Econ. Geogr.* 47, 101–20

4. SJOBERG, op. cit., p. 8.

5. Ibid., p. 110

6. Ibid., p. 97

7. Ibid., p. 83

8. Ibid., pp. 95–8

9. Ibid., p. 99

10. Ibid., pp. 95–6

11. Ibid., p. 101

12. Ibid., p. 99

13. ENGELS, F. (1892) *The condition of the working-class in England in 1844*, p. 95, 1952 edn (London)

14. JONES, G. S. (1971) *Outcast London* (Oxford)

15. SJOBERG, op. cit., p. 100

16. VANCE, op. cit., p. 107

17. Ibid., p. 101

18. Ibid., p. 105

19. Ibid., p. 103

20. Ibid., p. 105

21. Ibid., p. 105

22. Ibid., p. 105

23. Ibid., p. 106

24. Ibid., p. 101

25. Ibid., p. 106

26. Ibid., p. 105

27. Ibid., p. 106

28. Ibid., p. 107

29. Ibid., p. 113

30. GEORGE, M. D. (1925) *London life in the eighteenth century* (London)

31. Most notably those of Marx.

32. These concepts were formulated by F. Toennies. They are polar types representing, on the one hand, relationships which are formulated on the basis of historical experience and cultural norms, and on the other, relationships which

spring from the exercise of the 'rational will' on the basis of its desires for the future. The derivation of the concepts, and the illustration of their sociological significance, requires argument of an intricacy which would be out of place here, where it is sufficient to state that the change from one to the other in ordinary life represents the fundamental attribute of social modernization. See MANN, P. H. (1970) *An approach to urban sociology*, pp. 190–8 (London)

33. WRIGLEY, E. A. (1972) 'The process of modernization and the Industrial Revolution in England', *J. interdisciplin. Hist.* 3, 225–59

34. What Vance interprets as an outward movement of the wealthy from central London was mainly a westward and outward shift of the court, government and 'society'. Those who derived their wealth from work in the city itself continued to live centrally there until at least the late eighteenth century. Rudé maintained that 'there had long been a tendency for *poorer* tradesmen to move toward the *periphery*' (my italics); Saunders Welch stated in 1753 that the trade in old and ruinous houses was on the *outskirts* of the city, and Glass concluded that the wealthy central area and poor periphery were 'still visible in the 1830s'. See RUDÉ, G. (1971) *Hanoverian London* (London); GEORGE, op. cit., and GLASS, D. V. (1968) 'Notes on the demography of London at the end of the seventeenth century', *Daedalus* 97, 581–92

35. GLASS, D. V. (1966) 'London's inhabitants within the walls,' *Lond. Rec. Soc. Publs* 2, p. xxiii

36. HOSKINS, W. G. (1935) *Industry, trade and people in Exeter, 1688–1700* (Manchester)

37. BUTLIN, R. A. (1965) 'The population of Dublin in the late seventeenth century', *Ir. Geogr.* 5, 51–66

38. WELFORD, R. (1911) 'Newcastle householders in 1665: assessment of hearth or chimney tax', *Archaeol. Aeliana*, Ser. 3, 7, 49–76

39. For a recent review of the value and uses of the assessments, see PATTEN, J. A. (1971) 'The hearth taxes, 1622–89', *Local Popul. Stud.* 7, 14–27

40. Glass used tax liabilities as an index of social status in London, and Hoskins considered that a close correlation existed between the number of hearths in a household and the status, wealth and occupation of its inhabitant. GLASS (1966) and (1968) op. cit. and HOSKINS, op. cit.

41. HOSKINS, W. G. (1957) 'Exeter in the seventeenth century: tax and rate assessments, 1602–1670', *Devon and Cornwall Rec. Soc.*, N.S. 2, p. xvii

42. The ward map of Exeter has been taken from HOSKINS (1935) op. cit., p. 113, and the map of Dublin parishes from C. Brooking's map of Dublin, drawn in 1728. The Newcastle ward map was prepared by the author from a verbal description of the boundaries of wards given in WELFORD, op. cit.; the map 'Newe Castle' inset on Speed's map of Northumberland (1610); 'A plan of Newcastle' inset on the map of Northumberland by A. Armstrong and Son (1769), and a 'Town Plan of Newcastle upon Tyne' (1745), ref. MPF 267 in the Public Record Office. The extra-mural boundaries of wards in Newcastle were estimated from the plan of 1745, and for Exeter from a plan of 1744, which is reproduced in HOSKINS (1935) op. cit. The extramural parish boundaries of Dublin continued beyond the edge of Brooking's map, which omitted some of the very poorest areas of the city.

43. This procedure for deriving a set of 'true scores' from a number of highly correlated but different series of scores was suggested by Kendall. See SIEGEL, S. (1956) *Nonparametric statistics for the behavioral sciences*, p. 238 (New York)

44. HOSKINS (1935) op. cit., pp. 23–5

45. Nine markets are depicted on the plan of 1745, and these have been plotted on Figure 2. A topographical description of 1649 mentioned six markets: that in Sandhill for 'fish and other commodities'; that in Pilgrim Street for wheat and rye; that in the Side for 'milk, eggs, butter &c', and, in the large triangular space to the north west of St Nicholas' church, partially filled with rows of shambles, there were the oatmeal, flesh, bigg (barley) and oat markets. W. G., 'Chorographia: or a description of Newcastle upon Tine' (1649), reprinted in *The Harleian Miscellany* 3 (1809), 267–84

46. 'This town (a great part of it) placed upon the highest and the steepest hills that I have found in any great town; these so steep as horses cannot stand upon the pavements,—therefore the daintiest flagged channels are in every street that I have seen: hereupon may horses go without sliding', HAWKINS, E. (ed.) (1844) 'Travels in Holland, the United Provinces, England, Scotland and Ireland, 1634–35, by Sir William Brereton, Bart.', *Chetham Soc.* I, p. 86

47. The major inns were located on Newgate and Pilgrim Streets on the plan of 1745

48. GLASS (1968) op. cit., p. 583

49. HUNTER BLAIR, C. H. (ed.) (1940) 'The mayors and lord mayors of Newcastle upon Tyne, 1216–1940, and the Sheriffs of the county of Newcastle upon Tyne, 1399–1940', *Archaeol. Aeliana*, Ser. 4, 18

50. DENDY, F. W. (1911) 'The Struggle Between the Merchant and Craft Gilds of Newcastle in 1515', *Archaeol. Aeliana*, Ser. 3, 7, 77–101

51. DENDY, F. W. (ed.) (1901) 'Extracts from the Records of the Company of Hostmen of Newcastle upon Tyne', *Surtees Soc.* 105

52. DENDY, F. W. (ed) (1894, 1899) 'Extracts from the Records of the Merchant Adventurers of Newcastle upon Tyne', *Surtees Soc.* 93 and 101

53. Given in DENDY (1899) op. cit.

54. The company had for long been coextensive with the Merchant Gild. Theoretically, drapers dealt in cloth, the boothmen in corn, and the mercers in 'mercery'—precious goods brought over long distances.

55. Given in DENDY (1901) op. cit.

56. In Newcastle, as in many English cities, there existed the custom of 'foreign bought and foreign sold'. 'Strangers' or 'foreigners', those who were not freemen of the city, could not sell goods there except to a freeman, and they could only buy from freemen. Linked with this custom was that of 'hosting'—a group of freemen, the 'hostmen', had the duty of entertaining strangers and acting as their business agents whilst they stayed in the city in return for a percentage of the proceeds of any transactions made. To facilitate the easy collection of custom duties, a statute of 1529 enacted that no person could ship,

load or unload any goods anywhere within the tidal limits of the Tyne except at Newcastle. As a result, all coal owners must ship their coal from Newcastle, and this could only be done through the agency of the hostmen, who thereby gained a monopoly of the Tyne coal trade. This hitherto loosely articulated group within the merchant community was given separate company status by Elizabeth I in return for a grant of £80 and a tax of 1/- per chaldron on all coal shipped from the Tyne.

57. HOPE DODDS, M. (ed.) (1923) 'The Register of Freemen of Newcastle upon Tyne', *Newcastle upon Tyne Rec.* Ser. 3. A few additional occupations were obtained from WELFORD, op. cit. (mainly doctors of medicine and ministers of religion) and from HODGSON, J. L. (1914 and 1919) *Archaeol. Aeliana*, Ser 3, 11, 65–118 and 16, 151–4

58. Where a name appeared only once on both the hearth tax list and an admissions list, it was assumed that the occupation given in the latter was followed in the ward indicated in the former in 1665. This involves two presumptions. First, that the person whose name was given in the hearth tax return lived in the property in question and was not an owner who rented the house out. In general, the occupier was liable to the tax, but in the second Revising Act of 1664 it was stipulated that the tax on hearths in the houses of leaseholders who were exempt was to be paid by their landlords. It may be, therefore, that some persons who were listed with two hearths or less in a ward did not live in that ward, although the number of leasehold properties was not necessarily large, and it is not known how far this provision of the Act was actually put into practice. The second presumption is that there was little occupational mobility. Again, little is known about this, but it was probably not common; there were ordinances in Newcastle against changing craft, which could only be done by transferring to the appropriate gild and paying the required fine. It seems reasonable to suppose that the occupations and places of residence in 1665 of those persons who were mentioned only once on each list are, generally, known accurately from a matching of the lists.

However, such reasonable certainty, appropriate for 41 per cent of the taxed population, cannot be achieved for a further 10 per cent whose names appear more than once on one or on both lists. Such names need not necessarily be rejected completely, because it sometimes occurred that the different occupations which could be ascribed to a household were in the same occupational sub-group or category. These names were therefore classified as of uncertain occupation, and used in appropriate calculations. Some householders in 1665 were widows. If the widow's surname appeared only once in the admissions list, the entry has been assumed to be that of her husband and, as widows often continued their husband's occupation after his death, as Laslett has shown, his occupation has been ascribed to her household in 1665. If the widow's surname appeared more than once on the admissions list, then that household has been placed in the 'uncertain' category, and used in calculations for aggregate occupational groups where appropriate. See MEEKINGS, C. A. F. (1940) 'The Surrey hearth tax, 1664', *Surrey Rec. Soc.* 17; PATTEN, op. çit., and LASLETT, P. (1971) *The world we have lost*, p. 8 (London)

59. W. G. op. cit., p. 278

60. Those who were not members of the merchant gild could only buy what they needed for the practice of their craft or for the sustenance of their household, and they could only sell what they themselves had made. Only the merchants, then, could trade on a large scale as middlemen. This was the basis of their wealth. Their control of municipal government stretched back to the fourteenth century and survived a number of assaults from the craft gilds. A Royal Decree of 1515 entrenched them in an unassailable position. It reaffirmed the exclusive right of the merchants to act as middlemen, ordered that more than one trade could not be practised simultaneously, and that a change of craft required goods to the value of £10 and the payment of a fine. Thus were the craftsmen kept in their economically inferior position. The election of town officials was ostensibly liberalized in 1515. Twelve 'felawshippes or crafts' (the drapers, mercers, boothmen, tanners, skinners, taylors, saddlers, bakers, cordwainers, butchers, smiths and fullers) out of the thirty which then existed were each to present two 'moost proued men and moost discrete of theymself' to form a committee of 24. This committee was, in its turn, to 'electe, chose and name' four burgesses who were then to choose eight other burgesses. These twelve were then to choose a further twelve, and this group of 24 was then to elect the city officials. However, the nucleus of four selected by the original 24 must be 'Burgesses as hath been both Maires and Aldermen of the said Towne' already, and so must the eight elected by them. The erstwhile dominance of the merchants was thus perpetuated by this apparent liberalization of the franchise, which was again only slightly eroded in a later revision in the reign of James I. See DENDY (1911) op. cit.; DENDY, F. W. (1921) 'Gilds and their survival', in DENDY, F. W. *Three lectures on old Newcastle, its suburbs and gilds*, pp. 46–7 (Newcastle), and GROSS, C. (1890) *The gild merchant*, Vol. II, pp. 382–5 (Oxford)

61. DENDY (1901) op. cit., p. 41

62. W. G. op. cit., p. 278

63. WELFORD, op. cit., p. 56

64. This was certainly the case in Wigan, where a number of officers of craft companies appeared in the exempt list in the hearth tax assessment returns of 1664. (This situation was revealed by matching data on occupations and company office holders given in the Court Leet Rolls with the tax returns)

65. W. G. op. cit., p. 272

66. In the calculation of these and later statistics, the 'populations' of the wards were taken to constitute those persons on the tax list whose occupations are known

67. The gildhall was built on the river-ward side of 'the Sand-hill, a market for fish, and other commodities; very convenient for merchant adventurers, merchants of coals, and all those that have their living by shipping. There is . . . a long key or wharf, where ships may . . . unload their commodities and wares . . . [on] it, are two cranes for heavy commodities, very convenient for carrying of corn, wines, deals etc., from the key . . . In this market place are many shops and stately houses for merchants, with great convenience of water, bridge, garners, lofts, cellars and houses . . . In this Sand-hill standeth the town-court, or guildhall, where are held the guilds every year . . . where the mayor keepeth his court every Monday, and the sheriff hath his county-court upon Wednesday and Friday. In it is kept a court of admiralty, or river-court, every Monday . . . There is a court of Pic-powder during the . . . two fairs . . . Under the town-court is a common weigh-house for all sorts

of commodities . . . Near this is the town-house, where the clerk of the chamber and chamberlains are to receive the revenues of the town for coal, ballast, salt, grindstones etc . . . Next adjoining is an alms-house . . . Above which is the stately court of the merchant adventurers'. W. G. op. cit., pp. 276–7

68. Ibid., p. 278

69. In 1649, Pilgrim Street was described as 'the longest and fairest street in the town' and Westgate Street as 'a broad street and private', although the areas surrounding them were of much lower status. Ibid., p. 277

70. Ibid., pp. 272 and 277

71. The empty 'boxes' in the matrix were filled in by a computer routine devised by Mr N. Wrigley of the Department of Geography, Southampton University, who kindly ran the program for me.

72. The major exceptions were the relatively large houses of the manufacturing and service tradesmen in Fickett Tower and Durham Tower wards in the north-west; the relatively large houses of the merchant group in the two large wards of the north-east, and the relatively small houses of the merchants in White Friar Tower ward in the south-west. In the first case, the wards concerned were on main roads to gates, and the numbers of tradesmen who lived in them were small, so that one or two exceptionally large houses in an occupational group (a weaver with 8 hearths in Fickett Tower Ward, for example) could markedly affect the averages. In the second case, the two wards flanking Pilgrim Street contained, along that thoroughfare, relatively large numbers of mayors and hostmen (see Fig. 5B). The small positive deviations registered by these wards resulted from a combination of these large houses with the generally smaller than average houses of the other merchant adventurers who lived in what was, relative to the main concentration of merchants' houses, a peripheral area. The smaller than average houses of the merchants of White Friar Tower Ward might (but need not necessarily) indicate that the residential status pattern of the merchant core was itself sorted around the wealthy nucleus of Pink Tower ward.

73. This kind of social structure was probably common in British towns. The largest were ports before the Industrial Revolution, and, generally, 'the organization of [trade] was so closely connected with the earliest form of municipal constitution as to have made it possible to argue that constitution and the Gild Merchant were one and the same thing'. In medieval Southampton this merchant dominance was expressed in an exclusive residential area in that part of the town most convenient for them, just as it was in seventeenth-century Newcastle. UNWIN, G. (1904) *Industrial organization in the sixteenth and seventeenth centuries*, pp. 16–17 (Oxford) and PLATT, C. (1973) *Medieval Southampton*, pp. 264–6 (London)

74. LASLETT, op. cit., pp. 18–20

75. Ibid., pp. 23–6; WOOLRICH, A. (1968) 'The English revolution: an introduction' in IVES, E. W. (ed.) *The English revolution 1600–1660*, 1–34, (London) and SUPPLE, B. W. 'Class and social tension: the case of the merchant', ibid., 131–44. Supple argues that the merchants formed the only true 'class' group in seventeenth-century English society. It is difficult to see how this situation can be made conformable with theories which suggest that class affiliations were produced by the rise of capitalism, which also destroyed the merchant hegemony.

76. See DENDY (1901, 1921) op. cit. and ROWE, D. J. (1966) 'The records of the company of shipwrights of Newcastle-upon-Tyne 1622–1967', *Surtees Soc.* 181, Vol I, which give extracts from the proceedings and ordinances of some of the gilds in the mid seventeenth century.

77. VANCE, J. (1967) has dealt with this relationship in a stimulating paper in *Econ. Geogr.* 43, 95–127

78. The role of these institutions in maintaining social and economic functioning in English cities in the seventeenth century, when plagues reduced the populations of some towns by up to 50 per cent, resulting in a vast influx of migrants, and when the Civil War caused short-term economic and longer term political and religious upheaval, would repay study.

APPENDIX

The production of generalized maps and tables required the classification of occupations into groups within which strong affinities of some kind existed. Unfortunately, no single criterion could be applied to produce a classification of pre-industrial urban occupations which was suitable for this particular analysis. The classification given below resulted from a set of compromises: other compromises could have been applied to produce different classifications, but the groupings which have been devised are at least as appropriate to the needs of this study as any other set of categories.

Historians have usually classified pre-industrial urban occupations according to the raw materials used or handled in them. This procedure is inappropriate here because it cuts across the fundamental distinction between merchants and manufacturing craftsmen. Classes A and C reflect this distinction. Class A contains, besides the merchants, those who provided personal services which were largely outside the remit of the Merchant Adventurers monopoly, and who were not, therefore, disabled from achieving similar wealth and influence. Within Class C, the manufacturing craftsmen were classified according to the raw materials they worked on except for the shipbuilders, who were not classified under 'manufacturing: wood' because they operated on a scale which was completely different from that of the joiners and coopers, and they were influenced by locational requirements which were different from those of the main body of manufacturing craftsmen. The latter characteristic, at least, suggested that the shipwrights were more appropriately classified with the other shipping occupations.

Those occupations which were neither mercantile nor manufacturing posed considerable problems of classification. They comprise the shipping, victualling and building crafts, which have been lumped together in category B as 'shipping and services'. This group thus contains, basically, the residuals which could not be appropriately fitted into the other two major categories. There were, obviously, few functional links between these three kinds of activity (this is illustrated by the patternless nature of the location quotients of this group, mapped on Fig. 5A). Because the data for the sub-groups were treated individually, it mattered little whether these three kinds of occupation were grouped into one category or classified as three quite separate ones. So that the summary maps and tables could be produced in a standard format, the former procedure was adopted.

The occupations which are bracketed in column 3 are those with which the preceding craft was linked in a gild. If such crafts were given alone as occupations in the admissions list, they have also been listed separately below.

1 Category	2 Sub-group	3 Occupation
A. Merchants and personal service	1. Merchants	Mayor; hostman who was not a mayor, merchant who was neither a mayor nor a hostman
	2. Personal Service	Goldsmith and scrivenor; recorder; minister of religion; doctor; apothecary; physician and barber-surgeon (and wax and tallow chandler)
B. Shipping and services	1. Shipping	Shipwright; master mariner; mariner, and carrier and carriageman
	2. Victualling	Baker (and beer brewer); butcher; brewer; miller, and confectioner
	3. Building	Mason; slater; waller (and bricklayer and plasterer); pavior; house carpenter; plasterer; plumber, and glazier (and painter)
C. Manufacturing	1. Metal	Blacksmith; anchorsmith; spurrier and lorrimer; cutler; armourer; whitesmith; pewterer; locksmith; pulleymaker, and coiner
	2. Wood	Joiner, and cooper
	3. Clothing and Textiles	Weaver; fuller (and dyer); feltmaker; sailmaker; upholsterer; ropemaker, and tailor
	4. Leather	Tanner; Skinner (and glover); currier; saddler, and cordwainer

A SIMPLE MODEL OF LONDON'S IMPORTANCE IN CHANGING ENGLISH SOCIETY AND ECONOMY 1650-1750*

"Soon London will be all England": James I

E. A. WRIGLEY

TOWARDS THE END OF THE SEVENTEENTH CENTURY LONDON BECAME the largest city in Europe. The population of Paris had reached about 400,000 by the beginning of the seventeenth century and was nearing 500,000 towards its end, but thereafter grew very little for a further century. At the time of the 1801 census its population was still just less than 550,000. London, on the other hand, grew rapidly throughout the seventeenth and eighteenth centuries. Its exact population at any time before the first census is a matter for argument but in round figures it appears to have grown from about 200,000 in 1600 to perhaps 400,000 in 1650, 575,000 by the end of the century, 675,000 in 1750 and 900,000 in 1800.[1] London and Paris were much larger than other cities in Europe during these two centuries and each was very much larger than any rival in the same country. The

---

* I am greatly indebted to Dr. P. Abrams, Professor T. C. Barker, Mr. P. Laslett and Dr. R. S. Schofield for their comments on an earlier draft of this paper.

[1] There is a very useful compilation of estimates of the size of towns and cities in western Europe chiefly for the period 1500-1800 in E. Hélin, *La démographie de Liège aux XVIIe et XVIIIe siècles* (Brussels, 1963), Annexe 1, pp. 238-52. N. G. Brett-James summarizes the calculations of contemporaries and later scholars in *The Growth of Stuart London* (London, 1935), esp. pp. 496-512. He himself suggests figures of 250,000 in 1603 and 320,000 in 1625 (p. 512). John Graunt estimated the population of the capital to be 460,000 in about 1660: *Natural and Political Observations*, reprinted in C. H. Hull, ed., *The Economic Writings of Sir William Petty*, 2 vols. (New York, 1963 and 1964), ii, p. 371. Petty himself concluded that in 1682 London's population was already 670,000: *The Growth of the City of London*, in Hull, ed., *Sir William Petty*, ii, p. 460. Gregory King made a calculation of London's population in 1695 from the number of households arriving at a figure of 527,560: G. E. Barnett, ed., *Two Tracts by Gregory King* (Baltimore, 1936), p. 18. Creighton's estimates of London's population for 1603, 1625 and 1665 agree very closely with those of Brett-James and Graunt for the same periods: C. Creighton, *History of Epidemics in Britain*, 2 vols. (Cambridge, 1891 and 1894), i, p. 660. Mrs. George accepts figures of 674,500 for 1700 and 676,750 for 1750 based on the number of baptisms in the London parish registers: M. D. George, *London Life in the Eighteenth Century* (London, 1930), pp. 24 and 329-30. See also P. E. Jones and A. V. Judges, "London Population in the late Seventeenth Century", *Econ. Hist. Rev.*, vi (1935-6), pp. 45-63. The figures used in this text are rounded for convenience and are probably of the right order of magnitude, but nothing more can be claimed for them.

contrast between the size and rates of growth of the two cities is particularly striking when it is borne in mind that until the last half of the eighteenth century, when the rate of growth of population in England increased sharply, the total population of France was about four times as large as that of England.   In 1650 about $2\frac{1}{2}$ per cent of the population of France lived in Paris; in 1750 the figure was little changed.   London, on the other hand, housed about 7 per cent of England's total population in 1650 and about 11 per cent in 1750. Only in Holland does any one city appear to have contained such a high percentage of the total national population.   Amsterdam in 1650 was already a city of about 150,000 people and contained 8 per cent of the Dutch total.   But Amsterdam by this time had ceased to grow quickly and a century later had increased only to about 200,000, or 9 per cent of the total.[2]

These rough facts suggest immediately that it may be valuable to look more closely at the rapid growth of London between 1650 and 1750.   Anything which distinguished England from other parts of Europe during the century preceding the industrial revolution is necessarily a subject of particular interest since it may help to throw light on the origins of that extraordinary and momentous period of rapid change which has transformed country after country across the face of the globe.

I

It is convenient to begin by examining first some demographic aspects of the rapid growth of population which took place in London. The implications of London's growth can be seen from a very simple model.   The rates and quantities embodied in the model are at best approximations, and it is probable that within the next five years work already in train will make it possible to give much more precise estimates than can be made as yet; but it would require a radical revision of the assumptions used here to upset the general argument.

[2] See Hélin, *La démographie de Liège*, p. 242, and J. A. Faber, H. K. Roessingh, B. H. Slicher van Bath, A. M. van der Woude, and H. J. van Xanten, "Population Changes and Economic Developments in the Netherlands: a Historical Survey", *A. A. G. Bijdragen*, xii (Wageningen, 1965), pp. 58 and 110.   It should perhaps be said that only in countries like England, France and the Netherlands, if anywhere, does it make sense to relate city and national population totals.   In areas like Germany, Italy or Spain, political or economic fragmentation makes this a pointless exercise.   The only cities in Europe with populations of 100,000 or more *c.* 1650 apart from London, Paris and Amsterdam were Naples which was a very large city (250,000-300,000), and Palermo, Venice, Rome and Lisbon (all 100,000-125,000); none of these grew much in the following century.   By the mid-eighteenth century Vienna and Berlin were in this size class (*c.* 175,000 and 110,000 respectively), and perhaps Lyons.   See Hélin, *La démographie de Liège*, pp. 244, 247, 249 and 251.

We may note first that since the population of London rose by about 275,000 between 1650 and 1750 it will on an average have been increasing annually by 2,750.   Secondly, it seems clear that the crude death rate in London was substantially higher than the crude birth rate over the period as a whole.   The gap between the two rates is difficult to estimate accurately and varied considerably during the hundred years in question, being apparently much higher in the last three or four decades of the period than earlier.   The difference between the two rates is most unlikely to have been less than 10 per 1,000 per annum over the century as a whole, however, and may well have been considerably larger.[3]   For the purpose of illustrating the implications of the model we may assume that this figure held throughout.   Thus at the time when the population of London was, say, 500,000 the shortfall of births each year is assumed to be 5,000. At that time to make good this shortfall and to permit an annual increase of the total population of 2,750, the net immigration into London must have been about 8,000 per annum.   Towards the end of the period when the population of London was well above half a million and the gap between birth and death rates was at its greatest, the net figure must have been considerably larger than this.   At other times it may have been rather less.

[3] The uncertainty arises because of the problem of under-registration. Jones and Judges underlined this heavily in their examination of London's population at the end of the seventeenth century.   They were able to show wide discrepancies between totals of baptisms and burials drawn from the three available sources: the returns made under the Marriage Duty Act of 1694, the Bills of Mortality, and the counts made in parish registers at Rickman's behest in 1801.   See Jones and Judges, *Econ. Hist. Rev.*, vi (1935-6).   Glass has made estimates of the degree of under-registration of baptisms and burials in the parish registers and the collector's returns under the 1694 Act for two city parishes: see introduction by D. V. Glass to "London Inhabitants within the Walls, 1695", *London Rec. Soc. Publications*, ii (London, 1966), pp. xxxv-xxxvii. There is a convenient summary of some of the available data in George, *London Life in the Eighteenth Century*, App. 1, pp. 405-10. Gregory King made estimates based on a notional time of peace which imply only a rather small burial surplus in the capital (about 4 per 1,000); however, elsewhere he produced figures for the year 1695 which suggest a much larger shortfall of baptisms: *Two Tracts by Gregory King*, esp. pp. 27 and 43.   It is worth noting that Deane and Cole suggest a rate of natural increase for London in the period 1701-50 of −10·8 per 1,000 per annum and envisage an annual average net immigration into London of 10-12,000 (it should be added that they regard London's population as stationary in number during this half century): P. Deane and W. A. Cole, *British Economic Growth 1688-1959* (Cambridge, 1962), table 26, p. 115 and p. 111.   William Farr thought the London death rate in the later seventeenth century was 80 per 1,000 declining to 50 per 1,000 in the eighteenth century: W. Farr, *Vital Statistics* (London, 1885), p. 131.   Buer estimated that between 1700 and 1750 London needed an average immigration of 10,200 a year to maintain her population, and that during this period the ratio of deaths to births was 3:2: M. C. Buer, *Health, Wealth and Population in Eighteenth Century England* (London, 1926), p. 33.

In any population it is normally the young and single who migrate most readily. There is a growing volume of evidence that in England in the seventeenth and eighteenth centuries mobility before marriage was very high but was reduced once marriage had taken place.[4] In view of this, let us assume, as a part of the demographic model of London's growth, that the mean age of those migrating into London was twenty years. Given the mortality conditions of the day any large group of twenty-year-olds coming into London would represent the survivors of a birth population at least half as large again.[5] Some 12,000 births, therefore, in the rest of England and elsewhere were earmarked, as it were, each year to make it possible for London's population to grow as it did during this period. Once again this is a very rough figure, too high for a part of the century, too low for the later decades, but useful as a means of illustrating the nature of the general demographic relationship between London and the rest of the country.

One further assumption will make the significance of this relationship clearer. If the average surplus of births over deaths in provincial England was 5 per 1,000 per annum (and assuming for the moment that London grew by immigration from England alone), then it follows that London's growth was absorbing the natural increase of a population of some two-and-a-half millions.[6] The total population of England excluding London was only about five millions (varying, of course, a little over the century in question), and there were some areas, especially in the west and north, in which for much of this century there was either no natural increase, or even a natural decrease of population.

In view of the general demographic history of England at this time

[4] This appears very clearly in family reconstitution work based on parish registers. The analysis of successive nominal listings of inhabitants supports the same conclusion. See Peter Laslett and John Harrison "Clayworth and Cogenhoe" in *Historical Essays 1600-1750, presented to David Ogg*, ed. H. E. Bell and R. L. Ollard (London, 1963).

[5] The United Nations specimen life tables suggest that a birth population will fall to two-thirds its original number by the age of twenty when expectation of life at birth is forty: *Methods for Population Projections by Sex and Age*, United Nations, ST/SOA/Series A, Population Studies, no. 25 (New York, 1956). If expectation of life was substantially below this at this period (as it was at Colyton, for example, as I hope to show in a later publication), then a larger birth population would be needed to produce any given number of twenty-year-old immigrants into London.

[6] A rate of increase of 5 per 1,000 is a generous estimate for this period. Gregory King supposed that the annual number of births in England excluding London was 170,000 and of burials 148,000. Assuming the population of England without London to have been 4·9 millions, this suggests a difference between the two rates of about 4·5 per 1,000. But King uses different assumptions elsewhere and presents material which implies a rate of increase less than half as high. See *Two Tracts by Gregory King*, pp. 25 and 27.

London's demographic characteristics assume a singular importance. For there are some surprising features in English demographic history in the century 1650-1750. Family reconstitution studies show that in some parts of the country at least this was a time of very late first marriage for women. And the reduced fertility which is usually associated with a rise in the average age of women at first marriage appears to have been still further diminished in places by the practice of family limitation. Moreover, there is some evidence that age-specific mortality rates, especially of young children, were higher at this time than either earlier or later, so that natural increase was much reduced or was replaced by a surplus of deaths over births.[7]

The preliminary results of a large-scale survey of parish register material using straightforward aggregative methods[8] suggest that these trends were least evident in the home counties and the Midlands, the areas from which access to London was easiest, and it may prove to be the case that a substantial surplus of births continued to be characteristic of these counties throughout the century 1650-1750 but that instead of building up local populations the surplus was siphoned off into London to counterbalance the burial surplus there and to enable it to continue to grow quickly at a time when the rest of the country was barely holding its own.[9] The absence of any great upward press of numbers in England as a whole in this century meant that population growth did not frustrate a slow rise in real incomes, in contrast with the preceding hundred years.[10] Yet this did not prevent a very marked growth in the country's largest city.

One further implication of the demography of London's growth is worth stressing. Let us assume that there was a time when the population of London was 500,000 and the population of the rest of

[7] On these points see E. A. Wrigley "Family Limitation in Pre-Industrial England", *Econ. Hist. Rev.*, 2nd ser., xix (1966), pp. 82-109. This article was based on work done on the parish registers of Colyton in Devon. Preliminary work on reconstituted families of Hartland (Devon) also shows a late age of first marriage for women in the late seventeenth century. W. G. Howson has found the same phenomenon in parishes in the Lune Valley (personal communication).

[8] The survey is being carried out by the *Cambridge Group for the History of Population and Social Structure*. More than two hundred local historians have been kind enough to help in this work.

[9] The London apprenticeship records show that the proportion of apprentices coming from the north and west fell dramatically during the seventeenth century, while the proportion from the home counties rose. One reason for this may well have been the disappearance of a surplus of births in the north and west and its continuance nearer London. See L. Stone, "Social Mobility in England, 1500-1700", *Past and Present*, no. 33 (Apr. 1966), pp. 31-2. Marshall noted that the great bulk of the inter-county movement from Bedfordshire was to London: L. M. Marshall "The Rural Population of Bedfordshire, 1671-1921", *Beds. Hist. Rec. Soc.*, xvi (1934), p. 45.

[10] See Wrigley, *Econ. Hist. Rev.*, xix (1966), pp. 106-8.

the kingdom was 5,000,000. Let it further be assumed that the birth rate was uniformly at a rate of 34 per 1,000 (this is an arbitrary assumption but too little is known of the age and sex structure of these populations and of the prevailing age-specific fertility rates to provide substantially more accurate figures; and in any case the main line of the argument would be unaffected except by radical adjustments). If this were so, then the number of births taking place annually in London would be 17,000 and in the rest of the country 170,000. If we assume that all the children born in London remained in London, and if to the figure of 17,000 children born each year in London is added the 12,000 born in the provinces and needed to maintain London's growth, then it is apparent that the survivors to adult years of almost one sixth of all the births taking place in the country (29,000 out of a total of 187,000) would be living in London twenty years or so after the arrival of the birth cohort used as an illustration.

It does not, of course, follow from this that a sixth of the national total of adults lived in London. The infant and child mortality rates of those born in London were far higher than elsewhere so that many fewer of these children survived to adult years. Indeed the fact that this was so is one of the main reasons for the large inflow of migrants from outside London. The calculation assumes, moreover, that immigrants to London came only from England, whereas there was also, of course, a steady stream of young Scots, Welsh and Irish into the capital. Nor should it be forgotten that London was a great international centre with substantial Dutch, French and German communities.

On the other hand, all the calculations made above are based on figures of *net* immigration into London. The gross figures must certainly have been considerably higher since there was at all times a flow of migrants out of London as well as a heavier flow inward. If therefore one were attempting to estimate the proportion of the total adult population of England who had at some stage in their lives had direct experience of life in the great city, a sixth or an even higher fraction is as plausible a guess as any other.[11]

[11] See George, *London Life in the Eighteenth Century*, pp. 109-10 for an interesting discussion of the chief types of migrants into and out of London. She suggests that the settlement laws tended to encourage rather than prevent migration and that London exercised a strong attraction upon those dislodged from their original settlement. She also quotes a contemporary, Burrington, writing in 1757, who thought that two-thirds of London's adult population came "from distant parts". The records of the Westminster General Dispensary between 1774 and 1781 reveal that only a quarter (824 out of 3,236) of the married people served were London born. Of the rest, 209 were born in Scotland, 280 in Ireland and 53 abroad, a total of 542 in the three categories, or 17 per cent. The balance were born elsewhere in England or Wales (George, *op. cit.*, p. 111).

II

If it is fair to assume that one adult in six in England in this period had had direct experience of London life, it is probably also fair to assume that this must have acted as a powerful solvent of the customs, prejudices and modes of action of traditional, rural England. The leaven of change would have a much better chance of transforming the lump than in, say, France even if living in Paris produced the same change of attitude and action as living in London since there were proportionately four or five times fewer Frenchmen caught up in Parisian life than Englishmen in London life. Possibly there is a threshold level in a situation of this type, beneath which the values and attitudes of a traditional, rural society are very little affected by the existence of a large city, but above which a sufficiently large proportion of the population is exposed to a different way of life to effect a slow transformation in rural society. Too little is known of the sociological differences between life in London and life in provincial England to afford a clear perception of the impact of London's growth upon the country as a whole. Some things, however, are already known, and other points can be adumbrated in the hope that more research will resolve present uncertainties.

London was so very much bigger than any other town in the country that the lives of the inhabitants of London were inevitably very different from the lives of men living in the middle rank of towns, such as Leicester or Derby, where local landed society could continue to dominate many aspects of town life and the ties with the surrounding countryside were ancient and intimate. Family life in London, at least for the very large number who had come to London from elsewhere, was necessarily different from the family life of those who lived within five or ten miles of their birthplace all their lives. Near relatives were less likely to live close at hand. Households in the central parts of London were larger on average than those in provincial England. And this was not because the conjugal families contained more children but because other members of the households were more numerous. There were many more lodgers than in the countryside, as well as servants, apprentices and other kin in varying proportions according to the social type of the parish.[12]

Outside the household, moreover, a far higher proportion of

[12] The characteristic English provincial situation is becoming clear from work now being carried out by the *Cambridge Group for the History of Population and Social Structure* on listings of inhabitants of English parishes. This work includes the analysis of London returns compiled in 1695 under the Marriage Duty Act. Glass's analysis of some of these London parish listings, though only a first survey of the material, provides much valuable information about the city: Glass, *London Rec. Soc. Publications*, vol. ii.

day-to-day contacts was inevitably casual. Urban sociologists describe the characteristic tendency of modern city life to cause individuals in these circumstances to be treated not as occupying an invariable status position in the community, but in terms of the rôle associated with the particular transaction which gave rise to the fleeting contact. They stress the encouragement which city life gives to what Weber called "rational" as opposed to "traditional" patterns of action and the tendency for contract to replace custom. The " 'aping' of one's betters" which often attracted unfavourable comment at the time, and which has sometimes been seen as a powerful influence in establishing new patterns of consumption, is a common product of social situations like that in which the inhabitants of London found themselves at this period. Coleman has recently suggested that in the seventeenth century there was probably a backward-sloping supply curve for labour.[13] It would be fascinating to know how far the new patterns of consumption behaviour established in London may have helped to reduce any preference for leisure rather than high earnings. There is much literary evidence of the shiftless and disorderly behaviour of many members of London's population at this time, but there were important countervailing influences at work upon the bulk of the population. The shop, a most important, new influence upon consumer behaviour, was a normal feature of the London scene by the latter half of the seventeenth century.[14] Sugar, tea and tobacco had become articles of mass consumption by the early eighteenth century. Life in London probably encouraged a certain educational achievement in a wider spectrum of the population than might be expected. In 1838-9 fewer men and women were unable to sign their names on marriage than anywhere else in the country (marks were made as a substitute for signatures by only 12 per cent of grooms and 24 per cent of brides, whereas the national averages were 33 per cent and 49 per cent respectively). How long this differential had existed is not yet known but if it proves to have been true of earlier periods in London's history also, it suggests that the London environment put a high premium on at least a minimum degree of literacy.[15]

[13] D. C. Coleman, "Labour in the English Economy of the Seventeenth Century", repr. from *Econ. Hist. Rev.*, 2nd ser., viii (1955-6), in *Essays in Economic History*, ed. E. M. Carus-Wilson, ii (London, 1962), p. 303.

[14] See A. H. John, "Aspects of English Economic Growth in the first half of the Eighteenth Century", repr. from *Economica* (1961), in *Essays in Economic History*, ed. Carus-Wilson, ii, pp. 366 and 369.

[15] See Registrar-General, *First Annual Report of Births, Deaths and Marriages* (London, 1839), pp. 8-9. Dr. R. S. Schofield is engaged in a study of inability to sign based on a random sample of suitable source materials from the sixteenth century onwards. This will provide *inter alia* firm evidence about London in earlier centuries.

There were many ways in which seventeenth-century London differed from a modern city. Glass, for example, notes that in 1695 the proportion of wealthy and substantial households was highest near the centre of London and tended to fall with distance from the centre, being very low outside the city walls (apart from St. Dunstan in the West). "This kind of gradient is in contrast to that found in the modern city, in which the centrifugal movement of population has occurred particularly among the middle classes".[16] In this respect London was still in 1695 a pre-industrial city, but in general London was far removed from the classical type of pre-industrial city. Sjoberg's account of the typical pre-industrial city may serve as a means of underlining the "modernity" of London at this period. He draws illustrative material not only from the cities of Asia today, from ancient Mesopotamia and the Near East, and from the classical cultures of the Mediterranean, but also from medieval Europe.

Sjoberg's pre-industrial city is fed because the city houses the ruling élite. The élite "induces the peasantry to increase its production and relinquish some of its harvest to the urban community". It "must persuade many persons subsisting, relative to industrial standards, on the very margins of existence, under conditions of near starvation or malnutrition, to surrender food and other items that they themselves could readily use".[17] The farmer "brings his produce to the urban centers at irregular intervals and in varying amounts".[18] Within the city the merchants, those responsible for the organization of much of its economic life, are "ideally excluded from membership of the elite". A few manage to achieve high status under sufferance, but "most are unequivocally in the lower class or outcaste groups".[19] The chief reason for excluding merchants is that they necessarily meet all types of people, making casual contacts with men in all positions, and are therefore a menace to the stability of the existing societal arrangements.[20] Men are largely indifferent to the discipline of the clock and only half attentive to the passage of time. Almost all transactions, however trivial, are concluded only after long haggling.[21] There is little specialization of function in craft industrial production, though a good deal of product specialization.[22]

In the pre-industrial city the dominant type of family is the

---

[16] Glass, *London Rec. Soc. Publications*, ii, p. xxi.
[17] G. Sjoberg, *The Preindustrial City* (New York, 1960), p. 118.
[18] *Ibid.*, p. 207.
[19] *Ibid.*, pp. 120 and 121.
[20] *Ibid.*, p. 136.
[21] *Ibid.*, pp. 204-5, 209-10.
[22] *Ibid.*, p. 197.

extended family, though necessity may prevent it developing so fully in the lower classes as in the élite.[23]   Marriage takes place early, and before marriage a man does not reach full adult status.[24]   On marriage the bride normally expects to move into the household of her husband's family.[25]   "However, as industrial-urbanization becomes firmly entrenched, the large extended household is no longer the ideal toward which people strive.   The conjugal family system now becomes the accepted, and often the preferred norm".   This occurs because "a fluid, flexible, small family unit is necessarily the dominant form in a social order characterized by extensive social and spatial mobility".[26]

In his anxiety to correct the naive assumptions of some sociologists about cities in the past and in the developing world today, Sjoberg may well have been tempted to straitjacket his material at times in a way which does violence to history.   At all events not only London but all England had moved far from his archetypal pre-industrial society by the seventeenth century.   The conjugal family system was firmly established in England at that time.   On marriage a man and his wife set up a new household.[27]   And both sexes married late, later than in England today, and far later than in extra-European societies in which marriage, for women at least, almost invariably occurred at or even before puberty.[28]   Where three generations did live together in the same household this was not usually because a son on marriage brought his wife to his parents' home, but because a grandparent came to live in the household of a married son or daughter when no longer able to look after himself or herself, for example on the death of a spouse.

London shared these sociological and demographic characteristics with the rest of the country.   Three-generational households were possibly rather commoner in the wealthier parts of London than was usual elsewhere[29] but everywhere the conjugal family appears to have been the dominant form.   The status of merchants in London varied with their wealth but it would be difficult to argue that they were largely excluded from the ruling élite.   The provisioning of

[23] *Ibid.*, pp. 157-9.
[24] *Ibid.*, pp. 145-6.
[25] *Ibid.*, p. 157.
[26] *Ibid.*, p. 162.
[27] See P. Laslett, *The World We Have Lost* (London, 1965), pp. 90-2.
[28] See J. Hajnal "European Marriage Patterns in Perspective", in *Population in History*, ed. D. V. Glass and D. E. C. Eversley (London, 1965).   Also Wrigley, *Econ. Hist. Rev.* (1966) and, more generally, W. J. Goode, *World Revolution and Family Patterns* (New York, 1963).
[29] See Glass, *London Rec. Soc. Publications*, ii, pp. xxxii-xxxiv.

London was secured by an elaborate and sophisticated set of economic institutions and activities and many of the farmers who sent their produce to the London market geared their land to commodity production in a thoroughly "modern" fashion.[30] In short, whereas pre-industrial cities might grow large and powerful without in any way undermining the structure of traditional society, a city like London in the later seventeenth century was so constituted sociologically, demographically and economically that it could well reinforce and accelerate incipient change.

What might be called the demonstration effect of London's wealth and growth, for instance, played an important part in engendering changes elsewhere. London contained many men of great wealth and power whose sources of wealth did not lie in the land and who found it possible to maintain power and status without acquiring large landed estates.[31] Indeed in as much as it was the backing of London which assured the Parliamentary armies of success in their struggle with the king, London could be said at the beginning of the century 1650–1750 to have shown that it possessed the power necessary to sway the rest of the country to its will. In the provinces in the later seventeenth and early eighteenth centuries there were increasingly large numbers of men of wealth and position who stood outside the traditional landed system. These were the group whom Everitt has recently termed the "pseudo-gentry". They formed "that class of leisured and predominantly urban families who, by their manner of life, were commonly regarded as gentry, though they were not supported by a landed estate".[32] Their links with London were close and their journeys thither frequent. They were urban in their habit of life but would have been powerless to protect their position in society if London had not existed. London both provided them with a pattern of behaviour, and, because of its immense economic strength and prestige, protected them from any hostility on the part of the traditional elements in society. London was, as it were, both

---

[30] See Section III below.

[31] Stone in discussing the wealth generated by the great commercial expansion of the late seventeenth-century remarks: "The closing down of the land market suggests that, however it was distributed, less of this wealth than before was being converted into social status by the purchase of an estate, and more of it was being reinvested in long-term mortgages, commerce and banking". One reason for less money being invested in land was perhaps simply that rich Londoners no longer felt moved to use money in this way if their status did not suffer by refraining from acquiring land. See L. Stone, "Social Mobility in England, 1500-1700", *Past and Present*, no. 33 (Apr. 1966), p. 34.

[32] A. Everitt, "Social Mobility in Early Modern England", *Past and Present*, no. 33 (Apr. 1966), p. 71.

their normative reference group[33] and their guarantee against the withdrawal of status respect.

III

The social and economic changes of the seventeenth and eighteenth centuries reached their culmination in the industrial revolution. Although this was far more than simply an economic phenomenon, economic change was what defined it. It is natural, therefore, to consider the strictly economic effects of London's rapid growth as well as the demographic and sociological changes which accompanied it.

The importance of the London food market in promoting change in the agriculture of Kent and East Anglia from an early date has long been recognized. Fisher showed how even during the century before 1650 London was large enough to exercise a great influence upon the agriculture of the surrounding counties, causing a rapid spread of market gardening, increasing local specialization, and encouraging the wholesalers to move back up the chain of production and exchange to engage directly in the production of food, or to sink capital in the improvement of productive facilities. The influence of the London food market was "not merely in the direction of increased production but also in that of specialization, and in that direction lay agricultural progress" — "Poulterers made loans to warreners and themselves bred poultry. Fruiterers helped to establish orchards and leased them when established. Butchers themselves became graziers". Between 1650 and 1750 it is reasonable to suppose that the demand for food in the London market must have increased by about three-quarters since population increased roughly in that proportion. The increased demand was met from home sources rather than by import, and it follows that all those changes which Fisher observed in the preceding century were spread over a larger area and intensified.[34]

[33] To use the term employed by Runciman in a very lucid exposition of the concept of the reference group generally: W. G. Runciman, *Relative Deprivation and Social Justice* (London, 1966), chap. ii.

[34] F. J. Fisher, "The Development of the London Food Market, 1540-1640", *Econ. Hist. Rev.*, v (1934-5), pp. 56 and 63. The steady spread of the influence of London is well illustrated by the remark of a contemporary, John Houghton, who wrote *à propos* meat production for the London market, "The bigness and great consumption of London doth not only encourage the breeders of provisions and higglers thirty miles off but even to four score miles. Wherefore I think it will necessarily follow . . . . that if London should consume as much again country for eighty miles around would have greater employment or else those that are further off would have some of it": J. Houghton, *A Collection of Letters for the Improvement of Husbandry* (London, 1681), pp. 165-6. I owe this reference to the kindness of Dr. J. Thirsk.

Once more it is interesting to work initially in terms of a very crude model and review its implications, though in this case the orders of magnitude assumed are even more open to question than those embodied in the demographic model used earlier. Suppose, firstly, that in 1650 the population of London was 400,000 and the population of the rest of the country 5,100,000 and that in the country outside the metropolis the proportion of the male labour force engaged in agriculture was 60 per cent.[35] This would imply that 3,060,000 were dependent on agriculture (those directly employed plus their families), and that every 100 farming families supported a total of 80 families who earned their living in other ways. If in the next century the population of London rose to 675,000 and that of the whole country to 6,140,000[36] but the proportion engaged in agriculture outside the capital remained the same, then the agricultural population in 1750 would have numbered 3,279,000 and every 100 farming families would have supported 87 other families.[37] This in turn would imply a rise in agricultural productivity per head of about four per cent. This figure is certainly too low, however, since this was a century of rising exports of grain, especially after 1700. By 1750 exports formed about six per cent of total grain production; at the beginning of the century they were only a little over one per cent.[38] Grain was not, of course, the only product of agriculture, but there were parallel movements in some other agricultural products. Imports of wool, for example, fell markedly in the early eighteenth century, while

[35] This is once more rather an arbitrary figure. Different assumptions about its size produce slightly higher or lower estimates of increase in agricultural production per head. A higher percentage engaged in agriculture will result in a lower figure of increased productivity and vice-versa. The Tawneys' analysis of the Gloucestershire Muster Roll of 1608 suggests that a rather lower figure might have been appropriate: A. J. and R. H. Tawney "An Occupational Census of the Seventeenth Century", *Econ. Hist. Rev.*, v (1934-5), pp. 25-64 and esp. p. 39. Gregory King's work does not lend itself to a breakdown along these lines but is consistent with a figure of 60 per cent or slightly higher. This is true also of the analyses of listings of inhabitants being carried out by Mr. P. Laslett in Cambridge. Some of the listings give details of occupations. Stone's assumption, based partly on King, that 90 per cent of the population (presumptively in the mid-seventeenth century) were manual workers on the land is very difficult to accept. Even at the peak of the harvest period when men normally engaged in other pursuits might work on the land this would be an extraordinarily high figure. See Stone, *Past and Present*, no. 33 (Apr. 1966), p. 20.

[36] Brownlee's estimate, supported by Deane and Cole: Deane and Cole, *British Economic Growth*, pp. 5-6.

[37] This assumes that farming and non-farming families were of the same average size, but could be rephrased without damaging the sense of the passage if this assumption is denied.

[38] Deane and Cole, *British Economic Growth*, table 17, p. 65.

domestic production rose.   There was a sharp rise in the production of mutton, though not of beef, and some minor agricultural products, notably hops, were grown in greater quantities.[39]   All in all it is reasonable to suppose that these changes represent a rise of not less than five per cent in agricultural productivity per head.   This, in combination with the rise which must have occurred in meeting London's demands, suggests a rise of about ten per cent in agricultural productivity per head.

A rise of ten per cent in productivity is far from trivial.   It could have released a substantial amount of purchasing power into other channels as the price of foodstuffs fell and at the same time have made it possible for a substantially higher proportion of the population to be drawn into secondary and tertiary employment.   The rise, however, is almost certainly understated at ten per cent, since the percentage of the total labour force outside the capital engaged in agriculture probably fell somewhat, implying a still steeper rise in agricultural productivity per head.   It has been suggested, indeed, that the numbers engaged in agriculture actually fell in the first half of the eighteenth century.[40]   This is an extreme hypothesis. Suppose, however, that the population dependent on agriculture rose only from 3,060,000 to 3,150,000 between 1650 and 1750, and not to 3,279,000 as in the first variant of the model (that is the proportion engaged in agriculture fell over the century from 60 to $57\frac{1}{2}$ per cent of the total population outside London).   If this were the case, and making the suggested allowance also for growing exports and declining imports, then the rise in agricultural productivity per head would be about thirteen per cent during the century.   This is not an extreme figure.   Indeed it is very probably too low.   Deane and Cole suggest that the rise may have been as high as twenty-five per cent in the first half of the eighteenth century alone.[41]   But a rise in agricultural productivity even of this magnitude is a formidable achievement and goes far to suggesting how a pre-industrial economy can slowly lever itself up by its own bootstraps to the point where a rapid growth of secondary industry can occur.   The fact that income elasticity of demand for food is substantially less than unity makes it easy to understand how grain prices might sag in these circumstances

[39] For wool see Deane and Cole, *British Economic Growth*, p. 68 and B. R. Mitchell and P. Deane *British Historical Statistics* (Cambridge, 1962), pp. 190-1.   For mutton and beef, see Deane and Cole, *op. cit.*, pp. 68-71. For hops see T. S. Ashton, *An Economic History of England: the Eighteenth Century* (London, 1955), p. 240.

[40] Deane and Cole, *British Economic Growth*, p. 75.

[41] Deane and Cole, *British Economic Growth*, p. 75.

and how considerable the diversion of purchasing power into the products of secondary industry may have been.

It does not follow from the above, of course, that the considerable rise in agricultural productivity per head which appears to have taken place was due to London's growth in its entirety. What can be said is that the steady growth in demand for food in London as population there increased, necessarily caused great changes in the methods used on farms over a wider and wider area, in the commercial organization of the food market, and in the transport of food. It must also have tended to increase the proportion of people living outside London who were not engaged directly in agriculture since tertiary employment was sure to increase in these circumstances. Drovers, carters, badgers, brokers, cattle dealers, corn chandlers, hostlers, innkeepers and the like grew more and more numerous as larger and larger fractions of the year's flocks and crops were consumed at a distance from the areas in which they were produced. As yet it is difficult to quantify the changes in employment structure satisfactorily, but many parish registers began regularly to record occupations from the later seventeenth or early eighteenth centuries onwards,[42] and it is therefore a fairly straightforward matter to produce a picture of changing employment structure for this period for many parts of the country, given sufficient time and effort. Such an exercise may well reveal not only a slow fall in the proportion of men directly employed on the land, but also differences in the timing and speed of change related to the accessibility of the market.

There were other ways in which the immense demands of the London market helped to promote economic and technological changes in the structure of English production during this period. The inhabitants of London needed fuel as well as food, and before the end of the sixteenth century they were beginning to abandon wood for coal as the chief source of domestic fuel. The annual shipment of coal south along the coast from Tyneside and Wearside had reached about 650,000 tons by 1750, having doubled in the preceding hundred years.[43] This represented a very substantial fraction of the total production of coal in the north-east, and perhaps as much as a sixth of the total national production. Coal production in England was on a much larger scale during these years than in any

[42] In the case of marriages the occupation of the groom was given; in baptism and burial entries the occupation of the head of the household in which the birth or death had occurred. Frequently occupations were noted in only one or two of the series rather than in all three.

[43] J. U. Nef, *The Rise of the British Coal Industry* (London, 1932), ii, pp. 381–2.

other country in Europe, and the coal industry was the forcing house for many of the technical improvements which were to come to a fuller fruition during the classical years of the industrial revolution. Newcomen's engine was developed largely to meet the drainage problem in coal mines and found its largest sale among mine owners. And it was in the Newcastle area that the first railways were constructed to enable horses to pull much heavier loads from the pitheads to the coal staithes. The first beginnings of the new technology of the steam engine and the railway lay in the eighteenth-century coal mining industry, and one of its chief supports in turn was the large and steadily growing demand for coal afforded by the London coal market.[44]

Furthermore, the increased shipment of coal down the east coast to the Thames required a major expansion in shipping capacity. Nef estimated that during this period about half the total tonnage of the English merchant marine was engaged in the Newcastle coal trade.

> When we add, to the ships employed by the coal trade from Durham and Northumberland, the ships employed by that from Scottish and west-coast ports, it seems likely that, at the time of the Restoration, the tonnage of colliers had come to exceed the tonnage of all other British merchantmen. The coal trade from Newcastle to London was relatively no less important in the late seventeenth century than in the late eighteenth century, when, Adam Smith observes, it "Employs more shipping than all the carrying trades of England".[45]

Apart from serving as an important reservoir of trained seamen in time of war, the growth of the coal trade played a notable part in the expansion of the English shipbuilding industry and the development of vessels which could be worked by far fewer hands per ton of cargo.[46]

The crude quantification of the importance of the London coal trade can be approached in a different way. If output per man-year of coalminers at this time was about 200 tons in favourable circum-

[44] I have discussed these changes from a different viewpoint and at greater length elsewhere: E. A. Wrigley, "The Supply of Raw Materials in the Industrial Revolution", *Econ. Hist. Rev.*, 2nd ser., xv (1962-3), pp. 1-16.

[45] Nef, *op. cit.*, i, pp. 239-40.

[46] It is interesting to remember John's comment on the growth of the export trade in corn at this time: "Grain became a major bulk cargo and between 1730 and 1763 about 110,000-130,000 tons were, on an average, carried annually from English ports in ships which only occasionally exceeded a hundred tons burthen. This had its effect upon the more efficient use of shipping, upon investment in shipbuilding and upon the employment of dockside labour". Coal shipments along the coast at this time were running at about five times the level of corn shipments by tonnage. John, *Essays in Economic History*, ed. Carus-Wilson, ii, p. 364.

stances,[47] then by 1750 some 3,500 men must have been engaged in digging London's coal. Gregory King supposed that about 50,000 men were employed in his day as common seamen[48] and it is therefore probable that at least a further 10,000 men[49] were employed on the colliers easing their way up and down the east coast (though the ships were laid up in the winter so that the employment was heavily seasonal). In addition the movement of coal to the staithes must have been the livelihood of hundreds of carters, waggoners and coal heavers.[50] In all the total employment afforded by the London coal trade outside London (except in as much as the sailors were Londoners) may well have risen from about 8,000 in the mid-seventeenth century to 15,000 a century later. Including their families increases the numbers directly dependent on the coal trade to about 25,000 and 50,000 people respectively. The multiplier effect of the presence and growth of London is well illustrated by this example. Secondary and tertiary employment increased considerably at a distance as well as in London itself.[51] No doubt the flourishing state of the mines round Newcastle and the consequent local demand for food produced in miniature in that area the sort of changes in agriculture which London had already produced in the home counties at an earlier date.

London's importance as a centre of consumption, which prompted Defoe in 1724 to write of the "general dependence of the whole country upon the city of London . . . for the consumption of its produce",[52] sprang not only from its size but also from the relatively high level of wages prevailing there. Gilboy's work on eighteenth-century wage rates provides evidence of this. "The London laborer had the highest wages of any group we have examined. In the first part of the century, at least, he had surplus income to spend and there is every indication that real wages improved as the century

[47] Nef, *op. cit.*, ii, p. 138.
[48] *Two Tracts by Gregory King*, p. 31.
[49] The problem of moving coal in bulk by sea brought about a substantial saving in men employed per ton of cargo moved during the seventeenth century. For this reason it is likely that fewer men were employed on colliers than might be expected in view of their large share in the tonnage of the English merchant marine. See Nef, *op. cit.*, i, pp. 390-2.
[50] Nef, *op. cit.*, ii, p. 142.
[51] This is true of a wide range of manufacturing and service industries. Fisher, for example, noted that London had no malting facilities and few corn mills: "Consequently, a number of country towns found their major employment in the processing of the city's corn, and their inhabitants a regular occupation as middlemen": Fisher, *Econ. Hist. Rev.*, v (1934-5), p. 60.
[52] Fisher, *Econ. Hist. Rev.*, v (1934-5), p. 51.

progressed".[53]   When George remarked that "as early as 1751 it was said that the shoes sold in London were chiefly made in the country where labour was cheaper",[54] she was touching upon a general phenomenon.   Men and women were put in work over much of the home counties and Midlands because their labour was much cheaper than the labour of London artisans and journeymen.   The existence of a mass of relatively well paid labour in London played a major part in creating new levels of real wages and new standards of consumption in the century after the Restoration, when "there was a rise in internal demand which permanently affected the level of expectation of most classes in English society".[55]

Access to the London market was the making of many a manufacturer and a forcing house of change in methods of manufacture, in marketing techniques and in systems of distribution.   Josiah Wedgwood was drawn thither.

> [He] was quick to realize the value of a warehouse in London.   For high quality goods he needed a market accustomed to "fine prices".   He was not likely to find it in the annual market fairs of Staffordshire — the time-honoured *entrepôt* of their county's pots — nor among the country folk who haggled over their wares straight from the crateman's back or the hawker's basket, and to whom expense was the controlling factor in deciding their custom.[56]

But this did not isolate him from mass markets.   Once having secured the custom of the London élite he was able also to sell his less expensive lines to the middle and lower classes.   He studied closely the idiosyncracies of each group at home and abroad and produced goods designed to appeal peculiarly to each of them.

> By these means Wedgwood had created an enormous demand for his ware both ornamental and useful.   The upper classes bought both, but mainly the expensive ornamental wares, and in imitation of their social superiors the lower classes bought the useful.[57]

Moreover, his efforts to command a countrywide market drew him into canal construction and the promotion of turnpike trusts.[58]

Wedgwood was one of the most original and successful entrepreneurs of his age.   The actions of his fellows seldom show the same appreciation of the opportunities for new methods.   And his

[53] E. W. Gilboy, *Wages in Eighteenth Century England* (Cambridge, Mass., 1934), p. 241.   See also chaps. i and ii.

[54] George, *London Life in the Eighteenth Century*, p. 198.

[55] John, *Essays in Economic History*, ed. Carus-Wilson, ii, p. 373.

[56] N. McKendrick, "Josiah Wedgwood: an eighteenth century Entrepreneur in Salesmanship and Marketing Techniques", *Econ. Hist. Rev.*, 2nd ser., xii (1959-60), pp. 418-9.

[57] *Ibid.*, p. 429.

[58] *Ibid.*, p. 429.

product may have lent itself more than most to illustrating the sense in which a triumph in London opened up the markets of the whole country. Yet it is reasonable to quote his example, for his success hinged upon an economic and social fact of importance before Wedgwood's time — through the London market the whole country might be won.

> For a fashionable appeal in London had a vital influence even in the depths of the provinces. The woman in Newcastle upon Tyne who insisted on a dinner service of "Arabesque Border" before her local shopkeeper had even heard of it, wanted it because it was "much used in London at present", and she steadfastly "declin'd taking any till she had seen that pattern".[59]

The London market, of course, supported many industries within the city itself. Silk weaving at Spitalfields, brewing, gin manufacture, watch and clock making, cabinet making, the manufacture of soap, glass and furniture, and a wide range of luxury industries have all received notice. They all added to the economic weight of London, and furthered its growth, though few of them produced striking technological advances or were transformed into path-breaking industries during the industrial revolution. They were impressive in their range but were not for the most part greatly different in kind from the industries to be found in large cities elsewhere in Europe.

London's prime economic foundation, however, had long been her trade rather than her industry. English trade expanded greatly during the century and London enjoyed the lion's share of it. It has been estimated that a quarter of the population depended directly on employment in port trades in 1700 and, allowing for the multiplier effect of this employment, "it is clear that the greatness of London depended, before everything else, on the activity in the port of London".[60] London's merchants, not her manufacturers, dominated her activities economically and politically, and it has long been a momentous question how best to conceive the mechanism by which the large fortunes made in London from commerce helped to transform the national economy.

Many London merchants bought land in the country. Some in doing so hastened agricultural change. The banking and general commercial facilities of London were available to men throughout England and played some part in financing the agricultural and industrial changes which occurred in many parts of the country. The success of the London merchants fostered a change of attitude

---

[59] *Ibid.*, p. 420.
[60] R. Davis, *The Rise of the English Shipping Industry* (London, 1962), p. 390. See also pp. 34-5 on the rapid growth of English commerce and London's predominance among English ports.

towards trade.   It helped to fulfil one of the necessary conditions of rapid economic growth in Leibenstein's analysis — that "the rate of growth of the new entrepreneurial class must be sufficiently rapid and its success, power and importance sufficiently evident so that entrepreneurship, in some form or other, becomes an 'honorific' mode of life in men's minds".[61]   But it is doubtful whether the prime connection between the growth of London and the great changes going forward outside London is to be sought in points of this type. London's trading pre-eminence is perhaps better conceived as acting more powerfully at one remove.   It was the fact that the growth of her trading wealth enabled London herself to grow, to develop as a centre of consumption, and to dominate English society, which formed her greatest contribution to the total process of change in the country as a whole.   The relationship between rising trading wealth and economic and social change outside London was primarily, as it were, indirect, springing from the changes which the steady growth of London provoked elsewhere in ways already discussed.   While other big European cities during this century could do little more than maintain their population size, London almost doubled her population.   Already as large as any other European city in 1650, it was much larger than any rival a century later.   In order to meet the food and fuel requirements of a city of this size old methods in many cases were simply inadequate.   And the new methods developed often produced those substantial increases in productivity per head which form the most promising base for a continuing beneficent spiral of economic activity.

IV

It is always well to be chary of accepting explanations which explain too much.   The industrial revolution in England was a vastly complex congerie of changes so diverse that it would be absurd to suppose that any one development of earlier times can serve to explain more than a part of it.   It will not do to pyramid everything upon changes in the supply of capital, or the burgeoning of Non-conformist entrepreneurship, or an increase in upward social mobility.   Complicated results had, in this case at least, complicated origins.   It is therefore no part of this argument that the growth of London in the century before 1750 was the sole engine of change in the country, to which all the chief preconditions of the industrial revolution can be traced.   But London's growth is a fine vantage

[61] H. Leibenstein, *Economic Backwardness and Economic Growth* (New York, 1963), p. 129.

point from which to review much that was happening. The period between the rapid rise in population and economic activity which ended early in the seventeenth century and the onset of renewed rapid growth of population and production in the last third of the eighteenth century has remained something of an enigma in economic history. It was a period in which population grew little if at all over the country as a whole. In some areas for long periods it was probably falling. Many of the chief indices of production, when estimates of them are possible, show comparatively little change and certainly grew much less spectacularly than either before or after.[62] There was a slow, if cumulatively important, improvement in agricultural productivity because of the introduction of new crops like roots and clover, and because there was both a slow drift of land into enclosure and increasing flexibility of land use in the champion areas. Trade and industry expanded but in general at a modest rate.

How then should this period be understood? It was immediately followed by a period which saw the birth of a radically new economic system, the transition from the pre-industrial to the industrial world. Was England in 1750 greatly improved when compared with the England of the Commonwealth as a springboard for rapid economic and social change? Was the triggering off of the period of rapid growth connected, as it were, in great depth with the preceding period, or could it have occurred almost equally readily at a considerably earlier period? It is against a background of questions of this type that the growth of London appears so strategically important.

There were a number of developments tending to promote economic change and growth in the hundred years 1650-1750. Apart from the growth of London, for example, there were the agricultural advances which improved animal husbandry and lay behind the secular tendency of grain prices to fall (thus helping real wages to rise where money wages were unchanged or improved). Or again there is the probability that because of stable numbers and a modest increase in production the national product/population ratio rose significantly. The idea of critical mass has been invoked recently as a concept of value in conveying the nature of the importance of cumulative slow change in the period immediately preceding rapid industrialization.[63] It could be used appropriately

[62] For the second half of the period there is a good summary of available quantitative evidence in Deane and Cole, *British Economic Growth*, pp. 50-82.

[63] See D. S. Landes, "Encore le problème de la révolution industrielle en Angleterre", *Bulletin de la Société d'Histoire Moderne*, 12th ser., no. 18. This concept is discussed also in an article by F. Crouzet which clearly owes much to the idea, "Croissances comparées de l'Angleterre et de la France au XVIIIe siècle", *Annales, E.S.C.*, xxi (1966), esp. pp. 290-1.

of any of these progressive changes, but is particularly telling when related to London's growth. It is not so much that London's growth was independently more important than the other major changes which modified English economy and society during the century, as that it is a most convenient point of entry into the study of the whole range of changes which took place, especially since some aspects of London's growth can be quantified fairly satisfactorily. Both the changes in agriculture which took place and the failure of national population to increase are closely intertwined with the growth of London, but not with each other. Demographically the existence of London counterbalanced any "natural" growth of population in much of the rest of the country, and the necessity of feeding London created market conditions over great tracts of England which fostered agricultural improvement and reduced economic regionalism. The absence or slightness of population growth overall, had it not been for London's expansion, might well have inhibited agricultural change.

V

It is possible to write out a check-list of changes which by their occurrence in a traditional and predominantly agricultural society tend to promote social and economic change and may succeed in engendering the magic "take-off". On any such list the following items are likely to appear (the list is far from being exhaustive).

A. *Economic changes*

1. The creation of a single national market (or at least very much larger regional markets) for a wide range of goods and services, so that specialization of function may be developed and economies of scale exploited.

2. The fostering of changes in agricultural methods which increase the productivity of those engaged in agriculture so that the cost of foodstuffs will fall and real wages rise; so that a rising proportion of the workforce can find employment in secondary and tertiary activities without prejudicing the supply of food or raising its price inordinately; and possibly so that a larger export income can be derived from the sale of surplus food supplies abroad.

3. The development of new sources of raw material supply which are not subject to the problem of rising marginal costs of production in the manner characteristic of raw materials in pre-

industrial economies.[64]   This occurs when mineral raw materials are substituted for animal or vegetable products (for example, coal for wood) and may well be accompanied by important technological changes contrived to overcome novel production problems (for example, the Newcomen engine or the coke-fired blast furnace).

4.   The provision of a wider range of commercial and credit facilities so that the latent strengths of the economy can be more expertly, quickly and cheaply mobilized.   Under this head might fall, for example, the cluster of changes accompanying and reflected in the establishment and development of the Bank of England.

5.   The creation of a better transport network to reduce the cost of moving goods from place to place; to make it possible for goods to move freely at all seasons of the year in spite of inclement weather; to shorten the time involved and so to economize in the capital locked up in goods in transit; and more generally to foster all the changes of the type mentioned in (1) above.

6.   The securing of a steady rise in real incomes so that the volume of effective demand rises *in toto* and its composition changes with the diversion of an increased fraction of the total purchasing power into the market for the products of industry.   This is closely connected with (2) above.

B.   *Demographic changes*

7.   The interplay between fertility, mortality and nuptiality must be such that population does not expand too rapidly and this must hold true for some time after real incomes per head have begun to trend upwards.   If this is not so, the cycle of events which is often termed Malthusian can hardly be avoided — there is a great danger that real incomes will be depressed and economic growth will peter out.   This happened often enough before the industrial revolution. Leibenstein remarks with justice that ". . . historical evidence would seem to suggest . . . [that] it was the rate of population growth, whether or not induced by economic expansion, that ate up the fruits of expansion and resulted in expansion in the aggregate sense without much improvement per head".[65]   Too rapid population growth can, of course, be avoided by the existence of areas of surplus

[64] For a fuller discussion of the point see Wrigley, *Econ. Hist. Rev.*, xv (1962-3), esp. pp. 1-6.

[65] H. Leibenstein, "Population Growth and the Take-off Hypothesis", in W. W. Rostow, ed., *The Economics of Take-off into Sustained Growth* (London, 1963), p. 173.

mortality which counterbalance those of surplus fertility as well as by the existence of a rough balance of births and deaths in each area throughout the country.

C. *Sociological changes*

8.   The steady spread of environments in which the socialization process produces individuals "rationally" rather than "traditionally" oriented in their values and patterns of action.

9.   The establishment of conditions in which upward social mobility need not necessarily lead to what might be called the recirculation of ability within traditional society but can also produce a steady strengthening of new groups who do not subscribe to the same priorities or use their wealth and status in the same ways as the upper levels of traditional society.

10. The spread of the practice of aping one's betters. When consumption habits become more fluid and the new styles and wants of the upper ranks are rapidly suffused throughout the lower ranks of society, men experience a stronger spur to improve their incomes, and the first steps are taken towards the era of uniform, mass consumption. To be aware that a change in one's pattern of life is possible and to consider it desirable is a vital first step to the securing of the change itself. No doubt this awareness is never wholly absent, but it may be present in widely varying intensities and its increase is an important stimulant to economic change.[66]

This check-list is, of course, also a catalogue of the ways in which the growth of London may have promoted social and economic change in England in the period between the dying away of the economic upthrust of Elizabethan and early Stuart times and the sharp acceleration at the end of the eighteenth century. It may also be represented diagrammatically in a form which enables the inter-connection between some of the items on the list to be appreciated more concisely.

[66] George quotes Defoe's description of the "topping workmen" to be found in England, ". . . who only by their handy labour as journeymen can earn from fifteen to fifty shillings per week wages as thousands of artisans in England can . . . 'Tis plain the dearness of wages forms our people into more classes than other nations can show. These men live better in England than the masters and employers in foreign countries can, and you have a class of your topping workmen in England, who, being only journeymen under manufacturers, are yet very substantial fellows, maintain their families very well . . .": George, *London Life in the Eighteenth Century*, p. 157.

Many of the changes are connected with the growth of London in two directions, at once produced or emphasized by London's growth and serving in turn to reinforce the growth process, a typical positive feedback situation, to borrow a term from communication engineering. In some cases growth was possible only because of this mutual relationship. For example, the growth of London could not have gone very far if it had not produced substantial change in agriculture over large areas and brought about sufficient improvements in the transport system to make it feasible to maintain a reliable and moderately cheap movement of food surpluses from the home counties and East Anglia into London. In other cases there is no return connection between London and one of the aspects of social and economic change promoted by its growth. For example, the continued growth of London had much to do with the slightness of population growth over the country as a whole, but it would be difficult to argue that the reverse was also true. And in still other cases, even though no arrow is drawn in on the diagram, it is obvious that some degree of connection must have existed. A link may be presumed for instance, between higher real wages (6) and improved transport (5), or between new consumption patterns (10) and agricultural change (2). Only those connections which appear more direct and more important have been shown — though of course a connection between any two boxes can be shown by moving round the network: for example, there is no direct link shown between improved transport (5) and higher real incomes (6), but an indirect link exists via agricultural change (2) and by other more circuitous routes.

Sometimes, where a connection is shown only in one direction, the absence of a return arrow may seem arbitrary: for example in the case of new forms of social mobility (9) and "rational" not "traditional" behaviour (8). In several of these cases there was certainly some return effect, and with equal propriety but on different assumptions a return arrow might have been drawn. The act of judgement involved here demands careful scrutiny because the relationships which are expressed by a single arrow are of particular interest. Where there are arrows in both directions this implies an interconnection so intimate that in some ways it will prove pointless to distinguish between them. They are jointly parts of a larger situation which it is convenient to record separately for clarity's sake and for some analytic purposes. Where an arrow in only one direction exists, however, a clearer distinction, a lack of interdependence and in some cases a causal sequence is implied. For example, the

diagram suggests that the growth of London stimulated the development of "rational" modes of behaviour (8), but that this in turn did
not have any important direct return effect on London's growth
(though very soon an indirect path is opened up via (4), better
commercial facilities). This is a different type of relationship from
that between London and improved land and water communication
(5) which is represented as facilitating the growth of London directly.
The latter is shown as a chicken and egg situation, as it were; the
former is not. In the one case the positive feedback is direct; in the
other this is not so.

A special interest attaches to boxes (6) higher real incomes, (2)
agricultural change, and (8) "rational" rather than "traditional"
behaviour. They are key nodes in the system connected to more
boxes than others, and tied into the system by single as well as
double arrows. If the relationships are correctly stated it is these
aspects of the total social and economic situation which should prove
most repaying to future analyses (and possibly also (5) improved
transport). Unhappily the system embodies far too many subjective
judgements to justify any but conditional statements about it in its
present form.

The diagram underlines the poverty of our knowledge of many
things which it is important to know. Sometimes the absence of an
arrow betrays simple ignorance as much as an act of judgement.
For example, it is impossible to feel sure as yet about the nature of the
relationship between the demographic situation in the period 1650-
1750 and economic and social change. Some points seem clear.
It is reasonable to suppose that the relationship indicated in the
diagram between population balance and higher real incomes is
accurate. But other points are far from clear. It is very uncertain
whether the reverse relationship holds good — that is to say whether
higher real incomes tended to retard population growth, and in what
ways this effect, if it existed (and it would certainly be premature
to rule out this possibility), was produced.

This model is, like all models, intended as an aid to further thought.
It is not more than this. It may be noted, incidentally, that some
lines leading to the industrial revolution box, and more particularly
those leading back from the industrial revolution box, should be
viewed in a different light from other connections. The industrial
revolution did not get fully into its stride until after the period
discussed in this essay. Arrows pointing to it, therefore, show
circumstances tending to promote its occurrence. Those in the
opposite direction, on the other hand, cannot have existed before the

event itself, if its place in time is strictly defined. In a more general sense, however, they simply underline the positive feedback elements in the situation which grew stronger as time passed but were present from an early date. In contrast with this, the period of economic growth in the sixteenth and early seventeenth centuries produced relationships between major variables which might be termed typically those of negative feedback. The very growth of industry and population, by increasing the demand for food and industrial raw materials in circumstances where there were increasing marginal costs of production, and by oversupplying the labour market, drove up food prices, forced wages down, and increased the difficulties of industrial production, thus throttling back the growth process.

VI

The comparative neglect of London as a potent engine working towards change in England in the century 1650-1750[67] is the more paradoxical in that the dominance of Paris within France has long been a familiar notion in political history. Yet London was larger than Paris, was growing much faster, and contained a far higher fraction of the national population. All leavens do not, of course, work equally effectively in their lumps; and political dominance connotes different issues from economic and social change, but the irony remains.[68] A just appreciation of London's importance must await a fuller knowledge of many points which are still obscure. Meanwhile this short sketch of a possible model of London's relationship with the rest of the country will have served its purpose if it helps to promote further interest in the complexities of the changes to which no doubt it does only the roughest of justice.

Peterhouse, Cambridge   *E. A. Wrigley*

[67] See P. Laslett, "The Numerical Study of English Society", in *An Introduction to English Historical Demography*, ed., E. A. Wrigley (London, 1966), pp. 11-12 for a brief discussion of much the same point.
[68] It is symptomatic of the neglect of this topic that a work as perceptive and authoritative as Deane and Cole's recent analysis of British economic growth from the late seventeenth century onwards passes over the growth of London almost completely. Where London is mentioned at all it is incidental to some other main line of argument.

AGRICULTURAL CHANGE 2

HIGHER REAL INCOMES 6

SUITABLE DEMOGRAPHIC CONDITIONS 7

CHANGES IN RAW MATERIAL SUPPLY 3

INDUSTRIAL REVOLUTION

NATIONAL MARKET 1

IMPROVED TRANSPORT 5

GROWTH OF LONDON

BETTER COMMERCIAL FACILITIES 4

'RATIONAL' NOT 'TRADITIONAL' 8

NEW FORMS OF SOCIAL MOBILITY 9

NEW CONSUMPTION PATTERNS 10

The Links between London's Growth and the Industrial Revolution in England.

Coal Output in South-West Lancashire, 1590–1799[1]

By JOHN LANGTON

". . . perhaps the meagreness of data, particularly statistical data, makes causal analysis [of the Industrial Revolution] impossible."[2]

"Early statistics of production are little better than guesses."[3]

I

THE prefatory quotations epitomize one of the most cruel dilemmas of English economic history, a dilemma which is fully reflected in the current state of knowledge of the coal industry. No one doubts the central role of coal in the Industrial Revolution, but statistics of coal output before the mid-nineteenth century are meagre on both the national and the coalfield scales. Moreover, that those which do exist contain potentially serious flaws is admitted by their authors and by those who have subsequently used them. The pioneering work of Nef[4] remains the sole authority on the industry in the sixteenth and seventeenth centuries at both the national and the regional scales. However, at least for the inland coalfields, his estimates were generally based on a small sample of collieries and the evidence of output at those collieries was gleaned mainly from records of law-suits. Estimates founded upon evidence that must often be dubious and relates to a very small sample of the total colliery population obviously represent "conjectures rather than scientific data",[5] yet these conjectures are frequently quoted and are used as the only support of the hypothesis that "the [fourteenfold] increase in coal production in the various coalfields of Britain between mid-Tudor and late-Stuart times was as spectacular as any of the economic happenings of the period."[6]

No comparable body of coalfield estimates exists for the eighteenth century. Sets of national estimates have been calculated by Nef for the period 1760–80[7] and by the Coal Commission of 1871 for the whole century.[8] Nef's figures indicate a doubling of output from five million tons over those two decades, but the quantitative basis of the estimates is slight[9] and "it is impossible to say" whether

---

[1] I would like to express my thanks to Dr A. R. H. Baker and Prof. P. Koroscil, whose ability to spot logical flaws and verbiage contributed greatly to the final form of this article. They bear no responsibility for the views expressed.

[2] R. M. Hartwell, 'The Causes of the Industrial Revolution: An Essay in Methodology', repr. from *Economic History Review*, 2nd ser. XVIII (1965) in R. M. Hartwell, ed. *The Causes of the Industrial Revolution* (1967), p. 55.

[3] T. S. Ashton and J. Sykes, *The Coal Industry of the Eighteenth Century* (Manchester, 1964), p. 13.

[4] J. U. Nef, *The Rise of the British Coal Industry* (1932).

[5] C. Wilson, *England's Apprenticeship, 1603–1763* (1965), p. 80.   [6] Ibid.

[7] Nef, op. cit. II, 353–7.   [8] *Report of the Royal Commission on Coal in the United Kingdom* (1871), III, 32.

[9] The estimates for the "Midlands Coalfields" and Wales are pure guesses, and, generally, detailed estimates are made only for the decade 1781–90, the 1760 figure being produced in a single sentence.—Nef, op. cit. II, 353–7.

or not they approximate reality within an acceptable margin.[1] The Coal Commission figures, used by Ashton and Sykes and considered by them to be "the less unreliable of many estimates",[2] are based on London coal import data and consequently they "almost certainly" underestimate the growth of the industry.[3] Indeed, they contrast sharply with Nef's estimates, suggesting a less than three-fold increase from 1700 to 1770 and a doubling from 1770 to about ten million tons in 1800. Nef's estimates are too narrowly based to be treated with confidence, yet the Coal Commission figures yield almost ridiculously low rates of increase for the second half, and particularly the last thirty years, of the eighteenth century.

Regional statistics, even if they were of unimpeachable accuracy, could not help to resolve this problem. They could not be used to corroborate or refute national estimates. It has not yet been demonstrated that "there was an English economy rather than a collection of self-contained or trading regions within England" by the end of the eighteenth century,[4] and even if a cohesive national economy did exist regional rates of economic growth would differ.[5] In such a situation national aggregate data are of chimerical value, and regional statistics are more useful for testing hypotheses about the role of coal production in the Industrial Revolution. South-west Lancashire, focused on Liverpool, was one of the first important growth regions of industrial Britain. Accurate production statistics for this coalfield could provide considerable insight into the chronology and characteristics of early industrial growth.

II

This line of reasoning is rudely confronted by the second of the quotations which preface this essay. After the collection of a mass of quantitative and quasi-quantitative information on the south-west Lancashire mining industry one is acutely aware of the veracity of Ashton and Sykes's observation. It may be true that "of the varying approaches, those with a quantitative basis seem, in spite of their shortcomings, to offer the firmest foundation,"[6] and that "to give quantitative precision to variables is necessary before precise relationships can be defined, and statistically verifiable models of eighteenth-century growth can be formulated."[7] But statements such as these overlook the fact that it is not in the act of quantification itself that precision is achieved. The usefulness of lists of numbers in which each entry is open to wide error, within which range the true trend is free to ramble disguised and undetectable, is surely negligible. Indeed, to have bad statistics is probably worse than to have no statistics, and it may be that data of reasonable accuracy are just not available.

The horns of the dilemma are sharp, but a few further pricks are tolerable. The estimates presented below are intended to fulfil two major purposes. First, the discussion of the assumptions that are required, the nature of the evidence, and

[1] P. Deane and W. A. Cole, *British Economic Growth, 1688–1959* (Cambridge, 1964), p. 55n.

[2] Ashton and Sykes, op. cit. p. 13.   [3] Deane and Cole, op. cit. p. 59.

[4] R. M. Hartwell, 'Economic Growth in England before the Industrial Revolution: Some Methodological Issues', *Journal of Economic History*, XXIX (1969), 30.

[5] J. G. Williamson, 'Regional Inequality and the Process of National Development', Supplement to *Economic Development and Cultural Change*, XIII, no. 4 (1965), 4.

[6] M. W. Flinn, *Origins of the Industrial Revolution* (1966), p. 14.   [7] Hartwell (1967), op. cit. p. 8.

the complexity of the problem illustrate the difficulties involved in attempting to answer Hartwell's plea. As a corollary, it will exemplify the great range of error to which existing estimates, based on a much narrower range of source material, are liable. Secondly, the estimates for south-west Lancashire are intended to provide a body of quantitative information which is as reliable as, and hopefully more reliable than, that which exists to date on an industry which was one of the major pinions of England's economic "take-off".

The problems involved in the exercise may be conveniently summarized as devolving from, firstly, the quantity of data available; secondly, the nature of the mining industry of the period; and thirdly, the quality of the data.

It would be foolish to claim that the search for raw data was exhaustive. However, it did entail an examination of the bulk of the source material that could be expected to contain reference to the mining industry of the region during this period. The sample is thus as large as could be realistically assembled. Even so, there is insufficient evidence to allow estimates for single years, at least before the mid-eighteenth century. Like Ncf, one is forced to use the decade as a unit and to estimate annual outputs from data that refer to ten-year periods. The resulting series can thus only reflect medium- and long-term changes and is based on the assumption that collieries recorded in different years of a decade all worked continuously throughout the decade. This was not the case,[1] and one can only hope that potential overestimation resulting from this procedure will to some extent cancel the underestimation that results from working with a sample only. The sample is drawn from diverse sources, which range from accounts and other family business papers through law-suit records and taxation records to literary descriptions.[2] Moreover, the source-mix is similarly constituted through time until a preponderance of taxation records occurs in the late eighteenth century. It can thus be assumed that the sample approximates randomness as nearly as possible, approaching reality more closely than one based narrowly on single sources such as law-suits or accounts.

The industry of the time was not of a nature which is conducive to definitive statistical representation. The output series reproduced in Table 1 and Fig. 1 represent a varied spatial, chronological, and size range. They demonstrate that any average output figure denotes a mean with a high standard deviation, which, at least before the late eighteenth century (see Fig. 1), symbolized trendless fluctuations. On the assumption that such fluctuations were random their effects on aggregate coalfield production can be ignored, and the major consequence of this short-term variability is that there is a high probability that an isolated state-

[1] The more detailed records of the late eighteenth century allow rough estimates to be made of the ratio between the number of collieries recorded in a decade and the average number of collieries that worked in each year of that decade. This ratio was relatively stable for the last five decades of the century, being 2·01 in the 1750's, 2·03 in the 1760's, 1·89 in the 1770's, 1·97 in the 1780's, and 1·59 in the 1790's. Thus, if the decade was used as a unit in this period an over-estimation of up to 100 per cent would occur. Of course, no inferences can be drawn about the seventeenth century from these figures. On the one hand, the relative sparsity of the documentary records would probably have a greater negative effect on the denominator of the ratio than on the numerator, whilst on the other hand the more stable economic conditions would tend to lower the numerator relative to the denominator.

[2] A full itemization of the information on each colliery of the period can be found in J. Langton, 'The Geography of the South-West Lancashire Mining Industry, 1590–1799' (unpublished Ph.D. thesis, University of Wales, 1970), II, 10–135.

ment will misrepresent the mean output of a colliery by up to 30 per cent. An assumption of randomness would again allow this problem to be ignored, but such an assumption is not realistic when the sample of outputs for given years is

Table 1

Colliery location	Accounted years	Average annual output $\overline{X}$	Standard deviation σ	Coefficient of annual variation $V\left(\dfrac{\sigma}{\overline{X}} \times 100\right)$
1. Winstanley	1676–95	1,413	332	24%
2. Haigh	1725–38	4,705	1,485	32%
3. Eccleston	1747–56	2,944	990	34%
4. Prescot	1764–8	16,405	890	5%
5. Orrell	1788–99	36,121	9,653	27%
6. Kirkless	1791–9	8,421	1,864	22%

Sources: 1. Lancs. R.O. DDBa, Coal Pitt Accounts, 1676–95; 2. John Rylands Library, Haigh MSS, An account of what Cannel has been got . . . Sep. 28th. 1747 until Oct. 1st. 1748 and Cannel, 1749; 3. Wigan Public Library, Wrightington MSS, Eccleston Box, Dagnall Bundle, Accounts of Charles Dagnall's Colliery; 4. King's College Library, Cambridge, Prescot MSS, Prescot Hall Colliery, Accounts of Coal, 1763–81; 5. D. Anderson, 'Blundell's Collieries: the Progress of the Business', *Transactions of the Historic Society of Lancashire and Cheshire*, cxvi (1964), 113; 6. ibid.

Fig. 1. *Temporal Fluctuations in the Outputs of Collieries*

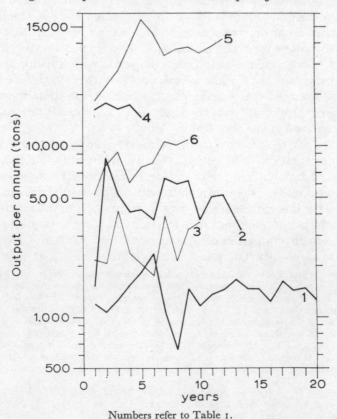

Numbers refer to Table 1.

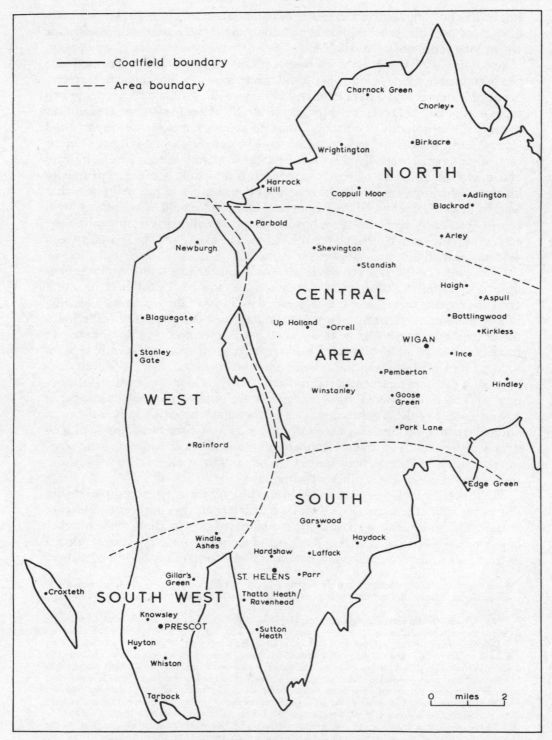

Fig. 2. *Reference Map, Showing Colliery Locations, Towns, and Regional Subdivisions*

small. The only antidote to this source of potential error is to use as large a body of data as possible as a basis for conclusions about the output of collieries for which long series are not available.

Accordingly, all information which provides some kind of index of colliery size has been used in the calculation of the following estimates. The data are extremely variable in precision and reliability, but they can be grouped roughly into two types on the basis of precision. First, there are the definite statements of output provided by accounts, law-suits, and miscellaneous sources such as reports and letters, and quantitative indexes which can be converted into output, such as receipts and rents. Secondly, there are the more numerous but less precise indexes of size, such as statements of weekly or monthly production, or of colliery capacity "if the trade will bear it", or statements of the number of pits or hewers that worked at a colliery. So that the largest possible sample could be assembled, both types of evidence have been used, but in recognition of their variable reliability each group has been plotted on separate graphs in Fig. 4 and the second type of evidence is used only as a supplement to the first.

Even evidence which is as ostensibly categoric as the first type contains potentially deep pitfalls for the unwary. One important source of possible error is that measure systems varied over the coalfield, with units of the same name varying widely in content. If measures are not standardized the outputs of collieries in the central area may be liable to up to 30 per cent underestimation relative to those of the south and south-west.[1] Furthermore, the precision of certain types of account and of statements in law-suits may be entirely illusory. "Receipt accounts" sometimes represented receipts *minus* wages and miscellaneous disbursements.[2] The totals entered in such accounts are obviously useless as sources of output data, but the exact composition of "receipts" is occasionally difficult to adduce where only summary accounts have survived. Statements made in law-suits were frequently abstracted from accounts and given by witnesses of no obvious partiality, but occasionally more than one total was given, with wide variation between the claims of different witnesses.[3]

These problems of interpretation pale into insignificance when compared with those that afflict the second group of data, which comprises imprecise indexes of output. This miscellany of information is dominated by quotations of the number of pits that worked at collieries and of the number of hewers that were employed in them. The former are the most common single form of expression of colliery

[1] This problem is fully discussed in a forthcoming paper in the *Transactions of the Antiquarian Society of Lancashire and Cheshire*. All outputs quoted in this article have been standardized to tons of 20 baskets of 120 lb.

[2] Lancs. R.O. DDBa, Coal Pitt Accounts, 1676–96; John Rylands Library, Haigh MSS, Bradshaigh Account Books, 1731–41, 1744–54, 1754–65, and 1765–74, and P.R.O. F.E.C./1/5/57 and 63–6.

[3] This difficulty can be illustrated from P.R.O. P.L.6/54/110 and 55/7, which refer to a dispute over a Sutton colliery. The plaintiff claimed that the defendant, who was his partner and had acted as auditor of the colliery, had not paid him as much money as was his due. He claimed that 1,000 works (3,000 tons) had been purchased "on trust" for which the defendant had received £300. It is not clear whether this money comprised receipts for one or two collieries in Sutton, or whether it was collected over one or more years. The lessors of the colliery witnessed that £30 rent was received for one colliery at 1s. per 60 baskets between 11 Sept. 1710 and 21 Sept. 1711. This represents an output of 1,800 tons, and I have considered this to be the most reliable estimate of the colliery's annual output. Nef, on the other hand, estimated the colliery's output at 5,000, using the receipts total, which he misread as £500, and an estimated selling price of 2s.–3s. per ton.—Nef, op. cit. 1, 62n.

size for the period before *c.*1750, the latter for subsequent decades, and Fig. 4 demonstrates that without these indexes information on colliery size would be very sparse, especially for the seventeenth century. Consequently, details of productivity per pit and per hewer are of more than intrinsic interest: to a significant degree their veracity will be reflected in the aggregate coalfield output estimates. The available evidence on pit and hewer productivity is itemized in Tables 2 and 3, which merit discussion.

Table 2. *Numbers of Hewers and Productivity at Coal Pits*

Colliery	Years	Av. no. of pits p.a.	Av. annual output per pit (o)	Vo	Av. no. of hewers per pit	Av. output per hewer (g)	Vg
Orrell	1600/1	1	1,040		2 or 3		
	1605	1			3		
Goose Green (Molyneux)	1624	1			2		
Goose Green (Pemberton)	1624	1			2		
Hindley	1624	1			3		
Wigan	1653	1			2		
Shevington (Rigby i)	1666	1			3		
	1669	1	1,100				
Shevington (Rigby ii)	1672	1			3		
Winstanley	1676–95	1·05	1,334	18%			
Eccleston	1686				2 in 1 pit		
Thatto Heath	1718–22	7	1,166				
Haigh (Baldwin–Young)	1728–30	1	413				
Westhead	1731	2	640				
Haigh (Langshaw)	1737–56	1	1,132				
Haigh (Holmes)	1744–7	1	480				
Haigh (Morris)	1745–51 and 1757	1	144				
Eccleston	1747–9	5·3	540	67%			
Prescot*	1750 (i)	2	2,800†				
	(ii)	7	3,120‡		4	780	
Orrell (Halliwell)*	1763–4		2,696	64%			
Winstanley	1766	2·5	1,589	35%	3·95	384§	21%
Haigh (Melling)	1768	1	1,192				
Haydock*	1769	4	2,145‖				
Orrell (Halliwell)*	1771–2	2·7	2,629	14%			
Orrell (Holme)*	1782–90	1·5	2,887	22%	4·1¶	704	23%
Orrell (Berry–German)*	1783–5	4·7			4·9		
Orrell (Hardcastle)*	1783–5	2			4·17		
Orrell (Warren–Blundell)*	1783–5	4			4·17		
Orrell (Culcheth)	1785	2			3		
Orrell (Blundell)*	1788–99	6·6	5,568	23%	4·1¶	1,357	23%

  * Steam-engine drained.   † Glass-coal pits, which were not continuously worked.
  ‡ House-coal pits, which were continuously worked.
  § Composed of two large pits which raised 2,125 and 1,920 tons p.a., had 4·9 and 4·29 hewers on average, and where the hewer outputs were 433·74 and 447·63 tons p.a. respectively; and one small pit, intermittently worked by 2·65 hewers at an output of 271·29 tons per hewer. Calculated from a forty-six-week weekly account × 52/46.
  ‖ Calculated from the statement that four pits raised 165 tons (per week?).
  ¶ Estimate comprising the average hewer complement of six Orrell collieries, 1783–5.

Fluctuation was marked around the mean output per pit of 1,656 tons per annum, the coefficient of variation (*V*) being 69·8 per cent. Such a mean has obvious limitations as a multiplier for the conversion of pit numbers to output estimates, especially when a high proportion of the variance was due to systematic variation in the number of pits worked and the type of drainage equipment used. More significant means can be obtained by abstracting variability due to these factors. The mean annual output of single-pit collieries was 854·4 tons per annum, but the coefficient of variation was still relatively high at 48·1 per cent. This is to be expected. A single pit producing at capacity probably raised *c*.1,000–1,300 tons per year, which is the modal range of the figures for single pits, but lower tonnages were raised if demand was below that level by reducing the number of hewers from three to two or even one,[1] and if drainage problems existed output was reduced by intermittent working.

Table 3. *Numbers of Hewers and Productivity at Cannel Pits*

Colliery	Years	Av. no. of pits p.a.	Av. annual output per pit (*o*)	*Vo*	Av. no. of hewers per pit	Av. output per hewer (*g*)	*Vg*
Aspull	1622–4	2			6 in 1 pit	200(?)*	
Haigh	1636	2			6		
	1645	2			5 in 1 pit		
	1687					390(?)†	
	1725–55	3·46	(i) 1,441	32%‡			
			(ii) 1,490	14%§			
	1748/9–1754/5	4·14	1,174	33%	5·1	227	21%
Kirkless	1750/1–1754/5	2·2	1,214	45%			
Ince	1792–3 1795–6 and 1799–1801		1,801	21%	8·3	(i) 217 (ii) 273‖	44% 15%

* Scowcroft pit employed six hewers on average, and produced, on average, 1,000 wain loads per year. The wain load was said to contain 24 baskets in Aspull at an unknown date.—L.R.O. DDGe(E)/245).

† Specified in the colliery orders, but not definitely achieved.

‡ Calculated from five-year moving means of receipts data which have been corrected for prior wage payments, and divided by current selling prices.

§ As (i) but ignoring years of exceptionally low output due to an underground fire and two years of exceptionally high output due to new pit openings.

‖ Calculated on the basis of the number of days actually worked by hewers.

The average output per pit at multiple-pit collieries was 2,056·3 tons per year, which was significantly higher than the maximum production of single-pit collieries. The coefficient of variation of 58·3 per cent was also significantly higher than that for single pits. However, a number of distinct groups were present within this category. The average annual output at multiple-pit works was higher than the maximum production recorded at single-pit collieries because it was strongly influenced by the high tonnages raised through the pits of the collieries that worked during the second half of the eighteenth century. Each of the works at which very high tonnages were raised was drained by steam engines,[2] and the

[1] This eventuality was sometimes specifically recognized in conditions of leasehold, as at Shevington in 1666 when the lessees covenanted that "they will keepe three getters Constantly at work if ye. sd. sale will Cary ye. sd. Coles away".—Lancs. R.O. DDHe/40/74.

[2] The first engine was built at Prescot Hall in 1744 (King's College Library, Cambridge, Prescot MSS, 1/v/40/1); at Orrell Hall in *c*.1764 (Wigan Public Library, Leigh–Pemberton MSS, 'Deeds reserving Rents and Coal Mines: Orrell', 'Mr. Porter's Account of Coals got at Hall Orrell'); at Haydock probably, though not certainly, in 1758 (John Rylands Library, Manchester, Legh MSS, Box 55, letter, Dodge to Legh, 8 Jan. 1758); at Holme's colliery in Orrell in 1774 (Lancs. R.O. DDBa,

logical inference is that steam-engine drainage allowed higher annual outputs from individual pits.[1] This conclusion is lent further support by negative evidence, for the low average annual pit output of *c.* 450 tons raised at the Dagnall colliery in Eccleston was the result of intermittent working due to drainage problems.[2] Earlier in the period, and on newly opened or naturally drained coal, per pit outputs at multiple-pit works that did not use steam engines seem to have been just over 1,000 tons per annum,[3] or the equivalent of the modal output of single-pit collieries.[4]

The following conclusions can thus be drawn from the pit productivity data. First, that a single multiplier for use on pit numbers is not acceptable. Secondly, that single-pit collieries produced less than 1,200 tons per annum throughout the period 1590–1799. The average output at such collieries was 854·4 tons per year, and this figure will be used as an estimate of the production of collieries of which it is known only that one pit worked. Thirdly, that multipliers of similar reliability cannot be postulated for multiple-pit works, and the following seem to be the most logical conclusions from the available data. During the seventeenth century, and later in the absence of evidence of unusual drainage difficulties, the average output per pit at multiple-pit collieries was relatively consistent at *c.* 1,250 tons per annum ($V=15\cdot8$ per cent). The mean output per pit at steam-engine-drained workings was more than twice as large. These averages will be used to convert statements of pit numbers at the relevant type of colliery to estimates of annual output.

Productivity per hewer was similarly variable, with the interesting additional factor that there was significant variation according to whether cannel or ordinary bituminous coal was mined.[5] Although pit outputs did not vary significantly with this parameter, twice as many hewers normally worked in cannel pits as in coal pits (see Table 3). Except for the doubtful figure of 390 tons per year specified in the Haigh colliery orders,[6] between 200 and 300 tons per hewer per

---

Accounts and Rentals / 20); and at the Warren–Blundell colliery at some time before 1774 (*The Liverpool General Advertiser*, 23 Dec. 1774). No evidence but tax records exists for the Berry–German or Hardcastle collieries in Orrell, but steam engines seem to have been a normal part of the equipment of the works in this area in the late eighteenth century (John Rylands Library, Haigh MSS, Box XI, letter, Earl of Balcarres to Mr. Stanhope, 1789).

[1] Due to the possibility of uninterrupted working. The difference made to output by "absenteeism" amongst the hewers of Ince cannel colliery is indicated in Table 3.

[2] Wigan Public Library, Wrightington MSS, Eccleston Box, Dagnall Bundle, Colliery Accounts, 1747–56, and numerous letters concerning drainage.

[3] As at the Park Colliery in Haigh, which was drained by the Great Sough of the Haigh cannel colliery, and the Bankes's Winstanley colliery, where extensive sough drainage had been developed from the early seventeenth century.

[4] Only the two-pit Westhead colliery of the Earl of Derby, situated in the almost undeveloped western area, raised per pit tonnages smaller than the single-pit mean.

[5] A number of factors can be suggested in explanation of this discrepancy. Cannel was an extremely choice fuel which was clean to handle, required no kindling, had a high calorific value, and burned with sufficient luminosity to light a room. Whenever possible it was carefully cut into large lumps, or "round cannel", which brought a higher price than small pieces. In addition, cannel was lighter in weight per unit of volume than ordinary bituminous coal, and the cannel seam was wet, gassy, and deep. Each of these factors would tend to lower the productivity by weight per hewer.

[6] This figure is based on the weight of coal which the Colliery Orders specified must be raised by each hewer in a full working year, which was probably in turn based on the assumption of continuous daily working through a six-day week for a year of about fifty weeks—clearly more exceptional than normal.—Wigan Public Library, transcription of the Haigh Colliery Orders by A. J. Hawkes.

annum were raised at cannel collieries, though variability from year to year at individual collieries was high in reflexion of the length of time spent by hewers on tasks other than hewing.[1] The "normal" single-pit coal-producing colliery employed a maximum of three hewers in the seventeenth century, and output per hewer was thus *c.* 415 tons per annum. The average figure for the three Winstanley pits of 1766 was lower, but at the two continuously worked shafts the mean was, at *c.* 440 tons per hewer per year,[2] slightly higher than the "norm" of the previous century. However, at the two steam-engine-drained collieries for which information is available, productivity per hewer was substantially higher,[3] and the averages for the collieries differ markedly. A productivity per man index is required if the outputs of the large canal-serving works are to be estimated.[4] An average of the two figures would obviously be of suspect veracity, especially as the Holme colliery in Orrell was completely atypical, in terms of size and entrepreneurship, of the canal-serving works of that township.[5] The rough and-ready expedient has been adopted of using the Blundell colliery's average productivity per man per year figure for collieries employing more than ten hewers, and the Holme average for collieries employing fewer than that number. This procedure obviously leaves much to be desired, but it is the most logical course of action, given the fact that without using the manpower figures of the late eighteenth century no reasonable estimate could be made of coalfield output after the opening of canals.

III

The numerical and output series which can be constructed from the information and assumptions elucidated in the previous section exhibit a marked change of trend in the mid-eighteenth century. The increase in colliery size is clearly marked even when represented on a semi-logarithmic scale, and the increase in colliery numbers that occurred between the 1740's and the 1750's (see Fig. 3) is by far the most significant break in the numerical series.[6] Thus, two clearly distinct periods of activity occurred, and these will be discussed in turn.

[1] Such as help with drainage, driving tunnels and endways, and opening up fresh reserves. When allowance is made for such "absenteeism" at Ince cannel colliery, where daily data were recorded, the mean output per hewer/year is raised by some 20 per cent and the coefficient of weekly variation falls from 44 per cent to 14 per cent.—Wigan Public Library, Euxton MSS, 6/3/23.

[2] Lancs. R.O. DDBa, Colliery Accounts, 1766.

[3] The reasons probably being that working was no longer interrupted by flooding and that specialists could be employed full time on non-productive jobs such as driving endways and tunnels and opening up new coal, thus cutting down the rate of "absenteeism" of the hewers.

[4] Fourteen out of the 15 indexes of output for the years 1780–99 which are portrayed on the lower graph of Fig. 4 represent conversions of hewer numbers derived from the Land Tax Assessment Returns.

[5] In the 1790's the average number of hewers recorded per year at the Holme colliery was 4·4 whilst at the next smallest collieries the averages were 19·2 and 24·8 (see Fig. 6). Moreover, the Holme colliery was the only one in Orrell worked by a member of the local gentry, the others being run by merchants, wool-staplers, bankers, coal merchants, and so on from Liverpool and Bradford. See Langton, op. cit. I, 323–6.

[6] According to the χ^2 statistic there is 0·10 probability (the lowest for any two adjacent decades) of such a difference occurring by chance in two randomly sampled totals from the same population. A 0·10 probability would usually lead to the acceptance of the null hypothesis that there is no significant difference between the number of collieries that worked in each decade. However, when the constancy of the trends over the five decades preceding and succeeding these two is taken into account, $\chi^2 = 4·96$ with d.f.=1. This value is significant at the acceptable probability level of 0·05.

1590–1749

This period, prior to the conventionally dated Industrial Revolution and to the building of canals, was not one of constant temporal trend or unvariegated spatial pattern. The trend in aggregate colliery numbers was upward, with discontinuities between 1610 and 1649 and between 1680 and 1699. The sparsity of output data is such that only the most tentative conclusions can be drawn about the direction and the rate of change in the size of collieries, which seem to have roughly paralleled the numerical trend, with some detailed non-correlation. It appears from the pit number data that the fall in colliery numbers from the peak of the 1620's was mirrored by an increase in the preponderance of single-pit workings, though this situation lasted until 1665, whereas colliery numbers increased after the 1630's. The numerical increase of the 1680's and 1690's was not paralleled by any perceptible growth in colliery size, whilst the shallow rate of numerical increase between 1720 and 1749 was accompanied by a marked increase in the size of collieries in certain parts of the coalfield.

The aggregate output figures which are the goal of this analysis are a compound of colliery numbers and size, but a simple multiplication of mean colliery output with the number of collieries that operated in a decade would not yield acceptable results. The colliery totals are samples, and the significance of fluctuations must be assessed on this basis; apparent changes in the number of working collieries may not be significant when the data are correctly treated as randomly sampled totals from unknown populations. Furthermore, the colliery size figures for the seventeenth century rely heavily on statements of pit numbers. It has already been pointed out that these are imprecise, and this was particularly the case in the seventeenth century when the only distinction recorded was usually one between single- and multiple-pit works. Fluctuations in single-pit production could be expected to be marked in a situation where demand pressure did not require, and flooding did not allow, the maximum scale of working continuously at all pits, and the exact number of pits operating at multiple-pit collieries is rarely known. Hence, even with a constant ratio of single- to multiple-pit collieries and numerical stability, aggregate coalfield output could have fluctuated markedly and a series produced by multiplying colliery numbers by the means would, for the seventeenth century at least, give a spurious impression of precision. The procedure adopted is to attempt to assess the significance of the breaks of 1620–49 and 1680–99 and to make "guesstimates" on the basis of those findings. It will yield results which are less ostensibly definitive, but more honest.

The exact significance of the apparent peak and trough of the 1620's, 1630's, and 1640's is elusive. The χ^2 statistic for the difference between the colliery totals for the 1620's and 1630's is significant only at the 0·25 level of probability.[1] However, when the consistency of the trends before 1620 and after 1630 is taken into account,[2] plus the shaky evidence of pit numbers, the question as to whether or not a significant fall in output occurred becomes tantalizingly open. Certainly, it would be impossible to conclude on the evidence available that production

[1] Ignoring copyhold workings—i.e. using the totals marked by the solid lines of the graphs in Fig. 3.

[2] A runs test yields interesting results. If the century-long series is tested by this method, randomness is indicated, but if it is broken at 1620–9 two series of significant trend are obtained. This suggests that there were two distinctly different periods of trend, confirming the conclusion that is obtained from a simple inspection of the graph.

increased, and the hypothesis that it declined is supported by the fact that a high proportion of the local gentry were catholic royalists, whose estates would suffer more than most during and immediately before the Civil War. The possibilities range from a fall of negligible proportions between 1620 and 1640 to an upper bounding figure of over 50 per cent.[1] To work to a finer margin is not feasible.

By the 1680's the number of collieries working the coalfield had apparently risen to the level achieved in the 1620's, paralleled by the ratio of single- to multiple-pit workings, so that taking the century 1590–1689 as a whole some growth probably occurred. In the 1590's total annual coalfield production was probably *c*.13,650 tons, and it is highly unlikely that it exceeded 27,000 tons.[2] In the 1680's it had probably reached *c.* 21,850 tons, with a maximum upper bounding figure of 49,500 tons.[3] The most likely conclusion is that output rose from *c.* 13,650 to *c.* 21,850 tons, but the maximum possible rate of growth was from 13,650 to 49,500 tons per annum. Nef's estimates of between 50,000 and 100,000 tons per annum in 1700,[4] with a fifteenfold rate of increase from 1550, seems highly optimistic, greatly exaggerating both the size of the industry at the turn of the eighteenth century and its growth-rate during the course of the seventeenth century. There is the additional strong possibility that output was as high in the 1620's as in the 1680's, and as low in the 1630's as in the 1590's. Figs. 3 and 4 demonstrate that spatial contrasts were present throughout the whole of the century, but they were muted. The majority of collieries, and the largest, surrounded Wigan in the central area or lay in the south-west around Prescot, and these two areas probably raised 75 per cent of the coalfield's output, shared equally between them.

The break in the trend of colliery numbers between the 1680's and 1690's is as inconclusive as that between the 1620's and the 1630's. When the decennial totals are taken in isolation the χ^2 statistic is not significant: when the constancy of the preceding and succeeding trends is additionally considered it is significant at the

[1] This figure can be derived after the following mass of assumptions has been made: that the fall in numbers with a 0·25 probability of chance occurrence is taken at face value; that the ratio of single to double pits did rise as the lower graph of Fig. 4 suggests and that this is deemed significant despite the small size of the sample on which it is based, and that the productivity of single- and multiple-pit collieries remained constant at 854·4 and 2,500 tons per annum. The totals then obtained, with the further assumption that the output of Haigh remained constant at 3,500 tons per annum, are 28,314 tons for the 1620's and 11,444 tons per annum for the 1630's. Obviously, little credence can be placed in these actual totals, but they do provide an approximation of an upper bounding figure for the magnitude of the possible fall.

[2] In the 1590's 11 collieries were recorded. At some time during the decade Prescot Hall raised *c.* 2,500 tons per annum (P.R.O. D.L.1/183/L/5); and Orrell colliery *c.* 200 tons (P.R.O. D.L.1/183/L/13); Sutton Heath colliery had two working pits and was thus of an equivalent size to Prescot Hall, and all later evidence suggests that Haigh must have been of a similar size. The aggregate output of these four collieries was thus about 7,700 tons per annum. If it is assumed that the remaining seven collieries were single-pit works with mean annual outputs of 854·4 tons the total coalfield output derived is 13,650 tons per annum. It could not have exceeded 27,000 tons, which is the figure yielded by the much less realistic assumption that the seven collieries were double-pit works.

[3] About 1,500 tons were raised annually at Winstanley in the 1680's (Lancs. R.O. DDBa, Coal Pitt Accounts, 1676–96) and *c.* 2,000 tons at Wrightington (Lancs. R.O. DDK/1743). From the data available it seems that 3,500 was the likely output of Haigh (see Table 3), and Hindley and Eccleston collieries were double-pit workings (P.R.O. P.L.6/44/81 and 38/107). On the assumption that all other collieries were single pits the total coalfield output was *c.* 21,350 tons per year. On the less realistic assumption that they were double pits the total was 49,500 tons.

[4] Nef, op. cit. 1, 60–4. The region as defined here incorporates two of Nef's "districts".

Fig. 3. *The Number of Collieries Working in Each Decade, 1590–1799*

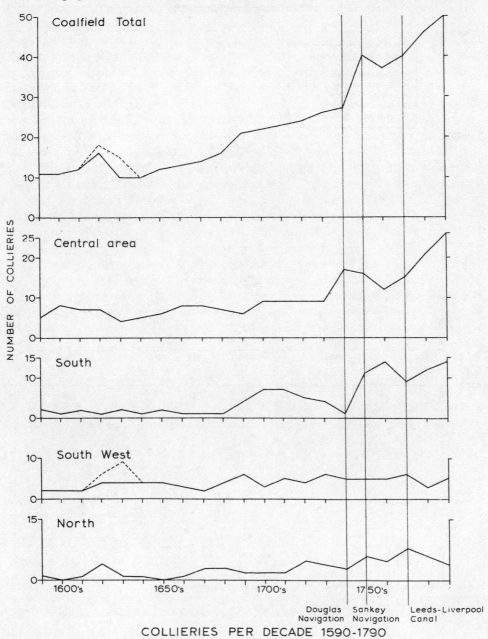

NUMBER OF COLLIERIES

Coalfield Total

Central area

South

South West

North

COLLIERIES PER DECADE 1590-1790

Douglas Navigation

Sankey Navigation

Leeds-Liverpool Canal

Dotted line depicts the total inclusive of collieries on copyhold ground, which were probably not usually recorded.

Fig. 4. *Average Annual Colliery Outputs as Recorded (upper graph)*
and Estimated (lower graph)

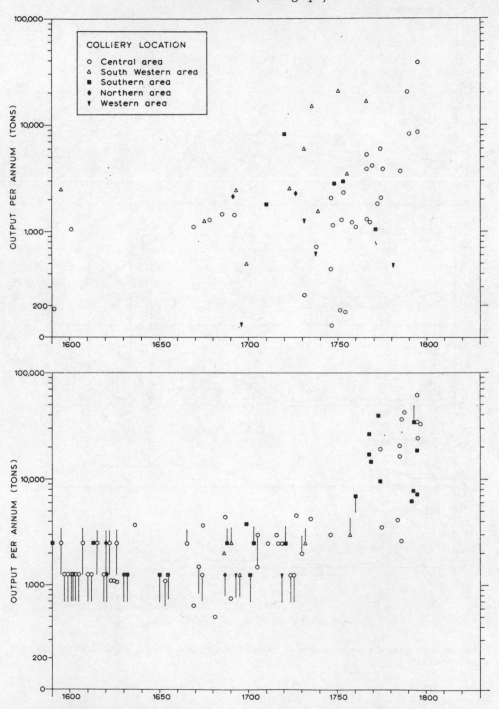

The direction of error to which certain estimates, principally made from pit numbers, are liable is indicated by vertical lines.

accepted probability level of 0·05. Moreover, though an increase in colliery size is clearly recognizable after the 1730's, the difference of 200 tons between the mean colliery outputs of 1590–1689 and 1690–1729 has a 0·75 probability of occurring by chance! But these aggregate trends, which display continuity until at least the 1730's, swamp significant changes even on this scale, and markedly quickening development began in small areas of the coalfield at least as early as the second decade of the eighteenth century.

These tendencies render the forty years before 1750, which are usually suspended in the limbo between Nef's early revolution in mining and the national economic upsurge conventionally dated after 1760, of great interest. Output began to grow perceptibly at an increasing pace in the two southern areas of the coalfield. The hitherto negligible southern areas witnessed an increase from one colliery in the 1680's to seven in the 1700's and 1710's, and at least one of these works raised more than double the erstwhile steady maximum output of 3,500 tons per annum, utilizing seven pits.[1] This growth of mining was linked with the supply of the northward-moving locus of the Cheshire salt industry[2] and was accompanied by the first significant influx of capital into the mining industry, Thatto Heath colliery being financed from Cheshire between 1691 and 1715.[3] After the opening of the Weaver navigation in 1732 the colliery population of the southern area declined and Thatto Heath was taken over by a local glass-maker.[4] The focus of growth shifted to the south-west, which then had the transport advantage to Cheshire as well as a greatly strengthened link with Liverpool after the building of the turnpike from Prescot to the port, which was also substantially completed by 1732. Fig. 3 demonstrates that the number of collieries in the south-west did not increase significantly after this twin stimulus. But the size of individual collieries greatly expanded: Prescot Hall raised less than 3,000 tons in 1721,[5] *c.* 6,000 tons in 1731,[6] *c.* 15,000 tons in 1735,[7] and at least 21,000 tons in 1750.[8] Liverpool capital was invested in the Whiston mines,[9] where the first steam engine on the coalfield was erected before 1729,[10] joined by a second at Prescot Hall in 1744,[11] and competition between these two large collieries became intense and

[1] 12,240 works were raised at Thatto Heath colliery between May 1718 and July 1722, so that an average of over 8,000 tons were raised yearly. In 1718 the colliery had an engine pit, three old but newly scoured pits, and four recently sunk shafts.—P.R.O. P.L.6/61/6.

[2] T. S. Willan, *The Navigation of the River Weaver in the Eighteenth Century* (Chet. Soc. Pub.), 3rd ser. III (1951), 2–4.

[3] The original lease of the Thatto Heath reserves was taken out by William Mascall of Frodsham. On his death the work was carried on by William Shaw of Sutton, Ann Mascall, and Richard Griffiths, a London apothecary. Shaw mortgaged the colliery to Richard Turner of Middlewitch in *c.*1714 to obtain working capital of £100. This was insufficient, and Turner took a one-quarter share of the enterprise in 1715, increasing his share to one-half after a third payment when Shaw encountered further difficulties, and Turner sent up horses from Cheshire for drainage work.—P.R.O. P.L.6/61/11.

[4] P.R.O. P.L.6/65/45.

[5] A rent of 1s. 8d. per work was worth "above £70 per annum".—King's College Library, Cambridge, Prescot MSS, 1/V/42/41 and 41/11.

[6] Ibid. 1/V/42/33. [7] Ibid. 1/V/74.

[8] "140 works per week besides what are sold to the Glass Houses at Liverpool".—Ibid. 1/V/42/18.

[9] They were purchased by the Liverpool salt-manufacturing and merchant family of Case, who developed them considerably during the eighteenth century.

[10] Lancs. R.O. DDWi, Box 12, 'Abstract of the Title of H. Case to the Manor of Whiston' (n.d.) (quoting from the will of Jonathan Case, 1729); DDK/406/90, and King's College Library, Cambridge, Prescot MSS, 1/V/42/35.

[11] King's College Library, Cambridge, Prescot MSS, 1/V/40/1.

bitter.[1] Rapid growth occurred in the output of the south-western area during the second quarter of the eighteenth century, accompanied by an increase in the size of productive units, technological innovation, and the emergence of a fiercely competitive economic structure. If "industrial revolution" means anything in terms of the mining industry it had surely occurred in the south-western area of the coalfield before 1750.

Elsewhere in the region the gradual trends of the seventeenth century continued on into the eighteenth. The colliery population of the central area expanded markedly in the decade following the opening of the Douglas for navigation from Wigan to Preston in 1742, almost doubling to 17. But, just as output increased in the south-west without numerical growth, so in this area the numerical increase greatly exaggerates the expansion of output. No colliery grew to the size of Prescot Hall, or even Thatto Heath; Haigh remained the largest works with an output only 30 per cent greater than that raised a century earlier;[2] no steam engines were built, and only one entrepreneur moved into the industry from outside the coalfield.[3] All the new collieries produced either cannel or smith's coal, which alone could compete in the coastal markets opened by the Douglas, or they were tiny collieries producing ordinary coal at Haigh,[4] the plethora of which perhaps illustrates the "demonstration effect" of the development of cannel mining in a classical diffusion situation.

Output calculations are difficult to make with confidence for the 1740's because of the spatial diversity of colliery size, and, in some areas, short-term temporal change. However, accounted outputs, estimates, or figures for the 1730's or 1750's which can be used in areas of little change for the 1740's are available for 12 of the 27 collieries that worked in the last decade of this period.[5] The assumption that Whiston colliery produced an equivalent amount to Prescot Hall seems logical,[6] and the further assumption that all other collieries of unknown size were single-pit works (they were all in relatively undeveloped areas)

---

[1] This bitter rivalry lasted from the 1730's until 1769, when the proprietor of Whiston colliery "Mr. Case, who has always acted with the spirit of a Rival & Competitor" carried out his threat to "turn them [i.e. Makin & Co.] out of possession of both the Mines & Estate" when he obtained the lease of Prescot Hall from King's College.—Ibid. 1/V/74, letter, Chorley to Smith, 25 Sept. 1769.

[2] The average output in 1748–55 was 5,005 tons per year.—John Rylands Library, Haigh MSS, An Account of What Cannel has been got . . . Sept. 28th 1747 until Oct. 1st 1748, and Cannel, 1749.

[3] T. Whitehead of Preston was a partner in a Shevington colliery on which a lease was taken out in 1731.—Wigan Public Library, Wrightington MSS, Box 10, 'Dicconson v Hesketh: Articles Coal in Shevington for 21 yrs., Janry. 29 1731'.

[4] Eight of the 20 collieries which worked in the central area in the 1740's and 1750's were small coal-producing collieries at Haigh, with average annual outputs ranging from 178 tons to 1,132 tons.—John Rylands Library, Haigh MSS, Bradshaigh Account Books, 1744–54 and 1754–65.

[5] The following outputs were accounted: Haigh (Langshaw), 1,154 tons p.a.; Haigh (Holmes), 480 tons p.a.; Haigh (Morris), 127 tons p.a.; Haigh (Prescot), 240 tons p.a.; Kirkless, 2,331 tons p.a.; Whiston (Earl of Derby), 2,001 tons p.a.; Prescot Hall, 15,000 tons p.a. in 1735 and at least 21,000 tons in 1750; Gillar's Green, 3,805 tons p.a.; Eccleston, 2,821 tons p.a. The following outputs can be estimated from receipts, hewer numbers, and so on: Shevington, *c.* 4,000 tons p.a.; Orrell, *c.* 2,304 tons p.a.—John Rylands Library, Haigh MSS, Bradshaigh Account Book, 1744–54; Lancs. R.O. DDK/2021/37; King's College Library, Cambridge, Prescot MSS, 1/V/42/41, 1/V/41/11, and 1/V/42/18; Lancs. R.O. DDSc/1/1; Wigan Public Library, Wrightington MSS, Eccleston Box, Dagnall Bundle, Accounts of Charles Dagnall's collieries, 1747–56; Lancs. R.O. DDBa, Up Holland Box, 'Hiring of Colliers 1744–8'; and John Rylands Library, Haigh MSS, Collieries Folder, 'Account What Coals Slate &c' (n.d.).

[6] They were the only steam-engine-drained works on the coalfield and the assignations "vast" and "large" were applied to Whiston by persons connected with Prescot Hall.

yields a lower bounding estimate of *c*. 78,000 tons per annum. The assumption that all collieries of unknown size were double-pit works yields an upper bounding estimate of *c*. 99,000 tons per annum. The four collieries of the south-west raised over half this total; the central area, with 63 per cent of the collieries and the only navigable water on the coalfield, raised between 30 and 40 per cent of the total.

1750–1799

An attempt has been made in Fig. 5 to demonstrate the year-by-year changes in the colliery populations of the various areas of the coalfield after 1750. Individual totals cannot be invested with too much credence, but the graphs ought to show regional contrasts and trends with a fair degree of accuracy. Fig. 4 illustrates the relative abundance of colliery output data for this half-century com-

Fig. 5. *The Number of Collieries Working per Year, 1750–99*

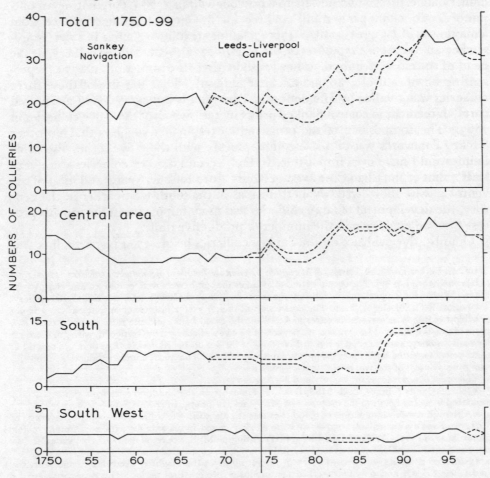

Dotted lines represent probable upper and lower limits in cases where no single total can be realistically estimated.

pared with the earlier period, but the bulk of the information does not compensate the speed and diversity of change so that, despite the wealth of evidence on colliery numbers and size, coalfield output estimates are more difficult to make and, if anything, less reliable than those of the earlier period.

The Sankey canal was opened in 1757, providing direct water access to Liverpool and the Cheshire saltfield from the southern area of the coalfield. A number of collieries were opened in the mid-1750's in anticipation of the waterway; by 1760 there were eight in the area and thenceforth no significant numerical change occurred before the opening of the Leeds and Liverpool canal in 1774. The increase in the colliery population which followed the opening of the Sankey was thus smaller than that which had followed the opening of the Douglas into the central area in 1742. The increase in output was considerably greater, though even its approximate magnitude is difficult to estimate because of a dearth of quantitative evidence on the collieries that were opened. Some of these collieries were undoubtedly as large as those of the south-west in the 1740's. Parr Hall colliery advertised for 20 hewers to work longwall in 1768 (representing an output of *c.* 27,000 tons per annum)[1] and receipts at Garswood colliery ranged from a maximum of £4,931 1s. 7½d. in 1766/7, falling steadily to £2,621 in 1773 (representing an output of *c.* 13,500–*c.* 23,500 tons in 1772).[2] Ravenhead colliery, at the head of the canal, required 30 hewers soon after its completion in 1773 (representing an output of *c.* 40,000 tons per annum).[3] That the size of these three collieries was rivalled by Haydock and Parr Hall is indicated by an attempted cartel agreement to control Sankey prices by the owners of these five collieries in 1763.[4] The composition of the projected cartel further suggests that no other Sankey coalworks was of a size commensurate with these five, otherwise price fixing would have been impossible. In fact, certain Sankey collieries were very small; that of Jonathan Case averaged only 1,012 tons per year,[5] and most of the ventures were short-lived.[6] Nonetheless, as in the south-west earlier in the century, the development of large collieries was more important in the growth process than an expansion in the number of productive units.

Quantitative evidence on the Sankey collieries before 1774 is sparse, flux was

[1] T. C. Barker and J. R. Harris, *A Merseyside Town in the Industrial Revolution: St. Helens, 1750–1900* (Liverpool, 1954), p. 35. The output estimate assumes that 20 hewers were employed and that, working in the efficient longwall manner, they were as productive as the hewers of Blundell's Orrell colliery.

[2] Lancs. R.O. DDGe(M)/1201. The conversion of these receipts into exact output estimates is not possible because coal was sold in Liverpool and on the canal bank, and the ratio between these two types of sale is unknown. In 1772, 4s. 3d. per ton of 25 cwt was charged at Garswood, with 3d. discount for ready money, and 7s. 4d. per ton in Liverpool or 6s. 8d. on board vessels. The first and second of these prices yield the higher and lower estimates respectively. The mean annual production, 1768–73, using the average of the two prices, was *c.* 15,000 tons.

[3] *Liverpool General Advertiser*, 23 July and 20 Aug. 1773.

[4] John Rylands Library, Legh MSS, Box 51, 'Thoughts on the Dublin Trade from Sankey' (n.d.) and 'Reply of Ra. Leigh to the proposals of Mr. Mackay, 9 Sept. 1763'.

[5] Although a minimum output of 6,000 tons was stipulated in the colliery lease only an average of 1,012 tons yearly was raised, 1770–3, and the colliery closed in accordance with a minimum selling price clause in 1773.—Wigan Public Library, Wrightington MSS, Eccleston Box, Old coal leases Eccleston and Sutton Bundle, Eccleston to Case, 31 July 1769, and appended note of 8 Oct. 1773.

[6] Nineteen collieries were recorded, 1757–73, yet no more than eight worked in any one year, the mean being 6·97, and only two worked continuously through that period. The ratio between the number of collieries recorded and the average number that worked annually was 2·73, compared with a ratio of about 2·00 for the coalfield as a whole.

rapid, and output estimates must thus be based largely on guesswork. The most realistic conjectures are that production rose from *c.* 80,000 tons in 1757 to *c.* 115,000 tons in 1765 to *c.*125,000 tons in 1773.[1]

The colliery proprietors of the south-west anticipated the opening of the Sankey canal with great foreboding,[2] but no colliery closed in the area between 1758 and 1770,[3] and competition for reserves in Whiston and Prescot remained intense. The output of Prescot Hall fell to an average of 16,500 tons per year, 1763–8,[4] which was still large compared with the majority of collieries, and at Whiston an agent was employed "to solicite and increase the Sale of Coal which was then greatly decreased".[5] Yet a new steam engine was built in 1767[6] and in 1769 a new colliery was opened at Whiston which for a short time worked simultaneously with the old.[7] Prescot Hall colliery closed in 1769, but the erstwhile proprietors obtained new reserves and opened up the steam-engine-drained Hillcock Street colliery in Prescot during the late 1760's and early 1770's.[8] This was not the only large new colliery of the area. James Gildart of Liverpool had a colliery comprising 11 pits and a steam engine in Whiston by 1770[9] and Charles Dagnall opened his works, which were eventually steam-engine drained, at Windle Ashes in 1759.[10] Although the latter had closed by 1773,[11] at that date there were three large collieries still at work in the south-west, and at least 60,000 tons per annum,[12] which was not lower than the pre-Sankey total, must have been raised in this area in the early 1770's.

The colliery population of the central area declined between 1750 and 1758, thenceforth remaining stable until 1773. This numerical decline represented the closure of the plethora of minute workings which had been opened after the Douglas was completed. But other collieries grew in size. Output at Orrell Hall

1 These figures are almost pure conjecture. They have been derived from the assumptions that Parr, Parr Hall, Haydock Wood, and Haydock Florida collieries raised *c.* 20,000 tons per year, as the scanty quantitative evidence suggests, and that Ravenhead produced 40,000 tons. It has been further assumed that collieries of unknown size raised 10,000 tons per year, which seem roughly commensurate with the heavy capital investment necessary to set up the drainage and haulage requirements of a canal-side works. These figures, when supplemented with the accounted outputs of Case's Sutton colliery and Laffack colliery (*c.* 7,000 tons p.a. in 1760—John Rylands Library, Legh MSS, Box 51 / letter, Leigh to Legh, 17 Feb. 1760) and the estimates made above for Garswood, yield the estimates given in the text.

2 King's College Library, Cambridge, Prescot MSS, 1/V/42/12–14.

3 The industry was more stable there than over the coalfield as a whole. The ratio of collieries working per year to the total number recorded was 1·94 between 1757 and 1774, and as low as 1·25 between 1757 and 1768.

4 King's College Library, Cambridge, Prescot Colliery Coal Accounts, 1763–81.

5 P.R.O. P.L.6/87/10.

6 King's College Library, Cambridge, Prescot MSS, 1/V/74, letter, Chorley to Smith, 25 Nov. 1767.

7 P.R.O. P.L. 6/87/10. The balance existing in the Whiston Carr colliery books in 1777 was £3,959 13s. 11¾d., which can be compared with a profit of £2,376 at Garswood on an output of *c.* 2,000 tons in 1768.

8 King's College Library, Cambridge, Prescot MSS, 1/V/74, 'Petition against the erection of an Engine', 15 Nov. 1774.

9 Lancs. R.O. DDWi, A Map and Survey of Land Lying in Whiston Belonging to James Gildart, Esq., 10 Oct. 1770.

10 Ibid. DDGe(E)/1257. The steam engine was built in 1766.—*Williamson's Liverpool Advertiser*, 28 June 1765 and 3 Oct. 1766.

11 *Liverpool General Advertiser*, 1 Feb. 1771.

12 It is highly unlikely that collieries with such vast reserves, numerous pits, equipment, and, in the case of the Case works, high profits, produced less—they may have raised far more.

colliery increased to *c*. 5,000 tons per annum[1] and the average at Haigh to *c*. 8,250 tons per annum in the early 1770's.[2] These collieries were smaller than the Sankey or Whiston works, but they were significantly larger than any which had previously operated in the central area. Symbolizing this growth in scale the steam engine was introduced at both collieries.[3] Again, aggregate output increases were achieved through colliery expansion rather than an increase in numbers: here a large numerical decline accompanied an increase in production from *c*. 29,000 to *c*. 36,000 tons per year between 1757 and 1773.[4]

The effect of the first canal thus corresponded with what would be expected; the area directly affected increased its output from less than 5,000 to *c*. 80,000 tons per annum. Less momentous were the non-occurrence of decline in the south-west, where the collieries lost their advantage in the Liverpool and Cheshire markets to the Sankey works, and the expansion in the central areas where maximum colliery size increased by 100 per cent and technological innovation advanced without any novel demand stimulus.

In October of 1774 "the Grand Canal from Leeds to Liverpool was opened amidst the acclamations of thousands of spectators—it is now navigable . . . to the great collieries at Wigan."[5] The massive expansion that was anticipated did not immediately occur. Indeed, after an initial small flurry the colliery population of the area hardly increased until the mid-1780's, and Fig. 6 demonstrates that the Orrell collieries, which dominated the supply of the canal, only began to grow rapidly towards their maximum size at about the same time—ten years after the canal was opened. After this decade-long lag large collieries grew apace and, as the population remained relatively stable,[6] output increased by a factor of ten to *c*. 380,000 tons per annum in the central area as a whole by 1799.[7]

[1] Wigan Public Library, Leigh–Pemberton MSS, Deeds reserving rents and coal mines, Orrell, 'Mr. Porter's Account of Coals got at Hall Orrell'.
[2] Calculated by dividing the selling price of cannel into the auditors' payments to the estate steward, corrected for disbursements between their receipt and payment. See Langton, op. cit. II, 171–3.
[3] At Haigh some time between 1765 and 1774 and at Orrell Hall in 1764.—John Rylands Library, Haigh MSS, Bradshaigh Account Book, 1765–74; Wigan Public Library, Leigh–Pemberton MSS, Deeds reserving rents and coal mines, Orrell / 'Mr. Porter's Account of Coals got at Hall Orrell'.
[4] Nine or ten collieries worked in the area. Of these, the outputs of the following six were recorded in the late 1760's and early 1770's: Winstanley, *c*. 3,800 tons; Haigh, *c*. 8,000 tons; Orrell Hall, *c*. 7,000 tons; Orrell (Holme), *c*. 2,500 tons; Haigh Park, *c*.1,250 tons, and Orrell (Jackson) worked through three pits in 1774, which would be the equivalent of *c*. 6,000–7,000 tons per year.—Lancs. R.O. DDBa / Colliery Accounts, 1766; John Rylands Library, Haigh MSS, Bradshaigh Account Book, 1765–74; Wigan Public Library, Leigh–Pemberton MSS, Orrell Coal Accounts, 1771–4; Lancs. R.O. DDBa / Accounts and Rentals / 20; *Liverpool General Advertiser*, 23 Dec. 1774. Given the location and entrepreneurial characteristics of the three or four other collieries that worked in the area an assumption that they produced *c*. 2,000 tons per year is logical. These known, estimated, and assumed sizes yield the total 36,000 tons per annum.
[5] *Liverpool General Advertiser*, 21 Oct. 1774.
[6] Although the total population remained stable, the colliery "turnover" was, at least in the early years, high, and the ratio between the mean annual colliery population and the total number of collieries recorded, 1774–9, was 2·33.
[7] The outputs of the Blundell collieries at Kirkless and Orrell were accounted at 10,937 and 42,480 tons per annum.—Anderson, op. cit. p. 113. The number of hewers employed at the Orrell collieries and the number of pits that worked at the collieries of Aspull and Haigh can be obtained from the Land Tax Assessment Returns. The multipliers elucidated in Section II of the article yield the following estimates of annual tonnages from these data. Orrell: Holme, 2,112; Hustler, 47,495; Clarke (Orrell Post), 65,163; Clarke (Gathurst), 43,425; Lofthouse, 44,781; Aspull, 6,000; Haigh, 8,000. Of the remaining five collieries of the area, Winstanley comprised huge reserves, was leased by Clarke & Co.,

Fig. 6. *The Growth of the Orrell Collieries, 1782–99*

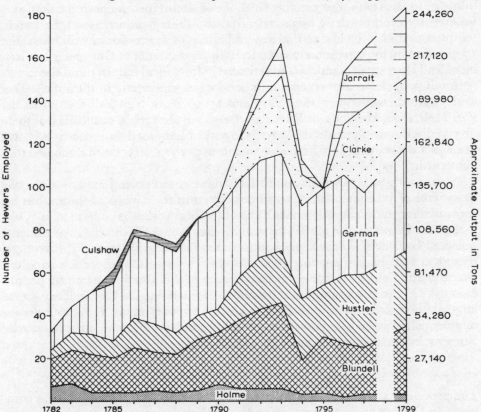

Source: Lancs. R.O. Land Tax Assessment Returns, West Derby Hundred, Orrell Townships, 1782–99 (1798 returns missing from series).

The Leeds and Liverpool canal allowed coal from the central area to compete with fuel from the south and south-west in Liverpool,[1] but again there is no evidence of catastrophic decline in the hitherto dominant supply areas. Perhaps decline did follow the opening of the new canal on the Sankey; at the very best, output stagnated as a combination of new competition in Liverpool, a financial slump in the port which caused bankruptcies on the Sankey,[2] and a new salt-

---

and sold to the canal, so that the assumption that it was of equivalent size to those in Orrell seems reasonable. Similarly, Standish and Pemberton collieries were large, owned by partnerships comprising Orrell coalmasters, and sold to the canal, and they too probably rivalled the Orrell collieries (30,000 tons p.a. assumed). Because of ownership characteristics, size of reserves, and/or distance from the canal, Shevington and Parbold were probably very small, and 2,000 tons per annum seems a realistic assumption. The sum of these totals is 380,000 tons.

[1] The Liverpool market of the Sankey was not seriously eroded immediately. 45,568 tons were shipped to the port on the Sankey in 1771, and this tonnage was not surpassed on the Leeds and Liverpool canal before 1783.—T. C. Barker, 'Lancashire Coal, Cheshire Salt and the Rise of the Port of Liverpool', *Trans. Hist. Soc. Lancs. & Ches.* CIII (1951), 95; J. R. Harris, 'Early Liverpool Canal Controversies', being pp. 78–97 of J. R. Harris, ed. *Liverpool and Merseyside: Essays in the economic and social history of the port and its hinterland* (1969), p. 97.

[2] Barker and Harris, op. cit. pp. 49–57.

making process which halved the fuel needs of the Cheshire saltworks[1] hit the industry in the south. But rapid revival, if not simultaneous compensation, was ushered by the growth of large-scale coal-consuming industries on the canal, tempted there by the low coal prices and site-rent concessions available in the 1770's, and by the expansion of salt output in consequence of Chryssel's development and buoyant demand.[2] Capital flowed in from local industry and the Liverpool salt proprietors and colliery numbers began to increase in the 1780's. Few of the Windle collieries of the 1780's and 1790's were even half the size of the Parr Hall, Parr, Haydock, or Ravenhead works of the 1760's, but the last of these survived without diminution. Aggregate output increased over the twenty-five years as a whole, probably from *c*.130,000 tons per year in 1773 to *c*.200,000 tons per year in 1799.[3]

In the south-west progress was probably more continuous. Jonathan Case, the proprietor of Whiston colliery, was bankrupted in the Liverpool slump, but his executors expanded the colliery.[4] Of the other four works that operated in Whiston, that of Gildart was almost as large as Case's if the Land Tax Assessments reflected colliery size accurately within individual townships, but the average, though not the maximum, outputs of the other three were considerably smaller.[5] No accounted outputs survive for the collieries of this area in the late eighteenth century. On the key assumptions that the twin steam-engine Case colliery was as large as the Orrell works and that the Land Tax Assessment Returns reflected relative colliery size within Whiston, output must have been about 100,000 tons per year in this area by the end of the century.

IV

The process of growth in the mining industry of south-west Lancashire was complex, and the data that have survived contribute more towards a recognition, rather than an exposition, of that complexity. Detailed reconstructions of the chronology of growth and its spatial variations are not, in this case, possible.

[1] Coal tonnages on the Weaver declined from 35,287 in 1772/3 to 18,102 in 1779/80. The new process, invented by Chryssel in 1776, halved the quantity of coal required to reduce one ton of salt.— Willan, op. cit. app. v, pt B; A. F. Calvert, *Salt in Cheshire* (1915), p. 123.

[2] The Weaver tonnage reached 84,863 by 1799.

[3] Output figures are very sparse, and exist only in the form of conversions of manpower figures of Windle collieries through the somewhat shaky multiplier derived from the output per man figures of the Holme colliery in Orrell. These collieries were certainly smaller than those of Orrell or those which had preceded them on the Sankey; the largest averaged 14 hewers per year, but the mean number for the four was only 8·7 per year compared with 40 at Ravenhead in the 1770's and an average of 31 at the six Orrell collieries in 1799. Other works were very large. The Ravenhead colliery supplied Greenbank Copper Works alone with 400 tons per week in 1784 and 700 tons per week in 1795. An estimate of aggregate output is best approached from the market end in this case. The Weaver took *c*. 85,000 tons, Warrington and the lower Mersey, minus Liverpool, had consumed 18,000 tons in 1773, and, on the basis of the Greenbank figures, the heavy industry of St Helens probably consumed somewhere in the region of 100,000 tons per annum. This is the best estimate that can be hazarded of Sankey production at the close of the eighteenth century.—Langton, op. cit. I, 245.

[4] All surface properties, except for 16 acres required for the operation of the colliery, were sold. Income from the colliery provided the money required to wind up the estate, build two new steam engines, pay off mortgages, and provide 4s. 3d. in the £1 to Case creditors in 1783.—Lancs. R.O. DDWi, Unsorted and unnumbered Box, 'Indenture of 26 Feb. 1801'.

[5] The Gildart colliery paid an average of £2 4s. 0½d. per year, 1783–99, and the Case colliery £2 15s. 3½d. The other three collieries paid between £1 and £2.—Lancs. R.O. Land Tax Assessment Returns, West Derby Hundred, Whiston Township, 1783–99.

Hartwell's plea for statistics to facilitate model-building has not been answered: the figures which can be provided are of insufficient rigour for inclusion in a model of the process of industrial growth. Assumptions must be made about the simultaneity of colliery operation, the significance of samples, sample means and equivocal trends, and about two key statistics of output per man. To these must be added some cavalier presumptions about the size of certain large collieries of the late eighteenth century for which no quantitative evidence exists. Even after these indulgences, only the most tentative estimates can be made, and many of them are open to 100 per cent error. The uncertainty to which the seventeenth-century figures are liable has been indicated in Fig. 7, where all the estimates have been plotted. (It must again be emphasized that the lower totals entered on the graph possess an overwhelmingly greater probability of accuracy than the

Fig. 7. *Estimates of the Annual Outputs of the Regions of the South-West Lancashire Coalfield between the 1590's and the 1790's*

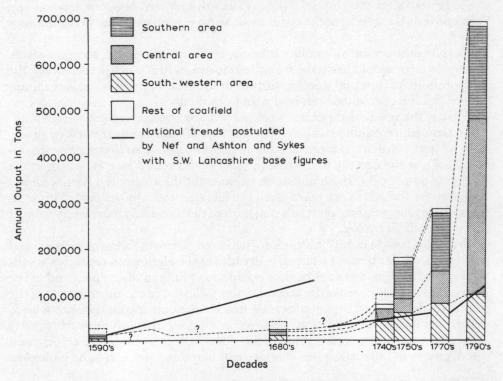

higher ones.) Even massive underestimation of these earlier figures would not, however, seriously affect the long-term trend.

This is not the case with the eighteenth-century figures which, as was mentioned earlier, are in some ways more dubious. Variations through space and in the rate of change were so great that it is not possible to make postulations about the possible range of error of the eighteenth-century totals similar to those for the seventeenth century. But two sets of canal haulage data lend some flimsy support to these later estimates. In 1771, 90,000 tons of coal were shipped down the

Sankey canal.[1] It was estimated above that the total output of the collieries of the area was 125,000 tons in 1773. That the canal accounted for 76 per cent of the output of the area before the local growth of large-scale coal-consuming industry seems a reasonable postulation. Statistics of coal shipment on the Leeds and Liverpool canal exist for the years from 1781 to the end of the period.[2] These fully support the conclusion that the growth of output was slow during the canal's first ten years. Only 31,401 tons were hauled on the canal in 1781, but the total had almost quintupled by 1790 and by 1799, 202,185 tons were shipped. The estimate of the production of the whole central area was 380,000 tons at the end of the eighteenth century. On the evidence of the canal tonnage figures this seems high. Before the canal was built the collieries of the area raised only *c*. 35,000 tons per annum, and it seems unlikely that the consumption of the population and industries of Preston and Wigan and its surrounding villages increased by the fivefold that would be required to lift local consumption to the size of the difference between the estimate and the canal tonnage figure. At best, therefore, it can be suggested that the output of the area lay somewhere between 240,000 and 380,000 tons by the end of the eighteenth century, both extremes being improbable.[3]

Despite serious doubt about the accuracy of many of the totals, any reasonably probable error would leave the major trends substantially unaltered. Given the acceptability of the estimates as indicators of the general trend of output, a number of definite conclusions can be drawn from them.

Firstly, the seventeenth century did not witness massive growth in the south-west Lancashire mining industry. The number of collieries increased relatively slowly, and neither the mean nor the maximum size of collieries grew significantly. Over the century as a whole production increased by somewhere in the region of 60 per cent. If the minimum estimate for the 1650's and the maximum estimate for the 1680's are taken, then the increase was 370 per cent. This is an improbably large figure, yet it falls well short of the fifteenfold increase postulated for this coalfield by Nef.

Secondly, no clear-cut "revolution" occurred. Growth followed a sequential pattern in spatial terms. In the early decades of the eighteenth century a seven-fold increase occurred in the colliery population of the southern area and in the maximum size of the collieries there. Decline followed in the third decade of the century, when output began to increase in the neighbouring south-western area, where an "industrial revolution" occurred in mining: in massive growth, greatly increased scale of the units of production, technological innovation, increased productivity to labour, capital infusion, and fierce competition—the hallmarks

---

[1] Barker, op. cit. p. 95 (quoting Thomas Pennant).

[2] Harris, op. cit. p. 97, for 1781–91, and Lancs. R.O. DP/175 for 1792–1800.

[3] This can be corroborated from other sources. In 1789 Joseph Preistley stated that 50 acres of four-foot coal were exhausted annually near the canal. One Cheshire acre yielded 3,200 tons per foot. There were 2·115 standard acres in a Cheshire acre in 1800 so that 302,600 tons must have been raised annually near the canal in 1789. This quantity was double the tonnage hauled on the canal to Liverpool in the same year. It seems, then, that the local and Preston markets were substantial by the late eighteenth century, and the figure of 380,000 tons for the total production of the area may not be so much of an overestimation as the canal tonnages suggest.—Lancs. R.O. DP/175; J. M. H. Bankes, 'Records of Mining in Winstanley and Orrell . . .', *Trans. Antiq. Soc. Lancs. & Ches.* XCIV (1942), 56; R. E. Zupko, *A Dictionary of English Weights and Measures* (Madison, 1968), pp. 3–4.

of the occurrence and aftermath of such a phenomenon. Rapid growth, with identical characteristics, took place in the southern area after 1757 and in the central area after 1774, though in the last case it began somewhat sluggishly. As the locus of development shifted across the coalfield so the rate of growth, the level of output achieved, and the median and maximum size of collieries at the locus increased.

Thirdly, the link between improved transport and the development of mining is overwhelmingly obvious. The spurts of growth were all generated by improved access to Liverpool and the Mersey. The situation was not, however, one of simple transport stimulus-mining response. It was access to Liverpool and/or Cheshire, rather than water transport itself, which was important. The Douglas, which opened into the Ribble and offered only circuitous access to Liverpool from Wigan, was responsible for a doubling of output in the central area. But this was small beer. The rate of increase in the south-western area following the Liverpool turnpike was much greater, and neither the growth of large collieries, the innovation of the steam engine, nor the infusion of capital into the industry were associated with the relatively modest expansion. However, even linkage with Liverpool was not alone sufficient to stimulate growth, as the slow development on the Leeds and Liverpool canal for the decade after 1774 testifies.

Fourthly, the greatest contribution to increased aggregate output was made by growth in the scale of the units of production. As a comparison of Figs. 4 and 5 demonstrates, expansion of the number of productive units was relatively unimportant.

Arguments which extend these conclusions shed some light on general hypotheses about the growth of mining and industry in general during the seventeenth and eighteenth centuries. Wrigley has demonstrated the crucial importance of easily expansible coal supplies in the Industrial Revolution. The corollary is that if coal supplies were not able to keep up with industrial and population growth then the pace of industrialization must to some extent have been slowed. The possibility that the supply of coal was not sufficiently elastic to keep pace with the potential rate of growth of demand is an eventuality rarely considered in analyses of British economic growth in the late eighteenth century. Despite the impressiveness of the series of large upswings in the coal output of south-west Lancashire, supply remained far below potential market capacity throughout the eighteenth century. Massive growth in output followed the construction of each of the three routeways between Liverpool and the coalfield, but each provided supplies which supplemented rather than replaced those of the erstwhile most cheaply linked collieries, and Liverpool, linked to a productive coalfield by two canals and a turnpike road, remained "short supplied often no better than half supplied" until at least 1789.[1] The mining industry, at least in south-west Lancashire, was not imbued with the capacity for full and rapid expansion up to the level of demand that was generated in the industrial and urban markets of the late eighteenth century.

The importance of increasing the scale of operations in the process of growth has been remarked upon, and the graphs of Fig. 6 demonstrate that expansion to maximum output was a protracted process that took a number of years. Even

[1] John Rylands Library, Haigh MSS, Box K1, letter, Earl of Balcarres to Mr. Stanhope, 1789.

so, "lumpy" investment was required to build or purchase the steam engines, wagonways, and flatts that were essential to large-scale colliery operations.[1] Unlike in the textiles industry, entry into successful competitive mining was not possible without substantial capital or credit backing. The expansion of mining on this scale could not usually be effected by the ploughing back of profits by existing firms, or by an insinuation into a system of circulating credit. As Pollard has demonstrated,[2] this was possible in the textiles and iron industries, but in mining not only were large lump sums necessary, but, as primary producers who normally sold to large purchasers "on trust", coalmasters acted as "long-stops" in the circulating debt and credit system, and this position pinched the industry's capital resources hard.[3] Thus, it is an entirely plausible argument that the short supply position was a product of stringent financial circumstances. The situation on the Leeds and Liverpool canal supports the validity of this conclusion. The slow expansion of the 1770's was associated with local financing of the industry, and the rapid growth of the 1780's and 1790's was accompanied by a massive influx of capital from Liverpool and Bradford.[4] The classic hypothesis that industrial growth was financed by the direct investment of mercantile capital is in this case unshakeable. The nature of the industry, the speed of its expansion, and the difference in size between pre-canal and post-canal workings required that this be so.[5]

The most obvious general conclusion indicated by the estimates themselves is that the trend of growth in the coal output of south-west Lancashire did not follow the national aggregate series produced by Nef and the Coal Commission of 1871, which have been superimposed on Fig. 7 for ready comparison. Throughout the seventeenth century there was virtual stagnation. The industry was of a fundamentally different type in terms of technology, the size of productive units, the magnitude of spatial contrasts, rates of growth, and capitalization, to that of the eighteenth century. References to oak trees and little acorns cannot cast doubt on the conclusions made obvious by these particular "sizes and quantities".[6]

---

[1] A large colliery of ten pits with a steam engine, wagonways of *c.* $\frac{1}{2}$–1 mile, and four flatts would have cost up to £2,600. The cost of pits (*c.* £500) could be spread, and flatts would be bought singly at *c.* £150, but the steam engine, wagonway, one flatt, and two pits would still cost up to £1,750. For the derivation of these costs see Langton, op. cit. 1, 306–13.

[2] S. Pollard, 'Fixed Capital in the Industrial Revolution, in Britain', *Jnl. Econ. Hist.* XXIV (1964), 299–314.

[3] John Rylands Library, Legh MSS, Box 59, letter, Gatley to Legh, 24 Feb. 1756, and Box 51, letters, Leigh to Legh, 17 Feb. 1760 and 2 May 1760, contain complaints about the difficulties resulting from the granting of "long credit" to industrial consumers.

[4] Eleven of the 12 collieries that worked, 1774–80, were financed and run either by the local gentry (6), by non-gentry coalowners or lessees who had mined since at least the opening of the Douglas (3), or by predominantly local partnerships formed in 1773 and 1774 (2). By 1799 only three out of 25 collieries in the area were definitely run by local capitalists: those of the Holmes in Orrell and the Dicconsons in Shevington were very small and the other, at Haigh, was owned by the Earl of Balcarres —hardly typical of local initiative and capital resources. All other collieries were at least partially financed by Bradford or Liverpool capitalists. See Langton, op. cit. 1, 324–6.

[5] When this point is considered in combination with the facts that Liverpool provided most of the initiative and much of the capital for the construction of the turnpike and canals, and provided the vast bulk of the market which was served by the area, the links between mercantile growth and industrial development might seem uncomfortably close to many contemporary analysts of the Industrial Revolution.

[6] Wilson, op. cit. p. 289, offers this analogy in support of his conclusion that the seventeenth century contained significant precursive economic growth to that of the eighteenth.

Neither does the growth of the south-west Lancashire coal industry in the eighteenth century "appear paltry when set beside the twentyfold growth . . . of the succeeding hundred years".[1] It matched it almost exactly! In fact, the growth-rate in Lancashire was almost exactly equivalent to that postulated for the national industry in the mid-eighteenth century by Nef, in contrast to the non-correspondence of the seventeenth-century figures. These correlations and non-correlations do not, of course, disprove the national estimates made by Nef for the seventeenth and the Coal Commission for the eighteenth century, nor do they support Nef's national estimates for the mid-eighteenth century. One would expect slower growth than the national norm in this region, land-locked and devoid of natural resources other than coal, in the seventeenth century. Similarly, one would expect more rapid growth than the national average in the second half of the eighteenth century because of the inexpensive haulage links with Liverpool and the Cheshire salt industry. What the wide discrepancies between the regional figures presented here and the existing national estimates do suggest is that to analyse the phenomenon of industrial growth in eighteenth-century Britain through national aggregates is to search for the needle by taking a detached perspective of the whole haystack.

St John's College, Cambridge

[1] Ashton and Sykes, op. cit. p. 13.